FRANZ GRILLPARZER'S DRAMATIC HEROINES
THEATRE AND WOMEN'S EMANCIPATION IN
NINETEENTH-CENTURY AUSTRIA

LEGENDA

LEGENDA is the Modern Humanities Research Association's book imprint for new research in the Humanities. Founded in 1995 by Malcolm Bowie and others within the University of Oxford, Legenda has always been a collaborative publishing enterprise, directly governed by scholars. The Modern Humanities Research Association (MHRA) joined this collaboration in 1998, became half-owner in 2004, in partnership with Maney Publishing and then Routledge, and has since 2016 been sole owner. Titles range from medieval texts to contemporary cinema and form a widely comparative view of the modern humanities, including works on Arabic, Catalan, English, French, German, Greek, Italian, Portuguese, Russian, Spanish, and Yiddish literature. Editorial boards and committees of more than 60 leading academic specialists work in collaboration with bodies such as the Society for French Studies, the British Comparative Literature Association and the Association of Hispanists of Great Britain & Ireland.

The MHRA encourages and promotes advanced study and research in the field of the modern humanities, especially modern European languages and literature, including English, and also cinema. It aims to break down the barriers between scholars working in different disciplines and to maintain the unity of humanistic scholarship. The Association fulfils this purpose through the publication of journals, bibliographies, monographs, critical editions, and the MHRA Style Guide, and by making grants in support of research. Membership is open to all who work in the Humanities, whether independent or in a University post, and the participation of younger colleagues entering the field is especially welcomed.

ALSO PUBLISHED BY THE ASSOCIATION

Critical Texts
Tudor and Stuart Translations • New Translations • European Translations
MHRA Library of Medieval Welsh Literature

MHRA Bibliographies
Publications of the Modern Humanities Research Association

The Annual Bibliography of English Language & Literature
Austrian Studies
Modern Language Review
Portuguese Studies
The Slavonic and East European Review
Working Papers in the Humanities
The Yearbook of English Studies

www.mhra.org.uk
www.legendabooks.com

GERMANIC LITERATURES

Editorial Committee
Chair: Professor Ritchie Robertson (University of Oxford)
Dr Barbara Burns (Glasgow University)
Professor Jane Fenoulhet (University College London)
Professor Anne Fuchs (University College Dublin)
Dr Jakob Stougaard-Nielsen (University College London)
Professor Annette Volfing (University of Oxford)
Professor Susanne Kord (University College London)
Professor John Zilcosky (University of Toronto)

Germanic Literatures includes monographs and essay collections on literature originally written not only in German, but also in Dutch and the Scandinavian languages. Within the German-speaking area, it seeks also to publish studies of other national literatures such as those of Austria and Switzerland. The chronological scope of the series extends from the early Middle Ages down to the present day.

APPEARING IN THIS SERIES

1. *Franz Grillparzer's Dramatic Heroines*, by Matthew McCarthy-Rechowicz
2. *Sebald's Bachelors: Queer Resistance and the Unconforming Life*, by Helen Finch
3. *Goethe's Visual World*, by Pamela Currie
4. *German Narratives of Belonging: Writing Generation and Place in the Twenty-First Century*, by Linda Shortt
5. *The Very Late Goethe: Self-Consciousness and the Art of Ageing*, by Charlotte Lee
6. *Women, Emancipation and the German Novel 1871-1910: Protest Fiction in its Cultural Context*, by Charlotte Woodford
7. *Goethe's Poetry and the Philosophy of Nature: Gott und Welt 1798–1827*, by Regina Sachers
8. *Fontane and Cultural Mediation: Translation and Reception in Nineteenth-Century German Literature*, edited by Ritchie Robertson and Michael White
9. *Metamorphosis in Modern German Literature: Transforming Bodies, Identities and Affects*, by Tara Beaney
10. *Comedy and Trauma in Germany and Austria after 1945: The Inner Side of Mourning*, by Stephanie Bird
11. *E.T.A. Hoffmann's Orient: Romantic Aesthetics and the German Imagination*, by Joanna Neilly
12. *Structures of Subjugation in Dutch Literature*, by Judit Gera

Managing Editor
Dr Graham Nelson, 41 Wellington Square, Oxford OX1 2JF, UK
www.legendabooks.com

Franz Grillparzer's Dramatic Heroines

Theatre and Women's Emancipation in Nineteenth-Century Austria

Matthew McCarthy-Rechowicz

Germanic Literatures 1
Modern Humanities Research Association
2018

Published by Legenda
an imprint of the Modern Humanities Research Association
Salisbury House, Station Road, Cambridge CB1 2LA

ISBN 978-1-78188-671-7 (HB)
ISBN 978-1-78188-672-4 (PB)

First published 2018

All rights reserved. No part of this publication may be reproduced or disseminated or transmitted in any form or by any means, electronic, mechanical, photocopying, recording or otherwise, or stored in any retrieval system, or otherwise used in any manner whatsoever without written permission of the copyright owner, except in accordance with the provisions of the Copyright, Designs and Patents Act 1988, or under the terms of a licence permitting restricted copying issued in the UK by the Copyright Licensing Agency Ltd, Saffron House, 6–10 Kirby Street, London EC1N 8TS*, England, or in the USA by the Copyright Clearance Center, 222 Rosewood Drive, Danvers MA 01923. Application for the written permission of the copyright owner to reproduce any part of this publication must be made by email to legenda@mhra.org.uk.*

Disclaimer: Statements of fact and opinion contained in this book are those of the author and not of the editors or the Modern Humanities Research Association. The publisher makes no representation, express or implied, in respect of the accuracy of the material in this book and cannot accept any legal responsibility or liability for any errors or omissions that may be made.

Trademark notice: Product or corporate names may be trademarks or registered trademarks, and are used only for identification and explanation without intent to infringe.

© Modern Humanities Research Association 2018

Copy-Editor: Dr Birgit Mikus

CONTENTS

	Acknowledgements	ix
	Abbreviations	x
	Translations	xi
	Introduction	1
1	Grillparzer and Women	25
2	Women and the Law	56
3	Women and Enlightenment	85
4	Female Rulers	115
5	Grillparzer and Kyriarchy	154
	Conclusion	187
	Bibliography	191
	Index	205

For my parents

ACKNOWLEDGEMENTS

This book started life as my doctoral dissertation at the University of Oxford. I would like to thank my supervisor, Prof. Ritchie Robertson, for his generous help, advice and support both during my studies and while I have been preparing this book for publication.

I would also like to thank my examiners, Dr Judith Beniston, Dr Kevin Hilliard and Prof. Helen Watanabe-O'Kelly, who offered helpful advice and suggestions at various stages of my doctoral studies.

I would not have been able to complete my D.Phil. without financial support from Exeter College, Oxford, and the Arts and Humanities Research Council. I am grateful to both institutions for their support.

The staff at the Taylorian Library, Oxford, and the Wienbibliothek im Rathaus, Vienna, were very supportive.

An amended version of the chapter on *Die Jüdin von Toledo* previously appeared in *German Life and Letters*, 69.3 (2016). I would like to thank the editors for permission to include this material here.

My editor at Legenda, Dr Graham Nelson, has been very helpful and supportive. Thanks are also due to Dr Birgit Mikus, who copy-edited the manuscript, and Legenda's anonymous reviewer, who provided useful feedback and suggestions for improvement.

I owe a huge debt of gratitude to my parents, John and Margaret, my brother, Aleksander, and Maciej, for their help, support and understanding over the past few years.

M.M.-R., London, January 2018

ABBREVIATIONS

ABGB *Allgemeines bürgerliches Gesetzbuch für die gesammten deutschen Erbländer der Oesterreichischen Monarchie* (Vienna: k.k. Hof- und Staats-Druckerey, 1811)

HKA Franz Grillparzer, *Sämtliche Werke*, Historisch-kritische Ausgabe, 42 vols, ed. by August Sauer and Reinhold Backmann (Vienna; Leipzig: Gerlach & Wiedling, 1908–16; Vienna: Schroll, 1916–48)

JdGG *Jahrbuch der Grillparzer-Gesellschaft*

SW Franz Grillparzer, *Sämtliche Werke: Ausgewählte Briefe, Gespräche, Berichte*, 4 vols, ed. by Peter Frank and Karl Pörnbacher (Munich: Hanser, 1960–65)

TRANSLATIONS

I used the below translations of primary works in German. In some cases, I have amended the translations from Grillparzer's dramas where they were not literal enough to convey meanings which were central to my interpretations of the original. These amendments have not been noted in the text, but were few and in each case minor. All other translations from primary and secondary sources are my own, including those from *Die Ahnfrau*.

JOHANN WOLFGANG GOETHE, *Iphigenia in Tauris*, trans. Roy Pascal, ed. by Martin Swales (London: Angel Books, 2014).
FRANZ GRILLPARZER, *A Faithful Servant of his Master*, trans. Arthur Burkhard (Yarmouth Port, MA: The Register Press, 1941).
—— *The Golden Fleece*, trans. Arthur Burkhard (Yarmouth Port, MA: The Register Press, 1942).
—— *Hero and Leander*, trans. Arthur Burkhard (Yarmouth Port, MA: The Register Press, 1962).
—— *The Jewess of Toledo. Esther*, trans. Arthur Burkhard (Yarmouth Port, MA: The Register Press, 1953).
—— *Libussa*, trans. Henry H. Stevens (Yarmouth Port, MA: The Register Press, 1941).
—— *King Ottocar, His Rise and Fall*, trans. Arthur Burkhard (Yarmouth Port, MA: The Register Press, 1962).
—— *Sappho*, trans. Arthur Burkhard (Yarmouth Port, MA: The Register Press, 1953).
IMMANUEL KANT, 'An Answer to the Question: "What is Enlightenment?"', in *Political Writings*, ed. by Hans Reiss, trans. H.B. Nisbet (Cambridge: Cambridge University Press, 1991), pp. 54–60.
FRIEDRICH SCHILLER, *Song of the Bell*, trans. W.H. Furness (Philadelphia, PA: C. Sherman, Printer, 1849).
—— 'What Is, and to What End Do We Study, Universal History?', trans. by Caroline Stephan and Robert Trout, in *Poet of Freedom*, 4 vols, II (Washington, D.C.: Schiller Institute, 1988), pp. 253–72.

INTRODUCTION

An unpublished manuscript in the Wienbibliothek im Rathaus lists sixty-seven wreaths and other tributes which were laid at Grillparzer's funeral.¹ Those who paid their respects included the Gesellschaft der Musikfreunde in Wien, the Theresianisches Gymnasium, and the management and members of the Hofburgtheater. We also find several women: Frau Iduna Laube, Frau von Littrow, Frau Baronin Ebner, Fräulein von Kudriaffsky and Fräulein Betty Paoli. Sophie Baronin Todesko remembered 'dem Ideale ihres Lebens' [the ideal of her life], while her sister, Frau Josefine von Wertheimstein, left a wreath 'in Liebe und Verehrung' [with love and admiration]. Frau von Gerold honoured the poet with a laurel wreath and a poem.

This devotion is surprising in the context of the misogynistic views which Grillparzer expressed in his diaries. W. E. Yates points to a discrepancy between his private writings and the 'sensitivity [...] to the tensions underlying the stirrings of the early Women's Movement' in his dramas.² Grillparzer was acquainted and on good terms with numerous intellectual women: Laube and Littrow(-Bischoff) were instrumental in the foundation of the Wiener Frauen-Erwerb-Verein; Ebner(-Eschenbach) was one of the foremost prose writers of the late nineteenth century; Paoli was a poet and journalist. How are we to reconcile Grillparzer's seemingly contradictory attitudes towards women?

Grillparzer's diaries, letters and unpublished prose sketches contain numerous references to women, and there are numerous entries which show that he did not always treat his paramours with respect and decency. However, these entries are tempered by an obvious interest in prominent and powerful women throughout the ages, an interest which is also reflected in his choice of dramatic material. It should also be noted that Grillparzer expressed other prejudices of his time, for example antisemitism and racism. In 1819, he wrote that 'die Orientalen' like riddles '[w]eil sie weniger denken als wir, und es ihnen daher wohlthut die Denkkraft manchmal aufzuregen ohne sie zu ermüden' [Orientals [...] because they think less than us, and it is therefore good for them sometimes to excite their powers of thought without exhausting them].³ In 1826, he wrote of the Jewish quarter in Prague: 'Schmutz. Schmutz. Schmutz. Man begreift warum dieß Volk keine Schweine ißt es wäre eine eigentliche Hyophagie (Anthropophagie).' [Dirt. Dirt. Dirt. One understands why this people eats no pork — it would actually be hyophagy (anthropophagy)] (Nr. 1495. *HKA* II/viii, p. 226).

Despite numerous romances, Grillparzer would never marry, and discarded lovers without onerous psychological consequences.⁴ Grillparzer's indifference in the face of his lovers' suffering is in some cases chilling. On the death of Marie Piquot, who had been infatuated with him, he was 'heftig erschüttert; obgleich mehr über das Unerwartete, als über die Sache selbst, obschon ich das Mädchen wahrhaft geschätzt hatte [...]' [violently shaken; albeit more by the fact that it was unexpected than by the event itself, although I had genuinely treasured the girl [...]] (1822. Nr. 1109. *HKA* II/viii, p. 48). When visiting the sickbed of Charlotte von Paumgartten, a former lover who married his cousin, Grillparzer was unmoved: 'Außer einem grimmigen Abscheu, den ich über meine eigene Theilnahmslosigkeit empfand, fühlte ich keine große Bewegung' [Apart from the severe revulsion I felt at my own apathy, I experienced no great emotion] (1827. Nr. 1614. *HKA* II/viii, p. 289). When Charlotte died, Grillparzer was moved to self-reflection and self-castigation rather than mourning: 'Ich war villeicht [*sic*] Mitursache ihres Todes. [...] Der einzige poetische Punkt in ihrem Leben war diese Liebe — und daran starb sie.' [Perhaps I was partially the cause of her death. [...] The only poetic element in her life was this love — and that is what she died of.] (16 September 1827. Nr. 1615. *HKA* II/viii, p. 290). In a rather sombre review of his romantic history, he lamented his inability to give his partners what they wanted from him and the unfortunate consequences: 'Ich habe auf diese Art das Unglück von 3 Frauenzimmern von starkem Charakter gemacht. Zwei davon sind nun bereits tot.' [In this way I have caused the unhappiness of three women of strong character. Two of them are already dead.] (1827. Nr. 1616. *HKA* II/viii, p. 291) In 1831, he lamented the passing of a time when women bore his mistreatment, and blamed them for enabling his bad behaviour: 'Einige liebenswürdige Frauenzimmer, die sich geduldig von mir mißhandeln ließen haben mich verwöhnt.' [Some kind women, who patiently let themselves be mistreated by me, spoilt me.] (Nr. 1921. *HKA* II/ix, p. 39.)

As Ian Roe writes, Grillparzer's life was far from conventional, and he did not conform to bourgeois ideals.[5] For example, his relationship with Kathi Fröhlich, the 'ewige Braut' [eternal fiancée] who would play a role in his life for almost fifty years, shows traits similar to those evident in his earlier affairs. Grillparzer admired Fröhlich's independence, but he could not accept a working woman as a wife, and so she gave up her stage career. Fröhlich and her sisters earned their own keep, which for the time was unusual, and she held progressive and feminist views.[6] The relationship was clearly passionate and explosive, and irritating for the poet: 'Warum mußte dieses Wesen in meine Hände gerathen, oder je darauf verfallen sich gleich auf gleich mir gegenüber zu stellen!' [Why did this creature have to fall into my hands, or ever think to compare herself with me as an equal!] (1831. Nr. 1933. *HKA* II/ix, p. 47)

Grillparzer's *Selbstbiographie* (1853), one of the biggest surprises among the unpublished works discovered on his death, also affords insight into his personality. This was not his first foray into the genre: in total he composed six pieces of 'conscious autobiography'.[7] None was published during his lifetime, and of these six attempts, only the *Selbstbiographie* attained any meaningful length. Arno Dusini argues that the *Selbstbiographie*, despite being one of the most remarkable works of autobiography, was more or less forgotten because of the ways it defies the conventions of autobiography.[8]

Sauer and Hartmann observe that Grillparzer's autobiographies are unique among his writings, being the only ones that were written on external impetus (*HKA* I/xvi, p. ix). The short text *Anfänge einer Selbstbiographie* [*Beginnings of an Autobiography*] (1822) was probably written after the bookseller Friedrich Arnold Brockhaus had requested an autobiographical note for his *Konversationslexikon* (*HKA* I/xvi, p. xiv); *Anfang einer Selbstbiographie* [*Beginning of an Autobiography*] (1834/35) in response to a request from the French literary historian Saint-René Taillandier (*HKA* I/xvi, p. xvi). These autobiographical writings were therefore ostensibly written with an audience in mind. However, none was submitted to the party which requested it, and it is not clear to what extent Grillparzer presents a censored image of himself. This makes them problematic sources as their objectivity is difficult to gauge.

Grillparzer's *Selbstbiographie* was written after the Akademie der Wissenschaften requested autobiographies of each member. It was only after a third request, in 1853, that Grillparzer reluctantly set to work. William A. Little argues that this reluctance stems from an aversion to making public the details of his life, rather than from an unwillingness to write an autobiography.[9] The Akademie's request carried more weight than those which preceded it, and Grillparzer had a duty towards the institution, but he still had to overcome his own reluctance before beginning (*HKA* I/xvi, p. xvi). Grillparzer started work on the *Selbstbiographie* in early 1853, and it was finished perhaps later that year, and certainly by the middle of 1854 (*HKA* I/xvi, pp. xii–xiii). It was written 'in rascher Folge, in einheitlichem Zuge' [in quick succession, in one go], with little preparation and few notes, and was never fully revised. In essence, it is a first draft (*HKA* I/xvi, p. xix). It covers the period between his birth and 1836, and Dusini notes that the closer Grillparzer comes to the period in which he was writing, a period he breaks off before reaching, the less he develops the episodes recounted.[10] Although he began under external impetus, Grillparzer continued writing the *Selbstbiographie* because he enjoyed it, and because he wished to develop his views on aesthetics, culture, and politics in a single work. It is not an '*apologia pro vita*'; nowhere does the poet attempt to defend or justify his actions. He attempts rather to clarify them and to show them in perspective.'[11] Diary entries find their way into the text, often with little revision, and the 1822 *Anfänge einer Selbstbiographie* was also used as a source. Although Grillparzer wrote the *Selbstbiographie* with no intention of publishing it, Little argues that he 'cannily foresaw that future literary historians and critics would scrutinize it'. This in part motivated him to write it. Hartmann and Sauer indicate that caution is needed when using the *Selbstbiographie* because it was written from memory, with only brief and occasional use of sources, and breaks off prematurely (*HKA* I/xvi, p. xlvii). Nevertheless, Heinrich Laube, who knew Grillparzer, writes that 'das Eine ist unverkennbar in dieser Selbstbiographie: die ungeschminkte Wahrhaftigkeit' [one thing is unmistakable in this autobiography: the unvarnished truthfulness].[12] Dusini argues that some scenes are 'erzählerisch arrangiert, rhetorisch effektvoll gegliedert und zu nahezu eigenständigen Geschichten ausgeformt' [arranged in a narrative fashion, organized in a way that is rhetorically effective and shaped into almost independent stories].[13] Hartmann and Sauer write that it lacks the 'romanartige Technik, das breite Ausmalen des landschaftlichen Hintergrundes, die reizende Ausführung der Liebesszenen' [novel-like technique, the broad description of the scenic background, the charming execution of the love scenes] (*HKA* I/xvi, p. xviii). Indeed, his relationships with women are almost completely ignored. As Little argues, the *Selbstbiographie* is Grillparzer's solution, as someone who was '[s]imultaneously attracted and repelled by self-revelation': he 'sought [...] to expose only the outer course of his life and remain silent on those intimate matters which conditioned his spiritual and artistic development.'[14] To be able critically to approach the *Selbstbiographie*, Little continues, we have to accept that 'Grillparzer's "Innerste" is a *noli me tangere* and that his refusal to discuss it is explicit'.[15]

The abundance of autobiographical writings, diaries, notebooks and correspondence has not translated into a surfeit of biographies of the author. In 1946 Douglas Yates noted the need for a biography of Grillparzer in English, but that such a work was not possible at the time.[16] The hope he expressed regarding the publication of a Grillparzer biography has remained unfulfilled. However, Grillparzer's contemporaries shared their impressions of the author in a number of biographical works. Heinrich Laube furnished the 1872 edition of Grillparzer's works with a brief biographical sketch. Personal experience and that of Grillparzer's friends, as well as the *Selbstbiographie*, which had been recently discovered, along with Grillparzer's diaries, were probably Laube's sources for this sketch. Laube covers his childhood, family life, education and career briefly. He mentions some themes of Grillparzer's life, such as the struggle with censorship, politics, his Austrian character and patriotism. Laube also talks about his personality: he was 'schüchtern und anspruchslos' [shy and modest], but also proud because he knew exactly 'wie viel er werth sei neben Anderen' [how much he was worth compared to others].[17] Katharina Fröhlich is the only love interest mentioned, and Laube asserts that Grillparzer wanted to marry and start a family, but could not due to financial issues. Laube does not fail to mention that Grillparzer's dramas fell out of favour at the Burgtheater, nor the revival which began in the 1850s under his, Laube's, directorship. Laube's relationship with Grillparzer, as well as his responsibility for the renewed interest in Grillparzer's works from the middle of the nineteenth century onwards should encourage caution when using this biographical sketch. To what extent is Laube's view of Grillparzer affected by their personal relationship? And could Laube's portrayal of the author be motivated by self-interest?

These issues must also be considered when discussing Laube's 1884 book *Franz Grillparzers Lebensgeschichte* [*Franz Grillparzer's Life Story*]. Laube sees the *Lebensgeschichte* as an extension and continuation of the *Selbstbiographie*, but also as a work which looks at Grillparzer's life from another point of view. The *Lebensgeschichte* deals with Grillparzer's life and works in a largely chronological fashion, with some thematic diversions. From the outset, Laube's tone is familiar. He refers to Grillparzer as '[u]nser Dichter' [our poet], and this tone calls into question his objectivity.[18] Laube also seems rather too dependent on Grillparzer's *Selbstbiographie*, other autobiographical writings, and diaries as sources for the biography, sources the partiality of which he does not question.

Three women writers of the period produced memoirs of their acquaintance with Grillparzer. In 1873, Auguste Littrow-Bischoff published *Aus dem persönlichen*

Verkehre mit Franz Grillparzer [*From my Personal Acquaintance with Franz Grillparzer*]. In 1875, Betty Paoli published *Grillparzer und seine Werke* [*Grillparzer and his Works*], and she also dedicated several essays to the author. And in 1916, Marie von Ebner-Eschenbach published *Meine Erinnerungen an Grillparzer* [*My Memories of Grillparzer*]. These works do not attempt to be biographies; rather, their authors recount their own personal experiences of Grillparzer, and caution is again necessary when analysing them.

Littrow-Bischoff recounts her visits to the poet between 1865 and 1871, the year before his death. Because she did not converse with Grillparzer with the aim of publishing a memoir, she leaves out 'alles, was im Sinne des Dahingeschiedenen als Vertrauensäußerung gelten konnte' [everything which the deceased could consider a confidence].[19] This selective reporting makes Littrow-Bischoff's memoir dubious as a source, and is compounded by her stated aim, namely the portrayal of 'das nur wenigen bekannt gewordene, aber dennoch gleichfalls wahrheitsgetreue Bild des ernsten Greises im Gewande der ihm ganz eigenthümlichen schlichten und liebenswürdigen Weise' [the picture, which was only known to a few, but is nevertheless likewise truthful, of the serious old man and his characteristic simple and kind manner].[20] Her attempt proves successful, and her memoirs provide an intimate account of the time they spent together. Her frequent visits led to a very close acquaintance with him. This relationship between Littrow-Bischoff and Grillparzer, which the former presents in her memoirs, again confirms that Grillparzer was not the enemy of educated, independent, public women.

Several of Paoli's essays, as well as a lengthy prose work, *Grillparzer und seine Werke*, deal directly with Grillparzer. In 'Studie über Grillparzer' [A Study of Grillparzer] (1872), Paoli presents a portrait of the poet which is at odds with the image of him in the popular imagination. He was not the closed personality which people believed him to be, and indeed 'das Spontane in seinem Wesen brachte es mit sich, daß er sich im Gespräche unbefangen gehen ließ [...] und keinen der humoristischen oder witzigen Einfälle, an denen er reich war, unterdrückte' [the spontaneous element in his being meant that he was uninhibited in conversation [...] and did not suppress any of his many humorous or funny ideas].[21] Already in his own lifetime Grillparzer had a reputation as a somewhat misanthropic individual, but Paoli recalls the fierce loyalty which he nevertheless inspired in his admirers: 'Eine gegen ihn gerichtete Unbill verletzte uns empfindlicher als jeder Tadel, der uns selbst treffen mochte.' [An injustice directed against him hurt us more than any reprimand which might concern us.][22] Paoli's *Grillparzer und seine Werke*, as its title suggests, is a mixture of memoir and literary analysis. She recounts conversations they shared to inform the reader about Grillparzer's creative life, his influences, and issues, such as censorship, which affected him.

Ebner-Eschenbach mentions several visits to Grillparzer in her diaries. In a short note on a visit in November 1864, she captures his lighter side: 'Er war sehr gesprächig und heiter. In einer Beziehung, sagte er, freue er sich seiner Taubheit, sie entschuldige sein Wegbleiben aus dem Reichsrat.' [He was very talkative and cheerful. He said that in one respect he was happy about his deafness, because it excused his absence from the Imperial Council.][23] She recounts their acquaintance at greater length in *Meine Erinnerungen an Grillparzer*, and paints a vivid and intimate picture of the author without denying his flaws. Ebner-Eschenbach provides more biographical detail than Paoli, including insight into Grillparzer's relationship with Katharina Fröhlich. Ebner-Eschenbach's account starts in the 1860s, when she asked Grillparzer if she could read him one of her dramas. She does not share his reaction or his judgment with her readers, but notes on a separate occasion that he expressed his happiness at the success of her drama *Doktor Ritter*, which was performed at the Burgtheater in 1869. It is unclear whether Grillparzer engaged with the works of Ebner-Eschenbach, but his pleasure at her literary success suggests that he was not opposed to women writers or women's writing.

Although Ebner-Eschenbach does not ignore Grillparzer's morose, melancholic attributes, she shows us his happy side as well, for example his reaction to a birthday present: 'Er [...] stand auf, legte den Arm um meine Schulter und gab mir einen langen, ernsthaften Kuß.' [He [...] stood up, put his arm around my shoulder and gave me a long, sincere kiss.][24] Ebner-Eschenbach's account also shows her devotion to the aged poet, a devotion shared by many, perhaps all, of the women who knew him in the later period of his life. Grillparzer was clearly fond of them in return. In a well-known aphorism, Grillparzer compared himself to Jesus because only women visited him. He referred to Littrow-Bischoff, one of these 'Pilgerinnen zum Grabe' [pilgrims to the grave], as 'die Astrologin' [the astrologer] on account of her husband's job as director of the Vienna Observatory, and Ebner-Eschenbach remarks that 'wir wußten sehr gut, daß jede von uns gelegentlich mit einem sehr boshaften Scherzworte bedacht wurde. Das änderte aber nicht das geringste an unsrer Liebe für ihn.' [we knew very well that each of us was occasionally thought of with a very malicious joke. But that did not change anything at all about our love for him.][25]

Although Laube's *Lebensgeschichte* has flaws, it remains the most comprehensive biography of Grillparzer in English or German. Grillparzer's love life, largely overlooked by Laube, has nevertheless attracted much biographical interest. Anna Tizia Leitich, for example, has written two books about the women in Grillparzer's life, *Zwölfmal Liebe. Frauen um Grillparzer* [*Twelve Times Love. Women around Grillparzer*] (1948) and *Genie und Leidenschaft. Frauen um Grillparzer* [*Genius and Passion. Women around Grillparzer*] (1965). Both are defined by Leitich's attempts to analyse Grillparzer's dramas, and his female characters in particular, through the lens of his personal life, and she argues that Grillparzer's female characters must have been inspired by the women he knew.[26] Heinz Politzer also provides a detailed resume of Grillparzer's love life, linking Grillparzer's affair with Marie Smolk von Smolenitz to his depiction of Rahel.[27] Yates, in his study *Franz Grillparzer. A Critical Biography* (1946), argues that similarities between Grillparzer's life and his work are almost 'too detailed and too sensational to be believed'.[28] More recently, Pia Janke has argued that speculative biographical details generally have little or no value for serious literary analysis. Janke criticizes the use of Grillparzer's love life as an analytical tool when studying his dramas, and the use of these dramas as sources for biographical study.[29]

Given the paucity of biographical works on Grillparzer, the reliance of these on the *Selbstbiographie*, other autobiographical writings, and diaries (which themselves were sources for the *Selbstbiographie*), and the lack of a comprehensive biography, Grillparzer's autobiographical works inevitably play a large role in the attempts of this study to understand his relationships with women. As mentioned above, the composition of the *Selbstbiographie* was quick and relied heavily on Grillparzer's memory, a fact which led to numerous factual errors in the text (*HKA* I/xvi, pp. xliv–xlvii) and which necessitates its cautious and critical use. However, Grillparzer by no means presents a universally flattering portrait of himself, which is perhaps an indication that, in accordance with the text's ostensible original purpose as a record for the Akademie, he strove for impartiality. Indeed, Grillparzer's diaries show that he was harshly critical of himself and aware of his flaws. This tallies with the image he presents of himself in these autobiographies, and with the image which his acquaintances present.

In two episodes from Grillparzer's childhood we see that, while women played important roles in his life at this stage, he already had the tendency to distance himself from women as soon as he was disappointed by them. Grillparzer inherited his father's 'hypochondrische Zurückgezogenheit' [hypochondriac seclusion] and spent his 'erste Jugend in fast völliger Einsamkeit'; 'beinahe ohne Umgang mit seinen Altersgenossen und durch Neigungsverschiedenheiten von seinen Brüdern entfernt gehalten' [early youth in almost complete solitude; almost without contact to his contemporaries and kept apart from his brothers by different tendencies].[30] A maid in his parents' household played an important role in his early education and the two would read together. However, she was sidelined once the young Grillparzer felt that his intellectual capacity had outgrown hers.[31] Just one transgression was enough to see the maid exiled from Grillparzer's presence and interest. His mother similarly proved a disappointing assistant in the young Grillparzer's literary adventures: 'Meine Mutter, zu der ich Vertrauen hatte, habe ich vielleicht manchmal um Erklärung angegangen, da sie mir aber für jeden Fall keine geben konnte, so blieb ich still und las fort.' [Perhaps I sometimes asked my mother, whom I trusted, for an explanation, but as she in each case could not give me one, I stayed quiet and kept reading.] (*HKA* I/xvi, p. 12–13.) His mother clearly functioned as a key reference point for her son, even if she could not be much help to him.

Grillparzer's remarks on women in general also display misogynistic tendencies. So, for example, he argues that male and female artistic judgments differ because women 'in der Regel keiner Abstraktion fähig sind, und nur das bewundern können, was sie zugleich auch vollkommen billigen' [as a rule are not capable of abstraction, and can only admire that of which they at the same time also wholly approve] (1821. Nr. 900. *HKA* II/vii, p. 351). Similarly, he copies an excerpt from Swift, presumably in a spirit of approbation, which plays on women's supposed vanity: 'Der Grund warum Männer sich gern schmeicheln lassen, ist gemeiniglich, weil sie eine schlechte Meinung von sich haben; bei Frauenzimmern ist es gerade das Gegentheil. Swift' [Love of flattery in most men proceeds from the mean opinion they have of themselves; in women from the contrary] (1822. Nr. 1060. *HKA* II/

viii, p. 26). He also argues that differences between the sexes mean that infidelity has varying results depending on the sex of victim and perpetrator: 'Die Frau eines untreuen Mannes bedauert man, über den Mann einer untreuen Frau spottet man.' [One pities the wife of an unfaithful man, one mocks the husband of an unfaithful woman.] (1822. Nr. 1216. *HKA* II/viii, p. 89.) Men, according to Grillparzer, do less damage than women when they are unfaithful, and this is because of difference between the sexes. Grillparzer seems to link this discrepancy to nature, when surely society is responsible for the attitudes towards adulterers and cuckolds.

Grillparzer's interest in historical women stands in contrast to his misogynistic statements. He read works by Françoise Bertaut de Motteville, whose *Mémoires* depict life at the court of Anne of Austria, and Madame de Genlis (Nr. 321. *HKA* II/vii, p. 141). Grillparzer's library contained the memoirs of Princess Wilhelmine of Prussia, Madame Roland (the subject of Ebner-Eschenbach's 1867 drama) and Jeanne de Valois-Saint-Rémy (notorious for her role in the Diamond Necklace Affair), as well as works on Marie Antoinette, Catherine II and Rahel von Varnhagen (*HKA* II/xii, pp. 112–13). Alongside numerous references to female rulers, in his notebooks and diaries he mentions the situation of women in Africa, ancient Egypt and Greece, and Europe. He notes: 'Große Achtung der Frauen in Egypten, doch Eingeschloßenheit der Vornehmern.' [Great respect for women in Egypt, but noblewomen are kept inside.] (1822. Nr. 1163. *HKA* II/viii, p. 68.) He mentions the education of Pindar under the guidance of Myrtis, and his eventual defeat by the poet Corinna, an anecdote which would surely have interested a male writer who was acquainted with so many female writers during his life, and who achieved fame with a drama focused on the life of Sappho (1822. Nr. 1144. *HKA* II/viii, p. 64). Grillparzer's reading of J.-B. Douville's *Voyage au Congo et dans l'intérieur de l'Afrique equinoxale* (1832) yielded many quotations on the lives of African women, including what he referred to as 'immoral dancing', and toleration of promiscuity. Grillparzer noted, for example, the '[g]roße Abhängigkeit der Weiber'; 'Galanterieen der Negerinnen' [great dependence of the women; gallantries of the Negresses]; that the more lovers a woman had, the more she and her husband were respected; and that the chiefs only let their daughters marry local men 'unter der Bedingung, daß wenn es dieser einmal belieben sollte, sich einem Weissen [*sic*] zu ergeben, sie es thun könne, und der Mann, wenn er es hindern wollte, in die Strafe der Sklaverei verfiele' [on the condition that, should she at some time wish to take a white man, she would be able to, and the husband, if he should want to stop her, would be punished by slavery] (1833. Nr. 2069. *HKA* II/ix, pp. 118–21). There is much here which might have intrigued the poet: paying a bride price; a society in which women's sexual freedom is encouraged; matrilineal inheritance; a husband's powerlessness in the face of his wife's desire for another man. Grillparzer's diaries show the extent of his intellectual interests, which ranged well beyond the borders of the Habsburg monarchy.

Grillparzer's diaries, notebooks and letters provide a wealth of material which contradicts his own misogynistic statements, and suggests that he was indeed interested in intellectual women. Germaine de Staël (1766–1817) features prominently in Grillparzer's notes. Although his reaction to de Staël was ambivalent, he read her work and did not consider her achievements trivial because of her sex. His analysis of the autobiographical work *Dix années d'exil* combines literary criticism with personal attacks against the author, citing her 'lächerliche Eitelkeit' [ridiculous vanity] and his disgust at 'das ganze Wesen dieser Frau' [the entire being of this woman]. For Grillparzer, de Staël was the epitome of writers 'die nicht ihren Gegenstand zeigen wollen, sondern sich' [who do not want to show their subject, but themselves], and he questioned the validity of her suffering (1822. Nr. 998. *HKA* II/viii, p. 10). Karin Hagl-Catling sees Grillparzer's 'emotionale Unsachlichkeit' [emotional lack of objectivity] in his assessment of de Staël as a result of her refusal to bow to censorship, which might have challenged his view of his own masculinity.[32] Grillparzer was also critical of the morality she advocated in the foreword to her novel *Delphine* (1802), which he labelled 'die Moral eines debauchirten Weibes' [the morality of a debauched woman] (1830. Nr. 1868. *HKA* II/ix, p. 19). He did, however, see fit to praise the content of the novel itself: 'Es ist ein Schatz von gefühlten und treffenden Bezeichnungen in dieser Delphine wie nicht leicht in einem andern Buche.' [There is a treasure of felt and appropriate descriptions in *Delphine* as you will not easily find in another book.] (1830. Nr. 1884. *HKA* II/ix, p. 23.)

On his travels, Grillparzer came into contact with the German writers Wilhelmine von Chézy and Ida von Hahn-Hahn. He was happy to reestablish the acquaintance with 'die leibhafte Frau von Chezy, Dichterin der Euryanthe u.s.w.' [Chézy, author of *Euryanthe* etc., in the flesh] (5 May 1836. Nr. 3017. *HKA* II/x, p. 67). Grillparzer's notes concerning Chézy display no animosity, and he recognizes her as an author. It is also clear that he was at least aware of European women writers of the age. Grillparzer met Hahn-Hahn during his trip to Constantinople in 1843. He noted: 'Sie scheint natürlich, wenigstens spricht sie so. Gefiel mir weit besser als ich erwartete.' [She seems natural, at least in the way she speaks. I liked her much more than I expected.] (1843. Nr. 3665. *HKA* II/ii, p. 41.)

The question of Grillparzer's attitude towards women becomes more complicated in the context of his contemporaries. In comparison with the playwright Eduard von Bauernfeld (1802–90), Grillparzer's positive pronouncements on women are less forceful and explicit. Karl Glossy writes that critics recognized Bauernfeld as an author who attempted to apply a 'Lustspielcur' [cure by comedy] as a solution to social problems.[33] In Bauernfeld's *Xenien*, written in the early 1870s, are two aphorisms which are stronger defences of women than we find in Grillparzer. The first, 'Gegenseitige Schwäche' ['Mutual Weakness'], reads: '"Schwachheit, dein Namen ist Weib!" so meint ein Dichter, ein großer;/ Aber das Weibchen, es weiß : Schwachheit, dein Namen ist Mann!"'[34] ['Frailty, thy name is woman!' so says a great poet; But the woman knows: Frailty, thy name is man!] The second, 'Stuart Mill', indicates Bauernfeld's approval of John Stuart Mill's views on women: '"Tauglich für jegliches Tun der Männer erklär' ich die Frauen!" — / Recht! Und ein Superplus noch: Kinder gebären nur sie.' ['I declare women fit for everything men do!' — Right! And one more thing: only they can bear children.][35]

As far as the *Frauenfrage* is concerned, Bauernfeld's *Bürgerlich und Romantisch* [*Bourgeois and Romantic*] (1835) provides an interesting contrast to the historicizing restraint of Grillparzer's dramas. Bauernfeld presents a discussion of the *Frauenfrage* directly and explicitly, and in a contemporary setting rather than in the mythical or historical settings which Grillparzer chose as part of his efforts to pass censorship. Perhaps Bauernfeld was treated with more latitude than Grillparzer as *Bürgerlich und Romantisch* is a comedy rather than a drama, but the contrast is nevertheless startling. The comedy centres on the character of Katharine, a female artist staying by herself in a spa town. At the opening of the drama, the councillor's wife and daughter, Cäcilie, discuss Katharine's arrival in the town. While Cäcilie seems enchanted with the idea of a female artist, her mother considers this a breach of morality: 'Eine reisende Malerin? Es klingt doch immer ein bißchen abenteuerlich.' [A travelling [female] painter? It does always sound a little adventurous.][36]

Against a misogynistic backdrop, Katharine tries to assert her independence. She explains her unusual behaviour to the Baron: 'Mein Vater galt für einen Sonderling. Er gab mir die Erziehung eines Knaben. Ich lernte reiten, schwimmen, klettern.' [My father was considered an oddball. He gave me a boy's upbringing. I learnt to ride, swim, climb.] (p. 320) It is this background which allows Katharine to assert her independence and challenge restrictions on her freedom:

> Wir armen Frauen! Warum sind wir die Unterdrückten? Haben wir nicht Verstand, Geist, Gefühl, so gut als die Männer? Besser als die Männer? Sollen sie Gesetze geben für uns und sie brechen gegen uns? Laß sie Gelehrte sein, Staatsleute und Soldaten, aber laß uns nicht ihre Sklavinnen werden. Ich habe keinen Vater, keinen Bruder, keinen Mann. Ich stehe allein in der Welt. Soll ich mich deshalb vor der Welt verbergen? [...] Ist es ein so großes Verbrechen, ohne männliche Begleitung spazieren zu gehen? Verlang' ich denn mehr? Und kann man weniger verlangen? (pp. 294–95)

> [We poor women! Why are we the oppressed? Do we not have reason, intelligence, feeling just as good as men's? Better than men's? Should they make laws for us and break them against us? Let them be the scholars, statesmen and soldiers, but do not let us become their slaves. I have no father, no brother, no husband. I am alone in the world. Should I therefore hide myself away from the world? [...] Is it such a great crime to go for a walk without a man by my side? Am I demanding more? And can one demand less?]

The Baron gives the context for Katharine's complaints, and for some of the difficulties which Grillparzer's female friends must have faced: 'Sie sehen, mein Fräulein, [...] wie schwer sich eine Dame, bei allem Geist und Witz, in der Welt allein behaupten kann. Die Tugend und Sittsamkeit selbst sind vor bösen Zungen nicht sicher, wenn sie ohne Paß und männliche Begleitung reisen.' [You see, my dear [...] how difficult it is for a woman, though she may have great intelligence and wit, to survive alone in the world. Even virtue and decorousness are not safe from evil tongues when they travel without a passport and a male companion.] (p. 332) Katharine's references to concrete problems of the time — a growing number of unmarried women, women's disenfranchisement, questions regarding men's and women's cognitive and emotional faculties, legal issues regarding majority — as well as the play's contemporary setting make this a much more direct engagement with the *Frauenfrage* than anything in Grillparzer's œuvre. As Roy C. Cowen writes, Grillparzer 'stops short of social realism as a criticism of specific conditions' and avoids contemporary settings.[37]

Grillparzer wrote many of his dramas with the intention of having them performed on stage, and, as the foreword to the first edition of *Die Ahnfrau* [*The Ancestress*] shows, he was well aware of their theatrical elements (*HKA* I/xiv, pp. 3–4). Grillparzer's struggles with the censors are well known, and, as diary notes testify, censorship was a major source of frustration in Grillparzer's life. In his *Selbstbiographie* he writes that, after early problems with the censors, it was natural to choose subject matter which would not pose such problems (*HKA* I/xvi, p. 203). His reaction to criticism of *Sappho*, also recounted in the *Selbstbiographie*, again suggests self-censorship: contemporary critics argued that the drama was not Greek enough, which was fine by Grillparzer, 'da ich nicht für Griechen sondern für Deutsche schrieb' [as I was not writing for Greeks, but for Germans] (*HKA* I/xvi, p. 203). His settings, then, were not contemporary, but the issues in them were. His decision not to release *Die Jüdin von Toledo* [*The Jewess of Toledo*], *Ein Bruderzwist in Habsburg* [*Family Strife in Hapsburg*] or *Libussa* during his lifetime, and the request that these manuscripts be destroyed on his death, is perhaps the biggest act of self-censorship he committed.

The Austria of Grillparzer's time had one of the strictest censorship regimes in Europe. Throughout the first half of the nineteenth century, censors adhered to the guidelines laid out by Franz Karl Hägelin in his *Denkschrift* [*Memorandum*] (1795). The regulations were tightened up in 1801, especially as regards printed works, and by the 1830s the petty restrictions of censorship had become a running joke. In general, censorship was stricter in the theatre than in publishing as performed works could have an immediate impact upon people of all classes, whereas printed books were in effect restricted to the educated classes.[38] Different theatres were also held to different standards: coarser language was allowed in the *Vorstadttheater* [suburban theatres], while at the Burgtheater every offensive part of a text was removed.[39]

One of the basic duties of theatre censorship was safeguarding public morality; all indecent language, including references to adultery, had to be eliminated. No references to the Church were allowed. The monarchy could not be disparaged, and portrayals of rebellion were banned. Political liberty as a subject was not permissible. Until 1848, all texts to be performed in a theatre had to be pre-approved. Special police agents attended rehearsals and first-night performances to make sure that the censors' changes had been incorporated.[40] The police ensured that in the Burgtheater both text and performance adhered to the highest moral standards. In 1822, Schreyvogel's adaptation of *King Lear* was banned as it portrayed the downfall of a monarch.[41] An application to stage Schiller's *Maria Stuart*, which violated Hägelin's principle that depictions of monarchs' executions could not be performed in monarchist states, was summarily rejected in 1810. The performance of a modified version was allowed in 1814 and strictly overseen by censors.

Many of those who took on the role of censor did so out of necessity, and in some cases police officers, civil servants, lawyers and members of other professions were assigned these roles alongside their existing duties.[42] Censors often complained that they received insufficient guidance regarding objectionable material, and erred on the side of caution from fear of punishments for allowing material to pass censorship which later generated complaints.

Despite the strict enforcement of censorship at the time, theatres in *Vormärz* Austria dealt with the issues which would lead to the Revolution of 1848 — at first indirectly, then more daringly, until the dissolution of the system of censorship towards the end of March 1848 made possible open criticism of the Metternich regime in Nestroy's *Freiheit in Krähwinkel* [*Freedom Comes to Krähwinkel*].[43] Günter Berghaus argues that theatre audiences in Vienna in the early 1830s were politically engaged and, although not inclined to revolution, dissatisfied with the political and social status quo, and that those in the suburbs had become the 'Ausgangspunkt einer politisch-oppositionellen Bewegung' [starting point of a political-opposition movement].[44] Nestroy, he writes, felt obliged to portray the social reality of post-Congress Vienna, 'und griff in seinen Stücken realhistorische Probleme auf, die das kleinbürgerliche — und nicht etwa das großbürgerliche — Publikum im Theater behandelt sehen wollte' [and in his plays he took up historical problems which the lower-middle-class — and not, for instance, the upper-class — audience wished to see dealt with].

Theatre and newspapers enjoyed a close relationship in the Vienna of the first half of the nineteenth century, and the importance of the theatre as a forum for discussion of political themes transformed theatre reviews into a medium of public debate.[45] The two institutions were also dependent on one another: no open political debate was possible, so the press depended on theatres for material; theatres depended on the press not just for critical coverage, but also for potential subject matter. Theatre criticism could be polemical, and the editors and publishers of journals which contained reviews, and theatre reviews in particular, were held responsible for their employees' content, and prohibited from publishing essays which were openly critical.[46] According to Meike Wagner, '[i]n dieser publizistischen Atmosphäre der übersteigerten Theater-Polemik brach sich das Konzept der Meinungspresse Bahn' [in this journalistic atmosphere of exaggerated theatre polemics, the concept of a press of opinion made headway].

Both theatres and the media brought the issue of women's emancipation into the open, often in a far more direct way than Grillparzer's dramas. Yates, for example, writes that Nestroy, in *Der Kobold* [*The Goblin*] (1838), 'is already in effect summarizing two of the main plaints of the *Vormärz* feminists', while in other plays he deals with 'relations between the sexes, spelling out the inequalities of social expectations and emphasizing the deceptiveness, unreliability, and self-indulgence of the male'. Yates argues that Nestroy, like Grillparzer, saw in the 'uneven battle of the sexes [...] the extent to which in early and mid nineteenth-century Austria the underprivileged were women'.[47]

Due to ubiquitous, harshly regimented censorship, Grillparzer's texts as we know them, and as they were performed at the time, may have presented merely the author's censored version of his own views. Unfortunately, only *Die Ahnfrau* survives in a complete first draft available to readers, and in the relevant chapter this is compared with the final version to identify elements which Grillparzer might have changed. In other cases, Grillparzer's notes and plans are analysed to the same ends. However, it is seldom possible to establish Grillparzer's own views, and the extent to which he portrayed them faithfully and openly in his dramas, from the dramas and his preparatory work alone.

One indication that Grillparzer may have self-censored the dramas he wrote for the stage comes from a play written in 1811. In *Wer ist schuldig?* [*Who is to blame?*], a one-act *Lustspiel* which was probably not written with public performance in mind, Grillparzer presents a marital feud in a presumably contemporary setting in Vienna. Holl expresses negative stereotypes of women, while his wife, Marie, inveighs against the male sex and women's subordinate social position:

>	Herrschsüchtiges und ungezügeltes Geschlecht!
>	So stempelt denn dein Wille jede That zum Recht?
>	Euch schmückt des Rühmes Kranz, euch blüht des Sieges Krone,
>	ihr herrscht im Haus, im Lernstuhl, auf dem Throne
>	die ganze Welt ist euer ungeheures Reich
>	[...]
>	indeß die Frau verbannt in Kindesstub' und Küche,
>	dem Herrn der Erde dient als kaum bemerkte Magd
>	[...]
>	Genug! In Wien wie in dem Lande der Chinesen
>	ist eine Frau das unglüksel'gste aller Wesen! (HKA II/iv, p. 98)

>	[Domineering and unbridled sex!/ Thus your will stamps every action as right?/ The wreath of fame adorns you, the crown of victory will be yours,/ you rule at home, at school, on the throne/ the whole world is your enormous realm/ [...] / meanwhile the woman is exiled to the nursery and the kitchen,/ serves the lord of the world as a barely noticed maid / [...] / Enough! In Vienna as in the land of the Chinese/ woman is the unhappiest of all creatures!]

In conversation with Holl, Marie also criticizes the institution of marriage: 'Für uns [Frauen] ist die Eh' wohl die schlimmste Lotterie,/ Verlieren können wir allein, gewinnen nie' [For us [women] marriage is the worst lottery,/ We can only lose, never win] (p. 127). She even seems to address the contemporary legal issue of women's majority:

>	MARIE: Die Zeiten sind vorbei
>	 wo man geglaubt, daß eine Frau nie mündig sei!
>	HOLL: Wie, mündig? O an Mund fehlt' euch's in keinen Zeiten,
>	 allein mit der Vernunft sind wir noch jetzt im Weiten. (p. 126)

>	[MARIE: The times are past/ when one believed that a woman could never come of age! HOLL: What do you mean, come of age? You women are never short of words,/ the problem is with your common sense.]

While Grillparzer's mature works often deal with the social role of women, and present women who do not conform to contemporary ideals, they do not directly address legal issues in the way that *Wer ist schuldig?* does, even if the import of Marie's words is somewhat masked by Holl's disdainful reply. Here, Holl responds with the misogyny which characterizes his statements about women. In a similar vein, he claims: 'Zwei Klaßen Weiber gibt's: Die Schlimmen und — die Schlimmern' [There are two types of women: the bad and the worse], and refers to his wife as 'ein Lexikon von Weiberschwächen' [an encyclopedia of female weaknesses] (p. 127).

Wer ist schuldig? shows that Grillparzer was aware of women's issues, and thinking and writing about them from an early age. It is also a more direct engagement with the *Frauenfrage* than in later dramas, and demonstrates a desire to position these issues in a contemporary setting. This suggests that Grillparzer censored the content of his dramas beyond giving them historical or mythological settings. The likelihood of self-censorship in issues related to the *Frauenfrage* suggests that Grillparzer's views may have been stronger than he felt comfortable portraying on the stage. The abundance of misogynistic statements in Grillparzer's private writings cannot be denied, nor can the fact that such statements outnumber by far his expressions of sympathy for women. It should, however, be noted that the vast majority of such statements originate from the first decades of his life, and in particular from his late teenage years and his twenties. Hagl-Catling identifies a time lag between his hostile and friendly behaviour, and concludes that he was more tolerant of female writers in his later years.[48] Dagmar Lorenz argues that, despite his 'Anwürfe gegen "die Weiber"' [accusations against "women"], Grillparzer was not anti-feminist or misogynistic.[49] It is not inconceivable that such opinions belong to his youth, and betray the strong influence of upbringing and social trends, and that he moderated and reversed these opinions as he matured. It is possible that his later female acquaintance, who feature in Chapter 1, contributed to this change in his attitude. However, even his juvenilia evidence his deep sympathy with the plight of women in patriarchal societies, and his contempt for brutish misogyny. Is it possible to reconcile the conflicting views on women which appear in private prose and public dramatic works?

In *Das Kloster bei Sendomir* [*The Monastery near Sandomierz*] (1828), Grillparzer himself helps us reconcile these disparate public and private conceptions of women. The frame story, in which an incognito Count Starschensky tells two travellers his story, offers some potential insights into Grillparzer's self-conception and his relationships with women. The tale begins with the arrival of two travellers at a monastery. A monk provides them with accommodation and victuals, and they ask him to tell them the history of the monastery. The monk tells the story of Count Starschensky, whose wife Elga cuckolded him, and tricked him into raising the child fathered by her former lover. On discovering this betrayal, Starschensky gave her the choice between death or salvation by murdering her baby daughter. When she showed herself more concerned with self-preservation than her daughter's life, Starschensky murdered her. Starschensky left his child with a local couple, sold his remaining property and founded the monastery. It is only when the abbot enters looking for Starschensky that the travellers, and the reader, find out that the monk-narrator and Starschensky are one and the same.

While caution is necessary when linking an author to one of his fictional characters, there are many similarities between Grillparzer and Starschensky. Starschensky begins his narrative with a description of himself (in the third person, as he does not wish to betray his identity), and in this description we see Grillparzer's diffidence, reserve, and desire for independence.[50] This third characteristic, in particular, suggests an overlap between author and protagonist as it reinforces Grillparzer's assertion that he could not consider marriage because he detested the sacrifice of privacy which it entailed. Grillparzer is perhaps indulging in self-mockery when he describes the count's chastity:

> Über Eines wunderten sich die Leute am meisten: nie hatte man ihn einem weiblichen Wesen mit Neigung zugetan gesehen, sichtlich vermied er den Umgang mit Frauen. Er galt daher für einen Weiberfeind; doch war er keiner. (*HKA* I/xiii, p. 9.)
>
> [One thing surprised the people more than any other: no one had ever seen him display affection for a woman, he visibly avoided contact with women. He was therefore considered a woman-hater, although he was not.]

Here, Grillparzer wryly pokes fun at his own catalogue of romantic exploits while anticipating and calling into question his reputation as a misogynist. If Grillparzer were to be accused of misogyny, it would not be because he avoided women. In the context of this study, this quotation raises important questions regarding Grillparzer's self-perception, particularly as it could be seen as a rejection of claims that he was anti-women. If we take Grillparzer and Starschensky to be one and the same person as far as the quality of not being a *Weiberfeind* is concerned, then in *Das Kloster bei Sendomir* Grillparzer is perhaps giving us a means of navigating the discrepancy between his private musings and his dramas, of correcting the inaccurate picture which emerges from this discrepancy.

Grillparzer's expressed views on women and his female protagonists must be seen in the context of wider debates on sex/gender and on the roles of men and women in society. Gender was a contentious issue at the end of the eighteenth century, at least partly in the wake of the French Revolution, which, according to Thomas Laqueur, created a 'genuine new feminism'.[51] However, this was accompanied by antifeminism and a new fear of women. The Revolution also formed new political boundaries and commensurate gender boundaries. The creation of a bourgeois public sphere meant that it was necessary to decide which sex could legitimately occupy it. Throughout Grillparzer's creative period, the *Frauenfrage* was a very controversial topic. As we will see, Grillparzer's life and work both replicate and reject contemporary ideals of womanhood. On the one hand, diary entries and his treatment of his love interests, including Fröhlich, betray his misogyny. On the other, he counted some of the most atypical women of the era amongst his acquaintance, and his dramas question a social order in which woman are marginalized and mistreated. In the following chapters, I analyse eight of Grillparzer's dramas, drawing on his other writings as well, in an attempt to explain the discord between his private views and the subversion of these in his dramatic works, and to analyse Grillparzer's problematization of prevailing social norms.

As has been stated already, the aim of this study is to investigate the degree to which Grillparzer incorporated criticism of the social position of women into his dramas. It is, therefore, primarily about Grillparzer's *ideas*. The aims of this study, and its primary interest in Grillparzer's ideas, inform the methodological approaches which have been chosen, and explain the omissions which have been made. The focus is on Grillparzer's dramas as texts, rather than as dramas written for a stage, and on Grillparzer's other writings, rather than on the dramas' reception. This is for the simple reason that Grillparzer could control *what* he wrote more closely than he could control how his dramas were performed or received. Similarly, Grillparzer's other writings — juvenilia, diaries, letters, prose — provide more insight into the reading, reflection and ideas which went into creating these dramas than can contemporary reception.

In order to understand better Grillparzer's ideas and their genesis, his notes, diaries, correspondence, fragmentary dramas, juvenilia and prose are analysed. This contextualizes the dramas which are the focus of the study, and helps to show that, although he made misogynistic comments, he was interested in women's social roles, and in powerful women from myth and history, from an early age. Two early dramatic works, *Wer ist schuldig?* and *Der Zauberwald*, also indicate that Grillparzer might have censored his later dramas, and removed or amended material that was explicitly critical of the contemporary social position of women. This analysis also makes up for the lack of early drafts of the dramas considered here. Analysis of drafts would have allowed the development of socially critical ideas to be studied. Unfortunately, only *Die Ahnfrau* exists in a complete first draft.

Original plans for a chronological progression through Grillparzer's works gave way to the thematic approach in which this study is presented. Not only does a thematic approach allow for similarities between texts to be exposed, but the development of many of Grillparzer's dramas over a period of decades makes a strictly chronological approach inappropriate. Analysis of Grillparzer's notebooks and diaries provided inspiration for the approaches taken in two of the four main sections. In 'Women and Enlightenment', I demonstrate Grillparzer's engagement with Kant, and argue that Enlightenment philosophy influenced *Ein treuer Diener seines Herrn* [*A Faithful Servant of His Master*] and *Des Meeres und der Liebe Wellen* [*The Waves of the Sea and of Love*]. In 'Female Rulers', I contend that interest in powerful female figures from history and myth was combined with his reading in political philosophy to produce his portrayals of Sappho and Libussa. Taking inspiration for the analytical approaches from Grillparzer's writings means his dramas are analysed in the context of ideas which interested him. This mitigates a lack of evidence that he actively portrayed social contract theory or Enlightenment philosophy in his dramas. In 'Women and the Law', I suggest that the contemporary legal situation of women is a useful tool with which to analyse *Die Ahnfrau* and *König Ottokars Glück und Ende* [*King Ottakar, His Rise and Fall*]. The final section, 'Grillparzer and Kyriarchy', consciously breaks with this approach, seeking analytical inspiration in the recent concepts of kyriarchy and intersectionality to understand the ways in which Grillparzer portrays complex interlocking patterns of discrimination and subjugation in *Das goldene Vließ* [*The Golden Fleece*] and *Die Jüdin von Toledo*.

Interest in Grillparzer's ideas influenced other methodological choices. The focus on Grillparzer's dramas as texts means that, in Chapter 1, the focus is on women writers rather than actresses. The actresses with whom Grillparzer was acquainted are considered. However, unlike Caroline Pichler, Johanna Franul von Weissenthurn and others, Sophie Schröder, Julie Rettich and Charlotte Wolter did not engage critically in print with the contemporary debates around the *Frauenfrage* which provide the broad context for this analysis of Grillparzer's dramas. Here it should be noted that I do not attempt to prove links between the women Grillparzer knew and their works, and his portrayal of female characters. Rather, the discussion of women Grillparzer knew serves to: show how women's rights were being debated at this time in Austria; demonstrate that women Grillparzer knew engaged actively with these debates in writing, and possibly also in salons Grillparzer would have attended; and suggest that Grillparzer was more open to intellectual, 'emancipated' women in real life than his diaries might make us think. The focus has been placed on female writers whom Grillparzer knew as their writings allow us to gain insight into the concerns of contemporary thinking regarding women's rights, and therefore to contextualize Grillparzer's dramas. This also explains why these women's fictional writings are ignored in favour of non-fictional writings. Their fiction does not engage with the *Frauenfrage* in the explicit way in which their non-fictional works considered here do. Fictional works would also need to be analysed through the lens of these non-fictional works. The limits of this study preclude the thorough and lengthy analysis of these fictional texts — Pichler's many historical novels, for example — which would be necessary. Additionally, it seemed at odds with the broadly feminist methodology of this study to treat fictional works by these women — works which are voluminous, and, although now largely forgotten, even by scholarship, were very popular in their time — as a sideshow in a work dedicated to a male writer.

Grillparzer's dramas, and their female characters more specifically, have been the subject of much scholarship, and this study owes a debt to those authors upon whose works it builds. A brief review of the key publications specific to the present study will afford an overview of what has already been accomplished, and highlight some of the gaps which I hope to fill.

The importance of Grillparzer's female characters was already recognized during his lifetime. In 1848, an anonymous writer in the *Sonntagsblätter* compared Grillparzer's 'edle[], oft großartige[] Frauengestalten' [noble, often magnificent female characters] with his male characters, all of whom appear 'mehr oder weniger erbärmlich' [more or less wretched].[52] Jaromir is 'unmännlich' [unmanly], Ottokar 'zerbrochen und männlich unwürdig' [broken and unworthy as a man]. The author concludes: 'Die Frauen sollten unsere[n] Grillparzer [...] lieben und verehren. Uns Männer hat er wenig verklärt.' [Women should love and honour our Grillparzer. He did not paint a pretty picture of us men.] In 1856, the English translator Archer Gurney wrote to Grillparzer, praising his portrayal of women, and of Sappho in particular: 'Ach, wie viel schulden Ihnen die Deutschen Frauen! Sie allein haben die Rechte des Geschlechts vertheidigt, und eben dadurch Sich den Haß der meisten Männer zugezogen.' [Oh, how much do German women owe you! Only you defended the rights of their sex, and through exactly that incurred the hatred of most men.] (Nr. 851. *HKA* III/iii, pp. 174–75.) In 1877, Bauernfeld called Grillparzer 'der weibliche Dichter *par excellence*' [the female poet par excellence] and noted that his female characters 'enthalten feine Züge, wohl auch Widersprüche, wie sie der Dichter dem weiblichen Herzen abgelauscht' [contain fine traits, and contradictions too, which the poet observed in the female heart] while his male figures excited little interest.[53] Reception by Grillparzer's contemporaries focuses on the ways in which Grillparzer's portrayal of women agrees with stereotypes and prejudices regarding the female character, rather than on the feminist messages which I see in these dramas.

Grillparzer's depiction of women has since been mentioned by many critics. Franz Forster notes that Grillparzer 'gehört überhaupt zu den großen Frauendarstellern unter den Dramatikern' [is one of the greatest interpreters of women among dramatists] and that his dramas often deal with 'die Situation der Frau in einer von Männern dominierten Gesellschaft' [the situation of women in a male-dominated society]. Forster identifies the frequent juxtaposition of a formidable woman and a weak man in Grillparzer's dramas. His female characters are 'eigenwillig, selbstbewußt, scharfzüngig, teils auch mit einem guten Anflug verbaler Aggressivität ausgestattet' [unconventional, self-confident, sharp-tongued, sometimes also equipped with a good trace of verbal aggressiveness].[54] Walter Weiss notes that Grillparzer favours 'seine Frauengestalten [...] und sich oft mit ihnen identifiziert, im Kontrast übrigens zu seinem biographisch belegten Verhalten' [his female characters [...] and often identifies with them, in contrast, incidentally, to the behavior demonstrated during his life].[55]

An early study dedicated to Grillparzer's female figures was Francis Wolf-Cirian's *Grillparzers Frauengestalten* [*Grillparzer's Female Characters*], which aimed to provide a thorough analysis of his heroines. She[56] finds it puzzling that no one had previously devoted a monograph to them, despite the fact that 'die Frauen Grillparzers vor seinen Männern eine größere Bestimmtheit, eine erhöhtere Lebenskraft, zum wenigsten ein ursprünglicheres Triebleben voraushaben' [Grillparzer's women have the advantage over his men of a greater determination, stronger vitality, and at least a more elemental instinctive existence].[57] Wolf-Cirian does not place Grillparzer's heroines in a social context, which is one major flaw which the present study aims to address. Anna Tizia Leitich argues that scholarship has overlooked Grillparzer's 'großartiges Frauenbrevier' [excellent guide to women], and that he depicts psychological developments 'die wir uns erst im Laufe der modernen Frauenbewegung sozusagen erobern mußten' [which we had to claim for ourselves, so to say, only in the course of the modern women's movement].[58] Brigitte Prutti goes further when she states that the 'beeindruckende Statur und das emanzipatorische Potential von Grillparzers mythischen Heroinen und Amazonen ist nicht zu leugnen' [impressive stature and emancipatory potential of Grillparzer's mythical heroines and amazons cannot be denied].[59]

Lorenz has dedicated several studies to Grillparzer's heroines, among whom are 'jene merkwürdig schillernden, androgynen Charaktere, denen [...] die ihnen angestammten Rollen zu eng sind' [curiously resplendent, androgynous characters

[...] whose traditional roles are too restrictive for them].[60] Lorenz sees Grillparzer as an iconoclastic figure whose dramas demand a critical and radical attitude towards Western society in order to effect change.[61] This analysis stands in opposition to the conclusions of Heinrich Laube and others. Laube, for example, writes that Grillparzer's works were not 'polemisch [...], ja nicht einmal theoretisch' [polemical [...] not even theoretical] and that even 'das feinste politische Mißtrauen konnte ihnen nur wenig Bedenkliches absehen' [the most sensitive political mistrust could see only little in them which was questionable].[62] In her 1986 study, *Grillparzer, Dichter des sozialen Konflikts* [*Grillparzer, Poet of Social Conflict*], Lorenz analyses several of Grillparzer's dramas from a feminist perspective. She argues that Grillparzer constantly questioned the division of life into public and private spheres, and so should be placed 'auf einer Linie, die von Kleist über Marx/Engels und Bebel hinreicht in das 20. Jahrhundert und den zeitgenössischen Feminismus' [on a line which reaches from Kleist through Marx/Engels and Bebel into the twentieth century and contemporary feminism]. In his dramas, 'die Übergänge von Mann zu Frau, männlichem und weiblichem Verhalten' [the boundaries between man and woman, masculine and feminine behavior] are fluid, and '[i]n der Hinterfragung der traditionellen Geschlechterrollen liegt die Kritik an der Machtverteilung' [his questioning of traditional gender roles contains criticism of the division of power].[63] She also notes that his heroines are far more complex and developed than those of his contemporaries. Lorenz argues that his acquaintances with emancipated women show he was open to new gender roles. Elsewhere, Lorenz suggests that Grillparzer's female acquaintance is the reason why he did not fill his dramas with 'ausgeleierten Klischees von Tugend, Treue, mütterlicher Opferbereitschaft, Passivität, Unterwürfigkeit' [worn-out clichés of virtue, loyalty, motherly willingness to sacrifice, passivity, servility] and other idealized male conceptions of femininity.[64] In part, the present study elaborates on these points and shows in detail the attitudes of Grillparzer's female acquaintances to the *Frauenfrage*.

In a 1991 article, Lorenz argues that Grillparzer's 'Reaktionen zu den Emanzipationskomplexen und sozialen Fragen [sind] unkonventionell, ja revolutionär [...]' [reactions to the complexes of emancipation and social issues [are] unconventional, even revolutionary].[65] She shows that the Fröhlich sisters, who provided for themselves financially, did not comply with the expectations of patriarchal society, and argues that Grillparzer's female characters reflect his circle. Lorenz writes that Grillparzer's experiences with the women he knew, particularly the Fröhlich sisters, helped shape the way he thought about women: he saw man as the 'Normalmensch[]' [standard human] but did not believe gender differences to be categorical or unchangeable.[66]

Hagl-Catling has produced a larger feminist-themed study of Grillparzer's dramas. Central to this is a psychological examination of Grillparzer. She argues that the opposition of a strict father and depressive, artistic mother sowed the seeds of self-alienation in the young Grillparzer, and that this resulted in 'einer lebenslangen, erst im Alter abklingenden Identitätskrise' [lifelong identity crisis which only subsided in old age].⁶⁷ She links these psychological issues with his heroines. Hagl-Catling identifies a lack of positive comments on female writers, and argues that a 'tief verborgene Misogynie' [deeply hidden misogyny] influenced his reaction to de Staël and other literary women.⁶⁸ She sees the various portrayals of women in *Die Jüdin von Toledo* as representative of Grillparzer's personal *Frauenbild* which contains 'Elemente des spätaufklärerischen, des romantischen und des bürgerlich-biedermeierlichen Zeitgeistes sowie Elemente des misogynen Frauenbildes der Wiener Gesellschaft des 19. Jahrhunderts' [elements of the late Enlightenment, romantic and bourgeois-Biedermeier *Zeitgeist* as well as elements of the misogynistic image of women prevalent in Viennese society of the nineteenth century].⁶⁹

Lorenz, Hagl-Catling, and others have posited Grillparzer's female acquaintances as possible influences on his female characters. Cowen mentions Grillparzer's 'deep attachments' to several women who might have influenced his portrayal of women.⁷⁰ Bruce Thompson writes that Grillparzer's love life was a focus for many critics because 'it provided him with the source material for [...] his depiction of female characters.'⁷¹ Masato Ikuta sees Grillparzer's experiences with women as the inspiration for his portrayal of the relationship between the sexes, but argues that 'im Werk der intersubjektive Konflikt überwiegend vom frauenemanzipatorischen Standpunkt dargestellt wird' [in his work conflict between protagonists is predominantly portrayed from the viewpoint of women's emancipation].⁷²

Grillparzer criticism has not been immune to the political vagaries of the decades since his death. A year after his death, he was already considered the great Austrian national poet.⁷³ It was Laube who initiated the author's 'fatale Beförderung zur österreichischen kulturellen Leitfigur' [fatal promotion to a leading figure of Austrian culture].⁷⁴ In a process designed to cement German cultural hegemony in the multicultural Habsburg lands, Grillparzer came to be seen as a symbol of the Austrian bourgeoisie. The canonization of Grillparzer served cultural politics by suggesting the intertwining of German and Austrian-German culture and supporting the claim that German Austria was the rightful heir of Weimar. In the 1930s and 1940s, Grillparzer and his works 'became ammunition in a war of words' as Austria first sought to distance itself from Nazi Germany, before being integrated into it after 1938.⁷⁵ The Viennese press often stressed his Austrian credentials in the 1930s. From 1938 onwards, National Socialist and antisemitic tones became increasingly dominant in the rejection of 'the image of Grillparzer the weakling', with some critics portraying him as a pan-Germanic ideal of strength and vitality. 1941, the 150th anniversary of Grillparzer's birth, was dominated by praise of the author as a man of 'Greater German' ideas. In the years after World War II his Austrian credentials were again promoted, and Austrian critics portrayed him as 'the classical Viennese'.⁷⁶ Ekkehart Krippendorff argues that the post-war celebration of Grillparzer as an Austrian national author was an insult: 'man [hat] ihn erneut tief beschädigt, weil gewissermaßen "ethnisiert" als eine Art besseren Heimatdichter' [again one damaged him deeply by, as it were, "ethnicizing" him as a kind of better national poet].⁷⁷

Josef Nadler, who is quoted in this study, established 'deutschnationale[], antisemitische[], antiziganische[] und antislawische[] Ideologeme als Grundlage einer neuen Literaturgeschichtsschreibung' [German national, anti-Semitic, anti-Romani and anti-Slavic ideologemes as the basis for a new literary historiography].[78] His work ascribed particular importance to theatre as a forum for specifically national issues, and attempted to interpret literature anew in the service of National Socialism; Grillparzer and his works became mere material for analysis. Key Nazi ideologies were built around Grillparzer, who was reinvented as a central figure in the new Nazi literary canon. Ernst Fischer, also quoted here, was a KPÖ member and government minister after the war, and his study of Grillparzer is an example of the post-war trend for emphasizing the Austrian qualities of Grillparzer's works and characters. For example, Fischer sees Grillparzer's heroines as 'Wiener Frauen und Mädchen; und aus den Tiefen der allumfassenden Volkerstadt steigen auch die Medea und die Jüdin von Toledo hervor' [Viennese women and girls; and from the depths of the all-encompassing imperial city arise Medea and the Jewess of Toledo].[79] Hildegard Essler, writing in Vienna during and after the war, shares this view.[80]

The present study shares its central aim with that of Pia Janke's 2000 article, 'Gescheiterte Authentizität' ['Failed Authenticity'], namely an interpretation of Grillparzer's heroines 'aus einer sozialgeschichtlichen Perspektive heraus, die das kulturelle Bewußtsein des 19. Jahrhunderts mitreflektiert' [from a sociohistorical perspective which reflects the cultural consciousness of the nineteenth century].[81] Janke sees this as a more suitable alternative to the common approach of making Grillparzer's romantic life central to literary analysis of his heroines. Janke identifies a major issue faced when placing Grillparzer's works in the context of the women's rights movement: it has yet to be proven that he engaged with this movement at all. Although this study cannot *prove* Grillparzer's engagement with the movement, more thorough analysis of Grillparzer's relationships with some of its proponents, and of the feminist writings of the women he knew, than has previously been attempted, allows Grillparzer's dramas to be placed more firmly in this context than has previously been possible. As I show, Grillparzer's friendships with many women who were involved in the Austrian women's movement suggest that he was not wholly inimical to the movement's aims.

Notes to the Introduction

1. [Verzeichnis der Kranzspenden zu Grillparzers Begräbnis.] Undated manuscript, Wienbibliothek im Rathaus, H.I.N. 82372.
2. W. E. Yates, 'Grillparzer and the Fair Sex', in *Grillparzer und die Europäische Tradition. Londoner Symposium 1986*, ed. by Robert Pichl et al. (Vienna: Hora, 1987), pp. 71–83 (p. 77).
3. Franz Grillparzer, *Sämtliche Werke*, Historisch-kritische Ausgabe, 42 vols, ed. by August Sauer and Reinhold Backmann (Vienna; Leipzig: Gerlach & Wiedling, 1908–16; Vienna: Schroll, 1916–48). Here: Nr. 594, II/vii, p. 236. All further quotations from this edition will be indicated in the body of the text by the initials *HKA*. Upper-case and lower-case Roman numerals refer to the part and volume respectively. Grillparzer's works are quoted as in the *HKA*, including his sometimes erratic and non-standard orthography and punctuation.
4. Anna Tizia Leitich, *Zwölfmal Liebe. Frauen um Grillparzer* (Vienna: Georg Fromme & Co., 1948), p. 37.

5. Ian F. Roe, *Franz Grillparzer: A Century of Criticism* (Columbia, SC: Camden House, 1995), pp. 31–32.
6. Dagmar C. G. Lorenz, 'Frau und Weiblichkeit bei Grillparzer', in *Der Widerspenstigen Zähmung. Studien zur bezwungenen Weiblichkeit in der Literatur vom Mittelalter bis zur Gegenwart*, ed. by Sylvia Wallinger and Monika Jonas (Innsbruck: Institut für Germanistik der Universität Innsbruck, 1986), pp. 201–16 (pp. 202–03).
7. William A. Little, 'Grillparzer's Excursions into Autobiography', *Kentucky Foreign Language Quarterly* 11 (1964), 142–51 (p. 143).
8. Arno Dusini, '"...wenn nicht vernichtet, so doch verkümmert...". Zur Struktur der Grillparzerschen *Selbstbiographie*', in *Autobiographien in der österreichischen Literatur. Von Franz Grillparzer bis Thomas Bernhard,* ed. by Klaus Amann and Karl Wagner (Innsbruck: Studien Verlag, 1998), pp. 27–43 (p. 28).
9. Little, 'Grillparzer's Excursions into Autobiography', p. 147.
10. Arno Dusini, *Die Ordnung des Lebens. Zu Franz Grillparzers "Selbstbiographie"*, (Tübingen: Niemeyer, 1991), p. 7.
11. Little, 'Grillparzer's Excursions into Autobiography', p. 149.
12. Heinrich Laube, 'Einleitung', in Franz Grillparzer, *Sämmtliche Werke*, ed. by Josef Weilen, 10 vols (Stuttgart: Cotta, 1872), I, v–xl (p. xxi).
13. Dusini, 'Zur Struktur der Grillparzerschen *Selbstbiographie*', p. 33.
14. Little, 'Grillparzer's Excursions into Autobiography', p. 148.
15. Ibid., p. 149.
16. Douglas Yates, *Grillparzer. A Critical Biography*, (Oxford: Blackwell, 1946), p. v.
17. Laube, 'Einleitung', p. xxx.
18. Heinrich Laube, *Franz Grillparzers Lebensgeschichte* (Stuttgart: Cotta, 1884), p. 1.
19. Auguste von Littrow-Bischoff, *Aus dem persönlichen Verkehre mit Franz Grillparzer* (Vienna: Rosner, 1873), p. 18.
20. Ibid., pp. 18–19.
21. Betty Paoli, 'Studie über Grillparzer' (1872), in *Grillparzers Gespräche und die Charakteristiken seiner Persönlichkeit durch die Zeitgenossen*, ed. by August Sauer. Schriften des Literarischen Vereins in Wien I. (Vienna: Verlag des Literarischen Vereins in Wien, 1904), pp. 243–71 (p. 244).
22. Ibid., p. 255.
23. Entry for 16.11.1864. Marie von Ebner-Eschenbach, *Kritische Texte und Deutungen*, ed. by Karl Konrad Polheim et al., 8 vols, *Tagebücher I. 1862–69*, ed. by Karl Konrad Polheim and Rainer Baasner (Tübingen: Niemeyer, 1989), p. 36.
24. Marie von Ebner-Eschenbach, *Meine Erinnerungen an Grillparzer. Aus einem zeitlosen Tagebuch* (Berlin: Gebrüder Paetel, 1916), p. 50.
25. Ibid., p. 45.
26. Anna Tizia Leitich, *Genie und Leidenschaft. Die Frauen um Grillparzer* (Vienna: Speidel, 1965), p. 10.
27. Heinz Politzer, *Franz Grillparzer oder das abgründige Biedermeier* (Vienna: Molden, 1972), p. 121.
28. Yates, *Grillparzer. A Critical Biography*, p. 57.
29. Pia Janke, 'Gescheiterte Authentizität. Anmerkungen zu Grillparzers Frauenfiguren', *Lenau-Jahrbuch* 26 (2000), 57–72, (p. 58).
30. Grillparzer, '[Anfang einer Selbstbiographie]' (1835), in *HKA* I/xvi, 17–20 (p. 17).
31. Grillparzer, '[Anfänge einer Selbstbiographie]' (1822), in *HKA* I/xvi, 11–15 (p. 12).
32. Karin Hagl-Catling, *Für eine Imagologie der Geschlechter. Franz Grillparzers Frauenbild im Widerspruch* (Frankfurt a.M.: Peter Lang, 1997), pp. 113–14.
33. Karl Glossy, 'Aus Bauernfelds Tagebüchern', *JdGG* 5 (1895), ix–xviii, 1–217 (pp. xiii–xiv).
34. Eduard Bauernfeld, *Bauernfelds ausgewählte Werke in vier Bänden*, 4 vols., ed. by Emil Horner (Leipzig: Hesse, no date), I, p. 113.
35. Ibid., p. 118.
36. Bauernfeld, 'Bürgerlich und Romantisch', in *Bauernfelds ausgewählte Werke*, II, pp. 289–349 (p. 290).
37. Roy C. Cowen, 'Franz Grillparzer', in *Major Figures of Nineteenth-Century Austrian Literature*, ed. by Donald G. Daviau (Riverside, CA: Ariadne, 1998), pp. 252–77 (p. 259).

38. W. E. Yates, *Theatre in Vienna. A Critical History, 1776–1995* (Cambridge: Cambridge University Press, 1996), pp. 25–27.
39. Julius Marx, *Die österreichische Zensur im Vormärz* (Vienna: Verlag für Geschichte und Politik, 1959), p. 57.
40. Norbert Bachleitner, 'The Habsburg Monarchy', in *The Frightful Stage. Political Censorship of the Theater in Nineteenth-Century Europe*, ed. by Robert Justin Goldstein (New York: Berghahn, 2009), pp. 228–64 (p. 234).
41. Ibid., pp. 31–32.
42. Katy Heady, *Literature and Censorship in Restoration Germany. Repression and Rhetoric* (Rochester, NY: Camden House, 2009), pp. 15–16.
43. W. E. Yates and Ulrike Tanzer, 'Theater und Gesellschaft im Wien des 19. Jahrhunderts. Zur Einführung', in *Theater und Gesellschaft im Wien des 19. Jahrhunderts. Ausgewählte Aufsätze. Zum 25-jährigen Bestehen der Zeitschrift* Nestroyana, ed. by W. E. Yates and Ulrike Tanzer (Vienna: Johann Lehner, 2006), pp. 7–18 (p. 10).
44. Günter Berghaus, 'Rebellion, Reservation, Resignation: Nestroy und die Wiener Gesellschaft 1830–1860', in *Viennese Popular Theatre: A Symposium*, ed. by W. E. Yates and John R. P. McKenzie (Exeter: University of Exeter, 1985), pp. 109–22 (pp. 109–10).
45. Yates and Tanzer, 'Theater und Gesellschaft im Wien', p. 10.
46. Meike Wagner, *Theater und Öffentlichkeit im Vormärz. Berlin, München und Wien als Schauplätze bürgerlicher Medienpraxis* (Berlin: Akademie, 2013), pp. 326–27.
47. W. E. Yates, 'Nestroy, Grillparzer, and the Feminist Cause', in *Viennese Popular Theatre: A Symposium/ Das Wiener Volkstheater. Ein Symposion*, ed. by W. E. Yates and John R. P. McKenzie (Exeter: University of Exeter, 1985), pp. 93–107 (pp. 104–06).
48. Hagl-Catling, *Für eine Imagologie der Geschlechter*, p. 119.
49. Dagmar C. G. Lorenz, 'Grillparzer, Dichter des sozialen Konflikts', in *Grillparzer oder Die Wirklichkeit der Wirklichkeit*, ed. by Bernhard Denscher and Walter Obermaier (Vienna: Historisches Museum der Stadt Wien, 1991), pp. 31–38 (p. 32).
50. Grillparzer, 'Das Kloster bei Sendomir', in *HKA* I/xiii, 5–33 (p. 9).
51. Thomas Laqueur, *Making Sex: Body and Gender from the Greeks to Freud* (Cambridge, MA: Harvard University Press, 1990), p. 194.
52. 'Grillparzers männliche und weibliche Charaktere', in *Wienerbote. Beilage zu den Sonntagsblättern*, 9.1.1848, p. 10.
53. Eduard Bauernfeld, 'Kleine dramatische Studien' [1877], in *Eduard von Bauernfelds Gesammelte Aufsätze*, ed. by Stefan Hock. Schriften des Literarischen Vereins in Wien IV. (Vienna: Verlag des Literarischen Vereins in Wien, 1905), pp. 227–65 (p. 253).
54. Franz Forster, 'Grillparzer — ein Dichter des Alternativen, mit besonderer Berücksichtigung des Dramas "Libussa"', in *Franz Grillparzer 1791–1991. Vorträge anläßlich einer Grillparzer-Gedenkfeier an der Universität Oslo 25.–26. September 1991*, ed. by Kurt Erich Schöndorf and Elsbeth Wessel (Oslo: Germanistisches Institut der Universität Oslo, 1993), pp. 37–66 (p. 44).
55. Walter Weiss, 'Opfer bei Grillparzer', *Études Germaniques* 47 (1992), 235–43 (p. 238).
56. There seems to be some confusion regarding Wolf-Cirian's sex. Most writers use masculine pronouns when talking about Wolf-Cirian, but Frederic E. Coenen asserts that she 'was a woman, not a man'. 'Review of *The Inspiration Motive in the Works of Franz Grillparzer. With Special Consideration of "Libussa"*', *Monatshefte* 49/3 (1957), 131–32 (p. 132).
57. Francis Wolf-Cirian, *Grillparzers Frauengestalten* (Stuttgart: Cotta, 1908), p. v.
58. Leitich, *Zwölfmal Liebe*, p. 19.
59. Brigitte Prutti, *Grillparzers Welttheater: Modernität und Tradition* (Bielefeld: Aisthesis, 2013), p. 309.
60. Dagmar C. G. Lorenz, 'Ambivalenz und Erkenntnis in Franz Grillparzers Werk', in *Grillparzer heute — wiederentdeckt oder vergessen?* (Vienna: Picus, 1993), pp. 51–66 (p. 60).
61. Dagmar C. G. Lorenz, *Grillparzer. Dichter des sozialen Konflikts* (Vienna: Böhlau, 1986), p. 111.
62. Heinrich Laube, 'Dramaturgische Briefe über das Burgtheater', *Blätter für Theater, Musik und Kunst*, 8.9.1865, p. 285.
63. Lorenz, *Dichter des sozialen Konflikts*, pp. 23, 28–29, 19.
64. Lorenz, 'Frau und Weiblichkeit bei Grillparzer', p. 201.

65. Lorenz, 'Dichter des sozialen Konflikts', p. 31.
66. Lorenz, 'Frau und Weiblichkeit bei Grillparzer', p. 203.
67. Hagl-Catling, *Für eine Imagologie der Geschlechter*, p. 98.
68. Ibid., pp. 111, 114.
69. Ibid., p. 260.
70. Cowen, 'Franz Grillparzer', pp. 265–66.
71. Bruce Thompson, *Franz Grillparzer* (Boston, MA: Twayne, 1981), p. 23.
72. Masato Ikuta, *Geschichte und Individuum in Grillparzers dramatischer Welt. Zur Entwicklung der Grillparzerschen Geschichtsdramatik* (Frankfurt a.M.: Peter Lang, 1990), p. 167.
73. Yates, *Theatre in Vienna*, p. 79.
74. Ekkehart Krippendorff, 'Grillparzer, der Fortschrittliche', in *Politics in Literature. Studies on a Germanic Preoccupation from Kleist to Améry*, ed. by Rüdiger Görner (Munich: iudicium, 2004), pp. 83–98 (pp. 87–88).
75. Roe, *A Century of Criticism*, pp. 13–17.
76. Ibid., p. 17.
77. Krippendorff, 'Grillparzer, der Fortschrittliche', p. 88.
78. Birgit Peter, 'NS-ideologische Metamorphosen am Beispiel von Heinz Kindermann: Ferdinand Raimund und Franz Grillparzer als deutsche Volksdramatiker', in *Der Dichter und sein Germanist. Symposium in Memoriam Wendelin Schmidt-Dengler*, ed. by Stephan Kurz, Michael Rohrwasser and Daniela Strigl (Vienna: New Academic Press, 2012), pp. 81–95 (pp. 81–82).
79. Ernst Fischer, 'Franz Grillparzer', in *Von Grillparzer zu Kafka. Sechs Essays* (Vienna: Globus, 1962), pp. 9–56 (p. 24).
80. Hildegard Essler, 'Die Frau Grillparzers' (unpublished dissertation, University of Vienna, 1945), p. 148.
81. Janke, 'Gescheiterte Authentizität', p. 59.

CHAPTER 1

Grillparzer and Women

The Nineteenth-Century *Frauenbild*

Before we proceed to examine Grillparzer's dramas and their relationship to the role of women in nineteenth-century Austria, we must get a better understanding of the real situation of women in this period, as this forms the framework within which these dramas must be viewed. This section focuses on the lives of several notable women, mostly writers, whom Grillparzer knew. The lives and works of these women give this study its socio-historical and cultural context. They show how intellectual women acquainted with Grillparzer managed their public careers, which issues they faced because of their sex, and how they approached the *Frauenfrage*. Their non-fictional works also grant insight into contemporary feminism.

The limits of this study prohibit a lengthy engagement with the gender debates of the late eighteenth and early nineteenth centuries, but a brief examination is necessary as these debates created the *Frauenbild* [image of women] against which Grillparzer's protagonists must be measured. They also created the atmosphere in which Grillparzer's female acquaintances wrote and published, and therefore the emancipatory import of these women's publications can only be appreciated against this background. This section sets out the broad European context of the gender debates, showing that these issues aroused much interest in England, France, Germany, and beyond. In the next section, responses to these debates by Austrian women known to Grillparzer are discussed. This shows two things: first, Grillparzer's dramas were written in the context of debates around the social role of women; and second, that these debates were very much a pan-European phenomenon in which texts from France and England were received and influenced thinking in German-speaking lands.

While it may seem strange that no Austrian texts are quoted in this introductory section, this is for the simple reason that Austrian texts on the *Geschlechtscharaktere* [sexual characteristics] were not definitive or groundbreaking. The Austrian texts discussed later in this chapter were responses to an existing debate, sparked by works such as Mary Wollstonecraft's *A Vindication of the Rights of Woman* (1792), Olympe de Gouges's *Déclaration des droits de la femme et de la citoyenne* [*Declaration of the Rights of Woman and the Female Citizen*] (1791), Johann Gottlieb Fichte's *Grundriß des Familienrechts* [*Fundamental Principles of the Rights of Family*] (1796), and Theodor Gottlieb von Hippel's *Ueber die bürgerliche Verbesserung der Weiber* [*On the Civic*

Improvement of Women] (1792), rather than texts which launched the discussion and were widely received outside their national borders. By contrast, Wollstonecraft's *Vindication* was widely read in Europe, including in Austria. Indeed, even today scholarship on the *Geschlechtscharaktere* tends to ignore the contributions discussed in this study, focusing instead on German, French and British works. Nevertheless, the Austrian texts discussed here should be seen in a wider European context. Despite the image of Austria as an intellectual backwater, and despite the efforts of the censors, foreign texts did penetrate the borders of the Habsburg Empire and were often widely received. Grillparzer read Kant as well as Rousseau and a number of English philosophers. Caroline Pichler and her mother both read Wollstonecraft's *Vindication* and de Gouges's *Déclaration*.[1]

Jean-Jacques Rousseau's writings, in particular *Émile* (1762), were important for the development of gender debates in Germany.[2] According to Rousseau, society was divided in such a way that men had to be educated for the world, and women for the home. Barbara Becker-Cantarino argues that Rousseau created a modern housewife who was exemplary in both spiritual and practical household matters. Rousseau's vision of the model woman was adopted wholesale by the German bourgeoisie, and it became the benchmark of real-world expectations. Women's role, defined from the male perspective, was not questioned, but became the goal of women's education. Under Rousseau's influence, numerous literary and educational figures published works on women's education and what it meant to be a woman.[3] These texts have as their goal the education of good wives and mothers as conceived of by men. Foreign to all participants was the idea of women's education for its own sake, or as preparation for a career. Mary Wollstonecraft's *A Vindication of the Rights of Woman*, which appeared in a German translation in 1793, was therefore greeted by incomprehension and the fear that its influence would create viragos.

One strand of scholarship holds that the period around 1800 saw a redefinition of femininity as the result of biological rather than sociological factors. Gerhard Dilcher writes of class as the most important social factor in *ancien régime* Europe.[4] People lived in a 'Rechtsordnung der Ungleichheit' [legal system based on inequality], the legitimacy of which was accepted as God-mandated, natural, or, later, as rational. Women's social position was therefore not only determined by their status as the other sex, but also, and perhaps more so by the confines of a class-based society. Then, in the late eighteenth century, 'the debate [about gender] became more deterministic by emphasizing biological, rather than social factors' and by the 1790s, gender was increasingly conceived in monolithic binary terms.[5] The result of this shift was the concept of the *Geschlechtscharaktere*, a term which describes the mental characteristics which were supposedly inherent to each sex. Michaela Krug also argues that the late eighteenth century saw the class-based social order giving way to a new one based on sex.[6] Rita Morrien talks of the period as a transitional culture in which gender difference came to be seen as a natural sexual characteristic rather than one of several social classifiers.[7] Ingrid Spörk writes that bourgeois ideology endowed gender difference with new meanings and values, 'da etwa das Bild der Frau aus der Negation des Ideologems des männlichen Bürgers entstand' [since, for instance, the image of woman emerged from the negation of the ideologeme of the male citizen].[8]

Irmgard Götz von Olenhusen challenges this narrative. Pre-modern societies in Europe, she writes, did not question male economic, political or cultural dominance, and it is therefore strange to credit bourgeois society of the late eighteenth and early nineteenth centuries with the creation of the gender binary, as some scholars have done.[9] According to Olenhusen, the two-sex model of the post-revolutionary and Romantic eras was based on pre-modern scientific understanding, and sex had always been self-explanatory as a distinction in class-based society.[10] It was the Enlightenment's ideas of equality and the dismantling of the Christian worldview which necessitated a new gender order.[11] In order to find biological grounds for denying women equality, the tenets of modern science were largely ignored as its practitioners created links between their prejudices and observable facts with the goal of establishing a supposedly natural gender dualism: 'Die modernen Naturwissenschaften haben das dualistische Bild von Mann und Frau nicht nur nicht erfunden, sondern weitgehend destruiert.' [Not only did modern science not create the dualistic image of man and woman, it largely destroyed it.][12]

The image of woman which these debates created came to embody the highest ideals of bourgeois society. Women became emblematic of a new approach to life and the world, but the old model of the *gelehrte Frau* [learned women] was not a suitable emblem. While some exceptional individuals in the sixteenth and seventeenth centuries had benefited from their status as erudite women, the term soon became one of abuse and scorn for women who were seen to be appropriating male academic privilege.[13] Women's diseases came to be regarded as indications that female physiology had been corrupted by unnatural lifestyles: 'Scholarship and reading [...] were unnatural, and carried dire health warnings.' These anatomical interpretations, argues Helen Fronius, were not the result of advances in knowledge, but of a political agenda which sought to justify men's cultural and political dominance and keep women in their place.[14]

Scholarship also displays conflicting views regarding the effectiveness of the *Geschlechtscharaktere* in fulfilling their regulative ends. Susanne Kord defines this period as the passage from an era of greater intellectual freedom to one in which all intellectual activity was considered incompatible with real femininity. Kord argues that the gender debates were successful in limiting women's activities, writing that they prevented women from participating in intellectual public life, and that women's public intellectual activity was 'judged as an assumption of male prerogative'.[15] Kord's research has identified the methods used by women writers of the age to hide or obscure their identities. They knew they were overstepping the boundaries of proper femininity and 'taten ihr Bestes, um bekannt zu werden, dabei aber unerkannt zu bleiben' [did their best to become famous, but remain unrecognized].[16]

More recently, scholars have begun to challenge the idea that widespread contemporary propagation of the doctrine of separate spheres led to effective exclusion of women from public life. Wendy Arons writes that women's active participation in the public sphere in the eighteenth and nineteenth centuries means that the separate spheres approach does not provide an accurate or adequate portrayal of women's lives in this period.[17] Similarly, Fronius contends that women were central to German literary culture from the very beginning, and focuses her study on the opportunities that were open to women, rather than on the ways in which they were excluded. Fronius argues that the real position of eighteenth-century German women writers has been obscured firstly by contemporary gender debates, and subsequently by modern feminist scholarship. She points to a rising number of women writers from the 1790s onwards to argue that, although dominant, the restrictive discourse of Humboldt and others did not go unchallenged.[18] Linda L. Clark argues that the proscriptions of Rousseau and others were reactive rather than preemptive, and appeared after men had seen that women were gaining recognition and financial benefit from their literary endeavours.[19]

The *Frauenbild* developed at the end of the eighteenth century survived into the nineteenth and dominated in the Biedermeier era.[20] Hagl-Catling writes that the period in which Grillparzer wrote reacted to instability by reinforcing the Rousseauian *Frauenbild* in order to crush women's growing subjectivity.[21] At the same time, however, Grillparzer lived in an age of rising female self-awareness, which he encountered not least in his immediate circle.[22] In the 1840s, there was only incipient debate on the emancipation of women in Austria.[23] Indeed, Richard J. Evans argues that it is surprising that a women's movement emerged in Austria at all, given the opportunities which Catholicism offered middle- and upper-class women in the female regular clergy, the stronger resistance to female public engagement in Catholic than Protestant societies, and the lack of impetus which Protestantism gave the women's movement in Germany.[24] When an organized movement emerged in the form of the Wiener Frauen-Erwerb-Verein [Viennese Women's Employment Association], it was at a time of political and economic instability after Austrian defeats in the Six Weeks' War, and the Verein, although its aims were economic, owed its existence to political circumstances.[25] The early feminists of the *Vormärz* aimed for the improvement of education and for women's legal independence; the end of marriages of convenience; and wider occupational openings.[26] But the demands of feminists at the end of the nineteenth century, which were largely similar, show how little progress had been made.

The strict regime of censorship which was in place in this period has already been noted in the Introduction, and it is possible that censorship was one reason for the relative paucity of printed discussions of the *Frauenfrage* in Austria. The *Frauenfrage* was, however, discussed, and it was partially via reviews of topical performances that discussion of women's issues moved from the stage to the press. In 1839, for example, the *Wiener Zeitschrift für Kunst, Literatur, Theater und Mode* published a review of Wilhelm Marchland's *Frauen-Emancipation* [*Women's Emancipation*] which, it said, 'erscheint neu und zeitgemäß, da die Emancipationsfrage auf allen Seiten auf der Tagesordnung ist und das Capitel der Gleichstellungen nur allzuhäufig abgehandelt wird' [appears new and modern, since the question of emancipation is on all sides on the agenda and the chapter of gender equality is dealt with only too frequently].²⁷ The reviewer displays common prejudices regarding the nature and social role of women when he mentions the protagonist's 'unweibliche[s] Benehmen' [unwomanly behaviour] which alienates her friends and makes her 'lächerlich' [ridiculous], and the contrast between her 'Unweiblichkeit und der edlen, ächten Frauennatur' [lack of femininity and the noble, true female nature], or praises Marchland for not allowing his heroine to become a 'widerwärtige[s] Mannweib' [repulsive virago]. A review in *Der Österreichische Zuschauer* praised the play's depiction of '[d]ie schöne, moralische Tendenz, den wahren Standpunkt weiblicher Würde und die Lächerlichkeit des Strebens, außer den Grenzen der Weiblichkeit Geltung und Glück zu suchen' [the good, moral tendency, the true position of feminine dignity and the absurdity of pursuing importance and happiness beyond the boundaries of femininity].²⁸ A year later, a review of Marchland's *Gefährliches Mittel* [*Dangerous Means*] noted that the author 'mit der schon einmal aufgefaßten Idee der Frauen-Emancipation auch dießmal beschäftiget war, und wirklich wird auch kaum Eine mehr von den vielen Chimären unserer Zeit zu so vielen lustigen Verhältnissen Veranlassung geben, als eben diese' [was here again concerned with the idea of women's emancipation — which he has already interpreted — and hardly another of the many chimeras of our time will give occasion to so many humorous circumstances as this one].²⁹ The reviewer continued, again giving vent to contemporary prejudices:

> Die Art, wie Frauen selbstständig handeln zu können glauben, und wie sie gleich wieder in der ersten Widerwärtigkeit zu ihren natürlichen Beschützern fliehen, ist hier auch wieder mit vieler Laune aufgefaßt und durchgeführt.
>
> [The way in which women believe they are able to act independently, and in which they flee to their natural protectors as soon as they encounter the first adversity, is here again interpreted and performed with high spirits.]

If, in the late 1830s, the *Frauenfrage* was 'auf allen Seiten auf der Tagesordnung', in the 1840s it became a dangerously potent and effective force, judging by some of the discourse in the press. In 1842, for example, an opinion piece in the *Österreichischer Zuschauer* wrote that '[d]ie Frauenemancipation, diese Hydra mit den tausend Köpfen [...] ist schon zu einer solchen Größe herangewachsen, daß wir wahrhaftig in kurzer Zeit nur zwei Klassen von Frauenspersonen unterscheiden werden: Amazonen und Odalisken' [women's emancipation, this hydra with one thousand heads [...] has already grown to such a size that, in a short time, we will truthfully only be able to differentiate between two types of women: amazons and odalisques].³⁰ The author foresees the advent of 'das freie, das absolute, das belesene, das heroische Weib' [the free, the absolute, the erudite, the heroic woman], but fears that this will mean the demise of the womanly heart which is 'voll Milde und Versöhnung, voll Zutrauen und Liebe, voll Hochherzigkeit und kindlicher Demuth' [full of mildness and reconciliation, full of trust and love, full of generosity and childish humility]. The author saw this outcome as inevitable if 'Putzsucht und Koketterie' [addiction to finery and coquetry] continued to be dominant forces in society, and 'wenn nicht [...] nöthigen Falls die ursprüngliche Gewalt und Macht des Mannes, des Familienhauptes, ihre alten Rechte behauptet' [if [...] in necessity the original force and power of the man, the head of the family, does not assert its old rights]. A review of Karl Ebner's *Versuch zur Vertheidigung der angebornen Rechte des Frauengeschlechtes* [*Attempt at Defending the Innate Rights of Women*] of 1845 presented a vision of a society divided by the *Frauenfrage*:

> Wenigstens müssen wir dieß annehmen, da sich noch in neuester Zeit einander ziemlich schroff entgegenstehende Ansichten geltend gemacht haben. Während die Einen dem Weibe nur hinter dem Kochtopf und am Waschtroge, oder an der Wiege des Kindes seine Stelle anweisen, schaaren [sic] sich die Andern unter das Panier der Frauen-Emanzipation und wollen dem zarten Geschlechte auch die Cigarre, das Rappier und die Jagdbüchse vindicirt sehen.[31]
>
> [We must at least accept this, since in recent times strongly opposing views have asserted themselves. While some instruct women to remain by the stove and the washing trough, or at their child's cradle, others rally under the banner of women's emancipation and want the fair sex's rights to the cigar, the rapier and the hunting rifle to be asserted.]

Exactly this exaggerated vision of women's emancipation was blamed when, in 1848, the *Wiener Zeitung* reported that a woman had been discovered walking around the city dressed as a man. She defended herself by claiming that numerous women were already doing the same in order to move around more freely in public. As she did not appear to be suspicious in any other way, the newspaper concluded that '[sie] scheint nur von einer verkehrten Idee der Frauen-Emanzipation angesteckt worden zu sein' [she appears simply to have been infected by a false idea of women's emancipation].[32] Not only do these commentators grossly misrepresent the aims of the contemporary women's movement, they also overstate its achievements and progress. They are, therefore, indications of the resistance which the women's movement had to contend with — a resistance which saw any change as catastrophe and reacted viciously to even the slightest progress made by the cause for women's emancipation.

Almost twenty years later, Louise Otto's book *Das Recht der Frauen auf Erwerb* [*The Right of Women to Employment*] gave a reviewer in the *Neue Freie Presse* the opportunity to claim that much had changed in the matter of women's emancipation, while demonstrating that this was not, in fact, the case. Writing in 1866, Karl von Thaler claimed that no one was now opposed to 'die bürgerliche Gleichstellung der Frau mit dem Manne, die Emancipation der Frauen im guten Sinne' [the civil equality of men with women, the emancipation of women in the good sense]; there was only disagreement regarding the means of achieving it.[33] According to Thaler, there was no longer any resistance to women in the workplace:

> Das Recht, zu arbeiten, will den Frauen Niemand mehr verkümmern. Factisch [sic] thut es auch heute Niemand mehr, aber die Frauen drängen sich eben nicht zu den neu eröffneten Erwerbszweigen heran [...]
>
> [No longer does anyone want to restrict women's right to work. In fact, no one does this any more, but women are not exactly rushing to the newly opened occupations [...]]

Thaler also wrote that, while there was disagreement on the question of whether it was in women's own interests to be granted access to all areas of employment, there was greater agreement that women's employment would lead them to be more moral, but less kind. He argued that one's opinion on the matter would depend on whether one looked at the relationship between the sexes primarily from a moral or aesthetic point of view.

Although Thaler railed against marriage for economic reasons — 'gewiß, das Mädchen, das bloß um der Versorgung willen heiratet, ist nicht besser als die verkaufte Dirne' [the girl who marries only with maintenance in mind is certainly no better than a sold prostitute] — he argued that any changes to women's education should be made with the aim of preparing women for their role as wives and mothers in the service of the family and the fatherland, and that these aims would be scuppered were women to earn money. For Thaler, work and family were incompatible — 'Wir sind für Frauenarbeit, ja, aber nicht für die Arbeit der Frauen, sondern der Mädchen und Witwen' [We support women's employment, but not the employment of wives, rather of girls and widows] — and he saw the women's movement as a force inimical to the traditional family:

> Veredelt sie [die Mädchen], bildet sie, trachtet nicht blos nach materieller, sondern geistiger Gleichberechtigung, rüstet sie mit Kenntnissen aus, die sie befähigen, sich selbst zu ernähren, wenn es sein muß, aber zerstört das Band der Familie nicht, indem ihr die Frau aus dem Kreise der Kinder reißt und in ein Bureau oder Comptoir setzt.
>
> [Ennoble them [girls], educate them, strive not only for material, but also intellectual equality, equip them with knowledge which will enable them to feed themselves if they must, but do not destroy the bonds of family by tearing women from the sphere of their children and placing them in an office.]

Despite Thaler's claims that women's right to work was now universally accepted, his starting point is the same as that of many writers both earlier and later in the century: women's primary social role as wives and mothers, their inherent weakness and need for male assistance, and men's desire to see in women not strength, 'sondern ganz vorzugsweise die Schwäche' [but preferably weakness].

Many of the women whom Grillparzer knew took part in these debates through their own writings, and it is possible to see the extent to which these women conformed to, or undermined, the role expected of them. Examining their lives and works will also show that many emancipated women were among Grillparzer's acquaintance.

Grillparzer's Female Friends

Grillparzer had steady contact with prominent women throughout his career, but it is helpful to differentiate between the friendships of his early years, which centred around Caroline Pichler (1769–1843), and those of his later years, which were defined by Marie von Ebner-Eschenbach and women in her circles. Here I also differentiate between the actresses and the female authors whom Grillparzer knew. To the former group belong Sophie Schröder, Julie Rettich and Charlotte

Wolter. Through Pichler, Grillparzer came into contact with her friends Therese von Artner (1772–1829), Marianne Neumann von Meißenthal (1768–1837), and Marie von Zay (1779–1842). These women published works of prose and poetry in various journals and in discrete volumes. Johanna Franul von Weissenthurn (née Grünberg, 1773–1847) was a popular actress turned dramatist who was friends with both Grillparzer and Pichler.

Many of Grillparzer's female friends from the later part of his life have already been mentioned in the Introduction. Of those, only Marie von Ebner-Eschenbach (1830–1916) can be said to enjoy the notice and respect of posterity. Iduna Laube (1808–1879) and Auguste Littrow-Bischoff (1819–1890) were prominent members of Viennese society, *salonnières*, and founding members of the Wiener Frauen-Erwerb-Verein. Betty Paoli (real name Barbara Elisabeth Glück, 1814–1894) was a successful poet and journalist who wrote extensively on the condition of women. Euphemia von Kudriaffsky (1820–1881) was a writer and painter and gave lectures on aesthetics. Sophie von Todesco (1825–1895) and Josephine von Wertheimstein (1820–1894), sisters from the Gomperz family, were prominent *salonnières*, and Wertheimstein was one of Ferdinand von Saar's patrons.

Several of these women led salons in Vienna, and there Grillparzer came into contact with literary and intellectual women of the age,[34] and would possibly have engaged with their writing. Salons played a central role in the literary culture of the age. They were a space in which members of different social classes, and men and women, could interact freely.[35] Salons provided a space in which interested parties could share knowledge and encounter new literary works, and they provided members with access to newly published works.[36] Members shared and circulated publications between them, and thereby promoted a form of equality among guests.[37] Salons also played an important role in receiving and translating foreign literature: Charlotte Greiner's salon helped to spread English and German literature, while the salon of her daughter, Caroline Pichler, did the same for contemporary French literature.[38] Although salons took place in the home, the *salonnière* did not embody the role of passive housewife, but was the intellectual cynosure, and helped to craft the literary, theatrical and musical offerings of the event.[39] Salons also played an important role in fostering relations between Austrians and their foreign guests. The German Georg Forster visited the Greiner salon,[40] while Pichler played host to the Schlegels and de Staël. At salons, politics and other issues were also discussed, including women's emancipation.[41]

Pichler's salon began in 1802, after she had become famous with her *Gleichnisse* [*Parables*] and the literary world desired to be in contact with her.[42] Pichler's salon was influenced by Romanticism, partly due to an influx of Romantics from Germany in the wake of the Napoleonic Wars.[43] The statesman Anton von Prokesch attended Pichler's salon, and recalled that she would read her literary works to the assembled audience before publishing them.[44] Weissenthurn also read her dramas at Pichler's salon.[45] It was also an important focal point for Austrian national writers in the first decades of the nineteenth century. Gertrude Prohaska writes that it was 'ein Verdienst Karoline Pichlers, ja vielleicht überhaupt ihre Lebensaufgabe gewesen,

Vermittlerin dieses patriotischen Gedankenguts zu sein' [one of Karoline Pichler's achievements, perhaps even her life's work, to be a conduit for this patriotic philosophy].[46] Pichler's salon gave preference to Austrian authors, particularly those writing on national topics, and without Pichler and her salon, they would not have been able to establish contact with each other.[47] The presence of Joseph Hormayr in particular meant that Pichler's salon was an important focus of anti-Napoleon sentiment.[48] Later in the century, the salon of Josephine von Wertheimstein was a focal point of opposition to Metternich's regime, and a meeting point for those of liberal views.[49] Although Grillparzer does not provide us with any information regarding his visits to the city's salons, we know that he was in attendance at Pichler's and Wertheimstein's. This means that he met the literary and intellectual women of the age, and that, although he does not seem to have read the works of the women he knew, he may well have been familiar with them, either through a book he received from a fellow guest, or because he heard these authors reading from their own works. His attendance at salons may have also exposed him to discussion of the *Frauenfrage*.

When discussing Austrian women writers' engagement with the gender debates, there can be no better place to start than with Pichler, who wrote about women's issues in several texts. She was a prolific writer in both fiction and non-fiction genres whose collected works comprise sixty volumes. Grillparzer and Pichler maintained a correspondence for a few years after 1818, and he even wrote to her during his 1819 trip to Italy. In 1844, he read parts of Pichler's *Denkwürdigkeiten* [*Memoirs*] 'mit Rührung und dem Gefühle nie vergessener und nie gebrochener Freundschaft' [with emotion and the feeling of never forgotten and never broken friendship] (*HKA* I/xvi, p. 23).

Pichler enjoyed a wide education, including modern languages, and even received music lessons from Mozart. Her mother's salon was one of the first places in Austria where Wollstonecraft's *Vindication* was discussed.[50] Pichler tempers this picture of a broad education by stressing that her parents taught her to consider 'Häuslichkeit [...] als die erste und wichtigste Bestimmung des Weibes' [domesticity [...] as a woman's first and most important purpose].[51] Pichler's productivity and success were admired by other writers. Therese von Artner, for example, praised her friend in a letter from 1820:

> Wie ganz anders ist es mit deinem litterarischen Wirken? Allenthalben kommen dir Antheil, Beyfall und Aufmunterung entgegen; das erhält und vermehrt deine Produktionskraft, die schon von der Natur so reich ausgestattet ist. Und dem Himmel sey dank, daß es so ist! So können sich Tausende wieder einer erquickenden Geistesnahrung erfreuen.[52]

> [How very different is it with your literary work? Everywhere you are greeted with interest, applause and encouragement; that maintains and multiplies your productivity, which is already so richly endowed by nature. And thank the heavens that it is so! Thus can thousands look forward to new refreshing intellectual nourishment.]

Several of Pichler's essays deal directly with the social role of women, and with women's education in particular. In 'Über die Bildung des weiblichen Geschlechtes' ['On the Education of the Female Sex'] she makes clear that she is writing within the larger context of contemporary gender debates which accepted that women's intellectual and physical capabilities determined their roles as wives and mothers. She argues that women's education should prepare them for these roles, and that anything which distracted women from their purpose was 'der Natur zuwider, und daher verwerflich' [contrary to nature, and therefore reprehensible].[53] Here, she appears to adhere to the idea that women's physicality destines them for particular social roles, and in doing so reaffirms the ideas of Humboldt and others who propagated this idea. On the same page, however, she offers a much less conservative view of gender constructs as she argues for the influence of historical and political developments on the social role of women. Social changes, she writes, destroy 'die altgewohnten Formeln', and the female sex '[kann] sich dem Einflusse derselben nicht entziehen; es muß daher mit dem Zeitgeiste fortschreiten [...] und die Mittel ergreifen, die ihm eine würdige und sichere Existenz schaffen können' [the long familiar formulas; cannot resist their influence; therefore it must march forward with the spirit of the age [...] and grasp the means which will enable it to create a dignified and safe existence].[54] Pichler is critical of the restrictions under which women are placed: if she hopes that change in the future will secure women a better existence, then she must take issue with the domestic limitations of contemporary Europe. In this second quotation, she argues against the deterministic idea of gender which she supported in the first. She sees gender as a social construct which can be reevaluated and changed, and is not the direct result of the physical body. For Pichler, in this quotation at least, gender belongs to the 'altgewohnten Formeln' which can be destroyed and envisioned anew. Support for this conceptualization of gender indicates that the characterization of Pichler as a conservative is not wholly accurate. Friedrich Weissensteiner, for example, argues that Pichler rejected the emancipatory ideals of German women such as Dorothea von Schlegel.[55] Yet here Pichler's own desire for greater freedom for women is clear.

Another essay, 'Kindererziehung' ['Child-Rearing'], also deals with the subject of women's education. Pichler criticizes the fact that many girls from the middle and upper classes received an education very similar to the one she herself received. Pichler does not fail to stress, albeit at the very end of this essay, that it is not her intention to restrict women's intellectual development and 'die Töchter des neunzehnten Jahrhunderts, gleich unseren Großmüttern, zu bloßen Nätherinnen [sic] und Köchinnen erziehen zu wollen' [raise the daughters of the nineteenth century, like our grandmothers, to be mere seamstresses and cooks].[56] She sees the nineteenth century as an age in which the educational opportunities of women have been widened, and this is a development which she welcomes. However, while women should be allowed to be more than just cooks or seamstresses, their true destiny should not be obscured by education. In calling for women to be educated just as well as men, 'nur in einer andern Richtung und in einer solchen, die sie nie von dem Hauptzwecke ihres Lebens und Wirkens entfernt' [only in a different direction, and one which will never distance them from the main purpose of their lives and works], Pichler echoes the 'different but equal' thinking which was common in this era.[57]

Pichler's contradictory attitude towards women extends to her attitude towards women writers. In an essay on Germaine de Staël's novels *Delphine* (1802) and *Corinne* (1807), Pichler sees a conflict between women's preordained role as wife and mother and their intellectual activities. Pichler emphasizes that she is writing in the context of wider debates which criticize any woman who finds 'eine edlere Verwendung ihrer Kräfte' [a more noble use for her powers] than housework.[58] Pichler's judgments on de Staël's heroines, however, indicate that she too imposed limits on women's behaviour and roles. Pichler claims that the portrayal of Corinne and Delphine as women motivated by the heart mitigates the horror which was aroused by such accomplished women. Corinne, the famous and adored poet and improviser, 'war zu weit aus der weiblichen Sphäre geschritten, um in irgend einen häuslichen Zirkel zu passen' [had stepped too far outside the feminine sphere to be suitable for a domestic setting].[59] Despite views which seem to favour the social rather than biological origins of gender and the *Geschlechtscharaktere*, Pichler's attitudes are rooted in the concept of male and female as binary opposites, each having defined social roles. Pichler therefore wonders why de Staël created two exceptional characters who have been alienated from their feminine destiny by 'höhere Geistesbildung und einen kühneren Schwung des Charakters' [higher learning and a bolder force of character] and will therefore never find domestic bliss.[60] Pichler, perhaps, fails to see the emancipatory message of the novels and de Staël's criticism of the limits placed on women. Women, writes Pichler, can and should develop their intellectual abilities, but only within the limits of what is suitable for them.

Pichler's friend, the actress and playwright Johanna Franul von Weissenthurn (1773–1847), whom George Reinhardt calls 'an alert woman in an age of transition',[61] was aware of the conflict which was perceived to exist between femininity and authorship. Weissenthurn was an actress, and later became a prolific author. Her plays were published in fifteen volumes between 1809 and 1848, and in total she composed sixty, forty-eight of which were performed at the Burgtheater.[62] Although not critically successful, they were very popular with audiences,[63] and between 1800 and 1853 they received no fewer than 912 performances.[64] In 1835, Bauernfeld wrote that her achievements 'im Felde des bürgerlichen Schauspiels und Lustspiels sind seit einer Reihe von Jahren in jedermanns Andenken' [in the field of bourgeois drama and comedy have been in everyone's memory for a number of years],[65] and a contemporary wrote that her plays, 'sind angenehm zu sehen, interessant, unterhaltend und belehrend' and that 'eine Gesamtausgabe ihrer Werke wäre sehr wünschenswert' [are pleasant to watch, interesting, entertaining and didactic; a complete edition of her works would be very desirable].[66] Emperor Franz was among her fans, as she recalls in an essay from 1840.[67] In 1829, Grillparzer wrote a poem commemorating Weissenthurn's fortieth anniversary at the Burgtheater (*HKA* I/xi, p. 88). The second stanza reads: 'Aber vierzig Jahr dem Spiele/ Holder Musenkunst geweiht,/ Sind nur Flügel zu dem Ziele,/ Teile einer Ewigkeit! — '

[But forty years dedicated/ To drama, the art of the fair muses,/ Are only the wings which lead to the destination,/ Parts of an eternity! —] By this time, she had already developed a reputation as a writer, yet Grillparzer's paean focuses solely on her work as an actress. Perhaps he was not familiar with, or did not value, her plays. Or perhaps he thought her talents as an actress far outshone her talents as a writer. Grillparzer nevertheless admired her talents, and valued her contribution to the Burgtheater.

Scholars have found very tentative criticism of women's social position in Weissenthurn's dramas. Ian Roe writes that the comparisons Weissenthurn invites between conventional and emancipated women 'might indicate an, admittedly very cautiously, critical female perspective'.[68] Reinhardt argues that Weissenthurn, in her comedy *Die beschämte Eifersucht* [*Humiliated Jealousy*] (1810), 'point[s] to the revolutionary and enlightened moral that men must include women in the call for "egalité"'.[69]

Critical reception of Weissenthurn's theatrical works reveals much about the attitudes of her contemporaries to women writers and shows the widespread influence of the *Geschlechterdebatten*. An 1818 review of Weissenthurn's *Johann, Herzog von Finnland* [*John, Duke of Finland*] reports that the drama was more or less popular depending on the 'Verschiedenheit der Ansichten des Publikums vorzüglich in Rücksicht auf den Einfluß des weiblichen Geschlechts, da die Frau Verfasserinn die Rollen der Marie und Katharina überaus glanzreich zu halten bestrebt gewesen ist' [differences in opinion among the public, particularly as concerns the influence of the female sex, as the lady author took pains to make the roles of Marie and Katharina extremely brilliant].[70] A reviewer in 1820 used a performance of *Ruprecht Graf zu Horneck* [*Ruprecht, Count of Horneck*] to criticize women who attempted the *Trauerspiel* [tragedy] genre. The reviewer claimed that *Ruprecht* was instantly recognizable as the work of a woman, that 'jedes Trauerspiel, das den Nahmen in der That verdienen soll, weit außer dem Kreise weiblicher Kräfte [liegt]' [every tragedy which does really deserve the name [lies] far beyond the boundaries of women's power], and that even 'weiblich gesinnte Männer' often fail in the genre due to 'die vorwaltende Weiblichkeit ihrer Natur' [feminine-minded men; the dominant femininity of their nature].[71] He further recommends that female writers stick to *Schauspiele* [dramas], a genre to which they have a well-founded claim because they take place 'nur zwischen den vier Wänden eines Gesellschaftszimmers [...], und also nothgedrungen die enge Häuslichkeit immer wiederkäuen [müßen]' [only between the four walls of a drawing room [...] and so of necessity must keep going over and over the narrow domesticity]. He finishes by claiming tragedy as part of the male domain,

> denn sollten die Damen je in ihrer Mitte einen weiblichen Shakespear [*sic*] aufzustellen vermögen, so kann das sicher gelten als Zeichen einer neuen Zeit, und — wohl dem Manne, der diese Revolution nicht erlebt!
>
> [for if women should ever attempt to put forward from their midst a female Shakespeare, that can surely serve as the sign of a new era and — lucky the man who does not experience this revolution!]

Despite this criticism of Weissenthurn and of 'unsuitable' female literary engagement, the reviewer cannot deny that Weissenthurn's plays were 'fortwährend so entschieden begünstigt' [constantly so decidedly favoured] by audiences.

Weissenthurn's critical approach to contemporary ideals of womanhood is evident in the preface to the first volume of her collected works. Here she grapples with the topic of women writers, and begins by reiterating the conflict with which Pichler deals:

> Oeffentlich als Verfasserinn aufzutreten, — der Schritt ist gewagt; er führt auf eine Bahn, die die sanfte Weiblichkeit scheuen sollte — er führt zum Krieg.[72]
>
> [To publicly appear as an author — that is a risky step which leads on a path which soft femininity should avoid — it leads to war.]

Weissenthurn here seems aware of her status as an interloper in what many considered a male domain. Almost as a defence, she reminds the reader of the numerous other women who have gone before her and published literary works which, she humbly writes, were far more worthy. Weissenthurn refuses to apologize for her writing, as that would be an admission of wrong-doing. Instead, she defends her literary career and defiantly refuses to cease writing, even if she is censured for doing so: 'Ich habe allerdings wider die Kleiderordnung gefehlt und — statt Strümpfe zu stricken, ein paar Federn stumpf geschrieben.' [I did indeed violate the dress code and — instead of knitting stockings, I blunted a few nibs.][73] In defence of herself, Weissenthurn also addresses herself directly to the critics. By not publishing anonymously, she fears putting herself at risk of censure. She plays up her helpless femininity, referring to herself as 'eine ganz Wehrlose' [a completely defenceless woman] who is determined to endure all criticism with humble silence.

Weissenthurn anticipates the criticism which was often directed at women writers in this period when she states:

> Wie lächerlich uns der Nahme einer Gelehrten macht, weiß ich nur allzuwohl, und wie freygebig deßhalb Jede, die etwas schreibt, damit beschenkt wird, weiß ich auch.[74]
>
> [I know only too well how ridiculous the name erudite woman makes us, and I also know how generously it is therefore applied to every woman who writes anything.]

Weissenthurn is reluctant to be seen as an erudite woman because of negative social attitudes towards such women. She shares Pichler's fear that activity outside the boundaries of femininity removes women from the binary gender construct. This cannot be Weissenthurn's fate, however, as she has nothing of erudition about her: 'Alle, die meine Stücke lesen, werden erfahren, daß sie sich nur auf Menschenkenntniß, und die, einer Schauspielerinn angemessene Lektür [sic] gründen.' [All who read my plays will discover that they are based only on knowledge of human nature and reading matter appropriate for an actress.][75] The fact that Weissenthurn distances herself from erudite women should not, however, distract from the social criticism which finds its way into this prologue.

The correspondence between these two authors, of which thirty-one letters remain, reveals nothing of this contradictory attitude to their writing. Rather, Pichler and Weissenthurn come across as defiantly defensive both of their writing and of their right to publish. Weissenthurn defends her own publications and criticizes the androcentric nature of literary institutions when she addresses male critics:

> Schämt euch! wenn ich auch nicht das Außerordentliche geleistet habe — nützlicher, als so manches was ihr geschrieben, war es doch, und Ihre Werke werden, trotz dem verderbten Zeitgeschmack, ewig leben.[76]
>
> [Shame on you! Even if I have not achieved anything extraordinary — it was certainly more useful than much that you have written, and your works will live on for eternity despite the corrupt taste of the times.]

Gone is the mock-apologetic tone of the introduction to her printed works, replaced with a firm declaration that she is a more capable author than many men and anger at the injustice of posterity. Writing about rehearsals for her drama *Die Freunde* [*The Friends*], Weissenthurn anticipates criticism because she is 'ein Fraunzimer [*sic*], die nicht wie gewiße Leute mit der Degenspitze — nur mit einem Fächerschlage antworten könnte' [a woman who would only be able to respond with a blow with a fan — not with the tip of a dagger like some people].[77]

Later in his life, Grillparzer was acquainted with Betty Paoli and Auguste Littrow-Bischoff, who were prominent figures in Viennese social circles and who authored books about their dramatist friend. Paoli was a well-known Viennese poet who befriended Grillparzer and Stifter. Eufemia von Kudriaffsky, a contemporary, remarked in a letter to Josephine Knorr that Paoli was 'eine interessante doch emancipirte Schriftstellerin' [an interesting but emancipated author].[78] For many years, she wrote for various Austrian and foreign newspapers on literature, art and the Burgtheater. In 1895, she was feted as 'die letzte große Erscheinung jener Epoche [...] welche mit der "Ahnfrau" anhebt und mit den "Neuesten Gedichten" Betty Paoli's abschließt' [the last great figure of that era [...] which begins with the *Ahnfrau* and ends with Betty Paoli's *Neueste Gedichte*].[79] Grillparzer considered Paoli to be Austria's greatest lyric poet.[80] In 1852, Grillparzer wrote an epigramm titled 'Die Dichterin': 'Willst du dich öffentlich entkleiden/ Wie Phrynes Beispiel weist,/ So prüfe vorher dich bescheiden/ Wie schön du etwa seist.' [If you want to undress in public/ As Phryne's example shows,/ Assess modestly before you do/ How beautiful you really are.] (Nr. 1301. *HKA* I/xii/i, p. 239) Backmann argues that this was a warning against Paoli's desire to write an autobiography, and was motivated by the fear that such an endeavor would not be well received (*HKA* I/xii/ii, p. 264). Perhaps the most significant evidence of Grillparzer's respect for Paoli is Laube's assertion that she was one of the few people with whom Grillparzer discussed *Die Jüdin von Toledo*, which was discovered on his death.[81]

Karin Wozonig identifies Paoli as an individual who surpassed the limits which society attempted to place on her, and who succeeded in creating opportunities for herself outside the confines of house and family.[82] Paoli's journalistic career is part of the unusual level of mobility which Wozonig mentions. Paoli's interests extended beyond art and literature, and her essays deal with important social and political questions, such as 'jene brennende Frage [...] die niemand besser als sie, die rastlose Kämpferin im Lebensstreite, beurteilen konnte: — die Frauenfrage' [that burning question [...] which no one could assess better than she, the tireless fighter in the struggle of life — the question of women's rights].[83] In choosing her pseudonym, Paoli alluded to the Corsican freedom fighter Pasquale di Paoli, embracing with this choice a 'foreign, male identity associated with revolutionary impulses'.[84] Geber considers Paoli to belong to the first generation of the women's movement, which manifested itself in the foundation of the Wiener Frauen-Erwerb-Verein in 1866. Paoli's engagement with the *Frauenfrage*, writes Geber, is characterized by a strategic feminism which uses the tools of enlightenment to end an iniquitous state of affairs: Paoli's 'vorgebliche Angepasstheit' [apparent conformism] granted her a prominent role in the media, and she could therefore communicate her message very effectively.[85] Helene Bettelheim-Gabillon argues that Paoli was interested in the *Frauenfrage* when 'jenes Wort, dem jetzt bereits ein etwas polemischer Beigeschmack anhaftet — noch gar nicht existirte' [that word, which already has a somewhat polemical overtone, did not yet exist].[86]

Paoli's journalistic success brought with it money, influence and power.[87] She used this power in the service of women, thereby giving the incipient women's movement a serious and respected forum for discussion.[88] In her articles, Paoli urges the Austrian government to create the basis for unmarried women's financial independence, and to open education and employment to women so that they are not dependent on marriage for survival.[89] Wozonig writes that Paoli does not argue for the destruction of the social order, but rather uses 'eine Abfolge subtiler Strategien, mit denen sie auf Ungerechtigkeiten und Diskriminierungen hinweist und Abhilfe fordert' [a sequence of subtle strategies with which she points out injustice and discrimination and demands remedy].[90] 'Eine Zeitfrage' ['A Contemporary Concern'], for example, which appeared in the *Neue Freie Presse* in 1865, calls for women to be better able to provide for themselves financially. Paoli is careful to distance herself from 'törichten und unsauberen Emanzipations-Gelüsten' [foolish and dirty cravings for emancipation], arguing that it is the right of every human being to utilize his or her talents for their own benefit and society's.[91]

In 'Ein Wort Pombals' ['A Word from Pombal'] (alluding to the 1st Marquis of Pombal, the enlightened eighteenth-century Portuguese statesman), Paoli decries the prejudices which prevent women from obtaining gainful employment. She finds it particularly strange that such prejudices should be so common in Austria, given that the law allowed for female rulers and that Maria Theresa occupied such an illustrious position in Austrian history. Despite, or perhaps because of her arguments for women's right to work, Paoli emphasizes that women only work '[w]eil die "ungestüme Drängerin, die Not", sie dazu zwingt!' [Because the 'impetuous pesterer, need', forces them to!], and because they have no one to rely on.[92] Like Pichler before her, Paoli argues for wider women's education as a way of underpinning financial independence, and the role of women as wives and mothers. Contemporary education, writes Paoli, fails to endow women with the ability to think and reason, yet society complains about 'die Oberflächlichkeit der Frauen, über ihren Mangel an Logik und Konsequenz' [the superficiality of women, about their lack of logic and consistency].[93] Aware of social concerns regarding 'gelehrte Frauen', Paoli is quick to reassure her readers that nothing could be further from her mind than *femmes savantes*: 'Beruhige dich, lieber Leser! Ich habe es nicht auf eine gelehrte, sondern nur auf eine vernünftige Erziehung abgesehen' [Calm down, dear reader! I do not have a scholarly education in mind, only a sensible one].[94] Paoli advocates women's education as the basis of a career for intelligent girls and women who must support themselves, but is careful elsewhere in the article to highlight the importance of women's education as the bedrock of the family.

Paoli's unpublished essay, 'Die Wandlungen der Frauenfrage' ['The Changes in the Women's Question'], is an excellent example of the pragmatic nature of the contemporary women's movement, which sought practical solutions to the problems faced by women while accepting contemporary ideas regarding the relationship between the sexes. Paoli argues that Wollstonecraft goes too far in desiring to see women's dependence on men eliminated: 'Diese Abhängigkeit wird immer bestehen, denn sie beruht auf einem Naturgesetz, nämlich auf der geringeren physischen Kraft des Weibes.' [This dependence will always exist, for it rests on a law of nature, namely the lesser physical power of women.][95] For Paoli, the contemporary women's movement has modest aims, and is a 'Brotfrage' [economic issue] which has 'ein Gewicht und eine Dringlichkeit, die nur von der Gedanken- oder Herzlosigkeit geleugnet werden kann' [a weight and urgency which can only be denied by thoughtlessness or heartlessness].[96] The women's movement has moved away from the aims of Wollstonecraft and George Sand, and seeks practical solutions: 'es [handle] sich vor allem darum [...], die Erwerbsfähigkeit der Frauen zu entwickeln und ihr weitere Gebiete zu erschließen' [the main issue is [...] developing women's capacity for work and developing further areas of employment for them].

Paoli's letters show that she did not let herself be restricted on the same terms she advocates for other women. In her correspondence with Leopold Kompert, Paoli negotiates publication of her work, and justifies her decision to write. In 1850, Paoli asks that her article be included, despite Kompert's negative views of female authorship, views she claims to agree with.[97] In another letter from the same year, she demonstrates that she does not shy away from self-publication. Not only does she publish literary works, but she actively seeks to have them discussed in the press:

> Ich bitte Sie, das Buch [*Nach dem Gewitter* (1850)] im Lloyd zu besprechen [...] Sie würden mich sehr verbinden, wenn Sie die Güte hätten, in ihrer [*sic*] Besprechung die schreiendsten Druckfehler hervorzuheben; das wäre zugleich eine Ehrenrettung für mich und eine erlaubte Rache an diesem scheußlichen Bösewicht von Setzer. — [98]
>
> [I ask you to discuss the book [*After the Storm*] in *Lloyd* [...] I would be very indebted to you if you would be so kind as to highlight in your discussion the worst of the misprints; this would at one and the same time rescue my honour and be a permissible act of revenge against that dreadful villain of a typesetter.]

By requesting that Kompert highlight the failures of the typesetter, Paoli locates the source of her honour in her writing, thereby subverting contemporary ideas which held that a woman's purity could be damaged by too much contact with the world. Her desire to seek revenge against the typesetter also defies contemporary gender ideals. After Kompert published his review, Paoli even wrote to tell him that it was not quite what she had envisioned: 'die Individualisirung mangelt. Ich glaube nicht, daß jemand, der meine Gedichte nicht kannte, sich durch die Recension einen richtigen Begriff davon zu machen vermöchte' [it lacks individualization. I do not believe that someone who did not know my poems would be able to get a good idea of them from the review].[99]

Paoli is not a feminist in today's understanding of the word, not least because she believes that every young woman accepts and welcomes her destiny as a housewife and mother. Rose asserts that in embracing this conservative feminism, 'Paoli astutely recognized the limits of her culture's tolerance for change', while Wozonig argues that, regardless of her own opinions, it was important for Paoli to refer positively to traditional gender ideals if she wanted her writing to be accorded a prominent place in publications.[100] She allowed those readers who would always see women as subordinate to consider her texts harmless: 'Dieselbe Taktik führt dazu, dass auf den zweiten Blick und bei Bedenken der Konsequenzen und Implikationen ihrer Argumente das durchaus revolutionäre Potenzial der Forderungen zutage kommt.' [The same tactic means that, when looked at again with consideration of the consequences and implications of her arguments, the very revolutionary potential of her demands comes to light.][101] Paoli's essays give us insight into contemporary discussions around the *Frauenfrage*, and allow us to place Grillparzer's dramas, and their portrayal of emancipated women, in an appropriate context. Notably, Paoli demonstrates that the discussion was concerned almost exclusively with designing practical solutions to the problems faced by (mainly single) women who struggled to support themselves, rather than with issues of equality or women's suffrage.

While some considered Paoli to be Grillparzer's Eckermann, others assigned this position to Auguste Littrow-Bischoff.[102] In a touching and emotional letter of 1866, Grillparzer thanks Littrow-Bischoff for a Christmas gift, and expresses warm affection for his friend:

> Nicht als ob ich nicht so unzählige Beweise Ihrer Theilnahme empfangen hätte, aber daß an dem Tage, der der häuslichen Freude gewidmet ist, Sie sich meiner erinnert hatten, das überraschte mich. Haben Sie von allen Östereichern [*sic*] allein ein so langes Gedächtniß, daß Sie sich der Zeit erinnern, wo ich noch etwas werth war [...] (1866. Nr. 1404. *HKA* III/iv, p. 279.)

> [It is not as if I had not received countless displays of your interest, but I was surprised that you thought of me on that day which is dedicated to domestic joy. Are you alone among all Austrians in having such a long memory that you remember the times when I was still worth something [...]]

Like Paoli, Littrow-Bischoff was a prominent figure in Vienna, and she also entered the debate on the social position of women. Additionally, she published a memoir, *Aus dem persönlichen Verkehre mit Franz Grillparzer* (1873), which concentrates on her acquaintance with the dramatist. She and her husband were the centre of a large social set, with guests at their salon including Paoli, Bauernfeld, Ebner-Eschenbach, Hebbel and Saar.[103] After her death, her friend Fanny Meißner-Diemer wrote that Littrow-Bischoff had been 'eine Vorkämpferin für die bessere Erziehung und für die Erwerbsfähigkeit des weiblichen Geschlechtes' and had shown 'daß höhere weibliche Bildung und häusliche Tugenden einander nicht ausschließen, wie es nur zu oft angenommen wird' [a pioneer of better education for, and economic activity of the female sex; that further education of women and domestic virtues are not mutually exclusive, as is all too often assumed].[104]

Littrow-Bischoff was 'eine vielseitig interessierte Frau und besonders sozialen Gedanken aufgeschlossen'[105] whose intellectual independence made her 'eine der Wegbereiterinnen der Emanzipation des 19. Jahrhunderts' [a woman with a variety of interests who was in particular receptive to social concepts; one of the forerunners of emancipation in the nineteenth century].[106] This activity brought her into contact with John Stuart Mill and Florence Nightingale in England. Littrow-Bischoff helped Nightingale with research into women's institutions in Germany and Russia, and she turned to Nightingale for help in writing an article on Mill.[107] Mill, to whom Littrow-Bischoff sent copies of her work in the hope that he would attach a preface to it, wrote that he was 'very happy to learn from your testimony that there is already a widely spread interest among German women for the cause of political & social equality of the sexes'.[108] In a second letter, Mill thanked her for her 'valuable contribution to the cause both of women & of education & I hope it is not the only one which they are destined to receive from you as a writer'.[109]

In *Die sociale Bewegung auf dem Gebiete der Frauen* [*The Social Movement as it Relates to Women*] (1868), published under her pseudonym Otto August, Littrow-Bischoff argued for more economic opportunities for women. She begins by identifying an obsession with theory, which did not originate in 'der Noth des wirklichen Lebens' [the needs of real life], rather than practice, as one of the reasons why the cause of women's emancipation had made little progress.[110] Like Paoli, Littrow-Bischoff distances herself from these theories, as well as from the idea of equal rights for women, which she argues would be a denial of women's nature. She writes that the focus of the contemporary women's movement is on allowing women the means to earn an independent living and protecting them 'vor dem Abgrund des Lasters und der Schmach' [from the abyss of vice and humiliation].[111] Pichler, writes Littrow-Bischoff, recognized that women never make it to the highest levels even 'in den [ihnen] zugehörenden Verrichtungen und Thätigkeiten' [in the duties and occupations which are within their sphere] such as dressmaking, hairdressing or cooking.[112] In arguing for greater emancipation, Littrow-Bischoff does not break new ground. Indeed, the similarities between her arguments and standpoint and those of Pichler several decades earlier indicate that, as in much of Europe, the arguments for women's emancipation did not change much over the course of the nineteenth century.[113] That Littrow-Bischoff's starting point and aims seem to be those of Pichler also shows the minimal impact of the 1848 revolution on the position of women.

Littrow-Bischoff's engagement with the *Frauenfrage* extended beyond authorship, and she was one of the women who, in 1866, founded the Wiener Frauen-Erwerb-Verein. Run exclusively by women and consisting almost exclusively of female members, the Verein's statutes listed its aim as 'die Unterstützung der wirtschaftlichen Thätigkeit der Frauen und Mädchen, sie mögen in Familien leben, oder auf sich allein angewiesen sein' [supporting the economic activities of women and girls, whether they live with their families or are dependent on themselves alone].[114] This aim was to be achieved by a variety of means, including 'durch Bekämpfung und Beseitigung der Vorurtheile und Hindernisse, welche mancher Frauenarbeit im Wege stehen', 'durch Berufs-, Gewerbs- und Handelgeschäfte der Frauen', and 'durch Förderung entsprechender Arbeit und Beschäftigung, insbesondere durch Gründung weiblicher Genossenschaften, Arbeitsnachweisungsanstalten u. dgl' [by fighting and eliminating the prejudices and obstacles which stand in the way of many forms of women's employment; through women's professional, commercial and trade activities; by supporting appropriate work and employment, in particular by founding female associations, employment agencies etc.].[115] Evans sees the Verein's cautious approach as a reaction to strict authoritarianism which could close the organization if its programme were too radical.[116] He notes that the Verein did not aim to have the *Allgemeines bürgerliches Gesetzbuch* (*ABGB*) amended, although he shows how that law book shaped the character of the Verein's work. Because of the legal powers the *ABGB* granted women over their property, the Austrian women's movement initially focused on improving the lives of unmarried middle-class women.[117] Impetus for the foundation of the Verein came less from theoretical and philosophical publications than from the terrible, increasingly documented conditions in which many women lived.[118] Unmarried women often relied on the kindness of relations for survival, and Littrow-Bischoff and others saw this as an undignified situation. For Margret Friedrich, the creation of the Verein shows that women had lost faith in the patriarchal, class-based social order.[119] She argues that the Verein 'trug mit seinem Wirken zur Entwicklung und Verbreitung einer bürgerlichen Frauenkultur wesentlich bei' [contributed significantly through its activities to the development and dissemination of a bourgeois women's culture],[120] and although it did not aim to achieve full equality or a revised division of social roles, the demand for work which was central to the Verein's activity marks the beginnings of the women's movement.[121]

Marie von Ebner-Eschenbach is the best known female friend from the latter part of Grillparzer's life. In 1847, Ebner's stepmother, Xaverine Dubsky, sent some of her poetry to Grillparzer, whose reaction was favourable: he praised the young woman's 'höchst glückliches Ohr für den Vers, Gewalt des Ausdrucks, eine, villeicht [*sic*] nur zu tiefe, Empfindung, Einsicht, und scharfe Beurtheilungsgabe in manchen der satyrischen Gedichte' [extremely good ear for verse, power of expression, a perhaps only too deep emotion, insight, and keen gift for judgement in some of the satirical poems].[122] What was missing was the maturity 'die den Dichter erst zum Künstler macht' [which is what turns the poet into an artist]. While Grillparzer claims that young women are generally ahead of their male peers as far as reason and intelligence are concerned, they lack 'Ordnung in den Gedanken' [order in their thoughts]. Here, Grillparzer cites a typical prejudice against women, but locates the cause in a lack of education rather than in women's physiology. Dubsky had hoped for a negative reaction, which would dissuade Ebner from continuing with her literary pursuits: writing was not considered appropriate for young aristocratic women, and her family was not supportive.[123] It was feared that the exclusivity of the aristocracy would be compromised if one of its members subjected herself to the scrutiny of the general public, and if a female aristocrat were to publish literary works, then the private sphere would be exposed to an intolerable extent.[124] Ebner-Eschenbach's family hoped that repeated bans would stifle her ambitions, and this attitude made her childhood and youth unpleasant.

Although by no means a feminist in today's understanding, Ebner-Eschenbach had a deep interest in the *Frauenfrage*. According to Izabela Surynt, the basis of Ebner-Eschenbach's ideas on the nature of women was the conviction that all human beings were endowed with intellectual and artistic abilities, 'deren Herausbildung jedoch durch soziokulturelle Bedingungen nicht für beide Geschlechter im gleichen Maße möglich sei' [the development of which is not, however, possible for both sexes to an equal extent due to sociocultural circumstances].[125] Surynt argues that Ebner-Eschenbach does not doubt that men and women think and see the world differently, women being more motivated by emotions and feelings, but she believes that both sexes have equal value. Her view that this difference gives women greater moral responsibility reflects the view of the conservative women's movement. Ulrike Tanzer argues that Ebner-Eschenbach's 'emanzipatorische[s] Credo' [emancipatory creed] saw women as equal partners in marriage, and that her work displays 'Modelle weiblicher Selbstverwirklichung und Geschlechterbeziehungen, die bestimmt sind von Gleichberechtigung und gegenseitigem Respekt' [models of female self-realization and gender relations which are influenced by equality and mutual respect].[126] Surynt sees an affinity between Ebner-Eschenbach's views and those of conservative activists, with whom she shared the opinion that while suffrage was not a goal of the women's movement, social change was unstoppable and women would eventually enjoy the right to vote.[127]

Grillparzer also knew a number of actresses, and his works show that he held Sophie Schröder, Julie Rettich and Charlotte Wolter in high regard. Like women writers, actresses did not conform to the bourgeois ideal of femininity which prevailed in the nineteenth century.[128] Because actresses had public careers outside of the areas deemed suitable for women's financial activity, they contravened the female *Geschlechtscharakter*, and were therefore in a precarious position *vis-à-vis* bourgeois society.[129] In addition, the fact that an actress's métier is dissimulation made her suspicious in private life: bourgeois society depended on the ability to categorize individuals, including on the basis of their sex, and authenticity was a mark of female nature. The rise of the bourgeoisie meant that the social standing of actresses became ambivalent, for they were skilled at role-play, which, in the context of bourgeois society, was an esteemed skill: playing the correct social role was essential for a social existence, and what Wozonig terms 'soziale Theatralität' [social theatricality] played a role in all areas of social interaction.

In a diary entry, Grillparzer recalls the change in his own attitude towards actresses, which, he claims, turned from admiration from afar to contempt upon making the acquaintance of some members of their class: 'ich [entfernte] mich mit Abscheu von ihnen [...], und, obschon ich nothwendig so oft in ihrer Nähe seyn mußte, nie irgend ein Verhältniß mit einer von ihnen gehabt habe' [I [distanced] myself with disgust from them [...] and although I was by necessity often in their vicinity, I never had a relationship with any of them] (1822. Nr. 1186. *HKA* II/viii, pp. 75–76). Katharina Fröhlich hoped to make a career as an actress, but Grillparzer would not allow it.[130] Indeed, Grillparzer's refusal to let Fröhlich pursue an acting career accords with Wozonig's conclusion regarding social acceptance of actresses: such a public career could not be tolerated after marriage.[131] Despite this apparent distaste for actresses in general, and for an actress-wife in particular, Grillparzer was on good terms with a number of actresses throughout his life. This indicates that Grillparzer's views on 'emancipated' women may have been more generous than those expressed in his diaries.

Sophie Schröder (1781–1868), the first actress to portray Bertha, Sappho and Medea, was bound to Grillparzer by mutual admiration. She was extremely popular, and did not completely adhere to contemporary expectations. Her correspondence shows how she forged a career for herself, actively contacting theatres and suggesting roles for herself, negotiating salaries, and defending herself in the face of theatres' contractual breaches. In 1824, she claimed to be writing at a time 'wo mich mein Volk zur Vergötterung erhebt. — Ja, mein Freund, man vergöttert mich, nicht wie ein irdisches Wesen werde ich hier behandelt' [when my people raise me up for idolization. — Yes, my friend, I am idolized, I am not treated like an earthly being here].[132] This popularity, perhaps combined with her forthright attitude, meant that while many actors earned twenty *Gulden* per week, Schröder could demand one hundred *Taler* per role.[133] In a letter of 1828, she refuses to be restricted to behaviours considered becoming for women, and also demonstrates that actresses were not necessarily required to conform to the expectations placed on other women:

> Den Einwurf, ein Frauenzimmer könne nicht allein reisen, lasse ich gar nicht gelten — ein Frauenzimmer vielleicht nicht, aber bei einer Künstlerin wird es keinem Menschen einfallen, etwas Indezentes darin zu finden.[134]
>
> [I will not allow the objection that a woman cannot travel alone — a woman perhaps not, but where an artist is concerned, it would not occur to anyone to find anything indecent in it.]

Schröder's love life was also unconventional. She had a relationship with Moritz Michael Daffinger, a painter nine years her junior. In an 1817 letter to Rahel von Varnhagen, whose husband was also a younger man, Schröder sets out her hopes and fears regarding the relationship, and the troubles which convinced her that there was no such thing as 'ganz vollkommenes Glück zwischen Mann und Weib' [quite complete happiness between man and woman].[135]

Despite Schröder's lack of conventionality, and his own avowed dislike of actors, Grillparzer held her in high esteem. In 1836, comparing English actors, who he felt had 'etwas festes, auf sich selbst beruhendes, männliches, das außerordentlich wohl thut' [something solid, based in themselves, masculine, that does one a lot of good], with their Austrian counterparts, Grillparzer wrote that 'unter den Wiener Schauspielern [ist] ein einziger Mann, Madame Schröder nämlich' [among the Viennese actors [there is] only one man, namely Madame Schröder] (Nr. 3048. *HKA* II/x, p. 86). After another performance in London, he wrote in his diary: 'Ich weiß außer der Schröder keinen imposanten Schauspieler in Deutschland' [Apart from Schröder I know no commanding actors in Germany] (Nr. 3126. *HKA* II/x, p. 124). In his *Selbstbiographie*, he recalls rehearsals for *Sappho*: Schröder 'bemächtigte sich der Haupt-Rolle, war Feuer und Flamme, und steckte Jedermann mit ihrer Begeisterung an' [took hold of the main role, was on fire, and infected everyone with her enthusiasm] (*HKA* I/xvi, p. 129). Ernst Wurm ascribes to Schröder's performance as Sappho a central role in the establishment of Grillparzer's fame.[136] In 1854, Grillparzer immortalized Schröder in a poem which demonstrates his respect for her:

> Zwei Schröder, Frau und Mann,
> Umgränzen unsers Dramas Lauf;
> Der Eine stand in Kraft als es begann,
> Die Andre schied, — da hörts wohl, fürcht ich, auf.
> (Nr. 1348. *HKA* I/xii/i, p. 252)

[Two Schröders, woman and man,/ Mark the course of our drama;/ The first was in force when it began,/ The second departed — there, I fear, it comes to an end.]

The male Schröder mentioned in this epigram is Friedrich Ludwig Schröder (1744–1816), a German actor who was famous for his Shakespearean roles. He spent some time at the Burgtheater in the early 1780s, and, when Sophie Schröder was performing in Hamburg, near to where he lived, he visited the theatre to see her perform. According to Sophie Schröder's son-in-law, their interaction had long-lasting, positive effects on her career (*HKA* i/xiii/ii, p. 279). This poem, then, clearly demonstrates Grillparzer's admiration for Sophie Schröder, for he places her in the context of a renowned Shakespearean actor and states that the end of her career marks the end of an era.

Schröder supported Grillparzer from the beginning of his career. After an early performance of *Die Ahnfrau*, in which Schröder played Bertha, she 'erbat dem aufgeführten Trauerspiele als dem ersten Versuche eines jungen Dichters die Nachsicht des Publikums' [asked the audience to show the performed tragedy leniency as the first attempt of a young poet'.[137] Indeed, the performance might not have happened at all had Schröder not interceded with the censors on behalf of the author, as Grillparzer reports in his *Selbstbiographie* (*HKA* I/xvi, p. 122). The importance of her support must have been obvious to Grillparzer, although there is no correspondence which evidences his gratitude. In a letter of 1824 requesting his presence at an event she was hosting, Schröder makes clear her respect for the playwright, and reveals the efforts to which she has gone to help him. She calls herself his 'Verfechterin' [champion]: 'Ja, tapfer habe ich für Sie gefochten, einer ist schon gänzlich besiegt aber der Andere ist, wie man bei uns sagt, noch etwas hartmäulich, aber es wird mir doch gelingen auch ihn noch zur Vernunft zu bringen.' [Yes, I fought courageously for you, one is already completely defeated, the other, as we say, still a little obstinate, but I will succeed in bringing even him to his senses.][138] Although the exact context of this letter cannot be established, it is clear that Grillparzer's behaviour towards Schröder engendered a strong sense of goodwill and affection.

Julie Rettich, née Gley (1809–1866), was another famous Burgtheater actress who portrayed Grillparzer's heroines. In the year of Rettich's death Paoli published a biography of the actress. Paoli is careful to stress Rettich's feminine characteristics and traditional upbringing: she was encouraged to cultivate 'die Fertigkeiten und Geschicklichkeiten [...], die dem Weibe insbesonders zukommen' [the skills and expertise [...] which particularly befit women].[139] Rettich fulfilled the expectations placed on her, and her 'angeborener Drang nach Thätigkeit fand in der Erfüllung ihrer kleinen häuslichen Pflichten ein erwünschtes Genüge' [innate need for activity found a desired satisfaction in the execution of her small domestic duties]. Rettich, Paoli claims, often talked about women's social roles: she opposed the limits which were placed on women, as well as the prejudices which denied women any capabilities, and prevented them from developing any.[140] According to Paoli, it was Rettich's 'unerschütterliche Ueberzeugung, daß die Fehler und Schwächen, deren man die Frauen zu beschuldigen pflegt, nicht in der Natur des Weibes begründet, sondern ihm in den meisten Fällen nur anerzogen seien' [unwavering conviction that the faults and weaknesses of which one tended to accuse women were not innate to the nature of women, but had in most cases only been instilled in them]. This confession leads Paoli to stress, again, Rettich's conventional character: 'Selbst das Muster einer Gattin, Mutter und Hausfrau, war sie weiter als irgend Jemand entfernt, das Weib seinem natürlichen Berufe entfremden zu wollen' [She herself was a model wife, mother and housewife, and was further than anyone from wanting to alienate women from their natural occupation]. As we have seen, Paoli was an advocate of increased rights for women, and Wozonig sees Paoli's biography of Rettich as critical of a society which restricts women's opportunities.[141] Paoli's description of Rettich should be taken with caution: Paoli may have seen portraying a popular actress as an advocate of better education for women as a way of gaining support for her cause. However, there is some evidence that Rettich was engaged with women's issues. In the Wiener Frauen-Erwerb-Verein, she advocated better vocational education for women.[142] And, in an undated letter addressed to the members of Grüne Insel, a group of artists and writers, she asked that women be included in their gatherings:

> Sollten wir Frauen, die selbst der Kunst nahe stehen, von den Rittern des Geistes aus ihrem fröhlichen Kreise ohne allen Ausnahmsfall ausgeschlossen sein und bleiben?[143]
>
> [Should we women, who are close to art ourselves, be and remain excluded without exception from her happy circle by the knights of the mind?]

Although Grillparzer criticized Rettich for her portrayal of Emilia Galotti, he recognized her as a 'bedeutende Schauspielerin[]' [important actress] (1860. Nr. 4255. *HKA* II/xii, p. 35), and admired her dramatic skill. In 1834, he wrote to Theodor Hell in Dresden, asking him to persuade Rettich — '[die] von mir hochverehrte[] Künstlerin' [the actress whom I admire greatly] — to perform in *Des Meeres und der Liebe Wellen*. He hoped Rettich knew that 'ein einfaches Nein meiner Hochachtung für sie nicht ein Iota entziehen wird' [a simple no will not reduce my respect for her one iota] (Nr. 429. *HKA* III/ii, p. 123). Grillparzer states his admiration for Rettich, but this letter also shows how much he relied upon talented actresses for the success of his dramas. *Des Meeres und der Liebe Wellen* was not successful in Vienna, but Grillparzer hoped that Rettich's talents would popularize it.

Charlotte Wolter (1834–1897) was one of the actresses who signed Rettich's letter to the Grüne Insel. Between 1862, when her tenure at the Burgtheater began, and 1887, she appeared 1764 times in 114 plays.[144] Among other roles, she portrayed Medea twenty times, Hero twelve, Libussa six, Rahel seven times, and Sappho on thirty-three occasions. She thus played a major role in Laube's revival of Grillparzer's dramas.[145] After her death, she was remembered as '[e]in erhabenes Vorbild, eine Fürstin auf dem Gebiete der dramatischen Kunst, die größte Tragödin ihrer Zeit' [a sublime paragon, a princess in the field of dramatic arts, the greatest tragedienne of her time].[146] In 1866, Grillparzer wrote a letter to Littrow-Bischoff, thanking her for a photograph of Wolter which he said was 'mir höchst schätzbar, da ich sie nie mit Augen gesehen habe' [very valuable to me, as I have never seen her myself] (Nr. 1404. *HKA* III/iv, p. 279). Two years later, now acquainted with Wolter after Littrow-Bischoff's introduction, in the epigram 'Dramatisch' ['Dramatic'] (1868), which Frank and Pörnbacher interpret as criticism of Friedrich Halm's directorship of the Burgtheater,[147] Grillparzer shows his admiration for the actress by portraying her as a guiding force and saviour of the institution:

> Der Weg ist schlecht, der Karren schwach
> Es geht so ziemlich holter-polter.
> Da hilft am besten Vorspann nach
> Als allerbeste Fräulein Wolter.
> (Nr. 1811. *HKA* I/xii/I, p. 348)

[The path is bad, the cart weak/ Things are pretty helter-skelter./ The very best Miss Wolter/ Gives a helping guiding hand.]

In addition to these famous women, Grillparzer's diaries and notes mention other actresses, performers and writers, and demonstrate his support for women who aspired to such careers. In 1836, he wrote in Wilhelmine von Chézy's album: 'Geistreich, wie der beste Schriftsteller, und gut wie die beste Frau. Wer schmäht noch über schriftstellernde Frauen?' [Witty like the best writers and good like the best women. Who still speaks ill of female writers?] (Nr. 610. *HKA* I/xii/i, p. 72). Not only does this seem to be encouragement for Chézy's own writing, it also rejects the idea that female authors are ridiculous or bizarre. In 1838, he wrote a poem for Josephine von Remekházy, in which he questioned her decision to become a writer: 'Du hast was Menschen haben,/ Die höchsten Schicksalsgaben,/ Des Wirklichen Gewinn;/ Und dennoch Dichterin?' [You have what people have,/ The highest gifts from fate,/ The true prize;/ And yet: a poet?] (Nr. 702. *HKA* I/xii/i, p. 95). It is unclear why he is less supportive here: perhaps he thought less of Remekházy's talents than of Chézy's, or perhaps he was all too aware of the difficulties which faced women writers. In a similar vein, he quoted lines from *Sappho* in the album of Fürstin Wittgenstein, possibly as a warning of the difficulties of a writer's life (Nr. 1553. *HKA* I/xii/i, p. 292). In 1851, he wrote to Mathilde Baronin Guretzki, who had sent him some of her poems. He replied with a warm and encouraging letter (Nr. 720. *HKA* III/iii, p. 73): 'aus vielen dieser Gedichte [leuchtet] ein wahres poetisches Talent hervor und der Hauptfehler der übrigen ist, daß der Leser fühlt, dieselbe Verfaßerin hätte dieselben Gedichte viel beßer machen können' [a real poetic talent [shines] forth from many of these poems, and the main failing of the others is that the reader feels that the same author could have written the same poems far better]. He mentioned the flaws he saw in Guretzki's poems, and attributed these to the fact that her 'patriotische Begeisterung' [patriotic enthusiasm] had overpowered the poetic. Guretzki wanted to publish the poems, and Grillparzer warned her to expect some criticism. However, he considered these poems novel:

> Übrigens ist die Erscheinung, ein weibliches Wesen von den Heldenthaten unserer Armee begeistert zu sehen, wieder so anziehend, ja neu, daß der Reiz dieser Empfindung, der selbst etwas heroisches hat, nur zu Gunsten der Verfaßerin wirken kann. Wozu kommt noch, daß, wie ich schon früher gesagt, Vieles mit dem Stempel des eigentlich Poetischen bezeichnet ist.
>
> [By the way, seeing a woman who is enthused by the heroic acts of our army is so attractive, even new, that the attraction of this emotion, which attraction itself has something heroic about it, can only work in the author's favour. And in addition, as I already said earlier, much of this is stamped with the mark of the truly poetic.]

Although there is little evidence that Grillparzer engaged with the works of Pichler or Weissenthurn, these examples show that he was familiar with the works of women writers, and did not necessarily dismiss them as trivial or irrelevant.

In 1808, Grillparzer lamented the death of the Burgtheater actress Betti Roose: 'Madame Roose ist tot, und mit ihr meine schönsten Hofnungen! — Blanka von Kastilien kann nie aufgeführt werden' [Madame Roose is dead, and with her my dearest hopes! — *Blanka von Kastilien* can never be performed] (Nr 33. *HKA* II/vii, p. 18). In 1831, he composed an epitaph for the actress Sophie Müller: 'Ihre Freunde haben sie betrauert, und wer sie kannte war ihr Freund.' [Her friends mourned her, and anyone who knew her was her friend.] (Nr. 1897. *HKA* II/ix, p. 27) He commemorated the death of the actress Therese Löwe with a poem (1830. Nr. 74. *HKA* I/ix, p. 102). He also supported other women who chose public careers. He ended a poem for Karoline Mayer, a singer who was trained by the Fröhlichs and would begin her career at the Burgtheater (*HKA* I/xii/ii, p. 135), on an encouraging note: 'Du kannst was immer du willst.' [You can achieve whatever you want.] (1844. *HKA* I/xii/i, p. 155) In a poem entitled 'Jenny Lind', Grillparzer paid tribute to the Swedish opera singer who performed in Vienna in 1846: 'Du bist nicht Farbe, bist das Licht,/ Das Farben erst verkündet/ Das wenn sein Weiß an Fremdem bricht/

Die bunte Pracht entzündet.' (1846. *HKA* I/x, p. 215) [You are not colour, but the light,/ Which proclaims colours,/ Which when its white breaks against other objects/ Ignites the colourful splendor.] And, when she was attacked by critics, Grillparzer defended her:

> Der Hund bellt an den Mond,
> Der leuchtet wie gewohnt,
> Gibt sich durch Strahlen kund
> Und bleibt der Holde Mond,
> So wie der Hund — ein Hund.
> (1846. *HKA* I/xii/i, p. 182)

[The dog barks at the moon,/ Which shines as always,/ Makes itself known in rays of light,/ And remains the fair moon,/ As the dog remains — a dog.]

While these women were not necessarily *intellectual* women, they nevertheless were outliers in nineteenth-century Austria. They chose careers which gave them financial independence as well as a conspicuous public profile. They did not adhere to the standards of femininity which prevailed at the time, and Grillparzer's friendships with, support for, and admiration of these women should therefore be seen as an indication that, despite the misogynistic expressions in his private writings, he was not hostile towards extraordinary women.

The limits of this study make it impossible to list in detail all the prominent women and female authors with whom Grillparzer was acquainted. In addition to the women mentioned here, many others could be added to demonstrate the extent to which Grillparzer knew the prominent intellectual women of his age: the authors Therese Artner, Marianne Neumann von Meißenthal and Marie von Zay, who were friends of Caroline Pichler; Emilie von Binzer, who published under the pseudonym Ernst Ritter and whose stories Grillparzer praised; the poet Josephine von Knorr, who introduced both Littrow-Bischoff and Ebner-Eschenbach to Grillparzer; or Ida Fleischl-Marxow, friend, advisor and patron to Ebner-Eschenbach and Paoli.

The overview presented here does, however, allow us to establish that Grillparzer was not hostile to emancipated women. He was friends with many such women, some of whom were public figures who published widely, or popular actresses. These women received support and guidance from the author they revered and respected, and immortalized him in heartfelt and intimate memoirs. The lives and writings of Grillparzer's acquaintances who argued for women's emancipation allow us to place his dramas in context. When talking about Grillparzer, careful use of words such as 'feminism' or 'women's rights' is important, and the works of Paoli, Littrow-Bischoff and Pichler allow us to place Grillparzer's dramas in the context of 'feminism' as his contemporaries, and possibly he himself, saw it. The women's movement in nineteenth-century Austria was concerned first and foremost with alleviating real suffering which resulted from women's inability to participate independently in the economic life of the nation. The demands of Paoli and others therefore centred on access to education and training, and then employment. These female authors did not argue for equal rights or suffrage, nor did they repudiate the differences between men and women. But their writing challenged the status quo, defended women's intellectual abilities, and demanded better, if not equal, rights for women. Their lives and work also show the extent to which, on an individual basis, contemporary restrictions could be rejected and individual freedom achieved.

Notes to Chapter 1

1. Caroline Pichler, *Denkwürdigkeiten aus meinem Leben*, 2 vols, ed. by Karl Blümml (Munich: Georg Müller, 1914), I, p. 48.
2. Barbara Becker-Cantarino, *Der lange Weg zur Mündigkeit. Frau und Literatur (1500–1800)* (Stuttgart: Metzler, 1987), pp. 156–58.
3. Ibid., pp. 159–60.
4. Gerhard Dilcher, 'Die Ordnung der Ungleichheit. Haus, Stand und "Geschlecht"', in *Frauen in der Geschichte des Rechts. Von der Frühen Neuzeit bis zur Gegenwart*, ed. by Ute Gerhard (Munich: Beck, 1997), pp. 55–72 (pp. 55–56).
5. Helen Fronius, *Women and Literature in the Goethe Era 1770–1820. Determined Dilettantes* (Oxford: Oxford University Press, 2007), pp. 17–18.
6. Michaela Krug, *Auf der Suche nach dem eigenen Raum. Topographien des Weiblichen im Roman von Autorinnen um 1800* (Würzburg: Königshaus & Neumann, 2004), p. 42.
7. Rita Morrien, *Sinn und Sinnlichkeit. Der weibliche Körper in der deutschen Literatur der Bürgerzeit* (Cologne; Weimar; Vienna: Böhlau, 2001), p. 7.
8. Ingrid Spörk, 'Gesten der Herrschaft — Zeichen der Macht. Zur Annektierung des Anderen bei Grillparzer', *Études Germaniques* 47 (1992), 215–34 (p. 216).
9. Irmtraud Götz von Olenhusen, 'Das Ende männlicher Zeugungsmythen im Zeitalter der Aufklärung: Zur Wissenschafts- und Geschlechtergeschichte des 17. und 18. Jahrhunderts', in *Ordnung, Politik und Geselligkeit der Geschlechter im 18. Jahrhundert*, ed. by Ulrike Weckel et al. (Göttingen: Wallstein, 1998), pp. 259–83 (p. 259).
10. Ibid., pp. 259–60.
11. For similar interpretations of the *Geschlechtscharaktere* as a reaction to Enlightenment ideas of equality, see Andreas Gestrich, *Geschichte der Familie im 19. und 20. Jahrhundert*, Enzyklopädie deutscher Geschichte Band 50 (Munich: Oldenbourg, 2010); Vibha Bakshi Gokhale, 'Geschlechtscharaktere', in *The Feminist Encyclopedia of German Literature*, ed. by Friederike Eigler and Susanne Kord (Westport, CT: Greenwood, 1997), pp. 211–12.
12. Olenhusen, 'Das Ende männlicher Zeugungsmythen', p. 261.
13. Hannelore Scholz, *Widersprüche im bürgerlichen Frauenbild. Zur ästhetischen Reflexion und poetischen Praxis bei Lessing, Friedrich Schlegel und Schiller* (Weinheim: Deutscher Studien Verlag, 1992), p. 49. On the differentiation between *gelehrte* and *gebildete* women, see also: Becker-Cantarino, *Der lange Weg*, p. 117; Susanne Kord, 'Erudite Woman/Gelehrte', in *The Feminist Encyclopedia of German Literature*, pp. 124–26.
14. Fronius, *Women and Literature in the Goethe Era 1770–1820*, p. 33.
15. Susanne T. Kord, 'Eternal Love or Sentimental Discourse? Gender Dissonance and Women's Passionate "Friendships"', in *Outing Goethe and His Age*, ed. by Alice A. Kuzniar (Stanford, CA: Stanford University Press, 1996), pp. 228–49, p. 233.
16. Susanne Kord, *Ein Blick hinter die Kulissen. Deutschsprachige Dramatikerinnen im 18. und 19. Jahrhundert* (Stuttgart: Metzler, 1992), p. 40.
17. Wendy Arons, *Performance and Femininity in Eighteenth-Century German Women's Writing. The Impossible Act* (New York: Palgrave Macmillan, 2006), p. 1.
18. Fronius, *Women and Literature in the Goethe Era 1770–1820*, p. 52.
19. Linda L. Clark, *Women and Achievement in Nineteenth-Century Europe* (Cambridge: Cambridge University Press, 2008), p. 12.
20. Marsha Meyer, 'The Depictions of Women in Gutzkow's *Wally, die Zweiflerin* and Mundt's *Madonna*', in *Beyond the Eternal Feminine. Critical Essays on Women and German Literature*, ed. by Susan L. Cocalis and Kay Goodman (Stuttgart: Hans-Dieter Heinz, 1982), pp. 135–58 (p. 136).

21. Hagl-Catling, *Für eine Imagologie der Geschlechter*, p. 91.
22. Ibid., p. 110.
23. W. E. Yates, 'Nestroy, Grillparzer, and the Feminist Cause', pp. 97–99.
24. Richard J. Evans, *The Feminists. Women's Emancipation Movements in Europe, America and Australasia 1840–1920* (London: Croom Helm, 1977), p. 30, p. 92; Richard J. Evans, *The Feminist Movement in Germany 1894–1933* (London: Sage, 1976), p. 3.
25. Evans, *The Feminists*, p. 92.
26. W. E. Yates, 'Nestroy, Grillparzer, and the Feminist Cause', pp. 98–99.
27. Review of *Frauen-Emancipation* by Wilhelm Marchland, in *Wiener Zeitschrift für Kunst, Literatur, Theater und Mode*, 28.5.1839 (p. 511).
28. 'Öffentliches Leben in Wien', *Der Österreichische Zuschauer. Zeitschrift für Kunst, Wissenschaft und geistiges Leben*, 31.5.1839, 666–67 (p. 666).
29. 'Theatersalon. Theater in der Josephstadt', *Der Humorist*, 3.9.1840, 711–12 (p. 712).
30. "Gelegenheitsworte für unsere Zeit. Die schöne Wienerin", *Der Österreichische Zuschauer. Zeitschrift für Kunst, Wissenschaft und geistiges Leben*, 11.5.1842, 549–51 (p. 549).
31. "Literarische Nachrichten", Review of Carl Ebner's *Versuch zur Vertheidigung der angeborenen Rechte des Frauengeschlechtes*, in *Wiener Zeitung*, 27.6.1845, 1371–72 (p. 1371).
32. 'Wien', in *Wiener Zeitung*, 8.9.1848, p. 606.
33. Karl von Thaler, 'Frauenarbeit. ("Das Recht der Frauen auf Erwerb." Blicke auf das Frauenleben der Gegenwart von Louise Otto)', *Bücher-Zeitung. Neue Freie Presse*, 23.11.1866, no pagination.
34. Gertrude Prohaska, *Der literarische Salon der Karoline Pichler* (in unpublished dissertation, University of Vienna, 1946), pp. 159–60.
35. Johannes Frimmel, *Literarisches Leben in Melk. Ein Kloster im 18. Jahrhundert im kulturellen Umbruch* (Vienna: Böhlau, 2005), p. 129.
36. Peter Seibert, *Der literarische Salon. Literatur und Geselligkeit zwischen Aufklärung und Vormärz* (Stuttgart: Metzler, 1993), p. 348.
37. Frimmel, *Literarisches Leben in Melk*, p. 130; Seibert, *Der literarische Salon*, p. 348.
38. Frimmel, *Literarisches Leben in Melk*, p. 130; Seibert, *Der literarische Salon*, p. 387.
39. Barbara Becker-Cantarino, 'Caroline Pichler und die "Frauendichtung"', *Modern Austrian Literature* 12 (1979), 1–23 (p. 8).
40. Frimmel, *Literarisches Leben in Melk*, p. 130.
41. Hagl-Catling, *Für eine Imagologie der Geschlechter*, p. 110.
42. Karl Blümml, 'Einleitung', in Caroline Pichler, *Denkwürdigkeiten aus meinem Leben*, I, vii–lxxxvii (p. xii).
43. Blümml, 'Einleitung', p. xv; Johann Sonnleitner, '"Krasse Sinnlichkeit und frömmelnde Tendenzen". Wiener Salonszenen und Ansichten der Romantik', in *Paradoxien der Romantik. Gesellschaft, Kultur und Wissenschaft in Wien im frühen 19. Jahrhundert*, ed. by Christian Aspalter et al. (Vienna: Facultas, 2006), pp. 256–72 (p. 259).
44. Hans Lohberger, 'Anton Prokesch über "Caroline Pichler und ihr Kreis"', *Blätter für Heimatkunde* 46 (1972), 80–83 (p. 81).
45. Prohaska, *Der literarische Salon der Karoline Pichler*, pp. 146–47.
46. Ibid., p. 68.
47. André Robert, *L'idée nationale autrichienne et les guerres de Napoléon. L'apostolat du Baron de Hormayr et le salon de Caroline Pichler* (Paris: Alcan, 1933), p. 322.
48. Sonnleitner, 'Krasse Sinnlichkeit und frömmelnde Tendenzen', p. 259.
49. Karlheinz Rossbacher, *Literatur und Bürgertum. Fünf Wiener jüdische Familien von der liberalen Ära zum Fin de Siècle* (Vienna: Böhlau, 2003), p. 157.
50. Hagl-Catling, *Für eine Imagologie der Geschlechter*, p. 110.
51. Caroline Pichler, 'Überblick meines Lebens', in *Sämmtliche Werke* (Vienna: Anton Pichler, 1828–45), 60 vols, xxv, *Prosaische Aufsätze. Zweyter Theil*, pp. 187–209 (pp. 193–94, p. 195, p. 196).
52. Therese von Artner to Caroline Pichler, 14.3.1820, Wienbibliothek im Rathaus, H.I.N. 347. Also cited in Magdalena Bauer, 'Therese von Artner und Marianne Neumann von Meißenthal. Zwei Repräsentantinnen der ersten Generation schreibender Frauen im österreichischen Raum. (Studien zu einer Doppelbiographie.)', 2 vols (unpublished dissertation, University of Vienna, 1992), I, p. 173.

53. Caroline Pichler, 'Über die Bildung des weiblichen Geschlechtes. Als Gegenstück zu dem Aufsatze: über den Volksausdruck: Ein ganzer Mann' [1810], in *Sämmtliche Werke*, xxiv, pp. 150–61 (p. 151).
54. Ibid., pp. 151–52.
55. Friedrich Weissensteiner, 'Karoline Pichler', in *Zwischen Idylle und Revolution. Ungewöhnliche Biedermeierporträts* (Vienna: Ueberreuter, 1995), pp. 257–66 (p. 261).
56. Pichler, 'Kindererziehung', in *Sämmtliche Werke*, lv, pp. 49–65 (p. 62).
57. Ibid., p. 63.
58. Pichler, 'Über die Corinne der Frau von Staël' [1807], in *Sämmtliche Werke*, xxiv, pp. 29–39 (p. 31).
59. Ibid., pp. 34–35.
60. Ibid., p. 35.
61. George W. Reinhardt, 'Female Self-Determination in the Early Dramas of Franul von Weissenthurn', in *Austria in the Age of the French Revolution 1789–1815*, ed. by Kinley Brauer and William E. Wright (Minneapolis, MN: Centre for Austrian Studies, University of Minnesota, 1990), pp. 151–62 (p. 160).
62. Ludmilla Antonia Steyskal, 'Johanna Franul von Weissenthurn als Schauspielerin am Burgtheater' (unpublished dissertation, University of Vienna, 1963), pp. 183–84.
63. Reinhardt, 'Female Self-Determination', p. 152.
64. Ian F. Roe, 'The Comedies of Johanna von Weissenthurn', in *The Austrian Comic Tradition. Studies in Honour of W. E. Yates*, ed. by John R. P. McKenzie and Lesley Sharpe, Austrian Studies IX (Edinburgh: Edinburgh University Press, 1998), pp. 41–57 (p. 42); Steyskal, 'Johanna Franul von Weissenthurn als Schauspielerin am Burgtheater', p. 184.
65. Bauernfeld, 'Die schöne Literatur in Österreich', in *Eduard von Bauernfelds Gesammelte Aufsätze*, pp. 137–75 (p. 158).
66. E. Norbert, 'Weissenthurn', *Die Gegenwart. Politisch-literarisches Tagblatt*, 22.5.1847, 545–46 (p. 545).
67. This anecdote appears in the essay 'Meine Ansicht über den Verfall der dramatischen Bühnenerzeugnisse'. Paul Alfred Merbach, 'Zwei Aufsätze von Johanna Franul v. Weissenthurn. Aus der Handschrift mitgeteilt', *JdGG* 24 (1913), 211–24 (p. 219).
68. Roe, 'The Comedies of Johanna von Weissenthurn', p. 49.
69. Reinhardt, 'Female Self-Determination', p. 160.
70. 'Johann, Herzog von Finnland', *Wiener Zeitschrift für Kunst, Literatur, Theater und Mode*, 31, 12.3.1818, 251–52 (p. 251).
71. 'Ruprecht Graf zu Horneck', *Wiener Zeitschrift für Kunst, Literatur, Theater und Mode*, 20, 15.2.1820, 158–59 (p. 159).
72. Johanna Franul von Weissenthurn, 'Vorrede', in *Schauspiele von Johanna Franul v. Weissenthurn, gebornen Grünberg, kaiserl. königl. Hofschauspielerinn*, 15 vols (Vienna: Degen, 1804–48), I, pp. iii–vi (p. iii).
73. Ibid., p. v.
74. Ibid., p. iii.
75. Ibid., p. vi.
76. Weissenthurn to Pichler, 8.3.1843, Wienbibliothek im Rathaus, H.I.N. 590.
77. Weissenthurn to Pichler, 21.4.1838, Wienbibliothek im Rathaus, H.I.N. 589.
78. Eufemia von Kudriaffsky to Josephine Knorr, 21.6.1861, Wienbibliothek im Rathaus, H.I.N. 39919.
79. Josef Lewinsky, *Gedenkrede auf Betty Paoli* (Vienna: Verlag des Vereins der Schriftstellerinnen und Künstlerinnen in Wien, 1895), p. 6.
80. Friedrich Beck, 'Betty Paoli', *Österreichischer Rundschau* 9 (1906), 260–72 (p. 264).
81. *Neue Freie Presse*, 28.1.1872, p. 2.
82. Karin S. Wozonig, *Die Literatin Betty Paoli. Weibliche Mobilität im 19. Jahrhundert* (Vienna: Löcker, 1999), p. 21.
83. Helene Bettelheim-Gabillon, 'Einleitung', in *Betty Paolis Gesammelte Aufsätze*, ed. by Helene Bettelheim-Gabillon, Schriften des Literarischen Vereins in Wien IX (Vienna: Verlag des Literarischen Vereins in Wien, 1908), pp. v–cxi (p. xciii).

84. Ferrel Rose, 'Betty Paoli', in *Major Figures of Nineteenth-Century Austrian Literature*, ed. by Donald G. Daviau (Riverside, CA: Ariadne, 1998), pp. 387–416 (p. 390).
85. Eva Geber, 'Mir aber ward solch sanfte Milde von der Natur nicht eingeflößt', in Betty Paoli, *Was hat der Geist denn wohl gemein mit dem Geschlecht?*, ed. by Eva Geber (Vienna: Mandelbaum, 2001), pp. 7–65 (p. 37).
86. Helene Bettelheim-Gabillon, 'Zur Charakteristik Betty Paolis. Nach alten und neuen Quellen', *JdGG* 10 (1900), 191–250 (p. 236).
87. Geber, 'Mir aber ward solch sanfte Milde von der Natur nicht eingeflößt', p. 48
88. Ibid., p. 55.
89. Karin Wozonig, 'Betty Paoli, die Lyrikerin als Journalistin', *The German Quarterly* 76 (2003), 56–67 (p. 65).
90. Karin S. Wozonig, 'Betty Paoli, Journalistin', in Betty Paoli, *Was hat der Geist denn wohl gemein mit dem Geschlecht?*, pp. 66–77 (p. 76).
91. Paoli, 'Eine Zeitfrage' [*Neue Freie Presse*, 4.11.1865], in Betty Paoli, *Was hat der Geist denn wohl gemein mit dem Geschlecht?*, pp. 80–87 (p. 80).
92. Paoli, 'Ein Wort Pombals' [*Neue Freie Presse*, 12.8.1866], in Betty Paoli, *Was hat der Geist denn wohl gemein mit dem Geschlecht?*, pp. 88–94 (p. 93).
93. Paoli, 'Über weibliche Erziehung' [*Neue Freie Presse*, 4.6.1869], in *Was hat der Geist denn wohl gemein mit dem Geschlecht?*, pp. 95–103 (p. 96).
94. Ibid., p. 99.
95. Paoli, 'Die Wandlungen der Frauenfrage', Undatiertes Manuskript, 12 Seiten, Laut Tagebuch Marie von Ebner-Eschenbach: 1885, in Paoli, *Was hat der Geist denn wohl gemein mit dem Geschlecht?*, pp. 113–20 (p. 116).
96. Ibid., p. 117.
97. Paoli to Kompert, 25.11.1850, in Stefan Hock, 'Briefe Betty Paolis an Leopold Kompert', *JdGG* 18 (1908), 177–209 (pp. 190–91).
98. Paoli to Kompert, 11.12.1850, ibid., p. 193.
99. Kompert's review was published in *Lloyd*, 20.1.1851. Paoli to Kompert, 31.1.1851, ibid., pp. 195, 197.
100. Rose, 'Betty Paoli', p. 401; Wozonig, 'Betty Paoli, die Lyrikerin als Journalistin', p. 66.
101. Wozonig, 'Betty Paoli, die Lyrikerin als Journalistin', p. 66.
102. Carl Steiner, 'Franz Grillparzer and Marie von Ebner-Eschenbach: A Father-Daughter Relationship', in *Für all, was Menschen je erfahren, ein Bild, ein Wort und auch das Ziel. Beiträge zu Grillparzers Werk*, ed. by Joseph Strelka (Bern: Peter Lang, 1995), pp. 211–29 (p. 212).
103. Angela Scheider, 'Auguste und Carl von Littrow. Detailstudie einer bürgerlichen Familie des 19. Jahrhunderts' (unpublished dissertation, University of Vienna, 1999), pp. 214–15.
104. Fanny Meißner-Diemer, 'Auguste Littrow-Bischoff. (Erinnerungsblatt einer Freundin)', *Neue Freie Presse* Nr. 9279, 24.6.1890, Abendblatt p. 2.
105. Scheider, 'Auguste und Carl von Littrow', p. 58.
106. Vladimira Bousska, 'Der Salon der Johanna Bischoff von Altenstern und ihrer Tochter Auguste von Littrow-Bischoff', *Meidling, Blätter des Bezirksmuseums* 42 (1996), 30–37 (p. 36).
107. Florence Nightingale to Edwin Chadwick, 21.6.1873, in *Florence Nightingale on Society and Politics, Philosophy, Science, Education and Literature.* Collected Works of Florence Nightingale, ed. by Lynn McDonald, vol. 5 (Waterloo, Ontario: Wilfred Laurier University Press, 2003), p. 410.
108. John Stuart Mill to Auguste Littrow-Bischoff, 9.8.1871, in John Stuart Mill, *Additional Letters of John Stuart Mill*, ed. by Marion Filipiuk et al. (Toronto: University of Toronto Press; London: Routledge, 1991), pp. 228–29 (p. 229).
109. Mill to Littrow-Bischoff, 25.10.1871, in *Additional Letters of John Stuart Mill*, p. 234.
110. Otto August (Auguste Littrow-Bischoff), *Die sociale Bewegung auf dem Gebiete der Frauen* (Hamburg: Hoffmann und Campe, 1868), p. 3.
111. Ibid., p. 4.
112. Ibid., p. 45.
113. Silvia Bovenschen, *Die imaginierte Weiblichkeit. Exemplarische Untersuchungen zu kulturgeschichtlichen und literarischen Präsentationsformen des Weiblichen* (Frankfurt a.M.: Suhrkamp, 1979), p. 66.

114. *Statuten des Wiener Frauen-Erwerbs-Vereines* (Vienna: Verlag des Wiener Frauen-Erwerbs-Vereines, 1866), unpaginated, I, Zweck des Vereines, Absatz 1.
115. *Statuten des Wiener Frauen-Erwerbs-Vereines*, I, Mittel zur Erreichung dieses Zweckes, Absatz 2.
116. Evans, *The Feminists*, p. 93.
117. Ibid., p. 94.
118. Margret Friedrich, 'Versorgungsfall Frau? Der Wiener Frauen-Erwerb-Verein — Gründungszeit und erste Jahre des Aufbaus', *Studien zur Wiener Geschichte, Jahrbuch des Vereins für Geschichte der Stadt Wien* 47/48 (1991/92), 263–308 (p. 263).
119. Ibid., p. 268.
120. Ibid., p. 271.
121. Ibid., pp. 282, 300.
122. Grillparzer to Gräfin Xaverine Dubsky, 1847, nr. 665, in *HKA* III/iii, p. 25.
123. Anikó Zsigmond, *Marie von Ebner-Eschenbach. Das Frauenbewußtsein einer österreichischen Aristokratin* (Szombathely: Maedinfo, 2001), p. 36.
124. Agatha C. Bramkamp, *Marie von Ebner-Eschenbach. The Author, Her Time and Her Critics* (Bonn: Bouvier, 1990), p. 28.
125. Izabela Surynt, *Erzählte Weiblichkeit bei Marie von Ebner-Eschenbach* (Opole: Wydawnictwo Uniwersytetu Opolskiego, 1998), pp. 67–70.
126. Ulrike Tanzer, 'Konzeptionen des Glücks im Werk Marie von Ebner-Eschenbachs', *Seminar* 47 (2011), 254–67 (p. 265).
127. Surynt, *Erzählte Weiblichkeit bei Marie von Ebner-Eschenbach*, p. 149.
128. Karin S. Wozonig, 'Betty Paoli und die schönen Frauen', *Nestroyana. Blätter der Internationalen Nestroy-Gesellschaft* 29 (2009), 72–81 (p. 72).
129. Ibid., p. 73.
130. Ebner-Eschenbach, *Meine Erinnerungen an Grillparzer*, p. 67.
131. Wozonig, 'Betty Paoli und die schönen Frauen', p. 80.
132. To Georg Winterberg, 27.7.1824, in *Briefe von Sophie Schröder (1813–1868)*, ed. by Heinrich Stümcke (Berlin: Selbstverlag der Gesellschaft für Theatergeschichte, 1910), p. 15.
133. Kord, *Ein Blick hinter die Kulissen*, p. 32.
134. To Friedrich Wilhelm Riese, 6.11.1828, in *Briefe von Sophie Schröder*, p. 29.
135. To Rahel von Varnhagen, 19.1.1817, in ibid., pp. 145–46.
136. Ernst Wurm, 'Grillparzers erste Medea — Sophie Schröder', *JdGG* 3/6 (1967), 121–37 (p. 130).
137. 'Schauspiel. *Die Ahnfrau*', *Wiener-Moden-Zeitung und Zeitschrift für Kunst, schöne Literatur und Theater*, 5.2.1817, 87–88 (p. 88).
138. To Grillparzer, nr. 342, in *HKA* III/ii, p. 21. Sauer dates this letter to 23.3.1828, and concludes that Schröder is probably talking about her efforts to defend Grillparzer's *Ein treuer Diener seines Herrn*, which had been received negatively (*HKA* III/ii, p. 342). The Wienbibliothek catalogue, however, dates this letter to the same date in 1824, which seems correct based on inspection of the manuscript. In this case, it is possible that Schröder was defending *König Ottokars Glück und Ende*, which at the time was being held up due to censorship issues.
139. Betty Paoli, *Julie Rettich. Ein Lebens- und Charakterbild* (Vienna: Sommer, 1866), p. 7.
140. Ibid., p. 22.
141. Wozonig, 'Betty Paoli und die schönen Frauen', p. 81.
142. Ibid.
143. Julie Rettich, 'Diktatschreiben an die Grüne Insel', no date, Wienbibliothek im Rathaus, H.I.N. 213829.
144. Constant von Wurzbach, *Biographisches Lexikon des Kaiserthums Oesterreich*, 58. Theil (Vienna: Hof- und Staatsdruckerei, 1889), pp. 91–92.
145. Yates, *Theatre in Vienna*, p. 76.
146. Ludwig Eisenberg, *Großes Biographisches Lexikon der Deutschen Bühne im XIX. Jahrhundert* (Leipzig: Paul List, 1903), p. 1148.
147. Franz Grillparzer, *Sämtliche Werke: Ausgewählte Briefe, Gespräche, Berichte*, 4 vols, ed. by Peter Frank and Karl Pörnbacher (Munich: Hanser, 1960–65), I, p. 1294. Further quotations from this edition will be indicated in the main body of the text using the acronym *SW* and the volume number.

CHAPTER 2

Women and the Law

In this section, I show that *Die Ahnfrau* [*The Ancestress*] (1817) and *König Ottokars Glück und Ende* [*King Ottocar, His Rise and Fall*] (1823) investigate contemporary legal issues which affected the lives of women: the issue of inheritance, and in particular the status of female inheritance, is central to *Die Ahnfrau*, and the role of marriage as a defining element of women's lives is important when discussing *Ottokar*. In both cases, Grillparzer displays sympathy with heroines who are disadvantaged by their subordinate legal standing. Bertha in *Die Ahnfrau* is undervalued by her father because patrilineal inheritance prevents her from carrying on the family line, and her ancestress, the spectre Bertha, was murdered because her adultery potentially interfered with this inheritance paradigm. In *Ottokar*, Margarete, Kunigunde and Berta are shown to be the victims of marital law and state policy which were created by and serve the interests of men.

The *Allgemeines bürgerliches Gesetzbuch* (*ABGB*) [General Civil Code] of 1811 laid down the law for all the lands of the Habsburg monarchy. The text deals extensively with family law, including divorce, and is therefore an important text for understanding the legal status of women in Grillparzer's Austria. The *ABGB* seems to be indicative of what historians have identified as a shift away from early-modern class-based social structures, which allowed women varying degrees of freedom based on their social standing, to social structures based solely on sex which emerged in the late eighteenth and nineteenth centuries. It 'statuierte einen Familientypus als allgemeingültige Norm' [established one type of family as the universal norm].[1] The *ABGB* is in parts a contradictory text, as far as the position of women is concerned, in some cases guaranteeing relative freedoms, in others creating a legal framework unsympathetic to women. This could stem from the history of its composition. When he began work on the forerunner to the *ABGB*, Karl Anton von Martini wanted to secure women equal rights in marriage, and greater rights in some areas of the law.[2] However, as work progressed and the political climate changed, these aims became impossible to achieve as the state aimed to eliminate basic rights and negate the impact of the French Revolution. The fundamental goals of the state in the period until 1848 were the establishment of an absolutist monarchical system and the maintenance of law and order.

The first chapter of the *ABGB* guarantees every individual 'angeborne, schon durch die Vernunft einleuchtende Rechte' [innate rights which reason makes evident]; slavery and serfdom are expressly forbidden as inimical to these freedoms.[3]

Women are not excluded from these basic rights; indeed, both sexes are guaranteed the same basic freedoms. Richard J. Evans argues that the Enlightenment influenced the partially liberal character of the *ABGB*.[4] Ernst Holthöfer notes that the *ABGB* allowed women independence, and was therefore more progressive than either the Allgemeines Landrecht für die Preußischen Staaten [General State Laws for the Prussian States] (1794) or the Code civil (1804).[5] The second chapter, which deals with marriage law, shows that the positions of men and women are not so equal when it comes to specific rights. On the one hand, there are some provisions which protect women. Paragraph 55 states that an agreement to marry is invalid if it has been coerced. Furthermore, the law does not foresee the automatic transfer of a wife's money and goods to her husband upon marriage (§1233). Husband and wife are legally entitled to maintain possession of the goods with which they entered the marriage, and may make no claims to that which their spouse acquires during the marriage. As Ursula Vogel writes, real law guaranteed wives full legal competence, which was present in Roman Law, a source of inspiration for the *ABGB*, but not in any other European private law regime of the period.[6] However, 'Im Zweifel wird vermuthet, daß der Erwerb von dem Manne herrühre' [Where there is doubt, it is assumed that property belongs to the husband].'[7] The assumption that the husband, and not the wife, would be the breadwinning party reflects not just the patriarchal presumptions of those who wrote the law, but also the limited opportunities for women's financial independence in this era. Despite these protections, the husband is responsible for controlling his wife's fortune, unless the opposite has been stated (§1238). Husbands are empowered to put a stop to their wives' frivolous or excessive spending, and even have them deemed 'Verschwenderinnen' [spendthrifts] in accordance with statutory provisions (§1241).

Paragraph 90 installs husband and wife as equals in marriage: 'Vor Allem haben beyde Theile eine gleiche Verbindlichkeit zur ehelichen Pflicht, Treue und anständigen Begegnung' [Above all, both parties have an equal obligation to marital duty, loyalty and proper treatment].[8] Paragraph 91, however, declares the man as the superior partner in the relationship. He is in charge of the household and must provide his wife with 'den anständigen Unterhalt' [proper maintenance] and represent her 'in allen Vorfällen' [in all events].[9] The wife's commensurate duties, stated in Paragraph 92, include obeying her husband and running the household.[10] Despite the apparent equality created by some paragraphs of the law, the *ABGB* emphasizes the subordinate role of women in marriage and the household. Gabriela Polak states that the law assumed that the private relationship between married couples would be largely determined by their respective sexes, which she sees as the result of contemporary ideologies.[11] Polak highlights the symbiotic nature of the relationship between theory and practice in gender matters. The rules governing marriage both originate in, and create, the self-evidence of marriage. The necessity of women's subjugation to the will of their husbands is also, argues Polak, to be found in the political situation of the time: an absolute ruler could not condone marriage as a partnership, nor could a patriarchal society promote women as leaders of men.[12] Indeed, as Hauch shows, women only appear in the *ABGB* as dependents: daughters, wives, mothers, orphans or widows. That independence in financial and legal matters was denied women indicates the importance of the public sphere and contemporary conceptions of it as a male domain.[13] Franz von Zeiller, who helped write the *ABGB*, explicitly states the relationship between the public and the private as the reasoning behind the division into male and female areas of activity: 'Die Echtheit dieser Grundsätze läßt sich, ohne weitere Ausführung, aus dem engen Zusammenhange zwischen der häuslichen und öffentlichen Ordnung, zwischen dem Wohle der Familien und der allgemeinen Wohlfahrt leicht von selbst einsehen' [The authenticity of these principles is easily enough understood, without further explanation, from the close relationship between domestic and public order, between the wellbeing of the family and general social wellbeing].[14]

A husband's obligation to represent his wife resulted from contemporary ideas regarding the superiority of men and their duty to protect the 'weaker sex'.[15] Again, we see that law and life exist in symbiosis: on the one hand, a husband's obligation to represent his wife resulted from the fact that, in the nineteenth century, it was not taken for granted that women would represent themselves in court;[16] on the other hand, this provision further excluded women from participation in public life.[17] For Ellinor Forster, the wording of Paragraph 91 nevertheless represents a decisive innovation. Husbands have the obligation, but not the right, to represent their wives, and can only do so with their permission.[18] This formulation provided for new levels of independence for women, at least in theory. However, Zeiller confirms that married women were not considered independent individuals: 'Bey der Fortdauer der Ehe wird die Frau in Hinsicht der Personenrechte als Eine Person mit ihrem Gatten betrachtet.' [On the continuation of the marriage, the wife is considered to be one person with her husband where individual law is concerned.][19]

The position of married women is not ameliorated by the law's refusal to recognize divorce, even if both parties should be in agreement.[20] A couple can separate for a number of stipulated reasons, for example infidelity, abandonment or severe maltreatment (§109), but a marriage between Catholics only ends with the death of one partner (§111). Non-Catholic Christians can demand a divorce according to the precepts of their religion if there are grounds. Paragraph 58 allows men to declare their marriage to be invalid if, after the ceremony, they discover their wife to be pregnant by another man.

The regulations regarding guardianships established by the *ABGB* deny women's intellectual abilities. Vogel argues that the influence of Roman Law is evident in this respect because it contained 'all jene Vorstellungen weiblicher Geistes- und Charaktermängel [...] welche über Jahrhunderte hinweg unverändert als zureichende Gründe der rechtlichen Unmündigkeit der Frau gegolten hatten' [all those ideas regarding women's defects of intellect and character [...] which over centuries had without change been accepted as sufficient grounds for women's legal minority].[21] Paragraph 191 declares minors, the mentally and physically disabled, and convicted criminals as incapable of becoming guardians, while Paragraph 192 adds women. Males and patrilineality are always preferred, and mothers are neither considered to be suitable sole guardians for their children, nor the guardian of choice. Despite this, fatherless children should be entrusted to their mother's care, regardless of whether she is the appointed guardian or not (§218). Paragraph 218 refers to children who have lost their father but whose mother survives as 'Waisen' [orphans]. This wording highlights the insignificance of women within the family unit.

Women were generally deemed incapable of performing such representative duties for their children, otherwise their opinions would be heard without the need for male intercessors and intermediaries. This lack of trust in women's judgment is confirmed by the fact that women who remarried while acting as guardians were compelled to report this change of circumstances (or have their co-guardian report it) to the responsible court for approval (§ 255). Although women's primary role in the nineteenth century was the care of children and the household, the law did not trust them to fulfil this duty without male supervision. The law was clearly discriminatory towards women. It limited their prospects to house and family, and even went as far as to deny them rationality. However, reality did not always reflect the law. Women were active in the public sphere, for example publishing literary works and earning money independently of their husbands.

Grillparzer's Infernal Feminine: *Die Ahnfrau* and the Problem of Female Inheritance

Despite the title of Grillparzer's debut play, *Die Ahnfrau*, the issue of inheritance, which is undoubtedly a central concern of the drama, has been overlooked by scholarship. Here, the social and historical context for Grillparzer's drama is brought to the fore, particularly as concerns the feminist approach of this study as a whole. Many of the themes which have been identified in Grillparzer's later dramas already find expression in 1817. Emphasizing social aspects, and in particular such as are related to the *Frauenfrage*, will demonstrate Grillparzer's early interest in the issue of women's position in society.

The lack of interest in the social aspects of this drama may be the result of critics' focus on moral, aesthetic and taxonomic problems, or from a dismissive attitude towards the drama.[22] R. K. Angress claims that attempts to extract from the play any themes related to sociology, psychoanalysis or the history of ideas demand too much from the drama and can only bring to light its inadequacies.[23] Norbert Griesmayer writes that *Die Ahnfrau* is characterized by 'deutliche Einheitlichkeit und Einfachheit' [clear uniformity and simplicity].[24] Reinhold Backmann also sees *Die Ahnfrau* in simplistic terms, stating that it 'ist in erster Linie ein Gespensterstück' [primarily a ghost play].[25] For the present analysis, neither the categorization of *Die Ahnfrau*, nor its aesthetics is of central importance.

Grillparzer's drama portrays the final days of the Borotin dynasty. Count Borotin, the last remaining male member of the family, laments the fact that his only heir is a daughter. Years earlier, his son disappeared and was believed to be drowned. Unbeknown to the family, Bertha's suitor Jaromir is actually her brother: he did not drown, but was abducted and adopted by the band of robbers who plague the surrounding areas. Boleslav, one of the bandits, is the adoptive father of Jaromir. In a fight between the two robbers and the king's troops, Jaromir accidentally stabs Borotin, his father, who later dies. Central to the drama is the ghost of the titular ancestress, also named Bertha, who was forced into marriage with a Borotin and later caught in an act of adultery with her former lover. She was murdered by her husband, but not before she gave birth to her lover's son, and now haunts the castle, awaiting the demise of the dynasty.

Die Ahnfrau is the only drama analysed here for which a full first draft is available in print. The drama's genesis is also unusual due to the heavy involvement of Schreyvogel. Sauer identifies five versions of Die Ahnfrau: the first is the manuscript which Grillparzer gave Schreyvogel, and which the latter made comments on; the second incorporated Schreyvogel's suggestions; the third was an abbreviated version of the second, intended for use in performances; the fourth was used for the first print edition of the drama, reversed some of these cuts, and contained other new alterations; for the sixth print edition, Grillparzer made a few important changes, and this represents the fifth and final version (HKA I/i, p. xliii). In the HKA, Sauer reprints the first and final versions, and these are the versions used here to ascertain the extent of the changes Grillparzer made to his original manuscript.

Schreyvogel's diaries evidence the extent of the assistance he gave Grillparzer. Between the middle of September 1816 and the end of January 1817, Grillparzer and Schreyvogel discussed Die Ahnfrau on at least nine occasions. On 15 September 1816, Grillparzer delivered the final act to Schreyvogel, who called it 'zu gräßlich und überhaupt noch formlos' [too terrible and furthermore still formless].[26] The next day, he wrote that the second half of the second act was 'sehr schwach und muß ganz verändert werden' [very weak and must be completely changed].[27] By 19 September, he had partially reworked the drama, which he wrote was 'als Composition doch noch sehr unreif' [still very immature as a composition].[28] On 22 September, he returned the manuscript to Grillparzer with his comments, and on 29 October he reported that Grillparzer had edited the first two acts 'ganz nach meinen Ansichten' [completely according to my opinions].[29] He and Grillparzer continued to discuss the drama, and on 30 January 1817, both were present at a rehearsal. Schreyvogel wrote that '[d]er dritte und vierte Akt müssen große Wirkung thun, — nur vielleicht zu gräßlich' [the third and fourth acts must have great effect — perhaps they are only too terrible].[30]

Schreyvogel does not indicate the nature of the changes he demanded, but Grillparzer, in his Selbstbiographie, recalls that Schreyvogel wanted the 'Schicksalsidee' [idea of fate] to be further developed, particularly 'der ganz unberührt gebliebene Umstand, daß das jetzt lebende Geschlecht geradezu die Frucht der Sünde der Ahnfrau sei' [the fact, which remained completely untouched, that the family now living was the fruit of the ancestress's sin] (HKA I/xvi, p. 121). Grillparzer was initially reluctant to make the changes, but did eventually acquiesce in Schreyvogel's demands, although in his Selbstbiographie he argues that they did not improve the drama, 'zum Teil auch darum, weil ich [die Änderungen] nur äußerlich anfügte' [also in part because I only made [the changes] superficially] (HKA I/xvi, p. 122). Indeed, Grillparzer would later reject the changes made at Schreyvogel's suggestion. In 'Widmung des Trauerspieles "Sappho" an Josef Schreyvogel' (1818) [Dedication of the Tragedy Sappho to Josef Schreyvogel] he stresses that he rejected changes suggested by Schreyvogel and that Sappho was all his own work, perhaps in an attempt to distance himself from Schreyvogel and repudiate the changes to *Die Ahnfrau* which his mentor suggested (HKA I/xiv, p. 25). In the *Selbstbiographie*, he writes: 'Genau genommen nun, findet sich die Schicksals-Idee gar nicht in der Ahnfrau' [Strictly speaking, the fate idea does not appear in *The Ancestress* at all] (HKA I/xvi, p. 125). And in a letter of 1868, he wrote that 'eine wohlwollende, aber sachunkundige Hand' [a well-intentioned but badly informed hand] encouraged him to develop the *Schicksalsidee* more than was necessary (HKA III/v, p. 62).

A comparison of the original draft (V1) of *Die Ahnfrau*, and the final version (V5) incorporating Schreyvogel's suggestions, shows how much these changes did to emphasize the *Schicksalsidee* and the theme of inheritance in the drama.[31] These differences are clear from the beginning. V5, for example, uses stage directions to show the similarity in appearance between Bertha and the ancestress, where V1 does not (p. 20, p. 161). V5 introduces the idea of the ancestress being forced into an undesired marriage by her parents, which is absent in V1 (p. 27, p. 168). Crucially, V5 introduces the idea that the current Count Borotin is a descendant of the ancestress's bastard child, which idea is also absent from V1 (p. 29, p. 169). This means that Borotin's worries about his origins and legitimacy in V5 are missing in V1 (p. 53, p. 186). V5 also lengthens Bertha's soliloquy at the end of Act II, where she foreshadows the revelation that she is related to Jaromir. This foreshadowing is not present in V1 (p. 73, pp. 195–96).

The theme of inheritance is strengthened in V5 in a number of ways. In V1, Jaromir sees the dagger as a means of helping him and Bertha escape and be together: 'Hat die Ahnfrau er getödtet/ Soll die Enkelin er befrein' [If it killed the ancestress/ It will free the granddaughter] (p. 215). In other words, in V1 Jaromir subverts the dagger's violent history and potential, instead choosing to use it to protect the ancestress's female descendant. In V5, the dagger becomes at once a sign that Jaromir is a member of the house of Borotin — he apostrophizes the dagger: 'An dem Morgen meiner Tage/ Hab' ich dich schon, dich gesehn' [At the dawn of my life/ I saw you already — you] (p. 96) — and a symbol of Jaromir's violent male inheritance, as will be discussed later, an inheritance he readily accepts. The emphasis placed on Jaromir's male inheritance means that Bertha's 'feminine' inheritance of kindness and mercy, introduced both by her pleas of mercy for the bandits, and by Jaromir's idealizing of Bertha's gentleness, plays a role in V5 (pp. 60–61) where it does not in V1. The inheritance theme is also strengthened in V5 by the inclusion of the captain's revenge motive after his own inheritance was destroyed by the robbers (pp. 59–60).

The motivation behind some smaller changes is less easy to identify. So, for example, V1 states that the Ahnfrau had an affair with a 'Knecht' [servant] (p. 168), while V5 refers merely to a 'Buhle' [lover] (p. 27). Perhaps the idea of a female aristocrat having an affair with a member of a lower class was deemed too dangerous for the stage. Where V1 refers to '[d]ie vor Gott geschworene[] Pflicht' of marriage [the duty sworn before God] (p. 168), V5 merely mentions the duties of marriage and omits the reference to God. This suggests that Grillparzer was self-censoring, possibly on the advice of Schreyvogel, who was employed as a censor, in order to excise anything which could possibly be deemed immoral or damaging to the social order. In V1, the count insists that the captain search his castle for the robbers, and the captain is embarrassed that the count could think himself under suspicion (pp. 194–95). In V5, however, the captain demands to search the castle, and the count is angered by the suggestion that there could be any link between himself and the criminals (p. 68). This change posits the state as a violent force which impinges on the private property of the nobility, and is perhaps a sign of Grillparzer's criticism of authoritarianism. This may also be linked to another change. In V1, the count accompanies the captain on his reconnaissance in order to protect society at large:

> Laß mich liebes Kind, wohin
> Mich der Unterthan, der Bürger
> Mich der Mensch gebiethend ruft,
> Dahin folg' ich, wärs zur Gruft! (p. 195)

[Let me go, dear child, there/ Where the subject, the citizen,/ The people command,/ I will go there, were it to my grave!]

In V5, this passage is removed, and Borotin expresses his duty as one to the king, rather than to the people. This change could have been removed from V1 in order to avoid potential censorship difficulties: Hägelin's *Denkschrift*, mentioned in the Introduction, and which influenced censorship throughout this period, forbade 'die Abwürdigung der monarchischen Regierungsform' [disparagement of the monarchical form of government], promotion of democracy or any other form of government, and disparagement of class-based societies.[32] Although the lines quoted from V1 are not particularly emphasized in the drama, their egalitarian import contrasts strongly with the amended passage in V5, and could have incurred the censors' wrath.

Although this comparative analysis indicates that a large part of the inheritance thematic I see in *Die Ahnfrau* was not in the original, but added at Schreyvogel's suggestion to increase the tragic and dramatic effects of the drama, it is also clear that the original version contained more material which was politically critical and potentially dangerous. This serves to remove *Die Ahnfrau* further from the confines of mere fate or ghost tragedies, and strengthens my argument that Grillparzer incorporated criticism of political and social conditions in this drama. It also provides fresh evidence of Grillparzer's self-censorship, which, as I argued in the Introduction, might have forced him to tone down some of the criticism of women's social position which I perceive in his dramas.

The drama's title points to the importance of themes such as inheritance and legacy in its conception. The word 'ancestress' is inseparable from the related ideas of heritage, provenance, and progeny, and yet precisely these key concepts have been too seldom investigated. Given the legal status of women in nineteenth-century Austria, inheritance through the female line was problematic, and this is reflected in Count Borotin's concern with his own legacy as the father of an only daughter. While the *ABGB* of 1811 guaranteed all children, regardless of sex, an equal share in a family's inheritance,[33] marriage entailed a woman's acceptance of her husband's name.[34] In the case of an only daughter, the family's wealth would be passed on to the next generation, but with marriage the family name would cease to exist.

The dynastic worries of Count Borotin in Grillparzer's drama mirror those of Emperor Charles VI in the early eighteenth century. The most notable example of female inheritance in Austrian history is that of Maria Theresa, only daughter of Charles VI. The problem of the succession occupied Charles VI for a large part of his reign, and the Pragmatic Sanction was the solution which emerged. The Pragmatic Sanction was an extension of the *Pactum mutuae successionis*, which Leopold I made both his sons agree to before Charles's departure for Spain in 1702.[35] The *Pactum*, which was to be kept secret, considered the Habsburg possessions in both lines as a whole, and declared that, should one of Leopold's sons die without male issue, the lands would be inherited by the survivor. Joseph I died eight years later with two female heirs. In 1711, Charles wrote a will which, in the event that he should not produce a male heir, provided for the succession of his daughters before those of Joseph I or Leopold I. Charles was reluctant to take any decisive steps in this matter as long as he could still hope for a son. However, drawn-out disputes at court between the widowed empresses Eleonore and Wilhelmine Amalia, and between the daughters of Joseph I and Leopold I, forced Charles's hand.[36] By 1713, Charles was the only surviving male member of the Habsburg house.[37] He gathered his advisors and acquainted them with the terms of Leopold's *Pactum*, adding an important clause which made the Habsburg lands indivisible and inseparable, and introducing the principle of primogeniture, in the male line in the first instance, then in the female.[38] Charles's declaration was named the Pragmatic Sanction in the tradition of similar documents from late antiquity, the Middle Ages, the Peace of Westphalia, as well as of Spanish declarations dating from 1615 and 1660.[39]

In the years between the death of his only son in 1716, and his own death in 1740, gaining acceptance of the Pragmatic Sanction by the crown lands of the monarchy and by the major European rulers demanded much of Charles's time. Charles's attempts at gaining European leaders' recognition of the Pragmatic Sanction are perhaps indicative of the problematic nature of female inheritance: this recognition was unnecessary as his authority allowed him to enact laws without asking for permission.[40] At the same time, Charles wanted to marry off the daughters of Joseph I. Their marriage contracts were formulated so as to exclude the possibility of future claims to the inheritance. European recognition for the Pragmatic Sanction came gradually.[41] In 1725, a treaty was signed with Spain, in which Philip V recognized the Pragmatic Sanction and guaranteed its execution. In the Treaty of Berlin (1728), Frederick William I guaranteed the inheritance of the Habsburg lands according to the Pragmatic Sanction, and was instrumental in securing the German Reichstag's acceptance in 1732. Great Britain recognized the Pragmatic Sanction as part of the Treaty of Vienna in 1731.

The relevance of such political concerns for the interpretation of *Die Ahnfrau* is made clear by Grillparzer's intertwining of public and private interests in the drama. The power structures and conflicts in the drama illuminate the role of the family as a microcosm of the state. For example, the captain wishes to use Borotin's castle as his headquarters in the fight against the bandits (ll. 1237–39), a request in which Borotin willingly acquiesces (ll. 1249–51). The family home is at once subordinate to the state, and an active participant in the state's power. The relationship is not, however, completely amicable, and the count takes umbrage when his castle, and therefore he himself, can no longer be seen as participants in the state's power, but become mere subjects and suspects:

> HAUPTMANN Streng gemessen ist mein Auftrag,
> Jede Wohnung zu durchsuchen,
> [...]
> Ich erfülle meine Pflicht.
> [...]
> Wer bürgt euch für eure Leute?
> GRAF Und wer euch, denkt ihr, für mich!⁴²
>
> [CAPTAIN: Strictly speaking my task/ Is to search every lodging/ [...]/ I am doing my duty/ [...]/ Who vouches to you for your people? COUNT: And who vouches to you, you think, for me!]

The public sphere enters the private and the relationship between the two becomes problematic. The captain's presence deprives Borotin of his private power. Bertha appeals to her father, asking that Jaromir be allowed to rest, but the power dynamics show that Borotin is no longer the real authority figure. In dedicating his castle to a public cause, he has had to abdicate his previous authority (ll. 1480–84).

Faced with a problem similar to that of Charles VI, Borotin's obsession with inheritance is present from the very first and accentuates the importance of this issue for the drama as a whole. In his opening speech, he laments the decay of his family, and its legacy, using the analogy of a rotting tree: 'Fallen seh' ich Zweig' auf Zweige,/ Kaum noch hält der morsche Stamm'' [I see branch upon branch falling,/ The rotten trunk is barely still standing] (ll. 2–3). Borotin thinks of inheritance in exclusively male terms: 'Was die Väter auch getan,/ Wie gerungen, wie gestrebt' [Regardless of what our fathers did,/ How they fought and strove] (ll. 12–13). It is something acquired by men, and passed down the generations from father to son; women, including Bertha, have no place in his concept of legacy. This mindset can perhaps be legitimated by the realities of life in nineteenth-century Austria. The material wealth, as well as the fame and renown which form an important part of inheritance in Borotin's understanding, originate in men's activity in the world outside the home, and the acquisition of an inheritance is therefore out of the reach of women, especially one who has never left the confines of her family's estate (l. 226). For Borotin, the legacy which a man passes down to his descendants is a faithful tribute to his own life, which keeps the memory of the ancestor alive in the consciousness of those who follow him (ll. 77–80). Within the drama, inheritance is seen as a bond between father and son, and Jaromir functions as a living symbol of inheritance. When Boleslav begs the count for mercy, in return he promises good news 'Die schnell euer Siechtum heilen,/ Euch mit Lust erfüllen soll' [Which will quickly heal your malady/ And fill you with joy] (ll. 2428–29). The news which Boleslav has to offer is that of the survival of the count's only son. Boleslav cannot help but see this news not only as something positive, but as something endowed with healing powers. While the lack of a male heir prompts the count to compare his family with a rotten tree, the news of a male heir should cure the count's malady. The count's reaction is not what Boleslav expected, for the count cannot but see himself as disinherited by Boleslav, even if his son is returned. As Boleslav himself confirms, Jaromir forgot his real family while under the aegis of the robbers (ll. 2481–83).

Borotin fears that Jaromir's character will have been damaged by his association with the criminals, in which case he would rather his son had died: whether Jaromir is dead or a criminal, Borotin no longer has an heir. While a dead son could not inherit, a criminal outsider would be unacceptable (ll. 2492–94). When Jaromir discovers the truth, his anger results from the idea that he has been deprived of his rightful Borotin inheritance:

> Schlichst dich Kirchenräuberisch
> In des reinen Kinderbusens
> Unentweihtes Heiligtum;
> Stahlst des teuren Vaters Bild
> Von der Gottgeweihten Schwelle,
> Setztest Deines an die Stelle!
> Ungeheuer! Ungeheuer! (ll. 2793–99)

[You crept like a church robber/ Into the unprofaned shrine/ Of the child's pure breast;/ Stole his dear father's picture/ From the threshold which was dedicated to God,/ And put your picture in its place!/ Monster! Monster!]

Jaromir, by means of religious references, conveys the idea of inheritance as a holy, God-given right and invokes the relationship between creator and creation. Fathers are particularly important figures for their sons, and by kidnapping Jaromir, Boleslav has sinned against a holy order and against the economic and social conventions governing inheritance. Jaromir's vilification of Boleslav and of his own former life of crime indicates his shift in allegiance following the revelation of his true origins. Now that he has been reunited with his true inheritance and has a role in established society, he scorns his former status as an outsider.

The robbers, who are in some ways more spectral than the ghost of the ancestress, are another indication of the social importance of ownership. While the ancestress appears on stage, and cannot therefore be considered as a manifestation of guilt or the obsession with legacy,[43] the band of robbers never appear as such, but are only represented by Jaromir and Boleslav. The robbers thereby become a symbol of society's obsession with property and inheritance. This sinister quality with which the bandits are endowed shows how deeply ingrained the importance of property is in the psyche of Borotin and others in this society. The fear of losing or being divested of one's property is all-encompassing, as also shown by Borotin's deliberations on the subject, and has resulted in the creation of these other ghosts, the robbers, as a numerous and powerful threat in the paranoid minds of the propertied elite. The great lengths to which the state and its representatives go to counter the misappropriating energies of the bandits are a further indication of the importance of property rights in this society.

In this context, Borotin's disregard for Bertha, despite the clearly affectionate relationship between the two, is more comprehensible. While he loves Bertha, she is useless to him in terms of inheritance. In the same way that Kreusa in *Das goldene Vließ* labels Medea's children orphans because their mother does not fit the mould of Greek motherhood, a patriarchal concept, so is Bertha a non-being because she can play no meaningful part in the Borotin inheritance. Borotin laments not that he will die without a son, but that he will die with no children whatsoever (ll. 62–69), an idea which is later reinforced with the exclamation: 'Und ich sterbe kinderlos!' [And I will die childless!] (l. 159). While a son would marry and bring home his bride (l. 124), thereby giving new life to the castle and propagating the name Borotin, Bertha, on being married, would probably be taken to her husband's home, where their offspring would carry his family name.[44] Only a male heir can secure the Borotin name a place in the future of the country, and this is what the duke desires. Carmen Stirnweis has identified Borotin's 'Fixierung auf einen männlichen, vollwertigen Nachfolger' [fixation on a male, fully adequate successor].[45] However, by disregarding the social context of Borotin's anxiety, she fails to identify the reasons for this: 'Der Graf betrauert ein totes Geschlecht, ohne das Leben zu bemerken, das in Form seiner Tochter neben ihm steht.' [The count mourns the end of his lineage, without noticing the life which stands in front of him in the form of his daughter.] While Bertha undoubtedly represents new life, she represents new life for the Eschens, Jaromir's fictional family, rather than for the Borotins. Borotin, unaware that Jaromir is his son, believes that the Borotins will die out regardless of whether Bertha has children. The cause of Borotin's anxiety is rooted in social realities which exclude women from playing a meaningful role in the future of their families.

Borotin is further dismayed by the fact that a female heir necessitates the destruction of his military legacy. Bertha, being a woman, cannot inherit this aspect of Borotin's legacy, and so the symbols must be buried (ll. 102–07). The importance of military honour for male inheritance is later reinforced by the captain. He has a score to settle with the band of robbers, who destroyed his family seat, and is determined to exact an appropriate punishment. The captain's plan for revenge is not simply to put the robbers to death, but to put them to a dishonourable death as the thieves that they are: 'Nein, dem Rad, dem Henkerbeile/ Sei ihr schuldig Haupt gebracht' [No, the wheel, the executioner's axe/ Shall receive their guilty heads] (ll. 1268–69). A death in battle would be an honourable death, the rightful inheritance of an honourable man, and therefore unfitting for criminals. The planned revenge thus goes beyond physical brutality and a death sentence. The captain proposes a punishment, namely a disinheritance, which mirrors his own disinheritance at the hands of the robbers.

Borotin chastises himself for his disregard for Bertha, which indicates that his opinion of her is at odds with society's:

> Kinderlos konnt' ich mich nennen,
> Und ich habe dich, du Treue!
> Ach, verzeih dem reichen Manne,

> Der sein Habe halb verloren
> In des Unglücks hartem Sturm,
> Und nun mit der reichen Hälfte,
> Lang an Überfluß gewöhnet,
> Sich für einen Bettler hält. (ll. 162–69)

[I could call myself childless,/ And I have you, you loyal person!/ Ah, forgive the rich man/ Who lost half of his wealth/ In the heavy storm of bad luck/ And now, with the valuable half,/ Long used to abundance,/ Considers himself a beggar.]

He clearly values his daughter highly and even permits her to choose her own husband (l. 188), but society at large does not see women as valuable individuals, and so a conflict arises in Borotin's perception of Bertha. For Bertha, excluded from the conveyance of the Borotin legacy to a new generation, marriage is the only way she can contribute to this process. To this end, much of Borotin's energy has been expended in ensuring that the eventual marriage is as profitable as possible (ll. 1084–90), and even when he has decided that Bertha is capable of making her own choice of husband, Borotin seems intent that the chosen man should be selected from among the country's nobles (ll. 186–87). The society in which the Borotins live is obsessed with class and inheritance, and members of the aristocracy would not want their children marrying social inferiors.

Given Borotin's obsession with male inheritance, questions regarding Bertha's female inheritance necessarily arise. On the one hand, and in stark contrast to the violence of the drama's male characters, Bertha's inheritance as a woman appears to be a certain humanity. The captain, who laments the destruction of his own inheritance (ll. 1258–60), wishes to exact brutal revenge on the bandits. Bertha responds to this proposed violence with a plea that the captain go about his duties with humanity: 'Nicht doch! Wollt ihr Menschen richten,/ Geht als Mensch ans blut'ge Werk!' [No, no! If you will execute men,/ Go as men to the bloody deed!] (ll. 1270–71). Jaromir cherishes Bertha's gentle nature which he wishes to protect from male influence:

> Wollt ihr dieses holde Wesen,
> [...]
> Mit der Rachsucht gift'gem Hauch,
> Mit des Hasses Atem trüben!
> Laßt sie süßes Mitleid üben [...] (ll. 1288, 1293–95)

[You want to pollute this fair creature/ [...]/ With poisonous vindictiveness,/ With the breath of hate!/ Let her practice sweet pity.]

Jaromir and Bertha are representatives of the opposed but complementary gender roles idealized in eighteenth- and nineteenth-century theoretical texts, and here Jaromir expresses his desire to uphold this status quo. Jaromir believes that Bertha's nature is susceptible to corruption when it comes into contact with male influences, an eventuality he is keen to avoid.

Grillparzer draws attention to another aspect of female inheritance, namely original sin. The ancestress in Grillparzer's drama, due to her own sexual transgressions, can be seen as a descendant of Eve. Not as lucky as Bertha in her parents, the ancestress was forced into a marriage with a man she did not care for, whom she then cuckolded (ll. 480–89). The murder weapon, a dagger, hangs in a prominent position and functions as a constant reminder of the deed and of the sexual transgression on which the house of Borotin is founded. Dagmar Lorenz argues that the ancestress's infidelity calls social structures into question.[46] This is particularly true as far as inheritance is concerned. By committing adultery and bearing another man's child, Bertha, the ancestress, deprived her husband of his rightful legacy. She usurped his role as the founder of the Borotin dynasty, and became its originator (ll. 113–14). Indeed, the Borotins of the drama are not Borotins at all, but rather the descendants of the ancestress and her lover (ll. 544–48). Given Borotin's obsession with inheritance, this enduring act of usurpation is shown to be particularly subversive. Borotin is clearly aware of the tales surrounding the ancestress's fate. In Act I, he names her as the founder of the dynasty (ll. 113–14), but later interrupts Günther's narration when the servant mentions her illegitimate offspring. Later, he is clearly troubled by the possibility of his own illegitimacy, and tries to rid himself of the thought (ll. 1104–08). Founding a dynasty, especially when we consider that Borotin's concerns originate in his daughter's inability merely to continue his line, represents female appropriation of male creative power. Within the power structures presented in the drama, female infidelity is shown to be a particularly dangerous transgression because it can disinherit and make illegitimate.

The omnipresent dagger is at once part of Bertha's material inheritance and a symbol of her inheritance as a woman, namely violence and oppression at the hands of men. Although Stirnweis does not see Bertha's maltreatment in terms of a 'female inheritance', as proposed here, she does see Bertha's situation as a repetition of the ancestress's. She interprets the ghost as a visible warning against the ancestress's fate, an 'instrumentalisierend[e] Ungerechtigkeit' [exploitative injustice] which now threatens Bertha.[47] She also suggests that the crime central to the drama is not the ancestress's infidelity, as is usually claimed, but 'ihre Zwangsverheiratung und Instrumentalisierung' [her forced marriage and exploitation] which precede it. As Stirnweis shows, the characters in the drama refer to the adultery as 'Sünde' [sin] while the murder is a mere 'Tat' [deed].[48] This hierarchy of evils is almost certainly linked to the subordinate social position of women in the society represented in the drama (and in Grillparzer's own society): 'Der Mord an der Ahnfrau belegt, daß der privilegierte Mann auch dann sicher ist, wenn er Faustrecht gelten läßt, solange er einen sozial Geringeren tötet' [The murder of the ancestress shows that the privileged man is safe even when he resorts to the use of force, as long as he kills someone who is socially inferior].[49] We are also reminded of Grillparzer's own views on the differences between male and female adultery, which were mentioned in the Introduction. Again, however, the issue of inheritance, and legitimate heirs, should be taken into account, as doing so helps explain the society's condemnation of the ancestress's deed: wives' extramarital affairs necessarily call into question the legitimacy of their issue, a state of affairs which cannot be tolerated by a society in which patrilineal inheritance is such a sacred principle. Conversely, the infidelity of Alfonso's ancestor in *Die Jüdin von Toledo* does not have a negative effect on Alfonso's own legitimacy, accentuating the societal double standard against female infidelity. The concept of patrilineality, which is central to *Die Ahnfrau*, can thus be seen as doubly misogynist. First, as has been argued, it relegates women to a mere supporting role in the family. Women's physiology makes them mere passive participants in the process. Women are absorbed by the family into which they are married and adopt their husband's name and identity. It is a woman's male relatives — brothers, cousins, uncles — who actively secure the future of the family name. Second, patrilineal systems of inheritance restrict women's sexual experience in order to guarantee the purity of resultant offspring. The *ABGB* 1811 lists proven infidelity as grounds for a separation, and allows for a marriage to be declared null and void, should the husband find his wife to be impregnated by another man after the ceremony has taken place.[50] Men's infidelities do not endanger the purity of the family line: the mothers of illegitimate children can easily be identified and their offspring sidelined. Before modern scientific advances, however, women had to be controlled by social and moral structures, such as those propagated by religions, to prevent contamination of the family line.

Bertha's inherited victimhood would not be possible without the corresponding masculine inheritance of violence, which has already been touched upon. The dagger is a constant reminder of the violent murder of Bertha's forebear, and so it is illuminating that Jaromir insists on possessing it. Desperate for weapons of some kind, Jaromir recalls the dagger. Despite Bertha's attempts to prevent him obtaining it, and the ghost of the ancestress which appears, Jaromir not only takes possession of the dagger, but appropriates it:

> BERTHA   Diesen Dolch! O leg' ihn hin!
> JAROMIR   Ich, den Dolch? Nein, nimmermehr!
>   Er ist mein, ist mein, ist mein!
>   Ei fürwahr ein tüchtig Eisen!
>   Wie ich ihn so prüfend schwinge
>   Wird mit Eins mir guter Dinge
>   Und mein innres Treiben klar. (ll. 2146–52)

> [BERTHA: This dagger! Oh, put it down! JAROMIR: I — the dagger? No, never!/ It is mine, is mine, is mine!/ Oh, in truth a capable blade!/ As I swing it in practice/ Suddenly I feel confident/ And I understand my inner turmoil.]

His appropriation of the dagger is shown in his assignment of new, positive, meaning to it, where previously the Borotins regarded it as a reminder of the horrors of the past. Labelling the dagger 'tüchtig', Jaromir shows his support for the deed which was committed using the weapon. Later, Jaromir shows himself to be prone to violence. Talking to the ghost, whom he mistakes for Bertha, he displays his short temper and violent tendencies (ll. 3230–40). The punishment Jaromir threatens, which is similar to that inflicted on the ancestress, disguises Jaromir's own inheritance with a specific and personal quality. Yet, when one considers that Jaromir and the ancestress's husband are not in fact related, the conception of masculine violence as the inheritance of Borotin men shows itself to be flawed.

Jaromir's violence is part of a more general male inheritance which serves as a tool of those who wish to oppress women.

Stirnweis argues for Jaromir's appropriation of the dagger to be read symbolically, for she sees the dagger itself as 'das symbolische Motiv für eine fundamentale Ungerechtigkeit' [the symbolic motif of a fundamental injustice].[51] While Stirnweis sees this fundamental injustice in specific events in the drama, namely the ancestress's forced marriage and Jaromir's treatment of Bertha, the universal context of the drama, that is, inheritance, indicates a more general criticism of the various kinds of maltreatment suffered by Bertha and her forebear at the hands of the men around them.

Bringing the central, and long ignored, issue of inheritance to the fore permits a broader analysis of *Die Ahnfrau* than is possible when the drama's social and legal context is not considered. Grillparzer portrays patrilineal inheritance as a construct which reduces women's freedom and importance. The society of *Die Ahnfrau* simultaneously demeans women and demands from them the highest levels of purity. Women's position as a marginalized group is shown to be the result of these demands: the violence committed against both Berthas goes hand in hand with these demeaning social structures. Bertha is of no use for the future of the Borotin family, and her existence as the sole heir to the name guarantees its destruction. On the other hand, however, female chastity and fidelity are highly prized, as only they can guarantee the purity with which the Borotin line is continued. The severity of the punishment inflicted on the ancestress is an indication of the high value placed by men on pure female sexuality as a guarantee of their children's legitimacy. The fates of Bertha and her ancestress demonstrate the dangerously limiting nature of life for women in patriarchal societies. Grillparzer's engagement with the *Frauenfrage* is thus already evident in his first mature dramatic work.

'Zum Schweigen und Gehorchen kam ich nicht!' Women, Marriage and Politics in *König Ottokars Glück und Ende*

The issue of inheritance which Grillparzer introduces in *Die Ahnfrau* is again visible in his historical drama *König Ottokars Glück und Ende*. In the figure of Ottokar, Grillparzer presents another dynastic leader who is deeply concerned with the future of his clan. Having married Margarete, his first wife, for her territorial possessions, he later regrets the decision when it becomes clear that the union will not produce heirs. Eager to precipitate the end of this marriage is Benesch von Rosenberg, a Bohemian nobleman and member of the Rosenberg family, who hopes to marry his daughter, Berta, to the king. Ultimately, however, Ottokar decides in favour of Kunigunde, granddaughter of the King of Hungary. The drama, in portraying these various unions and the fates of the three women linked to the king, examines the nature of marriage, particularly political marriage, and women's role in patriarchal political systems. This overarching political structure, hinted at but not explored in *Die Ahnfrau*, also allows for a comparison of Ottokar's and Rudolf's reigns, and of the role of women in both.

Previous scholarship has largely concentrated on the political and historical issues in the drama, and has tended to overlook the social issues. Much has been written on the parallels between the drama's content and events contemporaneous with Grillparzer's life. Contemporary audiences, and critics since, have seen in the drama's marital constellations reflections of the Habsburgs' political marriages. Mark Ward concludes that audiences would inevitably have made links between Grillparzer's characters and Napoleon, Josephine, and Marie-Luise.[52] Other critics have sought clues about Grillparzer's political beliefs. Alfred Doppler positions *Ottokar* in the context of 'Bühnenstücken, die das Herrscherhaus und den österreichischen Staat verherrlichten und die sich die Stärkung und Festigung patriotischer Empfindungen angelegen sein ließen' [plays which glorified the ruling dynasty and the Austrian state, and which made the strengthening and consolidation of patriotic feelings their concern], although Grillparzer's 'Einstellung zu dem Staat, auf den *Ottokars Glück und Ende* bezogen ist, war [...] nicht konservativ verherrlichend, sondern ambivalent und kritisch' [attitude to the state to which *Ottokar* refers was [...] not conservatively glorifying, but ambivalent and critical].[53] Doppler interprets Grillparzer's negative portrayal of the Bohemians as evidence of his conviction that the special interests of the Habsburg empire's various nationalities could destroy its unity.[54]

This is not to say that Ottokar's marriages have been ignored in scholarship. Bruce Thompson argues that the marriages' purpose is to make Ottokar a more pathetic character: 'Mothered by Margarethe, humiliated by Kunigunde, [Ottokar] is in each case the weaker partner.'[55] Harald Steinhagen writes that Ottokar does not feel any duty towards Margarete, and sees marriage merely as a means to an end.[56] On the contrary, his treatment of Margarete in particular has been examined, but the focus tends to be on the role of the divorce as a catalyst in Ottokar's downfall. Roe notes that the abrupt end to the marriage is followed by a swift decline in Ottokar's fortunes, and argues that his treatment of Margarete is symptomatic of his deep-seated inhumanity and cynicism.[57] Similarly, Konrad Schaum argues that any instance of lawlessness can threaten the stability of order and cause the loss of inner cohesion: 'Daher wird die sittliche Mißhandlung Margarethes zwar zum Wendepunkt seines Glücks, aber erst das Zusammenwirken vieler Kräfte aus dem Ganzen der Geschichte schafft den tragischen Prozeß.' [Therefore the moral mistreatment of Margarethe becomes the turning point of his fortune, but it is only the combination of many powers from the whole of history which creates the tragic process.][58]

Placing the focus on Grillparzer's female characters seems well justified when we consider that these roles are more important in his drama than in his sources. Vaclav Hajek's *Böhmische Chronik* was one source for *Ottokar*. The main outline of Grillparzer's drama can be found in this work, but the roles played by women are far smaller than those in *Ottokar*. Indeed, Kunigunde has several children, while it is hard to imagine Grillparzer's Kunigunde taking on the role of mother. Grillparzer also used the portraits of Ottokar and Rudolf in Joseph Hormayr's *Österreichischer Plutarch*. In his portrait of Rudolf, Hormayr gives much room to, and stresses the importance of, the many dynastic marriages in which the king paired his daughters, but barely mentions Margarethe or Kunigunde. Hormayr downplays the importance of Margarethe, writing that Ottokar gained the Austrian lands 'weniger aus dem Titel seiner Ehe mit Margarethen [...] dann aus freyem Willen des Landadels und der Gewalt seiner siegreichen Waffen' [less from the title of his marriage to Margarethe [...] than from the free will of the landed gentry and the force of his victorious weapons].[59] Hormayr calls Kunigunde 'eitler, unversöhnlicher noch als ihr Gemahl' [even prouder, more irreconcilable than her husband].[60] After Ottokar's prostration before Rudolf, she goads him, and suggests that he 'möge nur sein Lebelang [sic] bey ihren Frauen an dem Rocken weilen, — sie wolle das Heer führen wider den Feind' [may spend his life with her women at the distaff — she would lead the army against the enemy]. This portrayal of Kunigunde is very similar to Grillparzer's. In his biography of Ottokar, Hormayr again downplays Margarethe's importance. Margarethe's decision not formally to enter the convent and take the oath was influenced by the Pope, 'der sich ihrer als eines Werkzeugs bedienen wollte' [who wanted to use her as a tool] and who tried to marry her off.[61] For a while, she ruled Austria by herself, but without gaining the respect of the nobles, who 'dachten nun um so ernstlicher daran, ihr einen Gemahl und sich diesen zum Herrn zu geben, je dringender des Landes bisherige Leiden eine solche Gewißheit gebothen' [now thought more seriously about finding her a husband and making him their ruler, as the country's present suffering demanded such certainty with greater urgency].[62] Hormayr presents Margarethe's marriage to Ottokar as a decision taken by the nobles, rather than by Margarethe herself. In Grillparzer's drama, Margarete is an altruistic foil to Kunigunde. In Hormayr's version, however, Margarethe's demands are partly to blame for the end of her marriage: 'sie [forderte], der ungleichen Verbindung von jeher abgeneigt, zu oft Dank von dem Könige, den sie so groß gemacht, und von dem Lande, dem sie sich geopfert hätte' [she, who had always been opposed to the unequal union, too often [demanded] thanks from the king, whom she said she had ennobled, and from the country, for which she said she had sacrificed herself].[63] This behaviour, combined with Ottokar's desire for an heir, led him to seek divorce on the grounds that they were too closely related, and because Margarethe took an oath in the convent. Although there are similarities which testify to the influence of Hormayr on *Ottokar*, Grillparzer gives more prominence to the roles of Margarete and Kunigunde than do either Hormayr or Hajek. This would suggest that these female characters were of considerable interest to him, and that they therefore deserve more critical attention than they have hitherto received.

Marriage will be the central concern of this chapter on *Ottokar*. The legal issues surrounding marriage in Grillparzer's time have already been discussed in the introduction to this section on 'Women and the Law'. The *ABGB* of 1811, while holding both man and wife to the same degree of marital duty and fidelity (§90), establishes a clear, patriarchal hierarchy as the basis of marriage: 'Der Mann ist das Haupt der Familie' [The husband is the head of the family] (§91). The *ABGB* dedicates much space to family law, and dictates the procedure for ending a marriage. Or, rather, it states that a marriage cannot be nullified, even if both parties want this. As far as the state was concerned, marriage was not simply a personal arrangement between two individuals but an institution which had far-reaching effects on society as a whole. *Ottokar* demonstrates this principle.

The issues surrounding marriage which play such a central role in *Ottokar* were also of great interest to women writers at the time. Caroline Pichler, for example, wrote frequently on the subject. In 'Erinnerung an einige merkwürdige Frauen' ['In Remembrance of Some Unusual Women'] (1810) she cites Maria Theresa's luck in having avoided the terrible fate of a political marriage: 'Nicht, wie sonst bey Fürstentöchtern, war ihre Ehe das Werk der Staatskunst, und ihr glückliches Gelingen ein Werk des Zufalls. Nein!' [Her marriage was not, as is usual for the daughters of princes, the work of statecraft and its happy success the result of chance. No!][64] In another essay, 'Über Mißheirathen' ['On Mésalliances'], she laments various evils which had become prevalent in Austrian marriages. Pichler's definition of misalliance includes any marriage which is marked by a large difference, be it in age, social background, upbringing or education, between the partners. Although she believes that love and time can bridge many gaps, such an undertaking will always remain a 'Wagestück' [risky venture]. If there is any such discrepancy, writes Pichler, then it is much better that it be in the man's favour; this is in accordance with God's plan and nature.[65] In a letter to Marie von Zay, Pichler expressed concern about Marianne Neumann's upcoming marriage: 'Es ist mir vor allem nicht recht, daß sie ihm an Bildung überlegen ist — solche geistige *Mesalliancen*, besonders wenn das Übergewicht auf Seite der Frau ist — schlagen selten glücklich aus' [I am particularly uneasy about the fact that she is superior to him in education — such intellectual mésalliances, particularly when the superiority is on the woman's side — are rarely happy].[66] Marriages in which the woman is superior to the man in any way are 'traurig' [sad] and 'aller natürlichen Ordnung zuwider' [against all natural order], but Pichler is particularly disturbed by marriages in which the woman is the elder partner: 'Welche moderne Geistesrichtung oder Verkehrung ist es, die den männlichen Sinn [...] auf verwelkte alternde Gestalten lenkt?' [What modern school of thought or inversion is it, which directs the male interest [...] towards wilted, ageing figures?][67] The relevance of Pichler's comments for *Ottokar* is clear. On the one hand, Grillparzer displays the misery of political marriages, which take no account of personal preferences. Margarete, Berta and Kunigunde are pawns in a game for political power. Their feelings and desires are irrelevant, and love cannot play a role in the marriages in which they find themselves or to which they aspire. Furthermore, as in other dramas, Grillparzer portrays in *Ottokar* the consequences of marriages which are not based on some form of mutuality. Margarete's advanced age makes her incompatible for Ottokar as she is unable to give him the heirs he desires, while Ottokar and Kunigunde are divided by their cultures, a difference which manifests itself in their differing views of the role of women.

Ottokar's change of heart regarding the future of his dynasty causes trouble for the three women in the drama. While his marriage with Margarete was the result of territorial aspirations, by the beginning of the drama he is more concerned with the future of the dynasty and of his realm. Ottokar himself makes clear that his private decision, his divorce from Margarete, is necessitated by the political situation and by 'mein Land,/ Das in mir Ehen schließt und Ehen scheidet' [my land/ Which weds me, then unweds (p. 33)].⁶⁸ As in *Die Ahnfrau*, a male dynastic leader realizes the need for male heirs and does what he can to ensure the future of his line.

The first victim of Ottokar's political marriages is Margarete. In *Ottokar*, Grillparzer expands Margarete's role not just in comparison with his sources, but also in comparison with his 1818 poem 'Rudolf und Ottokar', where she is a dutiful housewife who 'schafft und spinnet emsig' [works and spins industriously] while Ottokar is in the field (*HKA* I/xi, p. 12). Grillparzer gives Margarete an active political role which is not present in his sources. Much as Ottokar's decision to divorce Margarete is motivated by politics rather than affairs of the heart, her decision to marry him was taken despite her wish to remain unmarried and was motivated by political considerations. Rather than territorial self-aggrandizement, however, Margarete sought to secure the safety of her compatriots by marrying Ottokar:

> Da traten zu mir hin, auf Haimburgs Schloß,
> Die Landesherrn und klagten ihre Not.
> [...]
> Von Weibern, Kindern, Blutenden, Verletzten
> Sah ich mit Schaudern, heulend, mich umgeben,
> Zu mir um Rettung flehend, die's vermochte.
> Da wollt ich alles und versprach es ihnen! (ll. 312–13, 323–26)

[Then in my Castle Haimburg there appeared/ My country's Lords, complaining of their need [...] Dense throngs of women, children, bleeding, bruised,/ Surged round as, horror-struck, I heard their cries,/ Entreating me to save them, for I could./ I would have risked my all, and so I promised. (p. 20)]

As Hans Gmür puts it, 'das Elend ihrer Untertanen zwingt sie zur Heirat mit dem mächtigen Ottokar' [The suffering of her subjects forces her to marry the powerful Ottokar].⁶⁹

In Act I, Zawisch von Rosenberg, a relative of Berta, gleefully announces the King's divorce from Margarete, who later airs her suspicions that the Rosenbergs' meddling was decisive in nudging Ottokar towards his decision (ll. 206–12). As becomes evident when Ottokar's reasons for divorcing Margarete are discussed, her behaviour has not in any way forced his hand: 'Ja, ich will gehn, doch bleibt die Ehe fest,/ Nichts ward verletzt, was ihren Bruch begehrte' (ll. 341–42) [Yes, I shall leave; our marriage, though, must stand./ No grounds exist that it should be dissolved (p. 21)]. Ottokar knew on marrying Margarete that she would not be able to produce heirs, but this fact did not deter him. Whereas territorial expansion was his goal before the marriage, the realization that heirs are necessary means that Margarete is no longer a suitable wife and must be removed from the picture (ll. 508–15). More explicitly than in *Die Ahnfrau*, Grillparzer indicates the analogous relationship of family and state. Ottokar claims his decision to divorce Margarete is not motivated by his attraction to a younger woman, but by his people's expectations of royal heirs and international alliances.

Although she suffers at the hands of her husband and sees the fate that awaits Berta, Margarete does not condemn the institution of marriage, but rather holds it up as sacred (ll. 288–91). Nor does Margarete cower before her husband. In conversation with Rudolf, Margarete displays knowledge of her legal position, rejecting the grounds for divorce listed by Ottokar. She refuses to forgive Ottokar's treatment of her, and defends her marriage against his claims. Ottokar, she argues, knew that she was no longer capable of bearing children before they were married, and was not concerned by this (ll. 257–61). She rejects Ottokar's claims that they are too closely related, and so should never have been married (ll. 276–78), and disputes the claim that the marriage is invalid because of an oath she took to her deceased husband before marrying Ottokar. While she did swear to remain chaste, it was not a solemn vow, the renunciation of which would break other religious rules (ll. 348–49).

Margarete's independence is most evident in her confrontation with Ottokar in Act I. The chancellor asks who will be representing her in the matter, to which she responds, 'Ich selbst!' (l. 539) [I shall, myself! (p. 30).] The chancellor's assumption that Margarete would have male representation, possibly in the form of Rudolf or Merenburg, who accompany her to the throne room, places the drama in the context of nineteenth-century Austrian law: the *ABGB* 1811 did not envision women representing themselves in legal matters. Margarete defends herself publicly against Ottokar's accusations, and warns him of the consequences of his actions. Even as Ottokar insults and derides Margarete, she shows herself to be a truly selfless character (ll. 616–18). Margarete also seems to have a better understanding of the reality of Ottokar's situation than he himself does. She warns him against those around him — 'Umringt seid Ihr mit Argen und Verrätern!' (l. 634) [You are beset by evil men and traitors (p. 34)] — and against furthering his plans: 'Ihr steht am Abgrund, glaubt mir, Ottokar!' (l. 637) [You face destruction, hear me, Ottokar (p. 34)] Yet she cannot divest him of his arrogance: 'Lehrt Ihr den Ottokar die Seinen kennen?/ Ich gehe meinen Gang, was hindert, fällt.' (ll. 635–36) [Would you teach Ottocar to know his men?/ I go my even way; what blocks it, falls (p. 34).]

Margarete is at once a pawn in Ottokar's plans for domination, and an independent player. She is not motivated by personal gain or private interest, but rather by the good of the population at large. She married Ottokar for this reason, and it is for this reason that she agrees to leave the court. Margarete seems at all times aware of the larger implications of her actions, and her discussion with Rudolf makes clear that she is familiar with the law. Berta, to whom we now turn our attention, is by no means Margarete's intellectual equal, nor does she have Margarete's strength of character, and as a result she is at the mercy of the scheming men around her.

It is Margarete's 'grenzenlose Güte' [endless kindness][70] which allows her to pity the fate of Berta despite her own problems. Recognizing Berta's role as a pawn in her family's game, Margarete does not blame her for Ottokar's decision (ll. 198–203, 218–20). The Rosenbergs' statements in Act I and their treatment of Berta confirm Margarete's suspicions. Benesch's first reaction to his daughter's appearance is dismissive and displays the misogyny present in many of Grillparzer's male characters: 'Ha, Närrin, du?/ Was willst du hier? Geh fort, auf dein Gemach!' (ll. 61–62) [You, foolish creature?/ What brings you here? Go home, stay in your room

(p. 8).] Discussions between her male relatives, even when they concern her own fate, are no place for Berta. Her uncle Milota later tries to take her away, but she begs Seyfried for protection. Clearly, Berta is accustomed to ill-use at the hands of her father and uncles. Zawisch mockingly praises the way in which his brother tried to tempt Ottokar with his daughter, before announcing that Ottokar has chosen Kunigunde as his second wife. Benesch is understandably infuriated and suspects treachery, but Zawisch cannot help but point out that it was Benesch's interference which has made the marriage possible (ll. 133–35). Although he turns to his brothers in an attempt at shifting the responsibility for the failure of the scheme, it is Berta whom Benesch blames most: 'Bringt sie mir her, das Mädchen bringt mir her!/ Sie soll nicht leben!' (ll. 142–43) [Bring her to me, bring me the girl, you hear?/ She shall not live! (p. 14)]

Benesch's plans to marry Berta to Ottokar display his lack of concern for her happiness. Berta has no value in and of herself, but is merely a means by which her male relatives hope to gain increased political influence. Benesch has placed Berta in Ottokar's eye as often as possible, in the hope that she might seduce him. In conversation with Rudolf, Margarete narrates the course of the Rosenbergs' campaign for influence, and in doing so partially exonerates her husband. For some time prior to Ottokar's decision, the Rosenbergs had been sowing dissent between the monarchs (ll. 206–09), and playing on the king's desire for an heir (ll. 210–12). According to Margarete, the Rosenbergs' campaign was so successful that the disintegration of the royal marriage is to be blamed on them rather than on Ottokar (ll. 215–17). Unfortunately for Benesch, his plan is only partially successful: while his meddling does induce Ottokar to divorce Margarete, it is not Berta, but Kunigunde, who is the new queen. Again, this marriage is more of a political than a romantic alliance. The Hungarian King Bela, recently defeated in battle by Ottokar, gives his daughter in marriage to the victor as a means of sealing the peace. Kunigunde's fate confirms that, for women in this society, marriage is not motivated by concerns for individual (female) happiness.

In terms of the scope of this study as a whole, Kunigunde is the most interesting of the three female characters in *Ottokar*. For Emil Staiger she is reminiscent of 'die lüsternen und machtgierigen Frauen des Barocktheaters oder der traditionellen Oper' [the lascivious and power-hungry women of the baroque theatre or the traditional opera] and could be confused with 'einem fast schablonenhaften Teufel von Weib' [an almost cliché devil of a woman].[71] Edmund Kostka labels her 'a beautiful but licentious woman devoured by carnal passions'.[72] W. E. Yates mentions her desire for self-determination and 'ungemein modern wirkende Erklärungen ihrer sexuellen Unbefriedigtheit' [her declarations of sexual frustration which seem very modern].[73] Brigitte Prutti also highlights her sexuality, calling her 'eine grausame Dominatrix und die Figuration einer kastrierenden weiblichen Sexualität, eine von Grillparzers kalten und abweisenden, letztlich aber doch verführbaren Frauen' [a cruel dominatrix and the figuration of a castrating female sexuality, one of Grillparzer's cold, but ultimately seductive women].[74] Prutti sees this sexuality as part of what makes Kunigunde so different from Margarete, and indeed her arrival on stage corroborates this. While Grillparzer does not indicate Berta's or Margarete's attire, Kunigunde's otherness is mirrored in her clothing. Disguised as a man in Bela's entourage, she is taken for his grandson. However, with the words, 'Nehmt Ihr mich unter Eure Krieger auf?' (l. 719) [Will you make room for me among your troops? (p. 40)] she removes her male clothing and reveals her identity. Kunigunde's cross-dressing marks her out as an exception to her sex, and, as she herself admits, she took on the disguise in order to avoid the exclusion which would otherwise have been her lot as a woman:

> Mein König, Ihr verzeiht die Überraschung.
> Sie wollten erst mich vor den Toren lassen,
> Doch triebs mich, hier zu sein, und also kam ich. (ll. 724–26)

[Your Highness will forgive me this surprise./ They wanted me at first to wait outside;/ But I wished to be present, so I came (p. 40)]

Grillparzer's dramas often rely on intercultural conflict, and *Ottokar* is no exception. There is the obvious political and military conflict between Ottokar and Rudolf, and, as Kunigunde discovers, the society into which she marries has a different opinion on the role of women than the society in which she was raised. Kunigunde rails against the inferior position of women in Bohemian society and highlights the more equal position which they are accorded in Hungary:

> Wär ich zu stolz nicht, meines Gatten Zorn
> In meiner eignen Sache aufzurufen,
> Wärs hier in Böhmen wie bei uns daheim,
> Wo auch die Frau ein Recht hat, eine Stimme,
> Und Macht, um zu vollführen, was sie denkt,
> Wo eine Königin nicht bloß des Königs Gattin,
> Wo sie Gebietrin ist; es sollt Euch reun! (ll. 884–90)

[If I were not too proud to stir to wrath/ My husband in affairs that are my own;/ If here one counted as at home with us,/ Where woman also has a right, a voice,/ The power to carry out what she conceives,/ And where a queen is not plain consort of a king,/ But really rules; you would regret your acts. (p. 49)]

Kunigunde's speech is reminiscent of Hero's optimism regarding her future in the temple ('Im Tempel hier hat auch die Frau ein Recht' [Here in the temple women also have rights], l. 279) and of Phaon's challenge to Sappho's authority ('Ist [Sappho] Gebiet'rin hier im Land?' [Is [Sappho] the ruler in this country?], l. 1641). In *Ottokar*, Hungary and Bohemia are contrasted in terms of social attitudes towards women, as are Colchis and Greece (*Das goldene Vließ*, 1819), Mytilene and Greece (*Sappho*, 1818) or the temple and wider society (*Des Meeres und der Liebe Wellen*, 1831) in other dramas by Grillparzer. Kunigunde's rights in Hungary seem to be more extensive than those of Hero in the temple, not least because she has not only rights, but also a voice and power to convert desires into action. She is, however, aware that her freedoms are limited in Bohemia, and threatens Zawisch with retribution at Ottokar's hands if he should again be so impertinent (ll. 910–11).

In conversation with her maid, Kunigunde offers insight into the widely differing fortunes which she encounters in Hungary and Bohemia. Her Hungarian youth was spent in the sort of freedom enjoyed by Medea in Colchis:

> [In Ungarn] galt ich noch! Frei streift ich in die Ferne,
> Dorthin, dahin, wohin der Wunsch mich rief.
> Mein alter Vater war mir gern zu Dienst,
> Zu Dienst die Fürsten, seine Sippen alle,
> Und was nur Mann hieß in dem weiten Reich.
> Und Leben war und Feuer, Glut und Mut! (ll. 967–72)

> [There I had worth, was free to stray afield,/ Here, there and yonder, as my fancy chose./ My agèd father served my beck and call,/ So did the princes, all his retinue,/ And each and every man from far and wide./ And life was there and fire, warmth and strength! (p. 54)]

As a member of the royal family, she enjoyed liberties denied to other Hungarians, while as a woman she gained the protection of men. Her royal status calls into question her assertion that Hungarian women in general have a greater level of freedom than Bohemian women. *Sappho* and *Die Jüdin von Toledo* both show the extent to which social status affects a woman's standing within a certain society — and within Grillparzer's dramas — but due to the courtly setting this issue plays little role in *Ottokar*. Kunigunde feels deceived by those who persuaded her to marry Ottokar. Expecting to find a youthful and energetic bridegroom, she was confronted with an old man who is sullen, bossy and violent, and expects her to be silent and obedient: 'Beim reichen Gott,/ Zum Schweigen und Gehorchen kam ich nicht!' (ll. 982–83) [God knows,/ I cannot sit in silence and obey. (p. 54)]

As in *Sappho*, age is again a catalyst for marital problems. While the Greek drama presents a constellation of young–younger–youngest (Sappho, Phaon and Melitta respectively), in *Ottokar* the schema is older–old–young (Margarete, Ottokar and Kunigunde respectively).[75] In both cases, a man is caught between two women. Just as Ottokar scorned Margarete because of her age, in turn Ottokar is scorned by Kunigunde because she deems him too old. In Act II, she confesses that she expected to find Ottokar a king in his prime, but was disappointed to find an aged man: 'Denn spielt ihm nicht schon graulich Bart und Haar?' (l. 979) [Is not his hair already grizzled grey? (p. 54)] In Act IV she reveals that she turned down a Cuman chief as she considered Ottokar's hand a better deal, but soon repented her choice:

> Ein kräftig freies Wesen kam ich her,
> Gar würdig wohl des Jünglings zum Gemahl,
> Und fand — ei nun, den König Ottokar! (ll. 2133–35)

> [I came here, spirited and fancy free,/ Well worthy of a partner, young in years,/ And found — Why now, I found King Ottocar! (p. 114)]

She feels no need to insult Ottokar further: the juxtaposition of Ottokar and youth is enough to convey her desires and the resigned disappointment she feels. As Staiger points out, Kunigunde's marriage to Ottokar was not motivated by concern for her compatriots, as was Margarete's. Rather, she hoped one day to become queen, even empress.[76] The realities of married life have left her severely disappointed in these ambitions, for Ottokar has not allowed her to be involved in the decision-making processes, treating her '[w]ie eine Magd, vielmehr als eine Fürstin' (l. 2139) [as a handmaid rather than as queen (p. 114)]. For Prutti, Kunigunde, with her 'unbefriedigten Freiheitswünschen und Emanzipationsansprüchen' is 'eine dezidiert moderne Gestalt' [unsatisfied desire for freedom and demands for emancipation; a decidedly modern character].[77]

It is this disappointment which leads Kunigunde into a flirtation with Zawisch and ultimately to a rejection of Ottokar. In *Sappho*, Phaon's youth relative to the heroine leads him into an amorous relationship with the younger Melitta. Similarly, Kunigunde flirts with Zawisch, a partner nearer her age, thereby transforming one of Ottokar's courtiers into his rival. Kunigunde is spurred on in her behaviour by her disappointment with Ottokar. The flirtation is also a rebellion against Ottokar's dominance over her, and in consorting with Zawisch Kunigunde turns the tables on the system which made her, Margarete and Berta into pawns. Zawisch becomes a pawn in her quest for revenge against her husband.

In Act II, Kunigunde and Zawisch flirt in the presence of a clueless Ottokar. Zawisch has refused to receive his prize from anyone but Kunigunde, and, aware that she has received his love letter, thanks her:

> O Königin, habt tausend, tausend Dank —
> (Langsam.)
> Im voraus für den Preis, den Ihr mir reichet. (ll. 1041–42)

[O Queen, accept a thousand, thousand thanks — / *slowly* / For the award you are about to give. (p. 58)]

The double entendre is lost on Ottokar, who chides Kunigunde for not awarding Zawisch quickly enough: 'Warum gebt Ihr den Preis nicht, Kunigunde?' (l. 1043) [Why not bestow the prize now, Cunigunda? (p. 58)], to which she replies: 'Ich wollte früher schon, eh' Ihr befahlt!' (l. 1044) [I started to, before you gave command! (p. 58)] Zawisch's audacity extends to purloining Kunigunde's ribbon, which represents a violation of her person. Ottokar is alarmed when he notices that only one of Kunigunde's arms is decorated with a bow, and offers a ring as a reward to the discoverer of the missing adornment. Queens give away diamonds, says Ottokar, but not their ribbons, which are a sign of a much more valuable treasure: chastity, or at least fidelity. In the context of Kunigunde and Zawisch's flirtation, Ottokar is right to worry about Kunigunde's dishabille, which reflects badly on her morality and his ability to keep her under control (ll. 1118–20). Kunigunde does not take well to being rebuked, and her response makes clear that her indulgence of Zawisch is both an act of self-determination and of rebellion against Ottokar. She defies Ottokar by permitting Zawisch to keep her ribbon and threatens to give herself to Zawisch as a sign of her autonomy:

> Auch mög er sehen, daß ich Herrin bin,
> Zu schenken was ich will; und wenn es mehr
> Als Schleife wäre, mehr als Diamant! (ll. 1127–29)

[And let him also understand my right/ To give what I desire, though it be more/ Than ribbons, more than diamonds and gold. (p. 63)]

At the end of the act, Kunigunde and her maid are alone on stage, but can hear

Zawisch serenading the queen. When asked whether Zawisch should be removed, Kunigunde lets him stay.

Kunigunde's private and political disappointments and her ambition provide the catalyst for Ottokar's disastrous political decisions. Ottokar sees Kunigunde's missing ribbon as a negative reflection on him, and she likewise feels shame because of his submission to Rudolf:

> Ich aber will nicht heißen: Knechtes-Frau;
> Nicht eines schnöden Dienstmanns Bette teilen;
> Will nicht, wenn mich der Kaiser heischt nach Wien,
> Die Schleppe tragen seiner Gräfin Hausfrau;
> Will nicht vor Rudolf knien, wie er getan. (ll. 2183–87)

> [I will not have me called a bondsman's wife,/ No longer share a vassal's shameful bed;/ Nor on the Emperor's summons to Vienna,/ Help bear his lowly housewife's courtly train;/ Nor will I kneel to Rudolph, as you did. (p. 116)]

Kunigunde expresses disdain not only for her unmanly husband, but also for the traditional domestic female role. Kunigunde is no less proud than her husband, who in this scene seems to realize that he is being cuckolded. Having discovered Kunigunde and Zawisch alone together, he hangs his head and says, 'Ist das mein Schatten? — Nun, zwei Könige!' (l. 2201) [Is that my shadow? — Well, two kings it seems! (p. 117)] This could refer to the political challenge he is facing from Rudolf, but it could also be an allusion to the queen's new lover.

In Act IV, we see the effect of Kunigunde's pride as a motivating force for Ottokar's decisions. Ottokar blames Kunigunde for challenging his authority and putting him in a position from which only extreme actions can save him:

> Sie hat den giftgen Stachel mir gesenkt
> In meine Brust, sie mag zugegen sein,
> Wenn ich ihn auszieh, oder im Bemühn
> Ihn drücke in das Innerste des Lebens! (ll. 2385–88)

> [She shot the poisoned shaft and rammed it home/ Within my breast; she shall be present now,/ When I withdraw it, or in my attempt,/ Drive it deep down where rests the source of life. (p. 125)]

Ottokar's motivation is no longer primarily political but private. He goes to war to appease his wife and to regain her respect. Kunigunde does not hesitate in the slightest when questioned by Ottokar, and calmly states that he must reject Rudolf's domination even if it means renewed war and Ottokar's death. Ottokar has already had a change of heart, and no longer seeks the territorial aggrandizement nor the prestige which formerly spurred him on. It is now Kunigunde who represents the force of cold ambition:

> KUNIGUNDE An Eurem Sarge will ich lieber stehn,
> Als mit Euch liegen, zugedeckt von Schande!
> OTTOKAR So stark? Ein Tröpflein Milde täte wohl!
> KUNIGUNDE Solang Ihr Euch nicht von der Schmach gereinigt,
> Betretet nicht als Gatte mein Gemach. (ll. 2401–05)

[CUNIGUNDA: Far better I should stand beside your bier,/ Than lie beside you covered in with shame. OTTOCAR: So hard? A drop of kindness would be sweet. CUNIGUNDA: Until you have been cleansed of this disgrace,/ You shall not share my chamber nor my couch. (p. 126)]

With these words she turns to leave, which prompts a panicked Ottokar to tear the letter of obedience to Rudolf — he expressly holds her jointly responsible for the consequences — and beg for her support: 'Und gebe mir die Kraft, die Ihr bewiesen!' (l. 2410) [And give to me the strength you have displayed. (p. 126)] However, once he receives Kunigunde's blessing, he is horrified by her and by what he has done to placate her:

> Ich sehe Blut an deinen weißen Fingern,
> Zukünftges Blut! Ich sag: berühr mich nicht.
> Gott hat das Weib aus weichem Ton gemacht
> Und: Milde zugenannt; was bist denn du? (ll. 2412–15)

[I seem to see on your white fingers blood,/ Blood still to flow; so keep your hands from me!/ God fashioned woman out of softer clay/ And named her Mercy; what, I ask, are you? (p. 126)]

He suddenly realizes how far removed Kunigunde is from his ideal of womanhood. Kunigunde's lack of femininity makes her an easy scapegoat for Ottokar's bad decisions and the war which will ensue. Ottokar cannot bear to be confronted with the symbol of his folly and pride, and he banishes her: 'Geh fort! Fort, sag ich! Fort!' (l. 2421) [Away, I say away! (p. 127)]

In a different context, Roger Bauer has already noted that Ottokar and Rudolf 'sind bei Grillparzer keine absolut antipodischen Figuren' [are not absolutely antipodal characters in Grillparzer's drama].[78] This also holds true in the context of their attitudes towards women. Ottokar's treatment of both his wives is evidence of his lack of regard for women. In contrast, Rudolf superficially appears to be a more just and enlightened ruler. He is keen to popularize this image of himself as a humane alternative to Ottokar, for example in Act III when he claims to be the representative of 'Recht [...] und Gerechtigkeit/ Im deutschen Land' (ll. 1751–52) [right and justice [...] in German lands (p. 96)]. Rudolf chastises Ottokar for his behaviour, and for his treatment of Margarete, which would suggest a more chivalrous attitude towards women. However, his behaviour towards women, and towards Kunigunde in particular, means that his ascendancy is at best ambivalent in nature.

Ottokar's treatment of Margarete allows Rudolf to appear as the proverbial knight in shining armour. At the end of Act I, Margarete is overcome by weakness, and appeals for help. Merenberg attempts to help, but retreats when admonished by Ottokar. Rudolf then defies the Bohemian king with words that demonstrate what supposedly differentiates him from Ottokar: 'Hier ist mein Arm, erlauchte Königin!/ Stets war bei Habsburg der Gekränkten Schirm.' (ll. 733–34) [Here is my arm, revered and gracious Queen!/ No Hapsburg but gives refuge to the wronged. (p. 41)] With these words, Rudolf positions himself as the defender of the weak and powerless. In this interaction with Margarete, Rudolf is easily able to assert his masculinity and portray himself as a chivalrous knight defending a damsel in distress. It is his realization that Kunigunde is not a woman to be so easily protected and restrained which causes him to judge her so severely. Kunigunde's appearance in disguise, and her justification for it, force Rudolf to utter a condemnation of her: 'Der rücksichtslosen, rohen Übereilung!' (l. 727) [What inconsiderate and ruthless haste! (p. 40)] His dismissive attitude towards women is best displayed in his interaction with Kunigunde in Act V. She has fled Ottokar and seeks asylum in Rudolf's camp. Rudolf is incredulous that she should have left her husband, but she claims that Ottokar became violent and that she had to beg for her life. Rudolf is not particularly disposed to aid her, and strongly suggests that it would have been more honourable to let Ottokar kill her:

> Gar viel Vertraun schenkt Ihr mir Königin!
> Denn Frauen kenn ich, sonst wohl hohen Muts,
> Die aber lieber tot von Gatten-Hand,
> Als daß sie flöhn zu denen, die ihn töten. (ll. 2762–65)

> [How great the confidence you place in me, my Queen!/ I know of women, some of courage too,/ Preferring death, though by a husband's hand,/ To life with those who seek the husband's death. (p. 148)]

In Rudolf's view, women cannot be separated from their husbands and should share their fate. This callous attitude towards Kunigunde's predicament demonstrates the similarities between the two men, rather than the supposed differences, and indicates that, at least for women, Rudolf's ascendancy will not institute positive changes. While Rudolf's chivalrous protection of Margarete appears to intimate that his attitude towards women is not that of surly and dominating Ottokar, his actions show that misogyny is common to both rulers.

In the drama's final speech, Rudolf anoints his sons as his successors, warning them against the pride which was Ottokar's downfall. It seems that the Habsburgs' reign of peace and humanity has arrived. However, although Rudolf is at pains throughout the drama to present himself as a more human, empathetic ruler than Ottokar, he is clearly just as proud as Ottokar, and his ambition for Habsburg territorial aggrandizement is at least as rapacious as the Bohemian's. For women, Rudolf's new order does not promise any significant improvements, for marriage and motherhood are the only possible roles for women in a dynasty which places such importance on heirs. Neither a Margarete nor a Kunigunde can expect a different lot in life after the transition from Ottokar's patriarchy to that of Rudolf.

Notes to Chapter 2

1. Gabriella Hauch, *Frau Biedermeier auf den Barrikaden. Frauenleben in der Wiener Revolution 1848* (Vienna: Verlag für Gesellschaftskritik, 1990), p. 23.
2. Ursula Floßmann, 'Die beschränkte Grundrechtssubjektivität der Frau. Ein Beitrag zum österreichischen Gleichheitsdiskurs', in *Frauen in der Geschichte des Rechts*, 293–324 (pp. 298–99).
3. *Allgemeines bürgerliches Gesetzbuch für die gesammten deutschen Erbländer der Oesterreichischen Monarchie* (Vienna: k.k. Hof- und Staats-Druckerey, 1811), I. Theil, §16, pp. 6–7.
4. Evans, *The Feminists*, p. 93.
5. Ernst Holthöfer, 'Die Geschlechtsvormundschaft. Ein Überblick von der Antike bis ins 19. Jahrhundert', in *Frauen in der Geschichte des Rechts*, 390–451 (p. 427).

6. Ursula Vogel, 'Gleichheit und Herrschaft in der ehelichen Vertragsgesellschaft — Widersprüche der Aufklärung', in *Frauen in der Geschichte des Rechts*, 265–92, p. 281.
7. *ABGB*, II. Theil, §1237, p. 357.
8. *ABGB*, I, p. 32.
9. Ibid.
10. Ibid., p. 33.
11. Gabriela Polak, 'Das Familienrechtsmodell des ABGB (1811) in Konfrontation mit den Modernisierungstendenzen bürgerlich-fortschrittlicher Frauenvereine bis zur 1. Teilnovelle im Jahre 1914' (unpublished dissertation, University of Vienna, 1991), pp. 54–55.
12. Ibid., pp. 56–57.
13. Hauch, *Frau Biedermeier auf den Barrikaden*, p. 23.
14. Franz von Zeiller, *Abhandlung über die Principien des allgemeinen bürgerlichen Gesetzbuches für die gesammten deutschen Erbländer der österreichischen Monarchie* [1816–20], ed. by Wilhelm Brauneder (Vienna: Manz, 1986), p. 38.
15. Polak, 'Das Familienrechtsmodell des ABGB (1811)', p. 65.
16. Ellinor Forster, 'Handlungsspielräume von Frauen und Männern im österreichischen Eherecht. Geschlechterverhältnisse im 19. Jahrhundert zwischen Rechtsnorm und Rechtspraxis' (unpublished dissertation, University of Innsbruck, 2007), p. 190.
17. Polak, 'Das Familienrechtsmodell des ABGB (1811)', p. 66.
18. Forster, 'Handlungsspielräume', p. 188.
19. Zeiller, *Abhandlung über die Principien des allgemeinen bürgerlichen Gesetzbuches*, p. 38.
20. *ABGB*, I, p. 33.
21. Vogel, 'Gleichheit und Herrschaft in der ehelichen Vertragsgesellschaft', pp. 282–83.
22. I. V. Morris, 'The "Ahnfrau" Controversy', *The Modern Language Review*, 62 (1967), 284–91 (p. 284).
23. R. K. Angress, 'Das Gespenst in Grillparzers *Ahnfrau*', *The German Quarterly*, 45 (1972), 606–19 (p. 606).
24. Norbert Griesmayer, *Das Bild des Partners in Grillparzers Dramen. Studien zum Verständnis ihrer sprachkünstlerischen Gestaltung* (Vienna: Braumüller, 1972), p. 70.
25. Reinhold Backmann, 'Entwicklungsgeschichtliches zu Grillparzers "Ahnfrau"', *JdGG*, 28 (1926), 22–42 (p. 24).
26. *Joseph Schreyvogels Tagebücher 1810–1823*, ed. by Karl Glossy, II, Schriften der Gesellschaft für Theatergeschichte III (Berlin: Verlag der Gesellschaft für Theatergeschichte, 1903), p. 203.
27. Ibid., p. 203.
28. Ibid., p. 204.
29. Ibid., p. 213.
30. Ibid., p. 236.
31. V1 refers to the original version of *Die Ahnfrau*, printed in *HKA* I/i, pp. 153–256. V5 refers to the fifth version, incorporating Schreyvogel's comments, printed in *HKA* I/i, pp. 9–148.
32. Karl Glossy, 'Zur Geschichte der Wiener Theaterzensur', *JdGG*, 7 (1897), 238–340 (p. 310).
33. *ABGB*, II, §732, p. 164.
34. Ibid., I, §92, p. 33.
35. Jean Bérenger, *Die Geschichte des Habsburgerreiches 1273 bis 1918*, trans. by Marie Therese Pitner (Vienna: Böhlau, 1995), p. 442.
36. Hanns Leo Mikoletzky, *Österreich. Das große 18. Jahrhundert. Von Leopold I. bis Leopold II.* (Vienna: Austria-Edition, 1967), p. 110.
37. Karl A. Roider, 'The Pragmatic Sanction', *Austrian History Yearbook*, 8 (1972), 153–58 (pp. 153, 156).
38. Bérenger, *Die Geschichte des Habsburgerreiches 1273 bis 1918*, p. 442.
39. Mikoletzky, *Österreich. Das große 18. Jahrhundert*, p. 111.
40. Ibid.
41. Bérenger, *Die Geschichte des Habsburgerreiches 1273 bis 1918*, pp. 443–44; Mikoletzky, *Österreich. Das große 18. Jahrhundert*, pp. 126–27.
42. Grillparzer, 'Die Ahnfrau', in *HKA*, I/i. 9–148. Here ll. 1454–55, 1459, 1461–62.
43. 'Ein symbolisches Gespenst stellt eine psychische Kraft dar; ein eigentliches Gespenst stellt die objektiv auftretende Macht der Toten vor.' Angress, 'Das Gespenst in Grillparzers *Ahnfrau*', p. 612.

44. The *ABGB* 1811 sees this as the only possibility for married women: '[Die Ehefrau] ist verbunden, dem Manne in seinen Wohnsitz zu folgen'. *ABGB* I, §92, p. 33.
45. Carmen Stirnweis, 'Verborgene Schuld in Franz Grillparzers *Die Ahnfrau*. Ein Beitrag zur Relativierung der angeblichen Schicksalstragödie', *JdGG*, 3. Folge 22 (2007–08), 80–108 (pp. 95–96).
46. Lorenz, *Dichter des sozialen Konflikts*, p. 37.
47. Stirnweis, 'Verborgene Schuld in Franz Grillparzers *Die Ahnfrau*', p. 101.
48. Ibid.
49. Lorenz, *Dichter des sozialen Konflikts*, p. 39.
50. *ABGB* I, §109, p. 40; §58, p. 21.
51. Stirnweis, 'Verborgene Schuld in Franz Grillparzers *Die Ahnfrau*', p. 104.
52. Mark G. Ward, 'Some Notes on Grillparzer's *König Ottokar* and the "entfernte Ähnlichkeit"', *German Life and Letters*, 34 (1981), 214–22 (p. 214).
53. Alfred Doppler, '*König Ottokars Glück und Ende*. Das Verhältnis von dargestellter Zeit, Zeit der Darstellung und gegenwärtiger Rezeption', in *Grillparzer und die Europäische Tradition. Londoner Symposium 1986*, 21–29 (p. 21).
54. Ibid., p. 25.
55. Thompson, *Franz Grillparzer*, p. 52.
56. Harald Steinhagen, 'Grillparzers *König Ottokar*. Drama, Geschichte und Zeitgeschichte', *Jahrbuch der Deutschen Schiller-Gesellschaft*, 14 (1970), 456–87 (p. 460).
57. Ian F. Roe, *An Introduction to the Major Works of Franz Grillparzer, 1791–1872, German Dramatist and Poet* (Lewiston, NY: The Edwin Mellen Press, 1991), p. 102.
58. Konrad Schaum, 'Grillparzers "König Ottokars Glück und Ende" — historische Tragödie und Zeitkritik', *JdGG*, 3. Folge 15 (1983), 51–63 (p. 55).
59. Joseph Hormayr, 'Rudolph von Habsburg', in *Oesterreichischer Plutarch, oder Leben und Bildnisse aller Regenten und der berühmtesten Feldherren, Staatsmänner, Gelehrten und Künstler des österreichischen Kaiserstaates*, 20 vols. (Vienna: Doll, 1807–14), I (1807), pp. 5–48 (p. 22).
60. Hormayr, 'Rudolph von Habsburg', p. 29.
61. Joseph Hormayr, 'Przemysl Ottokar der Zweyte', in *Oesterreichischer Plutarch*, XV (1808), 10–81 (p. 14).
62. Hormayr, 'Przemysl Ottokar der Zweyte', p. 14.
63. Ibid., p. 37.
64. Pichler, 'Erinnerung an einige merkwürdige Frauen' (1810), in *Sämmtliche Werke*, xxiv, pp. 96–137 (p. 111).
65. Pichler, 'Über Mißheirathen', in *Sämmtliche Werke*, lv. pp. 141–45 (p. 142).
66. Caroline Pichler to Marie von Zay, 28.3.1821, Wienbibliothek im Rathaus, H.I.N. 434.
67. Pichler, 'Über Mißheirathen', pp. 144–45.
68. Grillparzer, 'König Ottokars Glück und Ende', in *HKA*, I/iii, pp. 5–177, ll. 594–95.
69. Hans Gmür, *Dramatische und theatralische Stilelemente in Grillparzers Dramen* (Winterthur: Keller, 1956), p. 19.
70. Wolf-Cirian, *Grillparzers Frauengestalten*, p. 119.
71. Emil Staiger, 'Grillparzer. *König Ottokars Glück und Ende*' [1943], in *Franz Grillparzer*, ed. by Helmut Bachmaier (Frankfurt a.M.: Suhrkamp, 1991), pp. 69–87 (p. 79).
72. Edmund Kostka, 'Grillparzer and the East'. *Monatshefte* 47 (1955), 273–84 (p. 280).
73. W. E. Yates, '*König Ottokars Glück und Ende* und *Der Traum ein Leben*: Realitätsbezug und Rezeptionsproblematik', *Études Germaniques*, 47 (1992), 201–14 (p. 210).
74. Prutti, *Grillparzers Welttheater*, p. 329.
75. On the issue of age in *Sappho*, see Zdenko Škreb, *Grillparzer. Eine Einführung in das dramatische Werk* (Kronberg: Scriptor, 1976), p. 119.
76. Staiger, 'Grillparzer. *König Ottokars Glück und Ende*', p. 79.
77. Prutti, *Grillparzers Welttheater*, p. 330.
78. Roger Bauer, 'Grillparzers Aufklärung', in *Zwischen Weimar und Wien. Grillparzer — Ein Innsbrucker Symposion*, ed. by Sieglinde Klettenhammer (Innsbruck: Institut für Germanistik, 1992), pp. 13–30 (p. 17).

CHAPTER 3

Women and Enlightenment

In this section, I analyse *Ein treuer Diener seines Herrn* [*A Faithful Servant of his Master*] (1826) and *Des Meeres und der Liebe Wellen* [*The Waves of the Sea and of Love*] (1831) in the context of Grillparzer's engagement with Enlightenment philosophy. The influence of Enlightenment ideals on these dramas has previously received little critical attention, but here I argue that Enlightenment thought is an important tool for understanding them. Specifically, I show that Bancbanus's refusal to abandon obedience and act rationally is a central cause of the ensuing tragedy in *Ein treuer Diener*, and that, far from being thoughtless and impulsive, Gertrude is actually the voice of reason at the Hungarian court. Additionally, I highlight the Enlightenment ideals which play a strong role in Hero's attempts at fashioning for herself an existence independent of the dominant androcentric society in which she was raised. Lamps play an important symbolic role and allude to the importance of rationality in both dramas. In *Ein treuer Diener*, Bancbanus is frequently in possession of a *Blendlaterne* [dark lantern], the light of which can be regulated or concealed. At various points, Hero is seen tending a lamp which at once represents her rationality and her desire. The symbolic importance of light in both these dramas links them and suggests that Enlightenment thought can aid an interpretation.

Widespread Austrian reception of Kantian philosophy began after the publication of the second edition of the *Kritik der reinen Vernunft* [*Critique of Pure Reason*] in 1787 (first edition 1781) made this work more accessible.[1] By 1788, the *Kritik der reinen Vernunft* was widely known in Vienna.[2] Kantian philosophy played an important role in what Werner Sauer calls the 'Rückzugsgefecht[e] der Wiener Aufklärung' [rearguard actions of the Viennese Enlightenment] in the years between 1792 and 1795.[3] The star polemicist in these debates was none other than Joseph Schreyvogel (1768–1832), future director of the Burgtheater (1814–1832), ardent follower of Kant, and Grillparzer's theatrical mentor. Schreyvogel had begun a study of Kant around 1790, and soon proved his 'glänzendes Talent, die Kantische Philosophie in die publizistische Verteidigung der Aufklärung einzubringen' [brilliant talent for introducing Kantian philosophy into the journalistic defence of the Enlightenment].[4] Austrian reception of Kant grew considerably in a short period of time, and reprints of a selection of his works in Graz between 1795 and 1797 testify to a continued broad interest.[5] When the German philosopher Lazarus Bendavid held lectures on Kant in Vienna in 1793, it was almost a fashion among the city's polite society to attend.[6] In the 1780s, a young monk at Melk Abbey was interested in

Enlightenment philosophy, and these interests influenced the texts bought for the abbey's library.[7] The latest debates on Enlightenment philosophy were followed enthusiastically, and the abbey purchased Kant's *Kritik der reinen Vernunft* in 1788. The text was read. This purchase demonstrates the efforts taken by religious figures to keep up with the 'Diskussionen einer aufgeklärten kritischen Öffentlichkeit [...], wobei konfessionelle und territoriale Schranken keine Rolle mehr spielten' [debates of an enlightened and critical public [...] in which denominational and territorial limits no longer played a role]. In Klagenfurt, the family of Franz de Paula von Herbert engaged extensively with the Enlightenment. Herbert visited Weimar and Jena in the 1780s and 1790s to study Enlightenment philosophy, and knew Wieland and Schiller.[8] After his return to Klagenfurt, his home was regularly visited by German Enlightenment figures. Herbert's daughters also read Kant, and debated with visiting philosophers.[9] Herbert's sister was a Kantian, and had a brief correspondence with the philosopher. In Carinthia, seminarians attended the lectures on Kantian philosophy given by Friedrich Karl Forberg, the German philosopher, until they were officially forbidden to do so.[10] The sisters Ursula and Babette von Dreer had their volumes of Kant disguised as prayer books because they did not want to do without them in church.[11]

Grillparzer was well acquainted with Kantian philosophy. His first encounter with Kant occurred in 1805 when, at the age of 15, he entered the university. He was first required to complete two years' philosophical training. Later, during his legal studies (1807–1809), he undertook a study of Kant.[12] According to Franz Strich, however, this early encounter was not sufficient to allow Kantian philosophy to really take hold of Grillparzer. It would be Schreyvogel, the 'Vorkämpfer Kants' [champion of Kant], who would ensure that Kant took root in the young poet.[13] Schreyvogel had spent the years 1794 to 1796 in Jena, where he met Goethe and Schiller and acquainted himself with Kant's works.[14] Schreyvogel's enthusiasm for Kant comes across in this diary entry from 1818:

> Kants Religionslehre entschädigt mich wieder für vieles Schlechte, was ich lesen muß. In diesem Manne hat sich Gottes Wort für die Menschen ganz geoffenbart.[15]
>
> [Kant's religious theory compensates me once again for the many bad things I must read. God's word has completely revealed itself for mankind in this man.]

A year earlier, he had given Grillparzer Kant's major works with the hope that his protégé might find comfort in them. Strich writes that it was only after Schreyvogel's intervention that Kantian traces are to be found in Grillparzer's notebooks. The year 1819 proved decisive in the history of Grillparzer's study of Kant, and from then on Grillparzer's aesthetics were underpinned by the *Kritik der Urteilskraft* [*Critique of Judgment*].[16] A diary entry from 1832 testifies to Grillparzer's admiration for, and ongoing interest in Kant's work: 'Alles was ich philosophisches lese, vermehrt meine Achtung für Kant.' (Nr. 2012. *HKA* II/ix, pp. 78–79.) [All the philosophy I read increases my respect for Kant.] Störi notes that, although Grillparzer's references to Kant became more seldom, they never fully disappear and are present in his last years.[17] However, Störi also cautions against concluding that the frequent mentions indicate a more detailed engagement, for sometimes Grillparzer's notes do not go beyond the mention of Kant's name, and he never made such extensive extracts from the works of Kant or any other philosopher as he did from works of history or natural sciences.

Grillparzer, whose 'intellectual allegiance to the eighteenth century [is] so clearly manifested in his works, letters and conversations', also engaged with the ideas of Josephinism.[18] His father 'war in der josephinischen Periode aufgewachsen und mochte nicht viel auf Andachtsübungen halten' [had grown up in the Josephinian period and did not think much of religious practices].[19] Although August Sauer writes that Joseph II's ideals and beliefs had too powerful a presence in Austria to be forgotten after his death, and that the emperor's influence was felt strongly in Grillparzer's household, Günter Schnitzler argues that '[d]ie ohnehin kaum ausgeprägte Programmatik des Josephinismus [...] verliert recht bald ihre Gültigkeit', and that the Josephinism of Grillparzer's age was 'eine abgemilderte katholische nachjosephinische Spät-Spätaufklärung' [the in any case barely developed programme of Josephinism [...] quickly lost its validity; a tempered, Catholic post-Josephinian late Late Enlightenment].[20] Nevertheless, Grillparzer remained 'ein unermüdlicher Verehrer, Bewunderer, Verkündiger des Kaisers [...], auch ein Anhänger und Verkündiger der josephinischen Ideen' [a tireless devotee, admirer, proclaimer of the emperor [...] and also a supporter and proclaimer of Josephinian ideas], and the deeds of Joseph's successors were measured against his.[21]

Grillparzer, then, was familiar with Kant's ideas and Enlightenment thought more generally. Of particular interest for us is *Beantwortung der Frage: Was ist Aufklärung?* [*An Answer to the Question: 'What is Enlightenment?'*] (1784), a short essay in which Kant seeks to define enlightenment. For Kant, enlightenment is the process by which an individual leaves the state of immaturity ('Unmündigkeit') which he inhabits due to a lack of resolution and courage to use his own reason independently. This form of immaturity, which does not result from a lack of intelligence, Kant calls 'selbstverschuldet[e] Unmündigkeit' [self-incurred immaturity (p. 54)]. Concluding the first paragraph of his essay, Kant writes: 'Sapere aude! Habe Mut, dich deines eigenen Verstandes zu bedienen! ist also der Wahlspruch der Aufklärung.'[22] [The motto of enlightenment is therefore: *Sapere aude!* Have courage to use your *own* understanding! (p. 54)] According to Kant, many people live in a state of self-inflicted immaturity because they are lazy and fearful; sloth and fear are also the reasons why a minority can easily position itself as guardians over the immature majority. These guardians want to keep their wards in a permanent state of immaturity and prevent any attempts at emancipation. However, Kant believes that enlightenment is inevitable if people are given freedom: some will choose to throw off the yoke of ignorance, and once they have done so, proceed to encourage others. This is a slow and arduous process which can never be replaced with revolution, as revolution would not instigate 'wahre Reform der Denkungsart' [true reform in ways of thinking (p. 55)], but merely replace old prejudices with new as the 'Leitband[] des gedankenlosen großen Haufens' [leash to control the great unthinking mass (p. 55)].[23]

Kant's essay shows traits of the misogynist discourse regarding women's social role which flourished in the decades around 1800. Although Kant claims that the majority of people consider enlightenment a scary prospect, this is especially the case among women:

> Dass der bei weitem größte Teil der Menschen (darunter das ganze schöne Geschlecht) den Schritt zur Mündigkeit außer dem, dass er beschwerlich ist, auch für sehr gefährlich halte: dafür sorgen schon jene Vormünder, die die Oberaufsicht über sie gütigst auf sich genommen haben.[24]
>
> [The guardians who have kindly taken upon themselves the work of supervision will soon see to it that by far the largest part of mankind (including the entire fair sex) should consider the step forward to maturity not only as difficult but also as highly dangerous. (p. 54)]

Kant implies that women would be particularly susceptible to their guardians' scaremongering, but also criticizes men who discourage them from independent thought. However, Hero's desire for independence and determination to rely on her own intellectual powers, as well as Gertrude's invocation of rational self-determination, mark them out as proponents of enlightenment in the sense described here by Kant. By creating Kantian heroines, Grillparzer calls into question eighteenth- and nineteenth-century theories regarding women's mental and intellectual abilities. This further supports arguments for Grillparzer's dramas to be seen as his contribution to these debates.

'Auch eine Blendlaterne bringe mir': Gender and Rationality in *Ein treuer Diener seines Herrn*

As we shall see when discussing *Des Meeres und der Liebe Wellen*, Hero's lamp is a crucial symbol of the drama's Enlightenment context and content. In *Ein treuer Diener seines Herrn*, Bancbanus's dark lantern is no less important a symbol of the Enlightenment, although it indicates that the protagonist's relationship to rationality is more fraught than Hero's. Indeed, as I show, Bancbanus's dedication to his duty is at once a symptom of his self-imposed lack of rationality and an impediment to personal development. The dark lantern features prominently in Act IV of the drama. Bancbanus demands one from his servant when he wishes to enter the royal castle in secret.[25] He appears in the queen's rooms in a cloak and with the dark lantern in hand (p. 281), and at the beginning of the next scene the stage directions again state that he is in possession of the lantern (p. 284). The utility of such an object is obvious given that Bancbanus must conceal himself from the rebels. His lantern also fulfils a metaphorical function within the drama's investigation of rationality. The dark lantern serves to protect the flame, but can also be manipulated to prohibit the release of light, and represents the difficult relationship which Bancbanus and Gertrude have when exercising their reason. Bancbanus, entrusted with the maintenance of political order in his monarch's absence, is forced throughout the play to subordinate the exercise of reason to the obedience promised to Andreas. Gertrude is the voice of reason in the drama, yet her rationality is compromised by her love for Otto. Otto represents the complete lack of reason, for he is capricious in the extreme and motivated only by self-interest.

Much of what has been written on *Ein treuer Diener seines Herrn* has focused on Grillparzer's examination of the theme of loyalty. W. E. Yates, for example, argues that while Bancbanus's whole character is not defined by loyalty, this loyalty is the basis of his tragedy. His public duty seems paramount to him.[26] Thompson is more critical when he writes that Bancbanus 'is presented with grotesque irony, as a bumbling bureaucrat, a figure of fun for courtiers and servants alike'.[27] Coenen has claimed Kantian influences and writes that one of Grillparzer's motives in writing the drama was the 'dramatization of Kant's "categorical imperative", the great philosopher's epitome of all morality which was in accord with the author's devotion to the imperial house'.[28] Ritchie Robertson also sees Bancbanus in the context of eighteenth-century thought, writing that he is 'ein ins Mittelalter zurückversetzter Staatsbeamter josephinischer Prägung' whose behaviour is best understood 'im Rahmen des christlichen Stoizismus, der dem Ethos des josephinischen Beamtentums zugrunde lag' [a Josephinian civil servant in a medieval setting; in the context of Christian stoicism, which was the basis of Josephinian officialdom's ethos].[29] Meanwhile, Roe has shown that Bancbanus's sense of duty renders him unable, or unwilling, to approach the royal family in a critical manner.[30] In other words, Bancbanus's dedication to duty prevents him from exercising his reason freely; it functions in much the same way as the panels of the dark lantern. In the opening scene, for example, a servant claims to have seen Otto among the crowd outside the window. Bancbanus's answer shows the extent to which his loyalty has clouded his judgment:

> Hätt ichs gesehn mit diesen meinen Augen,
> Weit eher glaubt ich, daß ich wachend träume,
> Als Übles von dem Schwager meines Herrn! (ll. 41–43)

[If I myself had seen with these my eyes,/ I rather should believe I, waking, dreamed/ Than think such evil of my master's kinsman! (p. 8)]

Bancbanus allows his sense of duty to inhibit his rational abilities, and would rather blindly believe in Otto's probity than trust his own observations. In the Enlightenment context in which I place this drama, Bancbanus's attitude towards reason and personal responsibility provides a stark contrast to the behaviour and personality of the queen. Indeed, his reluctance to be rationally independent, which at first glance appears to be the result of his loyalty to the crown, may simultaneously be its prerequisite.

In Act I, Grillparzer characterizes his hero as a closed-minded, myopic individual. Bancbanus sternly castigates a servant who comments about the crowds on the street below, showing the extent to which he wishes others to be constrained by a devotion to duty:

> Was kümmert dich die Straße? Sieh du hier!
> Ein jeder treibe, was ihm selber obliegt,
> Die andern mögen nur ein Gleiches tun. (ll. 6–8)

[Why trouble with the street? Your task is here!/ Let every man but mind his own affairs,/ And all his neighbors do the same as he. (p. 6)]

Bancbanus's character is shaped by this single-minded and closely focused attitude. In the first conversation between Bancbanus and Erny, his younger wife, we see that his tunnel vision leads to problems in his marriage. The revellers outside the window mock the spouses in song, stressing the age difference between husband and wife. Erny is offended by the singers' words, but Bancbanus again shows himself unaffected by the events around him: 'Ich achte nicht drauf und rate dir ein Gleiches.' (l. 86) [I paid no heed at all and on you urge the like. (p. 10)] That he hastily departs to do the king's bidding, despite Erny's unease at being left in the besieged house, is the first indication that his devotion to his public role will force him to neglect his private role.

For Bancbanus, his public role trumps the private responsibilities with which he has been entrusted. Lorenz calls Bancbanus and Erny's relationship 'die einzige gute Liebesverbindung in Grillparzers Werk, die einzige, in der von Liebe und Vertrauen, von Kommunikation und Toleranz die Rede sein kann' [the only good loving relationship in Grillparzer's work, the only in which there are love and trust, communication and tolerance].[31] The opening scene casts doubt upon Lorenz's positive assessment. If Erny trusts her husband, Grillparzer shows this trust to be misplaced. While they talk to each other, Bancbanus is clearly preoccupied with duties of state and does not pay his wife the attention she deserves. Lorenz's characterization of the marriage as a father-daughter relationship, however, is particularly apt given what we learn in Act II:

> Als Nemaret, dein Vater,
> Im Tod zusammenfügte unsre Hände,
> Der blühnden Tochter und des Jugendfreundes,
> Dem Schutz dich anvertrauend eines Gatten [...] (ll. 838–41)

[As Nemaret, your father,/ Before he died, together placed the hands/ Of his fair daughter and his boyhood friend,/ Entrusting your protection to a husband [...] (p. 50)]

This description of the couple's history places their relationship firmly within the parameters of guardianship as understood in the *ABGB* 1811. Paragraph 21 of the *ABGB* took under special legal protection those 'welche wegen Mangels an Jahren, Gebrechen des Geistes, oder anderer Verhältnisse wegen, ihre Angelegenheiten selbst gehörig zu besorgen unfähig sind' [who, due to youth, mental affliction or other circumstances, are incapable of properly managing their own affairs themselves].[32] The first category included children under the age of seven and minors who had not yet reached the age of twenty-four, while those suffering from mental health problems ('Rasende', 'Wahnsinnige') or learning difficulties ('Blödsinnige') were also mentioned. The law provided for those whose fathers had died and who were unable to manage their own affairs by means of guardians (§187). Paragraph 188 defined guardians' duties as the care for those placed under their protection and the management of their wards' money. The specifics of such arrangements are discussed in intricate detail in the *ABGB* (§187–284). The salient points for our discussion are as follows: guardians were to be named by a child's father (§198); women were generally deemed unsuitable as guardians (§192), and mothers or grandmothers who took on a ward were required to have a male co-guardian assigned to them (§211); while minors owed their guardians respect and obedience, they could also complain to relatives or the authorities if these abused their power or did not adequately fulfil their duties (§217).

Bancbanus and Erny are joined not only by the bonds of matrimony, but also by Bancbanus's role as the guardian chosen by Erny's father. Even if Erny's father were still alive, Bancbanus's role as husband could, assuming similarities between the world of the drama and Grillparzer's world as governed by the *ABGB*, have entailed a certain amount of control over Erny's wellbeing and finances. However, the fact that Nemaret's main concern was for Erny's safety indicates that her relationship with Bancbanus is primarily that of guardian and ward, rather than husband and wife. Bancbanus's speech testifies to his feelings. Politzer notes that, until her death, he calls her 'Kind' [child] and seldom refers to her as a woman: 'Treibt es ihn, ihr seine Väterlichkeit als ein Prinzip einzuschärfen, an dem nicht gerüttelt werden darf?' [Does he feel the need to impress upon her his fatherliness as an unshakeable principle?][33] From Bancbanus's point of view, it would certainly make sense to instil in Erny a sense of his paternal role in her life if he considered himself first and foremost her guardian.

The exact nature of their relationship, whether principally a marriage or a guardianship, does not mitigate Bancbanus's neglect of Erny. Both as a guardian and as a husband, Bancbanus has an obligation towards Erny and is partially responsible for her safety and security. Her suicide in Act III shows how severely he failed in this duty. It is his inability to critically assess the royals, and in particular Otto, which makes Bancbanus oblivious to the danger which Erny faces. In Act II he again casts doubts on claims against the prince and bemoans the lack of respect for the royals (ll. 545–49). Although earlier in the act he opposed Gertrude's summary granting of petitions — 'Gewährt! gewährt! Lag diese Schrift nicht vor,/ So war nichts zu gewähren!' (ll. 449–50) [You granted the request? How could you grant it/ Without the testament I hold? (p. 30)] — and thereby royal prerogative, he here insists that the petitioner show respect for Otto because he is Gertrude's brother.

As Bancbanus deals with supplicants in Act II, his brother and brother-in-law storm into the room, angered by Otto's wooing of Erny (ll. 583–85). Bancbanus is resigned to the situation — 'Ich kann's nicht ändern!/ Kann ihn nicht ändern, wollt' ich's noch so gern.' (ll. 585–86) [Can I change that?/ Can I change him, no matter how I try? (p. 38)] — finds it self-evident that Erny should dance with Otto, as she was invited to a dance, and is confident that she will not reciprocate Otto's affections. Bancbanus's attitude does not change when faced with the appeals for protection from Erny herself. When she arrives at Bancbanus's side, she is 'erhitzt und schwer atmend' (p. 222) [her face is flushed and she breathes quickly (p. 40)], suggesting that her flight from the party was hurried. The speed with which she disappeared from the celebrations — as Otto says, 'Mit Eins war sie verschwunden' (l. 605) [She vanished all at once (p. 40)] — shows how unpleasant the prince's attentions were. Her first words on seeing Bancbanus are 'Hier, endlich hier! Nun,

Gott sei tausend Dank!' (l. 614) [Here, here at last! To God my deepest thanks! (p. 40)], and everything she says to him during this scene shows the extent to which she sees him as her protector: 'Nun ist es gut! Weil nur bei dir! O Gut!' (l. 619) [Now all is well! To be with you! How good! (p. 40)] and

> Ich weiche nicht von deiner Seite!
> So drück ich mich in deine Nähe, so.
> Trotz sei geboten, wer von hier mich trennt! (ll. 622–24)

> [I will not ever leave your side!/ Thus I will seek a refuge near you, thus./ And I defy him who would drive me forth. (p. 41)]

Bancbanus does not recognize the fear in Erny's words. He is more worried that, having exerted herself in dance, she might now become ill, and he chastises her: 'Du böses Kind, was machst du mir für Sorge!' (l. 618) [You naughty child, how much concern you cause me! (p. 40)] Again, we see that Bancbanus thinks of Erny as a child rather than his wife.

Bancbanus and Erny's problems partly stem from his inability or unwillingness to reconcile his two roles: the private role of guardian and husband to Erny, and the public role of regent. It is Bancbanus, in conversation with Erny, who makes clear that his public role necessitates sacrifices from both spouses in the public sphere:

> BANCBANUS Bancbanus' Weib steht gut in seiner Nähe,
>   Des Reichsverwesers Frau gehört zum Fest.
> ERNY   Gib sie zurück denn, dieses Amtes Bürde,
>   Sei Ernys Gatte bloß, mit ihr beglückt.
> BANCBANUS Was fällt dir ein? Weil du nicht gern beim Fest,
>   Soll ich von Hof, Unfrieden herrschen lassen
>   [...]
>   Dem Dienst folg ich, folg dem Feste du! (ll. 630–35, 640)

> [BANCBANUS: Bancbanus' mate may rightly stay with him,/ The regent's wife must share the courtiers' feast. ERNY: Then give it back, the burden of this office,/ Be Erny's husband only, quite content. BANCBANUS: What foolish words! Because you would not dance,/ Am I to leave, and let unrest grow rife/ [...]/ You seek the dance, I shall my duty do. (p. 41)]

Peter Lattmann argues that Bancbanus differentiates so absolutely between his public and private personae 'dass es scheint, als habe der Reichsverweser mit dem Gatten nichts gemeinsam' [that it seems as if the imperial administrator had nothing in common with the husband].[34] This attitude is clearly demonstrated in this scene, not least in Bancbanus's ascription to Erny of public and private personae analogous to his: Erny is at once 'Bancbanus' Weib' and 'des Reichsverwesers Frau', and each role requires different duties of her. This division of one individual into public and private personae is a key concern in Grillparzer's dramas and can also be seen in *Sappho*, *Des Meeres und der Liebe Wellen* and *Die Jüdin von Toledo* for example. For his part, Bancbanus is clear that he owes his primary obligation to the state, and he is determined to honour his promise to Andreas, 'trifft was immer zu.' (l. 639) [let what will ensue (p. 41).] According to Max Kommerell, Bancbanus's loyalty to Andreas is so central to his identity 'daß es am Ende scheint, als hätte das Göttliche in ihm Knechtsgestalt angenommen' [that in the end it seems as if the divine had taken on the form of a servant in him].[35] Bancbanus's relationship with Erny, and his inability to judge Otto accurately, prove to be catalysts for Erny's death rather than safeguards against harm, not least because it is precisely this relationship which puts Erny in danger. Erny, Otto confesses, is of less interest in her own right than because of her ties to Bancbanus: 'Beachtet man so wenig unser Tun?/ [...] / Ich will ihn reizen, will! und gält's das Ärgste!' (ll. 123–25) [Do they regard so little what we do?/ [...] / I must enrage him, must, let come what may! (p. 13)] and 'Den Mann zu ärgern gilts, der meiner Werbung/ Durch seine Sicherheit zu spotten scheint' (ll. 184–85) [My wish is to enrage the man who seems/ To mock my suit by staying calm and sure (p. 16)].[36]

Bancbanus's tenuous relationship with rationality does not prevent him from allowing Erny the exercise of free will. In part, he neglects her precisely because he believes her to be endowed with enough intelligence to fend for herself. Lorenz writes that 'Bancbans Insistieren auf dem freien Willen seiner Frau, gleich, was die Sitte diktiert, ist eine neue, fortschrittliche Haltung' [Bancbanus's insistence on his wife's free will, regardless of the diktats of custom, is a new, progressive attitude].[37] She goes so far as to call Bancbanus a 'feministischer Mann' [feminist man] whose revolutionary attitude towards his wife frightens her. Coenen agrees, and writes that Bancbanus 'is the modern husband who wants a "free" wife whom he trusts rather than a husband who considers his wife a chattel'.[38] Robertson notes that Bancbanus, rather than succumbing to jealousy, has faith in his wife's fidelity.[39] Bancbanus's attitude cannot, however, be seen quite as positively as Lorenz would wish, not least because the genesis of this attitude is unclear: does Bancbanus really believe that Erny can defend herself, or does this belief arise from his realization that his public duties preclude the protection she needs? In other words, is a self-sufficient Erny merely a fiction which assuages Bancbanus's unease regarding his inability to protect her?

Erny's words before her encounter with Otto in Act II show that she believes the prevailing opinion of her as a helpless woman to be mistaken:

> (Im Vorgrunde stehend, und die Locken an den Fingern aufwickelnd.)
> Sie glauben, weil ich selten sprech und wenig,
> Ich könne mich nicht wahren, nicht verteidgen.
> Mein Vater sprach wohl oft: sie hats im Nacken!
> Ich hab es auch. Ihr sollt noch wahrlich sehn! (ll. 663–66)

> [(stands at the front of the stage, turning her curls on her fingers) They think, because I speak not much and seldom,/ I cannot guard myself, cannot protect./ My father often said, Her neck is hard!/ And so it is. You shall have cause to know! (p. 43)]

Although Grillparzer undermines this confident assertion by presenting Erny playing with her hair, she shows herself determined to resist Otto's advances. After her encounter with Otto in Act II, Erny begs Bancbanus to punish and protect her, an idea which he finds laughable (ll. 812–19). As far as Bancbanus is concerned, such practices are foreign and unchristian. He goes on to suggest that the age difference between himself and Erny is enough to exonerate any misdeeds on her part, and almost seems to take her infidelity for granted.

Bancbanus is clearly not of the same species as Ottokar or Jason, for example, yet his 'fortschrittliche Haltung', to quote Lorenz, in matters of women's rights is nevertheless damaging to Erny. The freedom, or lack of protection, which he grants Erny is the result of love for her and regard for her as an individual, but it is also the result of his inability to recognize society for what it is. During his conversation with Erny, Otto betrays his objectifying view of women. He calls himself a 'Menschenkenner [...], Menschenforscher' (l. 699) [A connoisseur am I of human nature (p. 44)] who is particularly interested in women. He accuses women, and Erny in particular, of hypocrisy: 'Ihr aber scheinet Tauben, fromme Tauben,/ Und seids in Einem nur, in ewger Glut.' (ll. 705–06) [You women pose as doves, as pious doves,/ But are doves only in unstilled desire. (p. 45)] Otto's attitude towards women shows that not all share Bancbanus's progressive opinions, and that Bancbanus might actually be endangering Erny by failing to protect her. Otto's claim that Erny, like all women, is defined by sexuality is in his mind justification for his aggressively sexual behaviour towards her. Perhaps unsurprisingly, Otto is blind to the fact that the hypocrisy of which he accuses Erny is in all likelihood little more than her attempt at suppressing any sexual desires she might have in the name of female chastity and purity as demanded by society. Even Bancbanus, liberal though he seems in such matters, values female chastity highly: 'Die Ehre einer Frau ist eine ehrne Mauer,/ Wer sie durchgräbt, der spaltet Quadern auch.' (ll. 820–21) [A woman's honor stands like granite walls;/ Who pierces them, could cleave the living stone. (p. 50)]

It is not surprising that, considering the drama's focus on questions of duty, Bancbanus has received more attention in scholarship than the other characters. Gertrude, for example, has received short shrift from the majority of Grillparzer scholars. Politzer writes that Gertrude's desires have led her to disregard the limits placed on women,[40] while Yates remarks upon her lack of normal femininity.[41] Yates sees Bancbanus and Erny as characters defined by a high moral sense of duty, whereas Gertrude and Otto are essentially selfish. Kurt Frieberger labels the siblings 'die Maßlosen' [the immoderates] and sees in this the rationale behind Andreas's decision to leave the reins of power in Bancbanus's hands.[42] Peter Lattmann sees Gertrude's resolve as a mask which will fall as soon as her love for Otto triumphs over her. He sees in Gertrude's imperious behaviour an element of self-restraint: 'Eine prall mit Leidenschaft gefüllte Beherrschtheit ist ihr Wesen' [Her being is self-control filled to bursting with passion].[43]

While Thompson identifies Gertrude's tendency to allow emotion to cloud her judgment,[44] Wolf-Cirian sees her as the female character in Grillparzer's works who is most able to subordinate feeling to reason.[45] Yet for Wolf-Cirian, Gertrude's superior intellect and her knowledge thereof go hand in hand with an unfeminine hardness; in effect, Gertrude's intellect takes her out of the sphere of the feminine.[46] Wolf-Cirian sees in Gertrude's superior capabilities Grillparzer's criticism of unfeminine women. Here I argue for a revision of this opinion. In creating Gertrude, a woman who is more 'masculine', more independent and more rational than either Otto or Bancbanus, Grillparzer calls into question the validity of rigid gender dichotomies.

Gertrude's appearance in Act I provides much grist for the mills of those who would portray her as a particularly sensuous figure. As elsewhere in his dramas, Grillparzer uses costumes for illustrative purposes. Gertrude's nightgown is contrasted with Andreas's armour: she belongs in the private sphere, the home, while he is soon to enter the battlefield; her sensual apparel alludes to Andreas's duties as husband, while his armour shows his dedication to his political duties. Thompson sees this outfit as indicative of 'a hint of sensuality in her, of slovenliness, and of a disregard for the dignity of office'.[47] Andreas makes a distinction between his private and public personae similar to that made by Bancbanus:

> Schon eine Stunde gab dir der Gemahl,
> Der König darf dir keine zweite geben.
> Der Tag bricht an, das Heer erwartet mich. (ll. 216–18)

> [One hour of time your spouse has granted you,/ The king may not accord a moment more./ The dawn has come, the army stands in wait. (p. 18)]

Bancbanus and Andreas both prioritize their public roles: neither allows himself to be distracted by the needs or desires of his wife. Andreas renounces the conjugal pleasures which Gertrude offers as an enticement to stay, which refutes August Sauer's claim that Gertrude dominates her husband,[48] as does Andreas's refusal to endow his wife with any real power during his absence, a fact which does not elude Frieberger.[49] The wording of Andreas's speech makes clear that, although Gertrude will be regent in his absence, the real power will lie with Bancbanus:

> Sie wird im Rate sitzen,
> Vollziehn mit Unterfertigung das Geschäft.
> [...]
> Was Gnade gibt, empfängt man nur durch sie.
> In Sachen bloß des Rechts, und was noch sonst
> Des kühlern Blicks bedarf, und dies Papier benennt,
> Stell ich an ihre Seite zum Genossen,
> Der auch im Rate sitzt, und ohne den
> Nichts von dem übrigen auch wird verhandelt [...]
> (ll. 366–67, 369–74)

> [She will take a seat in council,/ Transact all business, sign all documents [...]/ And clemency is hers alone to show./ In matters of the law and what else needs/ Calm vision, as denoted in this brief,/ I place beside her as a trusty aide/ Who sits in council too and has a voice/ In every judgment that demands debate [...] (p. 25)]

The relegation of legal matters to subordinate status ('in Sachen bloß des Rechts') is designed to distract Gertrude's focus onto matters which she thinks important but which are secondary, while Andreas's delegation to Bancbanus of those matters which require impartial consideration shows a lack of confidence in Gertrude's ability to act as regent. As Frieberger writes, Andreas leaves the reins of government in Bancbanus's hands because he is aware of Gertrude's and Otto's lack of moderation.[50]

Gertrude's significance as both a proponent of reason and a practitioner of unreason results from her gender-defying self-identification. Grillparzer's dramas often depend on the subversion of nineteenth-century gender paradigms, presenting as they often do women of fortitude and courage opposite vacillating and capricious men, but Gertrude most explicitly grapples with an identity which fails to conform to society's expectations of her. Gertrude's account of her childhood shows the extent to which she was limited by her sex. Already in childhood she and Otto were consigned to separate spheres of experience, and it was only through imagination and identification with her brother that she was able to experience something outside the domestic arena:

> Ich grollte stets, daß ich ein Mädchen war,
> Ein Knabe wünscht' ich mir zu sein, wie Otto.
> Er wuchs heran, in ihm war ich ein Jüngling,
> In ihm ging ich zur Jagd, bestieg das Roß,
> In ihm lockt ich des Burgwarts blöde Töchter. —
> Ihr wißt, wie ich die Zucht als Weib gehalten,
> Doch tat mirs wohl, in seinem kecken Tun
> Traumweis zu überfliegen jene Schranken,
> In die ein enger Kreis die Weiber bannt. (ll. 322–30)

> [My plaint it was that I was born a girl;/ I wished to be a boy, a boy like him./ He grew, in him I felt myself a lad,/ In him I went to hunt and rode a horse,/ In him enticed the keeper's stupid daughters. — / You know how I have kept the woman's code,/ Yet I was pleased in all his daring acts/ To fly in dreams beyond the rigid bounds/ In which a woman's actions lie confined. (p. 22)]

Gertrude's conflicted self-image arises from the disparity between her capabilities and desires and the role she was expected to play. As a child, Gertrude resented her sex and its social limitations, and seems to have maintained the appearance of femininity despite much reluctance. This could in part explain her determination to be named regent in Andreas's absence, and it seems that Andreas reached his decision only after considerable lobbying on Gertrude's part.

Gertrude, like Eleonore in *Die Jüdin von Toledo*, displays considerable power as a manipulator of language and of men's conceptions of passive womanhood. On the one hand, Gertrude is proud of her unwomanly character, boasting to Andreas:

> Ihr nanntet oft mich stolz,
> Ein kühnes Weib, vergleichbar einem Mann.
> Ich wars, ich bins! Und doch — seht mich hier knien. (ll. 299–301)

> [You often called me proud,/ A daring woman, bold as any man./ I was, I am! And yet — you see me kneel. (p. 21)]

By kneeling she emphasizes her weakness and subordinate position, but in doing so impresses on both Andreas and the audience that this subordination is exceptional. She again shows that weakness is alien to her when she tells Andreas, 'Ihr seht mich schwach; ich schäme mich' (l. 311) [You see me weak; I am ashamed (p.

22)]. In employing an illusion of weakness with the aim of winning political gain, Gertrude embodies the femininity which inspires Alfonso's remark in *Die Jüdin von Toledo* that the fair sex 'ist stark erst wenn es schwach' [shows its strength by being weak]. Gertrude subtly questions the necessity of male dominance in politics while simultaneously manipulating Andreas's belief in the legitimacy of this principle to secure Otto's nomination as co-regent:

> Ihr habt erklärt,
> Ob nun mit Recht, mit Unrecht, stell ich hin,
> Daß manches sich ergibt im Kreis des Herrschers,
> Das rasch persönliches, selbsteignes Walten,
> Zutun und Fassen fordert und bedingt
> Und eines Männerarms bedarf. (ll. 233–38)

[You have explained — / If you were right or wrong I leave unasked — / That much develops in a ruler's sphere,/ Which calls for personal and rapid action,/ An independent manner, prompt dispatch/ Such as a man alone can give. (p. 19)]

Once it becomes clear how strongly Andreas opposes Otto's nomination, Gertrude skilfully changes tack, arguing that it will be she who manages Otto, thereby negating his role as her representative in inherently masculine matters of state:

> Gebt meinen Bruder mir als Reichsgehilfen!
> Gönnt ihm den Namen nur! Ich will ihn hüten,
> Er soll nichts tun, um was ich nicht gewußt.
> Wie einem Vogel man die Flügel schneidet,
> Nun hüpft er frei, und dünkt sich frei, und ists nicht.
> So will ich halten ihn, mit Liebe füttern,
> Und er soll Dank mir zwitschern, und gedeihn. (ll. 302–08)

[Appoint my brother, let him rule with me!/ Grant him the name at least! I shall keep watch/ And see that he does only what I know./ As one may clip the pinions of a bird,/ He then goes free, thinks he is free, though not,/ Thus will I keep him, feed him with love,/ And he shall twitter thanks to me and thrive. (p. 21)]

Although the siblings are now adults, the relationship has not advanced significantly, and as far as Gertrude is concerned Otto is still 'die Puppe, die ich tändelnd schmückte' (l. 319) [the doll whom I adorned at play (p. 22)]: now, however, Gertrude embellishes him with meaningless titles rather than jewellery. Gertrude lived through Otto in her childhood, and now she attempts to do the same. It is Gertrude, however, who is in control, and Otto is the powerless male figurehead which gives Gertrude's regency its legitimacy.

Although Andreas does not give Gertrude anything more than a ceremonial role, and leaves without installing Otto in any official position, it is only because he is strong enough to resist Gertrude's rhetorical onslaught. Before Gertrude's impassioned intercession on Otto's behalf, Andreas refused to invest him with any authority on the grounds that his immoderate nature was incompatible with the Hungarians' national character. After Gertrude's speech in which she declares her deep love for Otto, however, he promises to speak with Otto. It is clear that

Andreas remains unconvinced of Otto's suitability for the role of co-regent, for he says, 'Was machst du, Weib, aus mir?' (l. 335) [What would you make of me? (p. 22)] He eventually decides against giving Otto any power, but it is evident that the otherwise rational and moderate king has been affected by his wife's words.

While announcing Gertrude's role as his representative, Andreas makes her aware how exceptional the situation is: 'Die Königinnen saßen sonst am Kunkel,/ Solang ihr Mann im Feld.' (ll. 404–05) [Queens formerly were wont to sit and spin/ While husbands were at war. (p. 26)] This presumably is a sign that he recognizes her unusual strength of character. However, it is only when Gertrude and Otto are contrasted, and her rationality comes to the fore, that we really see how far her character deviates from nineteenth-century ideals. By contrasting the siblings as he does, Grillparzer undermines these ideals and the social realities which they underpin.

Gertrude ignores the role she plays in creating the irrational and immoderate Otto. In her metaphors, Otto is either a doll to be dressed up or a bird whose wings can be clipped. She deprives him of both freedom and rationality. It is clear that she actively encourages his dissipated lifestyle, stating in Act II, 'Was Scherz ist, tadl' ich nicht' (l. 502) [I chide none for a jest. (p. 33)], and later assisting in his plan to seduce Erny. The most interesting indication of the extent to which Otto is dependent on his sister comes at the close of Act II. Gertrude has separated Otto from Erny, ordering the latter to leave. Otto refuses to let Erny go, but Gertrude forbids him to follow her with the words, 'Du wirst [bleiben], denn ich befehl es.' (l. 902) [You will [stay], for I command — (p. 53)] Gertrude is permissive to an extent, but demands absolute obedience at what, to Otto, must seem arbitrary moments. Gertrude ascribes Otto's behaviour to madness, but it seems that it is precisely this accusation which induces mental instability:

> KÖNIGIN   Unsinniger! Wie weit geht deine Tollheit?
> OTTO   Und bin ich toll, so wahrt euch vor dem Tollen.
>   Du hasts gesagt, und so berühr mich nicht!
>   Hin auf den Boden werf ich meinen Leib,
>   (Er wirft sich zur Erde.)
>   Und mit den Händen greif ich in den Grund.
>   Nicht hören und nicht reden! Rase, stirb! (ll. 904–09)

[QUEEN: You reckless boy! Your madness goes too far! OTTO: If I am mad, then watch the madman well./ You call me mad, then keep your hands from me!/ I throw my body down upon the ground,/ (*throws himself on the ground*)/ And with my hands I dig into the earth./ I will not hear nor speak! Rave on and die! (p. 54)]

It is as if Gertrude's accusation of madness is understood by Otto as a command which he cannot but follow. But the mechanical way in which he acts his madness, with running commentary, betrays its falsehood. Otto's inability to act or think independently means he must accept Gertrude's explanation of his behaviour and conform to it.

Gertrude's role as an enlightenment figure in the play is best displayed in Act III. She has received word of Otto's illness, and discusses the matter with the doctor.

She declares Otto insane and reason the only cure: '[...] gegen Tollheit/ Gibt es ein einzig Mittel nur: Vernunft./ Er mag sich selber heilen, sagt ihm das.' (ll. 953–55) [madness needs/ One remedy alone: plain common sense./ The prince must cure himself, you tell him that. (p. 58)] She becomes even more resolute when she hears of Otto's violent outburst:

> Es ist genug! Das Rasen hab ein Ende!
> [...]
> Ob Wahrheit, oder Wahn, ob Kraft, ob Ohnmacht,
> Es sei im Klaren, und es sei geheilt. (ll. 984, 986–87)
>
> [It is enough! This frenzied rage must cease!/ [...] / Though it be fact or fancy, strength or weakness,/ Let it be clear and then let it be cured. (p. 59)]

Gertrude is here presented as the voice of reason, as opposed to Otto, who is characterized by weakness and madness. For Gertrude, sanity — or, as she puts it, truth — is indivisible from power, while weakness and insanity are bedfellows. Gertrude's attitude towards Otto's illness, that it is a self-inflicted ailment which he can cure himself, if he acts rationally, echoes Kant's essay, in which the philosopher describes *Unmündigkeit* as a self-inflicted evil.

Gertrude's role as a figure of enlightenment is more problematic than Hero's because she believes that rational behaviour can be enforced by royal command. When Gertrude enters Otto's room in Act III, she finds the curtains closed on his orders and demands that they be opened. The doctor objects, but Gertrude is insistent: 'Ich aber will's, gehorche!' (l. 999) [But I command. Obey! (p. 61)] With this command, Gertrude wins the battle of light over darkness. In conversation with Otto, she then declares that she will not tolerate his behaviour, '[a]m mindsten, wo ich Frau und Königin.' (l. 1037) [Here least of all where I am reigning queen. (p. 63)] Additionally, she declares her desire, 'Wunder zu versuchen!' (l. 1038) [to try a miracle (p. 63)], and commands Otto: 'Steh auf und sei gesund! sprech ich zu dir./ Steh auf, und zwar zur Stelle! Jetzt! Ich will's!' (ll. 1039–40) [Arise and walk! Be well, I say to you./ Arise without delay! I so command! (p. 63)] Gertrude's attitude towards rationality, which relies on enforced rational behaviour and even on the supernatural, defies the ideal laid down by Kant, which is dependent on an individual's free exercise of her intellectual capabilities. This stands in stark contrast to Hero's conviction in her own capability and her desire for an independent life of self-determination. As we shall see, Hero recognizes the tensions inherent in her role as a free-thinking individual who commands others. Gertrude does not see this contradiction. Despite Gertrude's advocacy for rational behaviour, it is her irrationality which leads to Erny's death. Gertrude loves her brother dearly, and this love finds expression in the leniency with which she treats him. She is desperate to dissuade him from leaving Hungary, and agrees to trick Erny into a private meeting with him. Yet her words show how conflicted she is over her complicity in Otto's machinations; she knows that she has not just effaced her royal dignity, but also acted irrationally:

> Nun aber hör! Ich weiß, was ich verletze,
> Wie sehr zu tadeln, daß ich mich gefügt,

> Verdammlich ist die Liebe, meine Liebe,
> Die du mißbrauchst, und doch so teuer mir. (ll. 1128–31)
>
> [But now give heed! I know the wrong I do,/ How much I merit blame that I consented./ Love is an evil, wayward thing, my love/ Which you abuse and yet is dear to me. (p. 67)]

Like Hero, Gertrude knows that her emotions are causing her to act irrationally. By allowing her love for Otto to override her better judgment, Gertrude fails Otto, who so clearly needs her guidance, and Erny, who commits suicide rather than be abducted by Otto. Bancbanus, on the other hand, is not aware of the negative repercussions for others of his own devotion to duty.

Gertrude and Bancbanus both fail those who depend on them when they act in an irrational manner. The difference between the two characters, however, lies in their awareness of their failings. Bancbanus allows his loyalty to the crown to blind him to his private responsibilities to Erny, and to the danger she faces. Such is the strength of his dedication to Andreas that he is barely aware that his role as regent prevents him from protecting Erny as he should. Gertrude, on the other hand, is aware that emotions affect her ability to act rationally, and decries the power they exert on her. Bancbanus's dark lantern, the light of which can be obscured at will, is an apt prop for this drama in which selective rationality plays such a central role. It is Bancbanus and Gertrude who prevent their own rational behaviour, thereby placing others in danger. In *Des Meeres und der Liebe Wellen*, Grillparzer investigates the nature of reason and the limits placed on its use by authority figures.

'Ich denke künftig selbst mir zu gebieten': Hero, Enlightenment Ideals and Female Emancipation

The aim of this section is to offer a new reading of *Des Meeres und der Liebe Wellen*. I highlight the Enlightenment ideals which play a strong role in Hero's attempts at fashioning for herself an existence independent of the dominant androcentric society in which she was raised. In addition to the issues discussed earlier, Kant's focus on enlightenment in matters of religion is also important for a study of this drama, insofar as Grillparzer's Priest heads an organization which seeks to inhibit the use of individual reason among the people of Sestos, and is therefore an opponent of Hero's enlightenment. For Kant, the freedom to use one's reason independently is a cornerstone of human progress; any attempts by individuals or groups to prevent others from exercising this freedom must be seen as an offence against humanity:

> Ein Zeitalter kann sich nicht verbünden und darauf verschwören, das folgende in einen Zustand zu setzen, darin es ihm unmöglich werden muss, seine (vornehmlich so sehr angelegentliche) Erkenntnisse zu erweitern, von Irrtümern zu reinigen und überhaupt in der Aufklärung weiterzuschreiten. Das wäre ein Verbrechen gegen die menschliche Natur, deren ursprüngliche Bestimmung gerade in diesem Fortschreiten besteht [...].[51]
>
> [One age cannot enter into an alliance on oath to put the next age in a position where it would be impossible for it to extend and correct its knowledge, particularly on such important matters, or to make any progress whatsoever in

enlightenment. This would be a crime against human nature, whose original destiny lies precisely in such progress. (p. 57)]

Although both are adherents of the same religion, Hero's aims stand in opposition to those of the Priest. For Hero, the ability to exercise her reason independently is, in part, the motivation behind her entrance into the temple. However, the temple is no less patriarchal and misogynistic than the lay society, the cruelty and oppression of which Hero hopes to escape by becoming a priestess. As the leader of this religious order, the Priest needs to maintain his authority — both as a religious figure and as a man — and doing so necessitates the suppression of Hero's intellectual and rational insurrection.

Hero may seem a strange choice as a proponent of Enlightenment. Indeed, it is not clear that this was Grillparzer's intention when he began the drama. In 1820, he wrote: 'Wie kein Mann [Hero] rühren kann, und sie Priesterin der Venus wird' [As no man can touch [Hero], and she becomes a priestess of Venus] (1820. Nr. 322. *HKA* II/vii, p. 141), which positions Hero's decision to enter the monastery as the result of romantic misfortune. This is hardly the explanation which Hero herself gives, namely that her decision was motivated by a desire to live independently and escape the oppression of the outside world. In the same note, Grillparzer stresses her sensuality, which although not absent from the final drama, does play second fiddle to her rationality: 'Vierter Akt. Hero mit dem Gefühle als Weib.' [Fourth Act. Hero with the emotions of a woman.] However, it would be another eleven years before the drama was finished, and Grillparzer's avowed central focus on Hero (*HKA* I/xvi, p. 231) means that he could have introduced more complex narratives. For many scholars, Hero represents an antithesis to Sappho. While Sappho is the remarkable poet who has been singled out by the gods' multifarious gifts, Hero is nothing more than average. For Politzer, her existence and decisions seem to be defined by negation: she enters the temple to escape her family. He describes her as spoilt and arrogant, arguing that she sees life as a priestess as a privilege rather than as an obligation.[52] For Kurt Adel, she is little more than a 'frohes und stolzes Mädchen' [happy and proud girl] at the beginning of the drama.[53] Coenen writes that Hero's 'self-sufficiency is not egotistical presumption, but the logical outgrowth of her immaturity and the melancholy outlook on life which her childhood experiences had given her.'[54] In Ernst Fischer's view, Hero feels she is destined for better things, even though she does not have Sappho's talent, and would be better suited for ordinary life than for the temple.[55] Lorenz paints a negative portrait of Hero: the young priestess has no intellectual or spiritual capacities which make her exceptional; she is a 'Durchschnittsmädchen' [average girl]; her difficulties do not result from her brilliance.[56] Indeed, Hero herself corroborates Lorenz's arguments: in the opening act, she acknowledges that she has not been given the gift of clairvoyance with the pragmatic utterance, 'Verschiednes geben Götter an Verschiedne;/ Mich haben sie zur Seh'rin nicht bestimmt.' [The gods give different things to different men;/ They have not destined me to be a seer. (p. 14)][57] Instead of a heavenly experience, she turns her hand to weaving wreaths of flowers. This episode highlights her affinity for action rather than contemplation. Later, Hero bemoans her lack of musical ability, not least, apparently, because music-making would provide a distraction from the thoughts that throng in her mind (ll. 1049–53). Yet Hero is far from the average woman, and even the Priest mentions her 'heller Sinn' (l. 1756) [clear mind (p. 92)]. Contrasting Hero with her mother cannot but lead to the conclusion that Hero is indeed an 'Ausnahmegestalt' [exceptional figure], to borrow a term from Lorenz, and that the quality which makes her so is her determination to forge for herself an independent, analytical existence far removed from that which her mother has endured.

In making his Hero an Enlightenment figure, Grillparzer strays significantly from his source material. Frank and Pörnbacher discern considerable similarities between Grillparzer's drama and Christopher Marlowe's *Hero and Leander* (1598), and cite this as Grillparzer's main source (*SW* I, p. 1244). Grillparzer himself mentions Marlowe's poem in his diary (1822. Nr. 1239. *HKA* II/viii, p. 96), although he does not indicate whether he read or was influenced by it. Grillparzer was also familiar with Schiller's ballad 'Hero und Leander' (1801), and the lovers' letters in Ovid's *Heroides* (*HKA* I/iv, p. ix). It is Ovid's Hero who comes closest to Grillparzer's. In Epistle XIX, from Hero to Leander, she mentions the unequal positions of men and women in society, although she does not question the status quo. Leander can distract himself in any number of ways, whether in the courts of justice or the palæstra, but for Hero, 'removed from these *pursuits*, nothing is left to do, even if I were inflamed less intensely, but to love.'[58] Marlowe emphasizes Hero's beauty — 'HERO the fair,/ Whom young Apollo courted for her hair'[59] — and devotes many lines to the pair's amorous exploits: 'O who can tell the greeting/ These greedy lovers had at their first meeting!/ He ask'd — she gave — and nothing was denied.'[60] In Marlowe's poem there is no sense of Hero as an intellectual and questioning being. The same can be said of Schiller's ballad, which focuses on the lovers' relationship, rather than Hero's intellect.

In the course of the conversation between Hero and her mother in Act I, a grim picture emerges of the life endured by the two women in their family home. Hero enjoyed a materially privileged upbringing: she refers to her father's house as 'reich' (l. 291) [spacious (p. 19)] and mentions servants (l. 292). Indeed, if we wish to put this upbringing in a nineteenth-century context, the material conditions of the household seem to be equivalent to those which prevailed in the homes of the Viennese bourgeoisie. That Hero's subjective appraisal of this household is so negative illustrates the extent to which she and her mother suffered at the hands of male relatives. Hero, talking to her mother, refers to the family home as 'deiner dunkeln Sorgen niedre Hütte' (l. 288) [gloomy cares beneath a lowly roof (p. 19)]. She has difficulty uttering the word 'father', preferring the formulation 'dein Gatte' [your husband (p. 19)] when speaking with her mother. Additionally, on first seeing her parents, Hero talks almost exclusively to her mother, even though it is her father who is more dominant.

Earlier in the first act, Hero recounts the cruel conditions of her childhood. Her father 'drängte mich, und zürnte ohne Grund./ Die Mutter duldete und schwieg.' (ll. 203–04) [harassed me and for no reason raged./ My mother suffered and stayed mute. (pp. 14–15)] Her brother used her as a 'Spielwerk seiner Launen'

(l. 208) [plaything of his whims (p. 15)]. Hero's father gives ample examples of his misogyny and disrespect for his wife. He displays his frustration and mocks her intellectual abilities (ll. 253–57). He is suspicious of Hero's private conversation with her mother, observing the women so closely that his wife becomes anxious. His behaviour also indicates the inherited quality of social misogyny which reigns in Hero's surroundings. Hero's father calls for her uncle's support for his misogynistic views (ll. 256–57), which both brothers presumably inherited from their father, and which the Priest later displays; and, as demonstrated by Hero's description of her upbringing, her brother imbibed and practised the misogyny he witnessed in his father. Konrad Schaum decries the conditions in which Hero and her mother live as 'die Tradition eines unmenschlichen Willensbarbarismus, der im Grunde nichts anderes als Gefangenschaft im Ich bedeutet' [the tradition of an inhuman and intentional barbarism, which essentially means nothing other than imprisonment in the ego].[61]

It is in the differing reactions of Hero and her mother to this patriarchal society that Hero's exceptional nature is best seen. As Lorenz points out, Hero's mother has internalized the demands of patriarchal society and can see no alternative way of life.[62] Hero's mother's statement, 'Das Weib ist glücklich nur an Gattenhand' (l. 320) [A woman to be happy must be wed (p. 20)], demonstrates this. Despite her own unhappy marriage, she cannot imagine any existence for a woman other than life at the side of a husband. Hero is infuriated by her mother's stance and rebukes her. In doing so, she makes the case for women's equality with men:

> Das darfst du sagen, ohne zu erröten?
> Wie? und mußt hüten jenes Mannes Blick,
> Des Herren, deines Gatten? Darfst nicht reden,
> Mußt schweigen, flüstern, ob du gleich im Recht,
> Ob du die Weisre gleich, stillwaltend Beßre?
> Und wagst zu sprechen mir ein solches Wort? (ll. 321–26)

> [You dare say that without a blush of shame?/ You, who must be aware of that man's glance,/ Your husband, lord and master; dare not speak,/ Must whisper, hold your tongue, though you are right,/ Though wiser far and better, self-contained./ You venture to address such words to me? (pp. 20–21)]

The force of such statements has not been missed by previous critics, even if they have been described in negative terms: Politzer, for example, writes that Hero's 'ungestüme[s] Emanzipationsbedürfnis' [impetuous need for emancipation] makes her sound like a suffragette.[63] For Ulrike Tanzer they remain positive, and she argues that Hero's statement is 'zweifellos bemerkenswert und konterkariert die zeitgenössischen Vorstellungen von den Geschlechtercharakteren' [without doubt remarkable and contradicts the contemporary ideas of the *Geschlechtscharaktere*].[64]

Hero's entrance into the temple is her attempt at finding a positive resolution to the question of women's position in society. Rather than following her mother's path, she renounces love and marriage in return for a life of independence. For Politzer, Hero's choice is inherently negative, as it is based on flight. He argues that she adheres to a family tradition in order to get away from her family, and that she demands the priestess's rights because she no longer wants to be daughter and sister.[65]

Lorenz also sees the decision in negative terms, asserting that the freedom afforded by the temple is a mere illusion and that Hero makes the decision as she wants to remain unmarried.[66] Gerhard Scheit sees things in a more positive light, writing that Hero's flight to the temple 'ist ja nichts anderes als der geglückte Ausbruch aus der Kleinfamilie' [is, after all, nothing other than a successful escape from the nuclear family], the patriarchal nature of which Grillparzer demonstrates.[67]

There is certainly factual truth in these statements, even if the conclusions reached are unnecessarily unsympathetic. There can be little doubt that Hero enters the temple to avoid the misogynistic atmosphere which dominates in the family home and an unhappy marriage of her own. But Schaum is more accurate in the positive value he gives to Hero's decision as an attraction to the promise of the temple's freedoms, rather than flight from the family home.[68] While she displays an aversion to marriage, she has not fled just anywhere, but to a place which, she hopes, will allow her a greater degree of autonomy. Furthermore, the fact that the independence offered by the temple is ultimately an illusion is a stronger indictment of a society itself than of a young oppressed woman who seizes a chance of freedom. Indeed, in a different context Hero later states: 'Was täuschte nie?/ Bleibt mir die Wahl, wähl' ich die süßre Täuschung.' (ll. 1717–18) [All things can [delude];/ If choice is mine, I choose the sweet delusion. (p. 90)] Not yet aware of the true nature of temple life, but all too well acquainted with the cruelty of life outside its walls, Hero's decision seems consistent with this principle.

In Hero's reaction to her father, Politzer identifies 'ein tief verborgenes, in Kindertagen und -träumen gesätes Mißtrauen' [a deeply hidden mistrust sown by childhood and its dreams].[69] Dorothy Lasher-Schlitt argues that Hero's inhibition 'wurzelt [...] im Groll gegen Vater und Bruder, deren Übelwollen und böse Launen sie nur mit einem Übermaß an Selbstbeherrschung ertrug' [has its roots [...] in her resentment against her father and brother, whose malevolence and bad moods she only endured with excessive self-control].[70] Hero's own statement in conversation with her mother provides ample evidence for her fear and mistrust of men, which is grounded in the childhood experiences of abuse at her brother's hands. On hearing of her brother's absence she affirms that she would now be twice as likely to return home; however, she believes that the remaining male population — 'Von gleichem Sinn und störrisch wildem Wesen./ Das ehrne Band der Roheit um die Stirn' (ll. 308–09) [Like-minded and of ruthless, brutal ways,/ The brazen band of roughness round their brow (p. 20)] — who are '[g]ewohnt zu greifen mit der starren Hand/ Ins stille Reich geordneter Gedanken,/ Wo die Entschlüsse keimen, wachsen, reifen' (ll. 311–13) [Accustomed to thrust stubborn, clumsy fingers/ Into the quiet realm of ordered thought,/ There where decisions sprout, take root, mature (p. 20)] would deprive her of freedom and rationality. Hero sees herself faced with the choice between a life of almost certain servitude in marriage, or the potential of personal freedom within the walls of the temple. The fact that she acknowledges the alternative to her mother's fate and seizes the opportunity with both hands is another indication of what singles her out. The subjugation which characterizes her mother was no doubt the result of an upbringing which degraded and devalued her in her own eyes, and inculcated her with the idea, which she attempts to pass on to Hero, that a woman can only survive at a man's side. We can assume that Hero's upbringing resembled her mother's, and yet she has come away with a sense of her own worth which prohibits her from subjecting herself to further maltreatment. Seen in this light, her decision to enter the temple is not so much the result of flight, but of the knowledge, won thanks to a mind willing to exert itself, that the temple offers her the best chance of self-realization.

The influence of Kant's concept of enlightenment can be seen in Grillparzer's portrayal of Hero as an independent and free-thinking individual. In the opening monologue she says:

> Hier, Hymenäus, der die Menschen bindet,
> Nimm diesen Kranz von Einer, die gern frei.
> Die Seelen tauschest du? Ei, gute Götter,
> Ich will die meine nur für mich behalten,
> Wer weiß, ob eine andre mir so nütz? (ll. 33–37)
>
> [Here, Hymenaeus, you that bind us mortals,/ Accept this wreath from one who would stay free./ You give to each the other's soul? How now?/ I think I should prefer to keep my own,/ Who knows? Another might not serve so well. (p. 8)]

This is a statement not only of a desire for independence, but also of great self-confidence. Her desire to remain unmarried derives from her early experiences and from the realization that any relationship would be unsatisfactory due to the qualities which define the men in her surroundings. This desire is also the result of her belief that she is capable of surviving as a single woman. Later, she more forcefully expresses the desire for independent intellectual existence as the motivation for her choice:

> Ich aber will mit heiterm Sinne wandeln
> Hier an der Göttin Altar, meiner Frau.
> Das Rechte tun, nicht weil man mirs befahl,
> Nein, weil es recht, weil ich es so erkannt. (ll. 331–35)
>
> [But I prefer to live with soul serene/ Here at the goddess' altar, whom I serve;/ To do not what I have been told is right,/ But what is right, as I have cause to know. (p. 21)]

The final two lines of this quotation have a particularly strong Kantian echo. Indeed, Grillparzer has here put in Hero's mouth what Kant defined as the motto of the Enlightenment: 'Sapere aude! Habe Mut, dich deines eigenen Verstandes zu bedienen!' [*Sapere aude!* Have courage to use your *own* understanding!] The temple is not just a refuge from the physical abuse suffered by women, but the only place where a woman can find intellectual peace.

Grillparzer does not present Hero's search for enlightenment as an untroubled endeavour. The first challenge to her desire to live a rational, self-determined existence arrives in the form of Leander. The final scene of Act III finds Hero alone in her tower. She acknowledges that she is attracted to Leander, and that the Priest was right to worry about the effects of her meeting with the strangers, but that her vocation precludes any romantic feelings (ll. 1006–09). She vows to avoid any attraction ('Neigung'). As a sign of this intention, she turns to her lamp and says:

> Und wie ich lösche deinen sanften Strahl,
> So möge löschen auch was hier noch flimmert,
> Und nie mehr zünd' es neu ein neuer Abend an. (ll. 1038–40)

> [And even as I quench your gentle rays,/ So also shall be quenched what here still glows,/ And no new eventide must kindle it anew. (p. 53)]

The lamp serves a double function — it is at once a symbol of rationality and of passion — and underscores the difficulties Hero has in negotiating the competing demands of enlightenment and romance.[71] Leander promptly arrives after this vow has been made, and the dangerous situation in which he finds himself alerts Hero to the depth of her feelings for him (ll. 1183–86). Hero, however, does not immediately fall victim to her emotions, but engages critically with what she feels: 'Was ist es, das den Menschen so umnachtet,/ Und ihn entfremdet sich, dem eignen Selbst' (ll. 1181–82) [What is it can benight a person so/ And make him strange, a stranger to himself (p. 59)]. Her conscious reaction to Leander's presence is annoyance rather than excitement, although she recognizes that her anxiety for his safety indicates desire, and she views her own emotional response as a negation of reason, and hence reprehensible. She underscores her aversion to emotion by avoiding physical contact with Leander ('Laß das! Berühr mich nicht!' [No, do not touch me! (p. 60)]) and again decrying love as unnatural:

> Das ist nicht gut,
> Was so verkehrt die innerste Natur,
> Auslöscht das Licht, das uns die Götter gaben,
> Daß es uns leite, wie der Stern des Pols
> Den Schiffer führt. (ll. 1187–91)

> [That cannot be good/ Which so would twist and turn our inmost self,/ Put out the light the gods have given us/ To lead us, as the steadfast pole-star guides/ The mariner. (p. 60)]

This demonstrates the importance of light as a metaphor in this drama. Rationality, which in this scene is under threat from emotion, is for Hero the god-given guiding light of human life. By having his heroine talk of rationality as a light which can be extinguished, Grillparzer creates parallels between the Priest and Leander, as both are male forces who are opposed to Hero's rationality. Leander, through the emotional response he elicits in Hero, affects her ability to act rationally, while the Priest, as we shall see, has a more actively hostile attitude towards Hero's intellectual independence. Despite the conscious resistance to emotions which Hero displays in this scene, she allows herself to be kissed, although she does not want the lamp to witness her submission to Leander's charms, and they spend the night together.

It is the Priest whom Grillparzer presents as the most obvious antithesis to Hero. He represents both the dominant patriarchal culture and the culture of religious obedience which prevails inside the temple walls, and is no less than Hero's brother an example of a self-appointed guardian.

Act I demonstrates the Priest's capacity to act in a caring manner towards Hero.

He knows that loneliness accompanies religious vocation, and tries to make Hero aware of the importance of female friendships. Hero's own declarations are evidence enough for the Priest that she has not fully comprehended the realities of temple life, and he tries to bring her to the realization of what is in store. Hero remains resolute in her decision, so the Priest tries to show her that her attitude towards religious service is too restricted and abstract; he wants to be sure, for Hero's sake and the sake of the temple, that she knows what she is committing to. At the beginning of Act III, on the evening of Hero's initiation, the Priest worries because he finds Hero less happy than he expected. He presents himself as a caring mentor for the young girl, however his choice of words — he calls himself Hero's 'zweite[r] Vater' (l. 997) [second father (p. 51)] — unwittingly positions him as an oppressive figure. This is reinforced by the emphasis he places on discipline, and the strict attitude he promises towards misbehaviour (ll. 998–1002). From the outset, the Priest is portrayed as a strict lawgiver and judge within the temple walls. In Act I, he chastises the servant girls with the words, 'Und ihr! und meidet zu begegnen/ Dem Zorne, der sein Recht und seine Mittel kennt.' (ll. 109–10) [You too! And dread to meet the wrath,/ That knows what rights it has and how they are enforced. (p. 11)] The personification of his anger endows it with severe force and power.

The Priest's authoritarian mindset results from his inability or disinclination to take the same critical attitude towards his religious duties that Hero develops. For him, religious practices are to be observed by the book, without the interference of human emotions or reason. The scene with the bird's nest in Act I allows Grillparzer to demonstrate the diverging methods and priorities of Hero and the Priest. The Priest orders that the nest be removed from the temple; Hero, noticing the effect this has on her mother, puts a stop to the eviction. She thereby arouses the anger of the Priest, who pointedly asks: 'Bist du so neu im Dienst,/ Daß du nicht weiß was Brauches hier und Sitte?' (ll. 347–48) [Are you so newly come,/ That you know nothing of our rules and customs? (p. 22)] This echoes his earlier justification for the removal of the nest with the words: 'So wills des Tempels Übung.' (l. 269) [The temple's practice so decrees. (p. 18)] The Priest, who imposes his will on his inferiors and thereby impedes the steps that Hero wishes to make towards a more enlightened existence, is himself 'unmündig', being as he is an uncritical servant of the tenets of his religion. Kant writes of 'Unmündigkeit' as a state which becomes comfortable for those confined in it, and from which they are genuinely incapable of escaping.[72] This is the case for the Priest. Although he is an unthinking slave of his religion, he benefits from the social position which he acquires as a result of his status as a religious leader. His 'Satzungen und Formeln' guide his life and actions, and by imposing them on his underlings, he secures the survival of the religion and of his own social dominance. This social dominance also finds expression in the Priest's attitude towards Aphrodite. In conversation with Hero's mother in Act I, the Priest emphasizes the abstract spiritual nature of the temple's adoration of Aphrodite. They do not worship a goddess of love '[d]ie Mensch an Menschen knüpft wie Tier an Tier' (l. 364) [That couples man with woman, beast with beast (p. 23)], but a goddess who inspires thought and reflection:

> Der Eintracht alles Wesens hohe Mutter,
> Geschlechtlos, weil sie selber das Geschlecht,
> Und himmlisch, weil sie stammt vom Himmel oben. (ll. 367–69.)

[High source of concord for all living things,/ Devoid of sex since she herself is sex,/ And heavenly, as she is heaven-born (p. 23)]

Aphrodite here is divested of any links to sex or sexuality: she neither possesses a sex of her own, nor does she inspire humans to love or sexual relationships. Sex is seen as dirty and animalistic, a form of interaction unworthy of an intellectual individual. This abstraction of the feminine emphasizes not only the contemplative nature of the temple, but also its patriarchal structure. Consequently, it does not bode well for Hero's chances of finding freedom within the temple's walls.

In combination with this authoritarian framework and patriarchal outlook, the Priest's anger becomes a dangerous force when he begins to blur the boundaries between earthly and heavenly power. In Act IV, the guard's account of strange nocturnal happenings arouses the Priest's suspicion and he realizes the possibility that Leander returned and seduced Hero. He is angered, but it is no longer human anger which he feels; rather, he recognizes the indignation of higher powers working through him: 'In meinem Innern reget sich ein Gott,/ Und warnt mich, zu verhüten, ehs zu spät.' (ll. 1365–66) [Some god within me stirs and counsels me;/ A warning! I must act before too late! (p. 70)] Act IV provides more examples of such blurred boundaries, and it becomes clear that, for the Priest, the gods are little more than a justification for his own actions. His willingness to abdicate personal responsibility provides a stark contrast to Hero's adherence to her own moral code; while the Priest remains willingly 'unmündig', Hero's justification comes from herself. As he sends Hero off with a list of chores, the Priest is already clear about his course of action: Leander must die if he tries to see Hero again. It is clear that he will be acting as judge and executioner; the gods barely get a mention in this soliloquy, and when they do, the word 'Götter' is expendable:

> Denn weil sie fern, leg' ich die Schlingen aus,
> Die ihn verderben, kehrt der Kühne wieder.
> Unseliger, was strecktest du die Hand
> Nach meinem Kind, nach meiner Götter Eigen? (ll. 1515–18)

[For, with her gone, I can prepare the snares/ That shall destroy him, should he dare return./ Unhappy lad, why did you stretch your hand/ To touch my child to whom my gods lay claim? (p. 78)]

On the evening of the fateful night, the Priest deliberately confuses divine and human power again. The Priest even considers a hypothetical situation in which he postpones his murderous plan, but rejects it on the grounds that Hero would continue to see Leander and would thereby fall ever closer to perdition:

> Gönn' ich ihr Zeit, und taucht ihr heller Sinn
> Auf aus den Fluten, die ihn jetzt umnachten,
> Denkt sie auf Mittel nur ihn zu erretten,
> Entzieht den Strafbarn unsrer Schlingen Haft,
> Und ist so mehr und sicherer denn verloren. (ll. 1756–60)

> [If I allow her time, if her clear mind/ Breaks from the clouds that shroud it darkly now,/ If she can think of means to rescue him,/ To snatch the culprit from our snare's confines,/ She is the more and then more surely lost. (p. 92)]

The Priest sees himself united in purpose with the gods to a collective 'wir'. That this is the only possible explanation is confirmed by his description in l. 1518 of Hero as his child and the gods' property. The Priest and the gods are the joint owners of Hero, and are united in the Priest's efforts to prevent the expropriation of this human property. This collaborative work reaches its conclusion at the end of Act IV. Looking at the light emanating from Hero's tower, the Priest utters the words: 'Der Götter Sturm verlösche deine Flamme.' (l. 1817) [Then may the gods send storms to quench the flame! (p. 95)] With this, he enters the tower, and the guard narrates as the Priest positions the lamp on the ledge, where it is exposed to the storm. The scene closes with a second appeal to the gods that they might finish off what he has started:

> Nun, Himmlische, nun waltet eures Amts!
> Die Schuldigen hält Meer und Schlaf gebunden,
> Und so ist eures Priesters Werk vollbracht:
> Das Holz geschichtet und das Beil gezückt,
> Wend' ich mich ab. Trefft Götter selbst das Opfer. (ll. 1830–34)

> [Now, Heavenly Powers, dispose as you ordain!/ Sleep and the sea hold fast the guilty pair;/ And so the duty of your priest is done./ The pyre is ready and the axe is raised./ I turn away. Strike, gods, yourselves, the victim. (pp. 95–96)]

The storm extinguishes the light of Hero's flame, Leander cannot navigate across the Hellespont, and is discovered, dead, the next day.

Despite the concern which he shows for Hero in the early parts of the drama, the Priest's unscrupulous abuse of religious authority and justification to provide himself with motivation for his actions shows him to be a monomaniacal tyrant. It is not as a result of his religious vocation per se that he values Hero's life. Rather, his role as a priest secures him a respected position within the patriarchal orders of both the temple and wider society on Sestos. Hero, at least in part, is a possession which he jealously guards and does not wish to cede to another man. The lack of compunction he displays and the callous manner in which he departs the scene show that his attitudes are stamped with the mark of a misogyny which would rather see a related woman dead than in the hands of an 'unsuitable' man. Grillparzer, by giving the Priest this complex motivation, and by framing him in an Enlightenment context, made the final version of the drama more nuanced than his plans suggest. A note from 1820 indicates that the Priest's motivation and actions would be simpler: having realized the nature of Hero and Leander's relationship, he 'beschließt, streng und ernst will er das Unerlaubte im Keime ersticken. [...] Der Priester löscht die Lampe aus' [decides to nip the forbidden behaviour in the bud, severely and seriously. [...] The priest extinguishes the lamp] (1820. Nr. 322. *HKA* II/vii, p. 141).

The Priest's appeals to the justification of heavenly powers are antithetical to Hero's philosophy of responsibility and autonomy. In conversation with the temple guard in Act IV, Hero disobeys the Priest's command with the words: 'Ich denke künftig selbst mir zu gebieten.' (l. 1687) [In future I take orders from myself. (p. 88)] This attitude is wholly compatible with the desire she expresses in Act I to act according to the judgments of her reason alone. While the Priest seeks to abdicate responsibility for his actions and their consequences, and elsewhere shows himself to be an unthinking follower of religious practice, Hero emerges as an Enlightenment figure insofar as she displays the will to defy those who would dictate her thoughts and actions and begin the difficult journey to rational self-determination.

Janthe is also an antithesis to Hero. While Hero represents Enlightenment values, Janthe is defined by the negative characteristics which the Priest associates with all women. The exchange between Hero and Janthe in the opening scene displays the antagonism between their opposing characteristics. While Hero makes sensible use of her time and puts her duties before pleasure, Janthe abandons her work to chase amusement: 'Wir waren früh am Werk und sprengten, fegten./ Da kam die Lust, im Grünen uns zu jagen.' (ll. 59–60) [We started work betimes, we swept and sprinkled,/ Then came the wish to run out doors to play. (p. 9)] This sort of frivolous behaviour and the attitude which would allow it are clearly anathema to Hero, and she chastises Janthe for neglecting her responsibilities (ll. 61–65). If Medea in *Der Gastfreund* defends her actions on the grounds that she acted according to her will at any given point, Hero here represents the subjugation of desire to duty.

Hero's behaviour allows Janthe many possibilities for jokes at her expense. She mocks Hero's arrogance which is a result of Hero's belief that she deserves to be a priestess: 'Verzeih, wir sind gemeines, niedres Volk./ Du freilich, aus der Priester Stamm entsprossen — ' (ll. 73–74), [Forgive, we are of lowly common stock,/ While you, descended from a race of priests — (p. 9)] and 'Ganz andre Freuden,/ Erhabnere Genüsse sind für dich.' (ll. 76–77) [Quite different pleasures,/ Far nobler satisfactions are for you. (p. 10)] The antagonism between Hero and Janthe can also be seen in terms of Kant's essay on enlightenment. It has already been argued that Hero represents the Enlightenment ideals of reason and independent thought. Janthe is not just a representative of a less reflective and introspective way of life, but also a threat to the ability of others to progress out of the state of ignorance. She is seen as the origin of frivolity not just by Hero, but also later by the Priest. Hero finds Janthe's behaviour disturbing, but even more worrying is the way in which she is able to involve the remaining servant girls in her schemes, distracting them from their duties and preventing them from acting rationally.

In the master-servant aspect of Hero's relationship with Janthe Grillparzer portrays another conflict between Hero's ideals of self-determination and the realities of life. Hero has just responded to her uncle's order with a profession of her intention to be her own master, when Janthe asks if Hero has any tasks for her. Hero replies,

> Ich nicht. Und doch! wenns selber dir gefällt.
> Geh nur hinauf, bereite mir die Lampe,
> Gieß Öl noch zu, genug für viele Zeit. (ll. 1689–91)

> [Not I. — And yet! If doing so should please,/ You may go up and there prepare my lamp, pour in more oil, enough to last for hours. (p. 88)]

Hero seems to realize that her desire to be self-determining is incompatible with a role in which she commands others. Her choice of words extends to Janthe the option of determining her own actions.

In Act IV, once the Priest has been made aware that Hero might have committed an indiscretion, he turns first to Janthe, whom he considers the source of evil in the temple:

> Von allem was sich Schlimmes je begab
> In diesem Haus, fand ich dich immer wissend,
> Belehrt durch Mitschuld, oder Neugier mindstens. (ll. 1377–79)
>
> [Whenever mischief happened hereabout,/ Of all the house I found you best informed;/ You shared the guilt or pried its secret out. (p. 71)]

For the Priest, Janthe's faults partly result from her sex. She is a 'Törin' (l. 1410) [fool]. He uses derogatory terms similar to those with which he abused Hero's mother in Act I, and indeed his estimation of her is no better or worse than his estimation of women in general: 'Die Torheit ruft. Folg ihr als Mensch, als Weib!' (l. 379) [Blind folly calls. Obey it as a person, as a woman! (p. 23)].

In the light of this antagonistic relationship between the Priest and Janthe, it is particularly appropriate that it is she who sees through the farce of his carefully arranged scheme and confronts him at the conclusion of the drama.[73] She lays bare the fact that he is responsible for Leander's death, and thereby also indirectly responsible for Hero's.

> JANTHE   Komm und schau
>   So sehn die Toten aus in diesen Landen.
> PRIESTER   Spricht das der Wahnsinn?
> JANTHE   Nein, er hört's.
>   Vorsicht'ger Tor, sieh deiner Klugheit Werke! (ll. 2103–07)
>
> [IANTHE: Come and look,/ If you would see what death can do and does. PRIEST: So madness speaks. IANTHE: No, madness hears./ Painstaking fool, see what your wisdom wrought. (p. 113)]

Janthe's view agrees with that of critics who also deem the Priest to be well aware of the consequences his actions will bring about. Lorenz claims that the Priest does not even believe in the gods, but himself plays the roles of god and fate.[74] Ulrike Tanzer states that he knows what will happen, but later distances himself from his responsibility.[75] Kurt Adel takes a more lenient approach: 'Der Priester vermochte die Strafe der Götter, wie er sie verstand, zu bewirken.' [The priest was capable of bringing about the punishment of the gods as he understood it.][76]

By analysing Grillparzer's drama in the context of its Enlightenment underpinnings, the true significance of Hero's entrance into the temple as an act of self-emancipation becomes clear. While this decision is in part taken as a means of escaping the oppression of a patriarchal society, it should be viewed more in terms of what Hero is looking for, rather than what she aims to avoid. In her naiveté, the temple appears to be a place where even she, a woman, can have rights, and where she will be free to nurture her development as a person, led by reason and conscience and not by the demands and desires of the men surrounding her. This intellectual independence is thwarted by the Priest, a representative of the patriarchal religion of the temple. The Priest cannot, or will not develop the critical attitude towards religion which Hero possesses. Inclusion in this discussion of Kant's essay on enlightenment allows for a better understanding of his role: religion is the tool he uses to extract obedience from, and subdue, those in the temple. By propagating this religion, he can justify the pressure for conformity and subservience which he exerts on his inferiors, suppressing independent thought and becoming what Kant calls a 'Vormund'. As in *Libussa* and *Sappho*, *Des Meeres und der Liebe Wellen* depicts the subjugation and, ultimately, death of a woman necessitated by the actions of a lesser man.

Notes to Chapter 3

1. Werner Sauer, *Österreichische Philosophie zwischen Aufklärung und Restauration. Beiträge zur Geschichte des Frühkantianismus in der Donaumonarchie* (Amsterdam: Rodopi, 1982), p. 108.
2. Ibid., p. 110.
3. Ibid., p. 139.
4. Ibid., p. 140.
5. Ibid., p. 143.
6. J. W. Nagl, Jakob Zeidler, Eduard Castle, *Deutsch-österreichische Literaturgeschichte*, 4 vols. (Vienna: Fromme, 1914–37), II/i (1914), p. 392.
7. Frimmel, *Literarisches Leben in Melk*, pp. 148–49.
8. Barbara Schöffmann, 'Immanuel Kant und die Aufklärung in Kärnten', in *Weimar — Jena — Klagenfurt. Der Herbert-Kreis und das Geistesleben Kärntens im Zeitalter der Französischen Revolution*, ed. by Wilhelm Baum (Klagenfurt: Kärntner Druck- und Verlagsgesellschaft, 1989), pp. 90–100 (p. 94).
9. Ibid., p. 95.
10. Wilhelm Baum, 'Einleitung', in *Weimar — Jena — Klagenfurt. Der Herbert-Kreis und das Geistesleben Kärntens im Zeitalter der Französischen Revolution*, ed. by Wilhelm Baum (Klagenfurt: Kärntner Druck- und Verlagsgesellschaft, 1989), pp. 6–21 (p. 11).
11. Ibid.
12. Walter Seitter, *Unzeitgemäße Aufklärung. Franz Grillparzers Philosophie* (Vienna: Kant, 1991), pp. 23–24.
13. Fritz Strich, *Franz Grillparzers Ästhetik* (Berlin: Duncker, 1905), p. 8.
14. W. E. Yates, *Humanity in Weimar and Vienna: The Continuity of an Ideal. An Inaugural Lecture delivered in the University of Exeter on 30 April, 1973* (Exeter: University of Exeter, 1973), p. 7.
15. Diary entry 17 April 1818, in *Joseph Schreyvogels Tagebücher*, p. 294.
16. Strich, p. 8.
17. Fritz Störi, *Grillparzer und Kant* (Frauenfeld: Huber, 1935), pp. 25, 28.
18. Yates, *Humanity*, p. 14.
19. Grillparzer, 'Selbstbiographie', in HKA I/xvi, pp. 63–231 (p. 71).
20. August Sauer, 'Akademische Festrede zu Grillparzers hundertstem Geburtstag. Gehalten in der Aula des Karolinums zu Prag am 15. Jänner 1891', in *Gesammelte Reden und Aufsätze zur Geschichte der Literatur in Österreich und Deutschland* (Vienna: Fromme, 1903), pp. 102–34 (p. 108); Günter Schnitzler, 'Grillparzer und die Spätaufklärung', in *Franz Grillparzer. Historie und Gegenwärtigkeit* (Freiburg i. Breisgau: Rombach, 1994), pp. 179–201 (p. 181).
21. Sauer, 'Akademische Festrede', p. 109.
22. Immanuel Kant, 'Beantwortung der Frage: Was ist Aufklärung?', in *Werke in sechs Bänden*, ed. by Wilhelm Weischedel (Frankfurt a.M.: Insel, 1956–64), VI, pp. 53–61 (p. 53).
23. Ibid., p. 55.
24. Ibid., p. 53.

25. Grillparzer, 'Ein treuer Diener seines Herrn', in *HKA* I/iii, pp. 183–314, l. 1448.
26. W. E. Yates, *Grillparzer. A Critical Introduction* (Cambridge: Cambridge University Press, 1972), p. 144.
27. Thompson, *Franz Grillparzer*, p. 56.
28. Frederic E. Coenen, *Franz Grillparzer's Portraiture of Men* (Chapel Hill, NC: University of North Carolina, 1951), p. 36.
29. Ritchie Robertson, 'Der patriotische Minister in Grillparzers *Ein treuer Diener seines Herrn* und Hebbels *Agnes Bernauer*', *Hebbel-Jahrbuch* (2010), 95–119 (p. 103).
30. Roe, *An Introduction*, p. 133.
31. Lorenz, *Dichter des sozialen Konflikts*, pp. 149–50.
32. *ABGB*, I, p. 8.
33. Politzer, *Das abgründige Biedermeier*, p. 187.
34. Peter Lattmann, *Franz Grillparzer. Untersuchungen zu seinem Drama* Ein treuer Diener seines Herrn (Zurich: Juris Druck+Verlag, 1971), p. 55.
35. Max Kommerell, 'Grillparzer. Ein Dichter der Treue' [1936], in *Franz Grillparzer*, ed. by Helmut Bachmaier (Frankfurt a.M.: Suhrkamp, 1991), pp. 88–98 (p. 92).
36. Cf. Robertson, 'Der patriotische Minister', p. 107.
37. Lorenz, *Dichter des sozialen Konflikts*, p. 157.
38. Coenen, *Franz Grillparzer's Portraiture of Men*, p. 39.
39. Robertson, 'Der patriotische Minister', p. 102.
40. Politzer, *Das abgründige Biedermeier*, p. 196.
41. Yates, *A Critical Introduction*, p. 133.
42. Kurt Frieberger, 'Bancbanus und Franz Deák', *JdGG*, 3. Folge 3 (1960), 94–105 (p. 99).
43. Lattmann, *Franz Grillparzer. Untersuchungen zu seinem Drama* Ein treuer Diener seines Herrn, pp. 27, 67.
44. Thompson, *Franz Grillparzer*, p. 58.
45. Wolf-Cirian, *Grillparzers Frauengestalten*, p. 136.
46. Ibid., pp. 135, 139.
47. Thompson, *Franz Grillparzer*, p. 59.
48. August Sauer, '"Ein treuer Diener seines Herrn"', *JdGG*, 3 (1893), 3–40 (p. 25).
49. Frieberger, 'Bancbanus und Franz Deák', p. 99.
50. Ibid.
51. Kant, 'Was ist Aufklärung?', pp. 57–58.
52. Politzer, *Das abgründige Biedermeier*, pp. 211–14.
53. Kurt Adel, 'Grillparzers Hero-Drama (und Kleists "Penthesilea")', *JdGG*, 3. Folge 7 (1969), 143–201 (p. 153).
54. Coenen, *Franz Grillparzer's Portraiture of Men*, p. 49.
55. Fischer, 'Franz Grillparzer', in *Von Grillparzer zu Kafka. Sechs Essays* (Vienna: Globus, 1962), pp. 9–56 (p. 37).
56. Lorenz, *Dichter des sozialen Konflikts*, pp. 51–57.
57. Grillparzer, 'Des Meeres und der Liebe Wellen', in *HKA* I/iv, 81–211. Here ll. 184–85.
58. Epistle XIX, Hero to Leander, in Ovid, *The Heröides or Epistles of the Heroines, The Amours, Art of Love, Remedy of Love, and Minor Works*, trans. by Henry T. Riley (London: Bohn, 1852), p. 209.
59. Christopher Marlowe and George Chapman, *Hero and Leander* (Chiswick: C. Whittingham, 1821), p. 3.
60. Ibid., p. 28.
61. Konrad Schaum, 'Grillparzers "Des Meeres und der Liebe Wellen": Seelendrama und Kulturkritik', *JdGG*, 3. Folge 11 (1974), 95–114 (p. 101).
62. Lorenz, *Dichter des sozialen Konflikts*, p. 53.
63. Politzer, *Das abgründige Biedermeier*, p. 214.
64. Ulrike Tanzer, 'Grenzgänge in Franz Grillparzers Trauerspiel "Des Meeres und der Liebe Wellen"', in *Grenzgänge und Grenzgänger in der österreichischen Literatur. Beiträge des 15. Österreichisch-Polnischen Germanistentreffens Kraków 2002*, ed. by Maria Kłańska et al. (Kraków: Wydawnictwo Uniwersytetu Jagiellońskiego, 2004), pp. 77–86 (p. 81).

65. Politzer, *Das abgründige Biedermeier*, p. 70.
66. Lorenz, *Dichter des sozialen Konflikts*, pp. 53–54.
67. Gerhard Scheit, 'Grillparzer und die deutschen Männer', in *Stichwort Grillparzer*, ed. by Hilde Haider-Pregler and Evelyn Deutsch-Schreiner (Vienna: Böhlau, 1994), pp. 51–58 (p. 53).
68. Schaum, 'Seelendrama und Kulturkritik', p. 99.
69. Politzer, *Das abgründige Biedermeier*, p. 214.
70. Dorothy Lasher-Schlitt, 'Grillparzers "Hero und Leander". Eine psychologische Untersuchung', *JdGG*, 3. Folge 3 (1960), 106–14 (p. 106).
71. On the lamp as a symbol of passion see Heinz Politzer, 'Der Schein von Heros Lampe', *Modern Language Notes* 72 (1957), 432–37 (p. 433).
72. Kant, 'Was ist Aufklärung?', p. 54.
73. Lorenz, *Dichter des sozialen Konflikts*, p. 57.
74. Ibid.
75. Tanzer, 'Grenzgänge', p. 82.
76. Adel, 'Grillparzers Hero-Drama', p. 159.

CHAPTER 4

Female Rulers

Grillparzer's historical dramas, by their very nature, feature queens — Margarete, Kunigunde, Eleonore and Gertrude — but two of his dramas in particular are the subject of this chapter on women rulers: *Sappho* (1818) and *Libussa* (1848). The inclusion of *Sappho* in this section may surprise, given that the focus is generally on her role as a poet, but I show that her role as a ruler is crucial to the drama. Central to my interpretation of these dramas is Grillparzer's interweaving of social, political and philosophical issues, and I show that the dramatist was influenced by the thought of Rousseau, Hobbes and Locke.

Both *Sappho* and *Libussa* are examinations of the predicament of the exceptional woman in a male-dominated society. The female ruler is an obvious trope for such an examination and was a popular motif in the nineteenth century, as Schiller's *Maria Stuart* (1801), Zacharias Werner's *Wanda* (1810), Kleist's *Penthesilea* (1808), as well as works such as Artner's *Rogneda und Wladimir* (1828) and Ebner-Eschenbach's *Maria Stuart in Schottland* (1860) and *Marie Roland* (1867) testify. Empress Maria Theresa, whom Grillparzer called 'diese wirklich gescheidte Frau' [this very brilliant woman] (1866. Nr. 4361. *HKA* II/xii, p. 74), loomed large in the Austrian psyche and serves as an obvious historical example of the powerful female ruler.

Grillparzer's private writings betray a keen interest in women who held positions of power. In notes on David Hume's *History of England* (1754–1761), Grillparzer mentions Matilda of England's attempts to secure political support for her claim to the throne (1812. *HKA* II/vi, p. 121). He notes that the wife of the regent of Forli defended the town of Cesena against papal forces in the fourteenth century: 'Endlich muß sie sich ergeben und büßt im Kerker für ihren Muth.' [Finally she must surrender and she pays for her courage in prison.] (1812/13. *HKA* II/vi, p. 262) While reading Douville's *Voyage au Congo*, he noted: 'In Dumbo regiert jederzeit ein Weib, zur Belohnung der Dienste, die das Geschlecht einmal in Feindesgefahr geleistet' [In Dumbo at any time it is a woman who rules, as a reward for the services which that sex performed when enemies threatened] (1833. Nr. 2069. *HKA* II/ix, p. 121). Elizabeth I and Mary Stuart, the subjects of Schiller's drama, also feature in Grillparzer's notes. He identifies parallels in the lives and political failures of Mary and Marie Antoinette, and their 'gemeinschaftliche[s] Schicksal verleumdet zu werden' [common fate of being slandered] (1836. Nr. 3224. *HKA* II/x, p. 159). Despite the misogynistic statements elsewhere in his notebooks, here Grillparzer identifies a fate common among female rulers: the contempt of posterity for them and their reputations. In the same entry, Grillparzer wonders at Elizabeth's putative plans to give her favourite, Leicester, to Mary in marriage.

Grillparzer mentions several female rulers who took on distinctly 'unfeminine' public roles. So, for example, he quotes the story of a queen who freed her people from foreign dominion, led her troops into battle, and was only defeated 'nachdem sie selbst tapfer in der Schlacht gefochten' [after she herself had bravely fought in the battle] (1822. Nr. 1167. *HKA* II/viii, p. 69). Nevertheless, he held to the idea that women, even as rulers, are inherently more emotional than men. When he heard about plans to emancipate Russian serfs, he assumed 'daß da gewiß ein Weib im Hintergrund stecke, und da die Kaiserin eine deutsche Prinzessin und daher gewiß höchst sentimental war, schloß ich, daß die Sache von ihr ausgehe' [that a woman was certainly behind this, and since the empress was a German princess, and therefore certainly very sentimental, I concluded that the matter was her idea] (1861. Nr. 4297. *HKA* II/xii, p. 52).

In 1822, he was reading widely in Bohemian history, and remarked on the prevalence of remarkable female figures: 'Merkwürdig ist, welche große Rolle in der alten böhmischen Geschichte die Weiber spielen. Ziemlich allgemein gilt jede ausgezeichnetere für eine Seherin.' [It is strange how large a role women play in old Bohemian history. It is quite generally thought that every outstanding woman was a seer.] (1822. Nr. 986. *HKA* II/viii, p. 8) He was intrigued by the story of Princess Elizabeth, daughter of King Wenceslaus III, who refused to be forced into marriage with a man of humble origins. She fled, and chose Johann von Luxemburg as her husband, who freed her and became king of Bohemia (1822. Nr. 974. *HKA* II/viii, p. 6). This historical anecdote may have been the inspiration for Grillparzer's heroines who refuse to accept the life others have planned for them, and in the case of Sappho and Libussa raise men to positions of greatness.

One figure in particular from Bohemian history seems to have piqued Grillparzer's interest: Drahomira. She is the subject of several diary entries, as well as of a number of dramatic drafts. In a dramatic fragment, Grillparzer summarizes the material: after her husband's death, Drahomira became ruler. She 'übernimmt [...] die Regierung zerstört Kirchen, ermordet Priester, läßt die Ludmilla die sich wiedersetzt auf dem Lustschloße Tetin ermorden' [takes over [...] the government, destroys churches, kills priests, has Ludmilla, who opposes her, murdered at the pleasure palace in Tetin]. She was deposed by German forces and fled to Brandenburg (1814/15. *HKA* II/iv, p. 309). In this draft version, Drahomira declares, 'Der Sinn nur macht den Herrscher, macht den Knecht' [The mind alone makes the ruler, makes the servant] (*HKA* II/iv, p. 320), a statement which calls to mind Hero's insistence on intellectual freedom. In a subsequent draft, 'Drahomira III' (1815/16), the heroine's character is more fully developed and her subversively unfeminine nature becomes clear:

> Erneute Frist ward mir gegeben
> Die nur sich endet mit dem Leben
> Wenn ich zerbreche dieses Landes Joch,
> Der eingedrungne Christenglaube
> Morsch und zertrümmert liegt im Staube

> Aus dem er Schlangenähnlich kroch
> Und auf der Kirche hingestürzten Trümmern
> Die Tempel uns'rer alten Götter schimmern.
>   (*HKA* II/iv, 363–72. Here: ll. 179–86)

[A new time was given to me/ Which will only end when life ends/ When I break this country's yoke,/ The intruder Christianity/ Lies rotten and shattered in the dust/ From which it crept like a snake/ And on the fallen ruins of the church/ The temples of our old gods shine.]

It is not clear why the several draft versions of 'Drahomira' did not become a full drama, but they show Grillparzer's interest in the types of heroine and theme which would become more developed in later works.

In both dramas under consideration in this section, a woman holds a position of preeminence in her society. This situation leads to, and perhaps even necessitates, gender conflict. Both Phaon and Primislaus find it difficult to tolerate their public subordination. The issue of gender conflict is one that interested Grillparzer from his youth onwards, and often features in his dramas. Like *Wer ist schuldig?*, *Der Zauberwald* [*The Magic Forest*], a short unfinished work from 1808, presents a more explicit engagement with the theme than is visible in Grillparzer's mature dramas.

Der Zauberwald is a take on Shakespeare's *A Midsummer Night's Dream* and concentrates on the conflict between Oberon and Titania. Oberon is a boorish husband who demands his wife's respect because of his status as husband rather than because his deeds are deserving. Titania, on the other hand, is wilfully defiant. Near the beginning of the drama, when the fairy monarchs' strife has already started, the chorus reminds Oberon of his position of power and tells him to consider 'daß in dieser Fehde/ ein schwaches Weib dein Gegener ist' [that in this feud/ your opponent is a weak woman].[1] Oberon, however, is not willing to stand down, and refuses to compromise his dignity and standing, even if it would achieve peace: 'ich selber liebe Ruhe, doch/ soll euer Herr den Naken beugen/ unter des Weibes niedres Joch' [I myself love peace, but/ should your lord bow his neck/ Under the woman's lowly yoke] (*HKA* II/iii, p. 88). He considers obedience a wifely duty, and interprets Titania's disobedience as ingratitude:

> Lohnst du so meine Liebe! — Ich habe dich auf die Stufe gehoben auf der du nun zu meiner Qual steh[s]t; ich habe dir die Macht gegeben, die du itzt zu meinem Schaden gebrauchst! — Ist das deine Dankbarkeit Schlange? (*HKA* II/iii, p. 90)
>
> [Thus you reward my love! — I lifted you up to the step on which you now stand to my torment; I gave you the power which you now use to my injury! — Is that your gratitude, snake?]

Two themes are introduced here which later reappear in *Sappho*: Oberon's conception of female dominance as a threat to masculinity, which is shared by Phaon; and criticism of ingratitude, which Sappho also considers particularly galling.

Titania is equally eager to carry her point. She refuses to be subservient to her husband, but shows herself willing to partake in a marriage of equals:

> Soll den[n] Titania immer weichen
> soll ich des Mannes Sklavinn sein
> Er mag die Hand zum Bund mir reichen
> und gern und willig schlag ich ein (*HKA* II/iii, p. 88)

[Should then Titania always yield/ Should I be my husband's slave/ If he wishes to give me his hand in union/ I will gladly and willingly accept]

Later, she mocks his anger by highlighting the absurdity of its cause:

> Ei seht doch boshaft wäre ich
> Mein theurer Herr und König
> gewiß wohl darum weil ich
> mich nicht zahm und unterthänig
> in eure Launen füge
> und meinen Hals nicht biege. (*HKA* II/iii, p. 91)

[Oh, see, I would be malicious/ My dear lord and king/ Certainly because I/ Do not submit tamely and subserviently/ To your caprices/ And do not bow my neck.]

Although *Der Zauberwald* was not developed further, it is an important indication that the teenage Grillparzer was already interested in the idea of gender conflict. While in the case of Titania and Oberon it is the man who has given the woman a position of importance, a situation which is exactly reversed in *Sappho* and *Libussa*, the text contains the genesis of later works which examine the topic in more sophisticated ways.

Grillparzer's later reflections on the female ruler are more complex partly because he depicts Sappho's and Libussa's sovereignty in the context of social contract theory. The imagery of social contract which Grillparzer introduces in both these dramas designates the heroines' domains as polities, governed not by an autocrat, but by an aristocratic leader who rules with the explicit approval of her subjects. It is not far-fetched to imagine that Grillparzer might have been influenced by contract theory. Grillparzer mentions Thomas Hobbes, and specifically *De cive* (1642), in a diary entry from 1824 (Nr. 1325. *HKA* II/viii, p. 137), and in 1836 he writes: 'Englische Lektüre. Durch Lockes gesunden Menschenverstand erheitert.' [Reading in English. Cheered by Locke's common sense.] (Nr. 3017. *HKA*, II/x, p. 67) His engagement with contract theory, however, preceded his work on *Sappho*, for he had translated excerpts of Jean-Jacques Rousseau's *Du contrat social* [*The Social Contract*] as early as 1808 (*SW* III, pp. 1188–97, p. 1369).

For Hobbes, the social contract allowed men to lift themselves above their mere natural condition, which he conceived as a state of war. In short, man in this state will and can do everything to preserve his life against the machinations of others. Hobbes's conception of the social contract, as laid out in *Leviathan* (1651), is of an arrangement whereby each individual lays down as many of his rights as do others, thereby guaranteeing each peace and security. Such an arrangement can only be fruitful if it is mutually agreed, for the individual who lays down his rights while others retain theirs exposes himself to attacks. The reciprocal nature of the social contract is very important, and Hobbes reiterates that, in accordance with the contract, an individual transfers some part of his rights to the rest of his community, but receives in return equivalent rights from each other member of the community. The aim of this transfer of rights is the preservation of each individual's life.

A society governed by this contract, however, cannot always rely on the individuals which compose it to abide by their word. There must, therefore, be a power which is set above all members of the society 'with right and force sufficient enough to compel performance' of contractual agreements made between its subjects.[2] The presence of this common power ensures that no individual, in being the first to offer up a part of her rights, becomes the prey of those who withhold theirs. This would be contrary to the right, which no person can ever sacrifice, of self-preservation. The presence of a power 'set up to constrain those that would otherwise violate their faith'[3] eliminates the fear that other contracting parties might not uphold their end of the bargain, and makes it possible for one individual to give up her rights as the first without endangering her life.

The only way Hobbes sees for such a common power to be created is for the subjects as a group to confer their power on one man or group of men. This individual or group is acknowledged as the representative of those who choose him, and each individual must accept as his own those acts sanctioned by the common power. Each individual subjects his will and judgment to this common power on the condition that every other individual does the same.[4] The individual upon whom this power rests is known as the 'sovereign', while all others are 'subjects'. Hobbes identifies two modes whereby an individual may become sovereign: he either benefits from the use of natural force; or, the mass of subjects agree to submit to his authority.

Locke put forward his ideas on the social contract in *Two Treatises of Government* (1689). Locke had read Hobbes, but scholars cannot say exactly when or to what extent. When writing his *Treatises*, however, *Leviathan* did have a positive impact on Locke.[5] Locke's point of departure, the state of nature, is a less menacing concept than Hobbes's, and Locke conceives of this state as merely a '*State of Perfect Freedom*' where men are free 'to order their Actions, and dispose of their Possessions, and Persons, as they think fit, within the bounds of the Law of Nature, without asking leave, or depending upon the Will of any other Man.'[6]

In accord with his intention of repudiating defences of the divine right of kings, Locke argues for a society governed by social contract. No legislative power shall be established other than by the agreement of the members of society, nor shall any law exist other than those created by the legislature in accordance with the trust placed in it by the commonwealth.[7] There are strong echoes of *Leviathan* in Locke's description of the process by which men leave the state of nature and form society. Men choose to relinquish their natural freedom, and enter into '*the bonds of Civil Society*' by agreeing amongst themselves to constitute a community which provides for their comfortable, safe and peaceful coexistence, and secures their property rights both against other members of the society and against any that are not.[8] This state of communal living, however, necessitates that each promise to abide by majority rule, otherwise the contract which binds all members in society would be meaningless.

For Rousseau, writing in the 1760s, the social contract also represented a means of elevating man from, and securing him against, his own nature. It is a form of association that can protect each of its members, along with his property, while also allowing him to be free as he was before he joined the association. The terms in which he expresses the task of the social pact are similar to those employed by Hobbes. Rousseau states that the essential core of the social pact is the submission of each individual to the 'general will' and the reception by society of each of its members as an indispensable element of the whole.

Rousseau uses several distinct terms to express the various relationships which exist in a state governed by the social contract. The associates of such a polity 'collectively take the name of *people*, and are individually called *citizens* as being participants in the sovereign authority, and *subjects* as being bound by the laws of the state.'[9] What was formerly known as a 'city', in Rousseau's terminology is named 'republic' or 'body politic'. The members of such an association call it 'state' when it is passive, 'sovereign' when it is active, and 'power' when comparing it with its like. Being a member of the sovereign, each individual is bound to the other individuals who constitute this entity; furthermore, the individual's membership of the state means that he is bound to the sovereign. As a result, from the time the contract is agreed, no member can be injured without the state being affected, nor can the state be attacked and the subjects remain unharmed.

On the subject of leadership in such a society, Rousseau diverges from Hobbes's view in not seeing leadership as the result of natural force or election. Rather, he traces the history of government to the earliest societies, which he claims were governed by the aristocracy. He subdivides aristocratic rule into three categories: natural, elective and hereditary, marking out elective aristocracy as the best of the three, for 'it is aristocracy in the true sense of the word.'[10] Government by aristocracy, elected on the basis of integrity, intelligence, experience and other qualities which inspire respect and admiration, is the best form of government according to Rousseau. If government is undertaken by a small group of the most intelligent citizens, the common good, rather than the benefit of the ruling power, will be served.

The female ruler, then, is a trope which interested Grillparzer deeply for all of his creative life. The numerous diary entries dealing with historical and mythical queens, and the lengthy engagement with figures such as Drahomira, show that female rulers, who were anathema to the prevailing gender constructs of the nineteenth century, presented themselves as prime dramatic material for the playwright at all stages of his career. In the following two chapters, I analyse Grillparzer's presentation of *Sappho* and *Libussa* in the context of contemporary gender debates and the social contract. *Sappho* and *Libussa* are more than dramas on the nature of female rule. The eponymous heroines function as examples of extraordinary women as a type, and therefore permit meditation on the role and position of such women in Grillparzer's Austria.

'Sie ehren Sapphon wie ein fürstlich Haupt': *Sappho* and the Social Contract

Scholarship has investigated *Sappho* primarily as a tragedy of the female poet or of the disappointed lover, and as an example of the apparent irreconcilability of art and love, particularly for women.[11] Alfred von Berger calls *Sappho* an 'einfache[s] und durchsichtige[s] Seelendrama' [simple and transparent psychological drama].[12] Norbert Griesmayer frames *Sappho* in terms of interhuman conflict when he contrasts the drama with *Ottokar*, where the characters act 'nicht nur im Raum des Zwischenmenschlichen, sondern auch in einem Raum des Staatlichen' [not only in the arena of the interhuman, but also in the arena of the state].[13] Superficially, the text itself supports such emphases. Sappho's suicide, which is partly the result of Phaon's rejection, favours her role as a scorned woman, while Rhamnes highlights her literary success:

> Wenn längst verfallen diese morschen Hüllen
> Und selber unsre Gräber nicht mehr sind
> Wird Sapphos Lied noch von den Lippen tönen,
> Wird leben noch ihr Name [...].[14]

> [When this soft flesh has long ago dissolved,/ And e'en our very graves have ceased to be,/ Will Sappho's songs still sounds from human lips,/ Her name still be alive, her name — (p. 91)]

As outlined in the introduction to this section, however, in this chapter I look at Sappho's role as ruler of Mytilene and the part that social contract theory played in the creation of this drama.

Grillparzer's writings on *Sappho* do not indicate that he focused on Sappho as a ruler, but they are contradictory. In a letter of 1818, he stresses that his heroine is primarily a poet and a lover:

> Sappho ist Dichterin! Daß Das hervorgehoben werde ist durchaus nöthig, die Wahrscheinlichkeit der Katastrophe hängt, wie ich glaube wesentlich davon ab. [...] Sappho ist in der Katastrophe ein verliebtes, eifersüchtiges, in der Leidenschaft sich vergessendes Weib; ein Weib das einen jüngeren Mann liebt. In der gewöhnlichen Welt ist ein solches Weib ein eckelhafter Gegenstand. (Nr. 104. *HKA* III/i, p. 99)

> [Sappho is a poet! It is absolutely necessary that this is emphasized, the likelihood of the catastrophe is, I believe, considerably dependent on this. [...] In the catastrophe Sappho is an infatuated, jealous woman who forgets herself in her passion; a woman who loves a younger man. In the real world, such a woman is a revolting object.]

In his *Selbstbiographie*, however, which was written several years later, he recalls his reaction to criticism of the drama. Some critics thought that Grillparzer focused too much on Sappho as a woman, rather than as a poet. Grillparzer writes that he welcomed this criticism: 'Ich war nämlich immer ein Feind der Künstlerdramen' [I was, you see, always opposed to artist's dramas] (*HKA* I/xvi, p. 130). He also writes that he wanted his Sappho to fall victim to 'eine[] wahre[] Leidenschaft und nicht eine[] Verirrung der Phantasie' [a true passion and not an aberration of the phantasy] which would not have been possible had he developed Sappho the Poet more thoroughly (*HKA* I/xvi, p. 131). A survey of eighteenth- and nineteenth-century reception of Sappho, however, supports my argument for a political Sappho. Although Frank and Pörnbacher conclude that Grillparzer did not conduct any research for *Sappho*, and do not identify any similarities with earlier adaptations of the material (*SW* I, p. 1308), Grillparzer's *Sappho* fits into two contemporary literary traditions. One the one hand, several other German-language adaptations of the Sappho material exist. On the other, wider European engagement with the material is another important context for Grillparzer's drama. An examination of these texts will show that, in creating a Sappho who was a political leader in the tradition of social contract theory, Grillparzer radically broke with tradition.

In 1793, Franz von Kleist published *Sappho. Ein dramatisches Gedicht* [*Sappho: A Dramatic Poem*]. He prefaces his work with a biographical sketch of his subject, as well as vignettes of other characters and an overview of Mytilenian society. Sappho's poems were familiar to all educated people, 'ihr Ruhm verbreitete sich mit unglaublicher Geschwindigkeit' [her fame spread with unbelievable speed].[15] Her poems kindled a love of poetry in the young people of Lesbos, and soon a group of female students had gathered around her.[16] When Phaon arrived in Mytilene, he was admired by all the women, but he 'sah über sie alle hin, und wählte Sappho' [ignored them all and chose Sappho]. Kleist writes that Sappho's misfortune was to be chosen as Phaon's 'Opfer der Verführung' [victim of seduction], and that she was weak enough to reciprocate.[17] The poet-admirers whom Sappho had spurned in Phaon's favour were angered, and wrote bitter satires against her.[18] These found a ready audience 'da Neid und Mißgunst ihre Hände im Spiel hatten [...] und die arme Sappho ward allgemein verlacht und verspottet' [since envy and resentment were involved [...] and poor Sappho was publicly mocked and ridiculed]. She found refuge in Phaon's love, but did not notice that this was diminishing. Phaon abandoned Sappho for one of her friends, but later returned 'aus Eigenliebe, um seinen Namen durch ganz Griechenland verbreitet zu sehen' [out of self-love, in order to see his name made famous through the whole of Greece].[19] Sappho welcomed his return, but he later left her a second time and went to Sicily. She followed him there and threw herself at his feet, but again he rejected her. She then committed suicide. Kleist's drama closely follows the story as laid out in his sources, and is a simple tale of love, betrayal and revenge in which Sappho's death is more directly related to Phaon's changing emotional attachment than in Grillparzer's *Sappho*.

Friedrich Wilhelm Gubitz's *Sappho. Monodrama* (1816) is a second example in the German tradition. This short work presents Sappho lamenting her desertion by Phaon, and therefore represents an even more restricted adaptation of the material than Kleist's. Gubitz's Sappho is a woman who has let her identity be entirely subsumed by that of her lover — 'Mein Dasein war in Deinem aufgelöst' [My being was dissolved in yours][20] — and who cannot therefore continue living once he has abandoned her. Sappho's poetry is linked to her love, and when Phaon has rejected her, she rejects her poetry, which she does by destroying her lyre and laurel wreath.

It is significant that Sappho sees her submission to Phaon as a source of shame not only for herself as a poet, but for the female sex in general: 'Durch dieses Fleh'n hab' ich mein ganz Geschlecht/ Und meinen Ruhm auf immerdar geschändet' [My entreaties have defiled all my sex/ And my fame for evermore].[21] Although she hopes that death will absolve her from the shame of submitting to Phaon, she says that she does not die because of his betrayal, but because she is no longer capable of love or trust. She jumps from a rock and is carried aloft.

The contemporary German tradition also brought forth Friedrich Gottlieb Welcker's *Sappho, von einem herrschenden Vorurtheil befreyt* [*Sappho, liberated from a prevailing prejudice*] (1816). The 'herrschender Vorurtheil' [prevailing prejudice] to which Welcker's title alludes was that of Sappho's non-heterosexuality, an 'unsäg-liche Gemeinheit, welche sich oft, vordem und neuerlich, über die Sappho ausge-sprochen hat' [indescribable wickedness which has often been expressed about Sappho, both in former times and more recently].[22] However, as Joan DeJean writes, Welcker never informs readers where and when this supposed prejudice was dominant, and she argues that at no point before Welcker did the image of a homosexual Sappho prevail. The majority of Welcker's book is dedicated to rejecting claims of sexual deviance aimed at Sappho, although at all times refraining from any mention of Sappho's homosexuality, or of female sexuality in general.[23] Indeed, DeJean remarks that Welcker, despite being credited with the foundation of modern Sappho scholarship, shows a consistent lack of interest in the poet, and provides no new information about her, even as he formulates 'what seems to be the first modern defence, even eulogy, of male homosexuality'.[24] If Grillparzer was aware of the charges against his subject, it is hardly surprising that the bisexual or homosexual theme does not surface in his own treatment of the material,[25] given that the strict censorship forbade plays to depict 'eine unsittliche Lehre oder eine wirckliche sittenlose That oder Verbrechen' [an indecent message or a real immoral act or crime], which at the time would surely have included same-sex relationships.[26] Welcker does, however, note that the citizens of Mytilene 'haben [Sappho] die höchste Auszeichnung erwiesen, welche der Stolz auf einen berühmten Mitbürger in jenen Zeiten eingeben konnte, indem sie sie auf ihre Münze prägen ließen' [accorded [Sappho] the highest honour which in those times pride in a famous citizen could give, by embossing her image on their coins].[27] There are no mentions of Welcker's work in Grillparzer's diaries or notebooks, but he may have been aware of the high social status which Sappho's poetic successes accorded her, and may have built upon this when he included a political element in his own drama.

The second literary tradition in which Grillparzer's Sappho must be placed is a larger European one. DeJean traces nineteenth-century engagement with Sappho to Germaine de Staël's salon, where the founders of philology, and notably the Schlegels, came into contact with two fictions of Sappho thanks to de Staël's lifelong interest in the poet.[28] The first of these fictions emerged in France in the decade prior to the French Revolution and portrayed a politically subversive Sappho who was forced into exile after a failed revolt against a dictator. De Staël herself tirelessly promoted this version. The invention of a political Sappho 'revitalize[d] the Sapphic plot by shifting its energy from sexual promiscuity to political sedition'.[29] The link between Sappho and political revolt originated in Jean Du Castre d'Auvigny's *L'Histoire et les amours de Sapho de Mytilène* [*The Story and Romances of Sappho of Mytilene*] (1724). Here, it is not Sappho, but her suitor Alcée, who is involved in a revolt against the senate.[30] In 1788, Jean-Jacques Barthélemy published *Voyage du jeune Anacharsis en Grèce* [*Travels of Anacharsis the Younger in Greece*], which 'enshrined [Sappho] as a political exile, a revolutionary who had fought alongside Alceus to overthrow tyranny'.[31] Although he had no evidence to support his conception of her, Barthélemy's portrait of a political Sappho captured the imaginations of numerous Sappho commentators, and was soon assimilated as historical fact, even by serious scholars.

An opposing vision of Sappho accompanied Napoleon's rise to power, notably in Italy.[32] This tradition, which began with Alessandro Verri's novel *Le Avventure di Saffo* [*The Adventures of Sappho*] (1782), shifted the focus from Sappho to Phaon: 'In this new fiction, there is no mention of Sappho's political activities; narrative energy is concentrated instead on a hypermasculinized Phaon.' Other works in this tradition include Etienne Lantier's *Voyages d'Anténor* [*The Travels of Antenor*] (1797) and Pierre-Jean-Baptiste Chaussard's *Fêtes et courtisanes de la Grèce* [*Celebrations and Courtesans of Greece*] (1801).[33] The authors of Napoleonic adaptations of the Sappho material remove her from the political sphere and assign her passive and demeaning roles, 'as if to guarantee against the threat of all female political activity, either conservative or revolutionary'.[34] These works were the precursors of the nineteenth-century German Sapphic tradition.

According to DeJean, it was de Staël more than any other writer who exploited the theme of Sappho's exile.[35] She sees the plots which de Staël creates for Sappho in *Delphine*, *Corinne*, and *Sapho* 'as the fulfilment, but more properly as the disclosure of the eighteenth-century French Sappho tradition.'[36] In *Corinne*, in DeJean's opinion the most developed Sapphic fiction of the turn of the century, 'the battle lines between literary women and the forces of the (Napoleonic) patriarchal order are drawn as nowhere else'.[37] De Staël's works show the influence of Barthélemy's political innovation, and reject the Napoleonic vision of an apolitical Sappho.[38] They also reanimate Sappho the writer, and reverse the model in Napoleonic fiction 'in which the obscure young woman is irresistibly attracted to the handsome, strong man'.[39]

DeJean sees not de Staël's version of Sappho, but that of the Napoleonic tradition as the foundation of the German tradition, a tradition which is often still dominant today and in which 'Sappho would never again be political, never again narratively or sexually active'.[40] A dispassionate Sappho was created to 'silence the speculation about female sexuality so threatening to the builders of empires'. Yet DeJean also identifies Grillparzer's *Sappho* as the beginning of the next phase of the Sapphic tradition, one in which German scholarship began to create fictions of the original writer.[41] One of the most discussed elements of Grillparzer's drama, Sappho's suicide as renunciation of sexuality and a sign of penance necessary to gain poetic immortality, is an important innovation in the tradition.[42] DeJean speculates that

Grillparzer's decision to reformulate Sappho's suicide as a ritual which frees her from the flesh and allows her to achieve immortality could indicate that Grillparzer was indeed familiar with the French versions mentioned here, or with Welcker's work.[43] Here, I argue that quite the opposite is the case: although Grillparzer's Sappho is most definitely a poet, she is also an important political figure in Mytilene. Grillparzer's drama would therefore seem to be part of the French tradition of a political Sappho, rather than the Napoleonic tradition of a passive Sappho which DeJean argues was so influential in the German-speaking world. Yet Grillparzer's drama is also innovative, for his Sappho is not a revolutionary who fights tyranny, but, as I show, the leader of a polity the foundations of which are located in social contract theory.

De Staël exerted an extraordinary influence on the German imagination around 1800, and was read by Grillparzer, and so deserves greater attention here. Both she and her novel *Corinne, ou l'Italie* [*Corinne, or Italy*] (1807) had a large and positive impact on German women writers of the time. The novel, which narrates the eponymous heroine's struggle to unite her literary career with her romantic life, was very popular upon publication, and between 1807 and 1810 fourteen editions or pirated versions appeared in France, England, Switzerland and Germany.[44] Judith Martin notes that many German women in both Biedermeier and Vormärz periods created their own *Künstlerromane* under the influence of de Staël and *Corinne*. Martin lists Johanna Schopenhauer's *Gabriele* (1819–1820), Ida Gräfin von Hahn-Hahn's *Gräfin Faustine* [*Countess Faustine*] (1840) and Luise Mühlbach's *Der Zögling der Natur* [*The Pupil of Nature*] (1842) as examples.[45] For both Mühlbach and Hahn-Hahn, reading *Corinne* was a formative experience which inspired their artistic dreams.[46] De Staël and her writings helped German women challenge the teachings that deemed them incapable of genius, and 'her exemplary status encouraged them to defy women's exclusion from public artistic activity and political commentary'.[47]

Grillparzer was among de Staël's readers. He had read *Corinne* by 1816, that is, one year before the composition of *Sappho*. His dislike of both the work and its author comes across in his diary entries. In 1816 he wrote:

> Ich habe dies Buch noch nicht ausgelesen, aber bis jetzt scheint mir der Plan einer der unglücklichsten die je entworfen worden sind. (Nr. 169. *HKA* II/vii, p. 78.)
>
> [I have not yet finished reading this book, but up to now the plan seems to me to be one of the most unfortunate which have even been drafted.]

Similarities between *Sappho* and *Corinne* are quite pronounced, and include Corinne's triumphal arrival in Rome, which is similar to Sappho's return to Mytilene; the juxtaposition in both works of an independent public woman with one who more obviously fits contemporary ideals; and the death, in both cases, of the heroine. Josef Nadler writes that Grillparzer found '[d]as eigentliche Thema des Dramas, die Liebestragödie der Dichterin' [the actual theme of the drama, the poet's love tragedy] in *Corinne* and that the features shared by the two works confirm de Staël's influence on Grillparzer.[48] Marianne Burkhard argues that the structural similarities between *Sappho* and *Corinne* imply the direct influence of the latter on the former. Burkhard even cites Grillparzer's admission in 1829 that there are similarities between the two works.[49] Pichler, who had met de Staël, wrote to Grillparzer after a performance of the drama that she saw de Staël herself in Sappho:

> in Schröder Sapho sah ich *Madame Stael* nach allen *Individualitäten* die ich von dieser Frau weiß. Gut, menschlich großmüthig, hingegeben, leidenschaftlich — unbedacht in der Wahl ihrer Liebe — eifersüchtig, und durch die Kunst dem Leben und der Wirklichkeit entfremdet [...] (1818. Nr 112. *HKA* III/i, p. 114.)
>
> [in Schröder's Sappho I saw *Madame de Staël* with all the *individualities* I know to be in this woman. Good, humanly generous, devoted, passionate — thoughtless in her choice of love — jealous, and through art estranged from life and reality [...]]

Later in his life, however, Grillparzer would expressly deny even a similarity between the works.[50] Whether or not any similarities exist between de Staël's and Grillparzer's heroines, and whether or not Grillparzer was influenced by her, de Staël and her work are important for several reasons: first, as we have seen, *Corinne* left myriad works by female writers in its wake; second, while *Sappho* scholarship focuses on the heroine's death, interpretations of *Corinne* seem more willing to accept as emancipatory the mere existence of a woman who lives from her literary works. Lori Marso, for example, writes that Corinne was de Staël's alternative 'vision of what politics could be, would be, if only we could value the feminine re-infused into the public sphere as a woman citizen'.[51] In the following interpretation of Grillparzer's *Künstlerdrama*, I take a similar approach. By putting *Sappho* in the context of contemporary gender debates and women writers, I argue against claims that Sappho's difficulties in uniting a literary career with a private life reflect the realities of Biedermeier Austria. Further, in examining the social and hierarchical structures of Sappho's polity, I argue that Grillparzer's portrayal of the woman poet as a ruler gives the drama an additional emancipatory facet.

Grillparzer's *Sappho* strongly reflects contemporary cultural ideas regarding gender and space. That the mores of Sappho's Greece markedly resemble those of Grillparzer's Austria has been remarked upon by more than one critic. Burkhard writes that it is the values of Grillparzer's own culture which determine Sappho's social role in the drama.[52] Politzer, meanwhile, comments on the distinctly bourgeois quality of the contractual terms in which Sappho conceives her relationship to Phaon. Sappho's language, argues Politzer, is littered with phrases taken from the Vormärz idiom of trade.[53] Steidele writes that the social order which Sappho's death restores has nothing to do with classical Greece, and everything to do with Grillparzer's reality, for it is the nineteenth-century social order which limits women's freedom in professional, social and sexual terms.[54]

The topography of *Sappho* is linked to the gendered framework of Sappho's society, which in turn is a reflection of Grillparzer's own. In I/i, Rhamnes places Sappho's society within the context of nineteenth-century mores when he says, 'Der Mann mag das Geliebte laut begrüßen,/ Geschäftig für sein Wohl liebt still das Weib.' (ll. 38–39) [A man may loudly greet the thing he loves,/ But woman serves and loves withdrawn and still. (p. 7)] This society is rooted in the binary oppositions of male-female, active-passive, public-private, and Rhamnes reformulates Schiller's famous lines in the 'Lied von der Glocke' ['The Song of the Bell'] (1798): 'Der Mann muß hinaus/ In's feindliche Leben/ [...]/ Und drinnen waltet/ Die züchtige Hausfrau.'[55] [The man must be out/ In hostile life toiling/ [...] And in [the house] presides/ The chaste gentle housewife. (p. 12)] There are also echoes of the opening monologue of Goethe's *Iphigenie auf Tauris* [*Iphigenia in Tauris*] (1787): 'Der Frauen Zustand ist beklagenswert./ Zu Haus' und in dem Kriege herrscht der Mann/ Und in der Fremde weiß er sich zu helfen. / [...] / Wie eng-gebunden ist des Weibes Glück!'[56] [Yet the lot of woman is pitiable./ At home and in war man is the master/ And abroad he knows how to fend for himself./ [...] How narrowly bound is the fortune of woman! (pp. 33–34)] In her monologue in III/i, Sappho reiterates the binary nature of gender relations. Men, unwilling to be constrained by the limitations of inner life — 'Zu eng dünkt ihm des Innern stille Welt' (l. 819) [too narrow seems the quiet world within (p. 42)] — throw themselves at life, hoping to find glory. Or, as the proverb goes, '*Dem* Mutigen gehört die Welt.' [Fortune favours the brave.]

Although Rhamnes first indicates that Mytilene is governed by a patriarchal code, Phaon is the main proponent of patriarchal society in the drama. In II/i he reveals the misogynistic atmosphere of his family's household. His father was a traditional paterfamilias who disapproved of women's active participation in public life. Writing on Staël's *Corinne*, Angelica Goodden argues that the deceased father of Oswald, Corinne's lover, is present in spirit and is 'an image of prohibition'.[57] Phaon's father, through the influence he has had on his son, is present in *Sappho* in much the same way. Phaon assures himself that even his father would abandon his prejudices regarding female poets, should he see Sappho (ll. 508–11). This upbringing has left its mark on Phaon. When insulting Sappho, he is unable to free himself from misogynistic metaphors. So, in III/vi, he compares her to Medusa — 'blinkt nicht ein Dolch in ihrer Hand/ Und noch zwei andre liegen tiefversteckt/ Dort unter den gesenkten Augenlidern?' (ll. 1154–56) [A dagger gleaming in her hand;/ She has two more besides that lie concealed/ Deep in her eyes beneath lowered lids (p. 56)] — and to Circe, claiming she laid her magic on him from afar (ll. 1164–74). Importantly, in this metaphor, Sappho's songs acquire negative connotations due to the comparison with Circe's spells. Phaon's background also helps explain why he is attracted to Melitta, who William C. Reeve argues is a caricature of nineteenth-century feminine ideals.[58]

Sappho appears on the stage in I/ii at the head of a triumphal procession. She is sumptuously dressed, rides in a carriage drawn by horses and carries a lyre: this is Sappho the poet, the public figure, returning victorious to her homeland. Welcomed by adoring crowds, she is at this point very much in the public sphere.[59] At the end of this scene, the townspeople leave and Sappho and Phaon are alone. She is still on stage when the curtain falls, and only reappears in II/v, where she is dressed in simple attire and without her lyre or wreath, the symbols of her public role. At some point in the intervening scenes, the setting of the play has moved from the external and public to the internal and private. Moreover, in the elapsed time Phaon has transferred his affections from Sappho towards Melitta, her servant. Sappho, entering the scene at this point, encounters Melitta and Phaon after their kiss.

It is while the public is becoming private that Phaon first catches sight of Melitta. When Phaon stumbles upon Melitta in the grounds of the palace, he does not at first recognize her. What draws him to her is their common longing for a distant homeland which, according to Phaon, unites those whom it afflicts. On seeing her face, however, he recognizes the servant who spilled wine during the feast. In his monologue in II/i, Phaon expresses his discomfort in Sappho's public world of glamour, and in Melitta recognizes another who is out of place in the public eye. Phaon, whom Sappho has elevated above his born station in life, is looking for someone of his own kind, someone who belongs to the private sphere. Both Phaon and Melitta use the phrase 'niedere[r] Herd' [lowly hearth] at different points in the play, a phrase which unites them in a common, lowly background. Phaon mentions the hearth of his parents' house where he first heard Sappho's songs sung by his sister (ll. 166–69). In II/iii, Melitta says, 'Der Sklavin Platz ist an dem niedern Herde' (l. 578) [The slave girl's place is by the lowly hearth (p. 27)]. That for both the humble hearth is a point of orientation cannot be a coincidence. Rather, it is an indication of their shared private, domestic preferences. In this sense, they both stand in opposition to Sappho.

The association of Melitta and Phaon with the lowly hearth, in contrast to the more dignified imagery of mountain peaks associated with Sappho, shows the richness of Grillparzer's social detail. Grillparzer has imbued the topography with social as well as gendered significance, and the image of the hearth marks both Melitta and Phaon as members of the lower social orders. As Yates writes, Sappho and Phaon are divided less by an age gap than by 'a still wider disparity in character and calling'.[60] That Mytilenian society is defined by a class hierarchy also goes some way to explaining how Sappho has been able to achieve such an esteemed position despite Rhamnes' formulation of prevailing gender roles. As Kerstin Aidenhoff and her colleagues write, Sappho is autonomous not because she rejects society, but because she is its ruler.[61]

In IV/viii Sappho's grounds become a public space. The stage has gradually filled with slaves and locals attracted by the furore over Phaon and Melitta's escape. In need of their assistance in apprehending the fugitives, Sappho is forced to give a speech in her capacity as a local ruler.

> Ha diese hier! Habt Dank, ihr Treuen, Dank!
> Gebt, Menschen! was die Götter mir verweigern!
> Auf meine Freunde, rächet eure Sappho!
> Wenn ich euch jemals wert, jetzt zeigt es, jetzt! (ll. 1516–19)

> [Ah! They are here! Thanks, loyal friends, my thanks!/ Let mankind give me what the gods refuse!/ Up, friends of mine, to help! Avenge your Sappho!/ If ever you have loved me, show it now! (p. 75)]

When she has finished speaking, they leave the stage and she is clearly fatigued by the effort she now needs, after dedicating herself to private life, to enter the public arena once again. Not only this, but the presence of crowds in her private space has weakened her, and their departure is a welcome relief: 'Sie gehn! Nun ist mir wohl! — Nun will ich ruhn!' (l. 1539) [They go! Now all is well — Now I will rest! (p. 76)] Her physical state is destroyed by this exposure to public life and she falls into Eucharis' arms. After a brief period as chatelaine, public life has become unbearable to her where once it invigorated her.

It is important to note briefly the toponymy which governs the drama's larger topographical scope. Both 'Lesbos' and 'Mytilene' are used, although not synonymously as some critics have subsequently done. In the drama, 'Lesbos' refers to the island as a geographical entity. So, in II/iv, Melitta says that the ship in which she was held captive approached the shore of Lesbos. 'Mytilene', conversely, refers specifically to the urban political entity which is governed by Sappho and located on Lesbos. In II/vi, Sappho tells Phaon that many of the girls she once educated are to be found 'in dem Kreise/ Von Mytilenes besten Bürgerinnen' (ll. 748–49) [in the ranks/ Of Mytilene's best and proudest matrons (p. 38)]. And, in V/iv, Rhamnes talks of the good that Sappho has done *Mytilene*'s citizens.

Grillparzer's use of the word 'Bürger' is also important, as it is an indication of the nature of Sappho's rule in Mytilene. The use of this word, and Sappho's description of her relationship to her subjects as 'Wechseltausch' [exchanges], indicate that Sappho's polity is defined by the pervading concept of a social contract between each citizen and his fellow citizens, and between each citizen and his ruler. Sappho's role as a ruler has not been ignored, but nor has it received substantial critical attention. Peter von Matt's matter-of-fact statement that Sappho is only fully portrayed as a ruler and as a priestess disguises the lack of critical attention which Sappho's role as ruler has received.[62] Aidenhoff and her colleagues are among the few scholars who have written in detail about Sappho as a ruler. They argue that Grillparzer's depiction of Sappho and Melitta's relationship, which they call 'ein[e] idealisiert[e] Sklavenhalterordnung' [an idealized slaveholding system], shows that it is a personal relationship which unites Sappho and her subjects, and that these subjects choose to be subordinate.[63] However, Aidenhoff et al. do not position these observations in the context of Grillparzer's readings in philosophy. Similarly, Caroline Anders notes that Sappho 'erscheint [...] obgleich nicht dynastisch legitimiert, als Adelige. Sie herrscht faktisch über die mytilenischen Bürger wie eine Fürstin und gebietet über alle ihrem Haushalt angehörenden Figuren.' [Appears [...] although not legitimized by belonging to a dynasty, as a noble. She effectively rules over the citizens of Mytilene and commands all those who belong to her household.][64] Pia Janke acknowledges Sappho's status as ruler, and that she is politically active. She also notes that her rule is based on mutual understanding rather than violence, but does not put this in a philosophical context.[65] Leitich also recognizes the consensual aspect of Sappho's rule when she writes that Sappho rules not because she commands, but because the people serve and admire her.[66]

The formulations of social contract theory discussed earlier inform my interpretation of the drama. Sappho is an elected leader insofar as the population of Mytilene has decided to invest her with the power, in the Hobbesian taxonomy, over those who have bound themselves together in the social contract. Sappho's speech at the beginning of I/iii is one of the many indications of the benevolent and consensual relationship between sovereign (in the Hobbesian definition) and her subjects:

> Siehst du, mein Freund, so lebt nun deine Sappho!
> Für Wohltat Dank, für Liebe — Freundlichkeit,
> So ward mir's stets im Wechseltausch des Lebens [...] (ll. 107–09)
>
> [You see, my friend, thus does your Sappho live:/ For favors thanks, for love, well — friendliness,/ Thus have I ever fared in life's exchanges (p. 10)]

The 'Wechseltausch des Lebens', the reciprocal give-and-take philosophy which dominates in Mytilene, demonstrates the influence of the social contract in the lives of the citizens who live under the watchful eye of their 'common power'.

Sappho's first speech in I/ii is full of love and affection for her people, and their reactions show that the feelings she expresses are mutual, a further indication of the influence of the social contract which binds ruler and ruled in a consensual relationship. For Sappho, the inhabitants of Mytilene are 'Freunde, Landsgenossen' (l. 44) [friends, compatriots (p. 8)], and it is only in their midst that she is able to develop as a person and an artist. The wreath she has won at Olympus ceases to become a burden when she has rejoined her fellow citizens, and is again the citizen ('Bürger') rather than the poet. The citizens of Mytilene express great pride in their ruler's talents, and one of the crowd cries out, 'Wohl uns, daß wir dich, Hohe, unser nennen!' (l.59) [Well that we call you ours, exalted one! (p. 8)] This reverence strongly suggests that it is Sappho's intelligence which marked her out as their leader in accordance with Hobbes's and Rousseau's formulations of the social contract.

This discussion of the political framework of Sappho's polity is important for my interpretation of the drama because I argue for a link between her position in Mytilene and her eventual suicide. I do not aim to dismiss interpretations which attribute her suicide to the irreconcilability of art and life, but rather to show that there are additional facets to Sappho's personality, and therefore also to her tragedy.

Werner M. Bauer identifies Sappho as the focal point of Mytilenian society: she is rich, powerful, and laden with prizes. She is the very opposite of a social outcast.[67] For Bauer, Sappho, '[d]ie "poetissa laureata" verfügt also über Besitz, Gesinde und auch politisch über ihre Insel, gemäß ihres kulturellen Ansehens' [the "poet laureate" has at her disposal property and servants, and she is politically in charge of her island, as appropriate to her cultural prestige].[68] Similarly, Aidenhoff et al. argue that Sappho is by no means outside Mytilenian society; rather, 'die persönliche Würde dieser Frau [garantiert] die Legitimität des sozialen Systems' [the personal dignity of this woman [guarantees] the legitimacy of the social system].[69] Despite his recognition of this element of Sappho's being, however, Bauer still attributes her death to the loss of her identity as an artist in tune with her society. As soon as she uses her public power — which she has gained from her poetic talents — to further her private aims, she is guilty of misuse of power. This misuse of political power, for Bauer, results in the loss of her artistic character. Although Bauer is right in asserting, as has been shown, that Sappho's power derives from her status as an artist, I disagree with Bauer's implicit assertion that art and politics are to be found in so symbiotic a relationship that the misuse of political power results in the loss of Sappho's identity as an artist. His interpretation may result from a common tendency to identify Sappho as a poet first and foremost, while relegating other aspects of her public persona to the sidelines. I would suggest that Sappho's misuse of political power — and breach of the social contract — leads to her further political role, which is based on an understanding between her and her subjects, becoming untenable. Aware of her transgressions against the order she is supposed to protect, and sentenced by Phaon, her political miscalculations contribute to her death.

Sappho's crimes amount to tyranny, which Locke defines as '*the exercise of Power beyond Right*, which no body can have a right to'.[70] Tyranny is '[w]hen the Governour, however intituled, makes not the Law, but his Will, the Rule; and his Commands and Actions are not directed to the preservation of the Properties of his People, but the satisfaction of his own Ambition, Revenge, Covetousness, or any other irregular Passion'.[71] Sappho's first violation against her society is the installation of Phaon, her lover, as a citizen. Sappho informs the Mytilenians of Phaon's investiture as a citizen with the words: 'Umsonst sollt ihr die Bürgerin nicht grüßen,/ Sie führt zum Dank euch einen Bürger zu.' (ll. 70–71) [You should not welcome the citizen in vain:/ In gratitude she brings to you a citizen. (p. 9)] Although Sappho has bound Phaon to her, he makes no such promises to the other citizens. Nor do the Mytilenians have a say in whether or not he should be welcomed into the polity. Furthermore, Sappho even sees the introduction of Phaon into Mytilenian society as something her citizens should be grateful for. She abuses her power in order to place the man she loves at her side.

Although Sappho does not install Phaon as leader of Mytilene, as Robert Pichl has claimed, their relationship is further complicated when Sappho gives Phaon the preeminent role in her private household, elevating him to a position above even hers:[72]

> Sieh um dich her, du stehst in deinem Hause.
> Den Dienern zeig' ich dich als ihren Herrn,
> Der Herrin Beispiel wird sie dienen lehren. (ll. 295–97)

> [Look round; the house in which you stand is yours./ I'll show you to the servants as their masters;/ From me, their mistress, they shall learn to serve (p. 16)]

Yet what we know about Phaon's upbringing would suggest that he is not at all suitable for such a role. Rhamnes certainly does not think Phaon fit to be in charge, and angers Sappho with his astonishment at her decision. Phaon's origins are anything but aristocratic, and he describes his parents' home as a cottage. It is Phaon who most frequently stresses the gulf which separates him from Sappho in terms of education, class and experience. He names Sappho 'Hellas' erste Frau' (l. 255) [Hellas' foremost daughter (p. 14)] and himself 'Hellas' letzte[r] Jüngling' (l. 256) [the last of Hellas' sons (p. 14)]. Although Phaon's ennoblement pertains only to the private sphere, this distinction emboldens him and encourages his later rebellion.

As the drama progresses, it becomes clear just how serious a mistake it was to introduce Phaon into Mytilenian society. Having been raised to such a high status without any contractual obligations to the other citizens, he scorns the conventions which have heretofore governed Mytilene. In Act V we see the true extent of Phaon's disregard for Sappho's polity. He has been apprehended by the people of Mytilene, and rails against his capture with the words, 'Bin ich nicht ein freier Mann?/ Wer gab das Recht ihr [Sappho] meinen Schritt zu hemmen?' (ll. 1621–22) [I am a free man after all!/ Who gave to her the right to stay my steps? (p. 82)] For Phaon, being a free man does not mean abiding by Mytilene's laws and customs; it means being above the law, and above even Sappho. His denunciation touches not just Sappho, but every citizen.

This self-importance is aggravated by misogynistic views inculcated in him as a child. His refusal to adhere to the terms of the social contract is compounded by his specific repudiation of Sappho as a woman and as a ruler. He alone among the male inhabitants of Mytilene cannot tolerate a woman's rule:

> Seid ihr so zahm, daß eines Weibes Rache
> Geduldig ihr die Männerhände leiht,
> Und dienstbar seid der Liebe Wechsellaunen? (ll. 1633–35)

> [Are you so tamed that to a woman's vengeance/ You men without protesting lend your hands/ And make yourselves the slaves of love's caprice? (p. 82)]

Phaon's prejudices against women and female poets, inherited from his father, mean that he cannot impute Sappho's actions to anything but her emotions. He even goes so far as to ask whether Sappho is the ruler in that country, to which the countryman answers, 'Sie ist es,/ Doch nicht weil sie gebeut, weil wir ihr dienen!' (ll. 1641–42) [She is,/ But not because she rules; because we serve her! (p. 83)] This is another indication of Sappho's consensual mode of government, which might be seen as a prototype for Libussa's polity in Grillparzer's later drama.

Sappho's second crime against Mytilene is the violence she inflicts upon Melitta. Although, as is clear from the designation of Melitta and others as slaves, there is a hierarchy of social classes in Mytilene, this does not excuse Sappho's behaviour towards Melitta. Indeed, the fact that Sappho refers to Melitta as '[d]ie Liebste [...] [v]on meinen Kindern' (ll. 740–41) [the dearest [...] [o]f all my children (p. 38)] makes her treatment of the latter seem all the more despicable. It is this behaviour that Bauer sees as the crime for which Sappho's death is atonement. By attacking Melitta in the hope of securing her own personal happiness, Sappho demands for herself a position above the law. As a result of this infraction, Phaon accuses Sappho of breaking the law, and in his condemnation of her, he destroys her 'eigentliche Existenz' [real existence], that is, her existence as an artist, and in doing so he sentences her to death.[73]

I take issue with Bauer's interpretation of Sappho's suicide for several reasons. First, the former of the crimes mentioned here is surely the more severe: by imposing Phaon upon the whole of Mytilenian society, Sappho rejects that society's very governing principles. In contrast to this, Sappho's attack against Melitta is a minor felony. Second, Bauer uses Phaon's tirade against Sappho (ll. 1685–94) to support his claim that, in essence, Sappho goes to her death guilty of crimes against art. Yet the two lines which precede this denunciation of Sappho the poet seem far more important. Phaon claims that she has become dehumanized and is no longer capable of compassion:

> So ist dein Busen denn so ganz entmenscht,
> Daß er sich nicht mehr regt bei Menschenleiden! (ll. 1683–84)
>
> [Is there no human feeling in your breast/ That it cannot be moved by human woe? (p. 85)]

Because it is clear from the very beginning that compassion and human kindness form the basic principles of Sappho's mode of governance, this accusation of heartlessness does more than destroy Sappho's artistic persona: it also invalidates her as a compassionate ruler who can claim to be invested with the authority of those she governs. I therefore suggest that Phaon's denunciation, which can, as Bauer does, be interpreted as a death sentence,[74] is a punishment for her own renunciation of Mytilene's guiding principles. The scene in which Sappho commits suicide certainly corroborates such an interpretation: she goes to her death with the insignia of the poet and of the ruler: 'Sappho reich gekleidet wie im ersten Aufzuge; den Purpurmantel um die Schultern, den Lorbeer auf dem Haupte, die goldne Leier in der Hand' (p. 368) [Sappho, richly dressed as in the first act, the crimson mantle about her shoulders, the laurel wreath on her head, the golden lyre in her hand (pp. 94–95)]. The death of this compassionate ruler was enforced by the least worthy of all her subjects as a punishment for crimes she would never have committed, had she not elevated him to so lofty a position. And herein lies both Sappho's tragedy, and Grillparzer's sympathy with her. Although Phaon's actions single him out as a base individual, he usurps Sappho's power and authority, destroying in the process a woman far superior to him.

Grillparzer's *Sappho* fits into a larger European context. The Sappho theme was very popular around 1800, when her life and works aroused some serious, as well as some not so serious, scholarly interest. Two other German-language versions of the material emphasize Sappho's romantic relationships, while French versions in the eighteenth century created a political Sappho. De Staël served as a contemporary Sappho figure whose life and writings encouraged a generation of German women writers, and of whose *Corinne* there are echoes in Grillparzer's drama. De Staël, in writing *Corinne*, was herself writing against a trend of Napoleonic Sappho fictions which championed an unpolitical Sappho whose artistic powers were dependent on Phaon. Grillparzer develops existing traditions of a political Sappho, but creates a political leader rather than a revolutionary, and does so in the context of earlier European writings on the social contract. Grillparzer's Sappho is portrayed as a successful and beloved ruler whose power is based on the consent of her citizens. This allows *Sappho* to be seen in the context of *Libussa*, which also shows a consensual female ruler divested of her power by a man.

'So nennt mich eure Fürstin und ich bins': *Libussa* and the Tragedy of the Extraordinary Woman

Libussa, for August Sauer Grillparzer's 'tiefsinnigstes Werk' [most profound work], is one of the author's most studied dramas, and has been approached by a large number of critics from various angles.⁷⁵ Gisela Stein sketches the plurality of themes which, over sixty years ago, had already been linked to the drama when she writes that *Libussa*

> has variously been taken to exemplify the contrast of culture and barbarism, the police and the legal state, the "vita activa" and the "vita contemplativa", the synthesis of Hegelian antitheses, the transcription of Kantian ideas on the development of mankind, the struggle of individualism and collectivism and the path into a great nihilism.⁷⁶

Franz Forster notes that Grillparzer often portrays opposition between a powerful woman and a weak man and argues that *Libussa* is his most interesting examination of the position of women in male-dominated societies.⁷⁷ Developing this argument, Libussa and Primislaus have often been interpreted as representatives of opposing ideologies or worldviews. Ruth Florack sees this as a facet which is absent from earlier versions of the Libussa myth. She argues that the central figures are 'Repräsentanten gegensätzlicher Normenhorizonte; sie verweisen auf eine gesellschaftliche Grundopposition der Restaurationszeit: Adel und liberales Bürgertum' [representatives of conflicting sets of norms; they point to a fundamental social opposition of the Restoration: nobility and liberal bourgeoisie].⁷⁸ Masato Ikuta writes that, in the relationship between the sexes, Grillparzer sees 'die Möglichkeit eines weitgehenden Einverständnisses, konstatiert jedoch einen Rest von Unüberbrückbarkeit' [the possibility of broad agreement, but establishes a remnant of irreconcilability].⁷⁹ Despite the ending of the drama, Ritchie Robertson argues that *Libussa* 'is revolutionary in realising the goals of women's emancipation: some women are educated, and all are equal with men'.⁸⁰

Forster sees *Libussa* as a historical drama because it is a drama about the state.⁸¹ Lorenz suggests several potential historical contexts for the drama: the victory of patriarchal over matriarchal societies; a revision of Prague's founding myth; or as a reference to Napoleon and Marie Luise's politically motivated marriage.⁸² For Ulrich Fülleborn it is not a historical drama, but 'ein Drama der Geschichte überhaupt' [a drama of history itself].⁸³ Yixu Lü rejects this interpretation and argues that rather than a metaphor for historical change and progress, *Libussa* documents the changes occurring in the nineteenth century and has a specific historical context: bourgeois society's progression towards modernity.⁸⁴

Grillparzer himself was aware of the complexity of the drama and the ideas which surface in it. In 1822, he had already conceived of Libussa and Primislaus as representatives of opposing world views. He sees Libussa's 'begeisterte Weisheit' [enthusiastic wisdom] as the opposite of Primislaus's 'Verstand' [reason], and writes: 'Primislaus ordnet und schlichtet. Libussens Zeit ist vorbei' [Primislaus orders and reconciles. Libussa's time is past] (Nr. 981. *HKA* II/viii, p. 7). He had also decided to include a gendered aspect to the drama. Libussa's 'Frauenherschaft [*sic*] des Gefühls und der Begeisterung' [matriarchy of feeling and enthusiasm] represents a 'goldenes Zeitalter' [golden age] which is destroyed by the Bohemians' demands for rights and property law. Libussa is forced to take a husband: 'Spottend frägt sie schon: was denn die Herrschaft des Mannes über die Frau rechtfertige?' [Derisively she asks what it is that justifies man's rule over woman] (1822. Nr. 1035. *HKA* II/viii, p. 20). This shows that Grillparzer intended for readers and audiences to engage with these topics, and indeed this formulation in his diary is more direct than in the drama itself, possibly suggesting another incident of self-censorship. In winter 1825/26, he wrote: 'Das Ganze läuft Gefahr aus dem Kreise der menschlichen Gefühle hinaus in das Reich der bloßen Ideen zu spielen.' [The whole thing is running into danger of leaving the sphere of human feelings and entering the realm of mere ideas.] (Nr. 1412. *HKA* II/viii, p. 184) He also worried that his attempts to portray the idea of Primislaus's superior endurance was unsuccessful, especially since, as he wrote,

> Das weibliche Geschlecht thut es dem männlichen in allem gleich, wenigstens in einzelnen Fällen. Wissen und Verstand, Muth und Entschloßenheit, alle diese Gaben besitzt, in seinen Erlesenen, auch das sogenannte schwächere Geschlecht, alle diese Gaben besitzt auch Libussa, Primislaus steht ihr sogar in mancher davon nach.

> [The female sex is in all things equal to the male, at least in individual cases. Knowledge and reason, bravery and resolve, the so-called weak sex also possesses all these gifts in its highest specimens. Libussa also possesses all these gifts, and in some of them Primislaus is even her inferior.]

As well as offering insight into the creation of *Libussa*, this statement is perhaps the clearest expression in Grillparzer's writing of the potential equality of the sexes. In 1831, he was still frustrated with the plethora of ideas in the drama. He found the plan unsatisfactory, and the drama as a whole uninteresting: 'Bloßes Gedankenzeug, nicht einmal streng abgegränzt, beinahe ohne Gefühls-, wenigstens ohne Leidenschafts-Motive.' [Mere intellectual nonsense, not even rigorously differentiated, almost without an emotional motive, at any rate without a motive of passion.] (Nr. 1930. *HKA* II/ix, p. 45.) Grillparzer ordered the destruction of *Libussa* in his will of 1848 because it had been written 'in Zeiten des härtesten Geistesdruckes, in langen Zwischenräumen, mehr um mich zu beschäftigen, als mit eigentlicher Hingebung und Begeisterung' [in times of harshest mental stress, with long intervals, and more to occupy myself than from true devotion or enthusiasm]. It was supposed to establish his 'Gedankengang im allgemeinen' [train of thought in general] (Nr. 684. *HKA* III/iii, p. 42). This means that Grillparzer not only did not want *Libussa* to be performed after his death, but that he did not write it with performance in mind.

Heinrich Laube was one of the few people to read the entire manuscript of *Libussa* before Grillparzer's death. In 1853, he wrote to Grillparzer and praised the drama's 'innere Reife' [inner maturity] (Nr. 768. *HKA* III/iii, p. 112). He also saw that it was a drama about the social roles of the sexes, and how these play out on a national level:

> Die Didaktik derselben [...] wächst so natürlich aus dem Stoffe und verschlingt

Mannes- und Weibesbestimmung mit Volks- und Staatsleben so eigenthümlich,
daß das Ganze wie ein völlig Neues anmuthet.

[Its didactics [...] grows so naturally from the material and intertwines male and
female destiny with the life of the nation and of the state so idiosyncratically
that the whole seems to be something completely new.]

This shows that at least some contemporaries were aware that Grillparzer's dramas discussed issues of women's social position. Laube also comprehended the drama's complexity: 'Es hat zuviel Gehalt, als daß es leichthin einstudirt und abgespielt werden könnte'; the actors 'müssen den Inhalt verdaut und nicht bloß hinabgeschlungen haben.' [It has too much content to be easily rehearsed and performed; must have digested the content and not just devoured it.] This would mean giving the actors a long time to prepare, and Laube, writing in April, suggested a performance in the autumn at the earliest. Laube also agreed with Grillparzer's assessment of the drama, namely that it would be an 'Ehrenerfolg' [honourable success] rather than a 'rauschender Erfolg' [rousing success]. Grillparzer must have expressed concerns regarding the political nature of the drama, perhaps because it features a Czech national foundation myth at a time when ethnic concerns were prominent in multinational Austria,[85] but Laube brushes these aside, writing that 'politisch kein Schatten von Bedenken darin ist' [politically there is nothing questionable in it], because Grillparzer's conception was 'so hoch und weit, daß es ganz unverfänglich bleibt' [so high and wide that it remains completely innocuous] (Nr. 768. *HKA* III/iii, p. 113).

Libussa, like *Sappho* before it, was written as part of an existing literary tradition. Grillparzer was familiar with a number of German-language versions of the Libussa material, as well as with Vaclav Hajek's *Böhmische Chronik* [*Bohemian Chronicle*], which was his most important source. Frank and Pörnbacher identify works by J. K. A. Musäus, Clemens Brentano, Karl Egon Ebert, and J. C. Bernard as sources for Grillparzer's *Libussa* (*SW* II, p. 1254). A brief overview of these sources will show that Grillparzer's introduction of Libussa as a regent in accordance with social contract theory was his addition to the tradition.

The *Böhmische Chronik* became increasing influential for German and Czech writers from the end of the eighteenth century onwards: Czechs, wanting to construct a national identity, found in Hajek a history of their people, while German literature in Bohemia used the *Chronik* to oppose both conflict between the constituent nationalities and centralization concentrated in Vienna.[86] This was part of a larger trend in which German writers actively received Slavic literature.[87] Herder first recognized the value of the Libussa myth, and Musäus popularized it in Germany.[88] Not only Grillparzer, but also Clemens Brentano and Carl Egon Ebert, whose works are discussed below, found their source material in Hajek.[89] Hajek explains how Libussa became the Czechs' leader and judge in simple terms. On the death of their father, Libussa and her two sisters asked the people whom they wanted as ruler. The people replied that the sisters should draw lots, which they did, and Libussa was accepted as ruler. Some Czechs, doubting that a woman could defend her people, demanded a male ruler, but they were convinced by others that

Libussa was indeed the best possible ruler, and so they reaffirmed their allegiance to her. These same fears resurfaced later, and Libussa agreed that a man would rule in a stricter fashion; she promised to marry the man the people chose. The people chose Primislaus, and Libussa kept her word. Primislaus 'lehrete alles Volck seine Rechte [...] und machte diese halb wilde Leute seiner Herrschung unterthan' [taught all the people his laws [...] and subjected these half-wild people to his rule].[90] When Libussa knew that she was close to death, she '[t]hät ihrem Volcke also große Danksagung daß sie ihr Treu und Gehorsam geleistet, bittende, sie wolten ihrem Herrn und Fürsten dergleichen thun' [gave great thanks to her people for showing her loyalty and obedience, and asked them to do the same for their lord and prince].[91] Hajek also deals with the period after Libussa's death, which was marked by conflict between the sexes. The women, led by Wlasta, one of Libussa's servants, feared that Libussa's death meant that their lot would be much harder, and they revolted. A seven-year war ensued, which the women lost despite some victories in battle.

Johann Karl August Musäus, in his *Volksmärchen der Deutschen* [*Folk Tales of the Germans*] (1782–1786), similarly pays little attention to the way in which Libussa becomes ruler of the Bohemians. He writes that Libussa 'nahm mit dem bescheidenen Erröten, welches den weiblichen Reizen den höchsten Ausdruck von Grazie mitteilt die Herrschaft über das Volk an' [took on rule over the people with the modest blush which lends the female charms the highest expression of grace], and that 'der Zauber ihres wonniglichen Anblicks machte jedes Herz ihr untertan' [the magic of her blissful appearance made every heart subservient to her].[92] Libussa 'saß auf dem Throne wie die Göttin Themis mit Schwert und Waage, und sprach das Recht ohne Ansehen der Person mit untrüglichem Urteil' [sat on the throne like the goddess Themis with sword and scales, and proclaimed the law regardless of the standing of the person with infallible judgment].[93] Primislaus also features in Musäus's version, although in a less important role than in Hajek or Grillparzer, and was 'ein rechtes Muster eines folgsamen unterwürfigen Ehegemahls, der seiner Herzogin weder das Hausregiment noch das Landesregiment streitig machte' [a fitting example of an obedient and submissive husband who did not dispute his duchess's rule in the house or in the country].[94]

In 1792, Johann Friedrich Ernst Albrecht's *Die Töchter Kroks, Böheims Fürstinnen* [*Krok's Daughters. Bohemia's Princesses*] was published anonymously. Albrecht's approach seems somewhat confused, and it is unclear whether he is approaching the subject matter as historical fact or myth. His declared aim is adding to the work of the 'Geschichtsschreiber' [chroniclers], who, he claims, do not pay enough attention to the private lives of Libussa and her sisters. According to *Die Töchter Kroks*, Libussa was tasked with governing Bohemia because the gods wanted it so. But this is not exactly a sign of the gods' approval, for as Libussa says, they did not want her sisters to be burdened with ruling, but free to do 'was mehr als herrschen ist' [that which is more than ruling].[95] The author presents a more developed and complex relationship between Libussa and her subjects than in the texts already discussed. Libussa rules because she has been chosen by the gods, but with the people's best interests at heart:

> [Die Götter] haben mir das Versprechen gethan, so ich nach ihren Willen keusch und recht lebe, so wollen sie mich stets lehren, was des Volks Wohl ist. Des Volks Wohl aber ist mein Wunsch und mein Wille.[96]
>
> [[The gods] promised me that, if I live chastely and well according to their wishes, they will always teach me the well-being of the people. But the people's welfare is my wish and my intention.]

Libussa links the gods and the people, for in obeying her, she says they obey the gods. In what could be seen as a precursor to Grillparzer's later intertwining of the myth with social contract theory, Libussa also asks the people, 'Wollt ihr dem euch unterwerfen, was ich in ihren Namen für Recht spreche?' [Do you want to subject yourselves to that which I in their name declare right?] The people agree to the conditions which Libussa suggests, and so she becomes ruler through a combination of divine revelation and popular support.

In Joseph Carl Bernard's *Libussa* (1823), the eponymous protagonist is already ruler at the beginning of the opera, and no real information is given regarding the relationship between ruler and subjects. As in *Die Töchter Kroks*, here Libussa also rules because she has been chosen by the gods.[97] However, her nobles are not happy with the situation, and Domaslav in particular 'nützt' [] jede Gelegenheit, des Weibes Herrschaft dem Volke verhaßt zu machen, bis dieses endlich einen Herrn mit Ungestüm verlangt' [used [] every opportunity to make the woman's rule unpopular among the people, until with impetuosity they finally demand a man].[98] The animosity of the nobles towards female rule has been amplified compared with its appearance in Hajek, and appears to stem from a much more virulent misogyny:

> Ihren Thron will ich erwerben,
> Sollt' ich drüber selbst verderben,
> Und zu meinen Füßen
> Soll die Stolze büßen
> Ihren Übermüth![99]
>
> [I want to acquire her throne/ Should it be my undoing,/ And kneeling at my feet/ The proud woman shall pay/ For her arrogance.]

Clemens Brentano's *Die Gründung Prags* [*The Foundation of Prague*] (1815) was another adaptation of the myth prior to Grillparzer's. Emanuel Grigorovitza argues that Brentano's creativity in adapting the myth means that Grillparzer, despite the freedoms he took in relation to the myth, cannot deny his dependence on this forebear.[100] As in *Die Töchter Kroks* and Bernard's *Libussa*, Brentano's Libussa is also a ruler by divine intervention. Although Libussa's subjects welcome her as their ruler, Brentano does not detail the relationship as closely as Grillparzer does. However, his Libussa, like Bernard's, sees links between divine will and the will of the people, and claims to stand 'in des Volks, der Götter Schutz' [under the protection of the people, of the gods].[101] These versions of the myth, in which divine intervention dictates that Libussa take up the reins of government, represent an alteration to the myth as it is related by Hajek, and provide an interesting contrast to Grillparzer's later innovation, in which Libussa rules thanks to chance, but explicitly formulates a methodology of government in which her people acquiesce.

Hajek's *Chronik* mentions the wars between the sexes which followed Libussa's death. These wars also feature in *Die Töchter Kroks*, where Wlasta, one of Libussa's servants, tries to make herself queen. But it is Karl Egon Ebert's *Wlasta. Böhmisch-nationales Heldengedicht* [*Wlasta. Bohemian National Epic*] (1829) which most fully utilizes this aspect of the myth. His epic poem takes place in a post-Libussa age, where women are dominated by men and long for the return of the matriarchy:

> Und wahrlich, Nacht ist's jetzo, und Tag ist's einst gewesen,
> Da noch Libussa herrschte, vom Himmel auserlesen,
> Von einem Gott erwählet, der gleich vertheilt die Rechte,
> Und der nicht fragt beim Geben: von welcherlei Geschlechte?[102]

[And truly now it is night, and once it was day,/ When Libussa still reigned, chosen by heaven,/ Elected by a god who distributed rights equally,/ And when giving does not ask: of which sex?]

Here again we see the idea of Libussa as a ruler by divine right, rather than by the people's will. Libussa had taught the Bohemian women the arts of fighting and riding, and let them hunt game 'wenn wir vor Kampflust schäumten' [when we seethed with belligerence]. The Bohemian men were sidelined under Libussa's reign, and were cowed by the women's power. But the situation was reversed after Libussa's death, and their new state of subjugation leads the women to a revolt against their male rulers. Ebert portrays a number of battles between the men and women of Bohemia in which both sides show bravery and endurance as well as brutality and violence. Despite some successes, Wlasta and her army of maidens are defeated, and patriarchal order is restored.

These adaptations of the Libussa myth which pre-date Grillparzer's version demonstrate two important points. First, that prior to Grillparzer, there had been no detailed examination of the link between Libussa and her subjects. Writers justify her rule by invoking divine intervention, or luck, or a combination of the two. In the case of *Die Töchter Kroks*, we even have a ruler whose position is explicitly welcomed by the people. However, in none of these works are an explicit contract or a declaration of intention formulated, as in Grillparzer's drama. This then is Grillparzer's important addition to the myth, which will be examined shortly. Second, by comparing Grillparzer's works with those which preceded it, it is clear that, although he mentioned 'Jungferkrieg' [maidens' war] in an 1822 note on *Libussa* (Nr. 1035. *HKA* II/viii, p. 20), to a large extent he excised the Amazon material from his version, as Udo Köster has previously noted. Köster sees this as a positive step, for the Amazon material brings with it negative connotations:

> Eine Geschichte der Amazonen ist immer auch die Geschichte ihrer Vernichtung, und die grundsätzliche Delegitimierung der Amazonen [...] macht es unmöglich, das alternative Prinzip einer weiblichen Herrschaft mit positiven Konnotationen darzustellen.[103]

[A story about the Amazons is always also the story of their destruction, and the fundamental delegitimization of the Amazons [...] makes it impossible to present the alternative principle of female rule with positive connotations.]

Grillparzer's decision to end his drama with Libussa's death could, however, also have been motivated by the fear that portrayals of graphic violence meted out by women would anger the censors.

Although Grillparzer's *Libussa* deals with a number of complex issues, as noted above, its content can be summarized simply enough. On the death of King Krokus, one of his three daughters, Libussa, Kascha and Tetka, must assume his crown. All three are engaged in supernatural practices and live isolated from the world. When her sisters refuse, Libussa accepts and institutes a new political regime. Her subjects are dissatisfied with her rule and demand she take a husband. She chooses Primislaus, a peasant who saved her from drowning and who brings with him ideas for the creation of a modern and industrialized state. Estranged from everything which was familiar to her, Libussa dies when making a prophecy during the foundation of Primislaus's new town, Prague.

I argue here that Libussa's reign should be seen as a manifestation of the ideas propounded by social contract theory. My interpretation is therefore partly in agreement and partly at odds with those of other scholars who have already written about the new era which Libussa seeks to initiate. Walter Weiss notes that Libussa represents a different world order than the patriarchal one in which she lives.[104] Lü argues that Libussa justifies her social reorganization 'lediglich mit ihrer Zugehörigkeit zum weiblichen Geschlecht und mit dem Wesen der Frau: Milde und Sanftmut, die jede Art von Zwang und Gewalt verabscheut' [merely with her affiliation to the female sex and with the nature of woman: mildness and gentleness which detests every type of force and violence].[105] This interpretation ignores the content of Libussa's two speeches in Act I, which show Libussa's reign to be founded primarily on her people's acquiescence. Fülleborn notes that Libussa detests violence, but his claim that her government should be seen 'offensichtlich als die volle Verwirklichung von Freiheit, Gleichheit und Brüderlichkeit [...], d. h. der Ideen der Französischen Revolution' [evidently as the full realization of liberty, equality and fraternity [...] i.e. the ideas of the French Revolution] fails to take into account Libussa's preeminent position.[106] Lorenz also sees Libussa's polity in the context of the French Revolution, and argues that Libussa takes an interest in her subjects' lives and sees herself more as *prima inter pares* than as a ruler.[107] Frederic Coenen misunderstands the nature of Libussa's polity when he calls it 'rather hazy communism'.[108] Anna Kuhn warns against labelling Libussa's state a matriarchy and suggests 'Frauenherrschaft' [rule by women] as a more suitable alternative.[109] Julia Neissl agrees, as matriarchy would mean 'eine Umkehrung des Patriarchats [...]: also ein System mit Hierarchien und Unterdrückung der Männlichkeit. Dies passiert auf keinen Fall' [a reversal of patriarchy [...]: i.e. a system with hierarchies and oppression of masculinity. In no way does this happen].[110] Neissl's take is surely accurate, for while Libussa is a woman ruler, and while she seeks to change the society she inherits from her father, there is no indication whatsoever that men *are* oppressed, even if the male nobles *feel* that they are suffering at her hands.

From the beginning of the drama on, it is clear that the three sisters live in elected separation from the world. In the second scene, in the sisters' castle, the stage directions indicate an 'aufgeschlagenes großes Buch' [large open book (p. 11)] lying on the table.[111] Dobra and Swartka, the sisters' maids, display their familiarity with their mistresses' interests as they discuss astrology and interpret the movements of the stars as prophecies of Krokus's death. This stands in contrast to the simplicity of Primislaus's environment, as portrayed in the opening scene, and as such is an early indication of his and Libussa's differing origins. The arrival of the peers of the realm with news of Krokus's death gives the maids an opportunity to emphasize the gulf that separates the sisters from the rest of the Bohemian populace. Biwoy, one of the peers, demands that the sisters be roused, and Dobra responds by setting up the wladiken as savages: 'Am Tor der Einsicht tobt und lärmt der Wilde,/ Hört er am liebsten doch der eignen Worte Klang.' (ll. 133–34) [At wisdom's gate the savage raves and cries;/It seems he ever loves the sound of his own word. (p. 13)] The sisters, then, not only live separated from the world, but see themselves as distinct from, and superior to other Bohemians.

The sisters' world before Libussa's ascension to the throne is a metaphor for the domestic sphere in which Grillparzer's female contemporaries were supposed to find their life's meaning. The sisters find fulfilment in the narrow confines of their castle and in their engagement with potions and prophecies; nothing could be further from their minds than the assumption of temporal rule in their father's footsteps. Both Kascha and Tetka are exclusively concerned with their metaphysical practices, and both refuse to accept the Bohemian crown because they are wedded to the preternatural. Kascha, refusing, highlights her interest in magic and nature, and repudiates the value of earthly goods (ll. 209–14). Tetka rejects the importance and validity of an earthly reign and criticizes the practicalities of *Realpolitik*. No less than Kascha, she sees the trappings of human society as inferior to the knowledge and insight available to her in the natural world (ll. 220–23). They are equally confident that Libussa will have no interest in succeeding their father, and attempt to warn the peers who have come to find Krokus's heir.

When Libussa finds her way back to the castle, she reveals the guilt she feels for leaving her dying father and declares her intention to mourn him. Kascha is quick to point out that one of their number will be excluded from their mourning, and when Libussa asks whom, Kascha replies: 'Die, welcher obliegt mehr als [Krokus] beklagen:/ Zu folgen ihm in seiner harten Pflicht.' (ll. 326–27) [She who has higher duties still than mourning him:/To follow in the paths that he found hard. (p. 24)] Libussa quickly voices her unwillingness to become ruler, but Kascha points out the she and Tetka have already declined, and suggests they draw lots to decide. Each sister will put her belt into a bowl, and the sister whose belt is the last to be blindly drawn will take the crown. They soon discover, however, that Libussa's trinket has been taken from her belt, which she realizes is Primislaus's doing. Kascha therefore ostracizes and criticizes Libussa, and wonders at her behaviour: 'Die Nacht im Wald, in Bauerntracht gehüllt,/ Verloren deines Vaters Angedenken.' (ll. 373–74) [The night spent in the wood, in peasant garb,/Lost the memento that your father gave! (p. 26)] Libussa defends herself, saying, 'Mein Vater lebt, ein Lebender, in mir,/ So lang ich atme lebt auch sein Gedächtnis.' (ll. 375–76) [My father lives in me, a man alive;/As long as I shall breathe his memory lives. (p. 26)] Kascha paints Libussa as a frivolous, careless young girl who does not properly love her father: 'Die Liebe knüpft sich gern an feste Zeichen,/ Der Leichtsinn liebt was schwankend so wie er.' (ll. 377–78) [Love ever seeks to cling to lasting tokens;/Frivolity that's mutable loves change. (p. 27)] Kascha decides that Libussa's loss disqualifies her from their circle and that she cannot partake in their draw. Libussa, who did not relish the idea of ruling, accepts Kascha's decision defiantly:

> Ich soll nicht losen? Und ich will es nicht.
> Wo sind die Männer aus der Czechen Rat?
> Den Vater will ich ehren durch die Tat,
> Mögt ihr das Los mit dumpfen Brüten fragen:
> Ich will sein Amt und seine Krone tragen. (ll. 387–91)

> [You say I may not draw? Nor will I then./ Summon the councillors who wait below./ Through deeds I'll honor to my father show;/ Brood ye o'er lots in dull-eyed meditation,/ I shall assume his office and proud station. (p. 27)]

Although Libussa is very impassioned, it is hard to see her decision in an entirely positive light. Much as Hero's decision to enter the temple was less a positive affirmation of the joys of monasticism, and more a thorough rejection of the secular world outside, so Libussa's decision, well justified though it is, seems motivated more by anger at Kascha's words than by genuine desire to rule. Indeed, considering Libussa's initial rejection of the role, and her only grudging later acceptance, it is difficult to agree with Ulrich Fülleborn who writes that Libussa accepts the role 'spontan, in einem bewußten Akt selbständiger Entscheidung' and becomes '[d]as moderne, in Freiheit verantwortlich handelnde Individuum' [spontaneously, in a conscious act of independent decision; the modern individual who in freedom acts responsibly].[112] Hans Gmür is closer to the truth when he writes that Libussa's sense of duty makes her assume the role of monarch, even though she knows that her powers will atrophy in contact with the world.[113]

Libussa's decision was made possible by her experiences outside the castle and with Primislaus, which act as a catalyst and make her more willing to separate herself from her sisters. In a second speech, she reiterates the importance which her recent experience of the external world has for her:

> Denk' ich von heut
> Mich wieder hier in eurer stillen Wohnung
> Beschäftigt mit — weiß ich doch kaum womit —
> Mit Mitteln zu den Mitteln eines Zwecks,
> Mit Mond und Sternen, Kräutern, Lettern, Zahlen,
> Dünkts allermeist einförmig mir und kahl.
> [...]
> Mit Menschen Mensch sein dünkt von heut mir Lust,
> Des Mitgefühles Pulse fühl' ich schlagen,
> Drum will ich dieser Menschen Krone tragen.
> (ll. 396–401, 404–06)

> [If from today/ I think myself again in your still dwelling,/ Concerned with — aye, I hardly know with what — / With means that serve the means to some

far end,/ With moon and stars, with herbs, with letters, numbers,/ It seems at most monotonous and bare./ [...] To live with men will henceforth please me best,/ I am partaker in the fate men share;/ These men are human, I their crown will wear. (p. 28)]

Libussa not only takes on the crown, but delivers a harsh criticism of her sisters' world. Kascha and Tetka are so removed from the world that their spells and prophecies are but 'Mitteln zu den Mitteln eines Zwecks' [means that serve the means to some far end]. She also rejects the validity of their mourning, which is nothing but 'dumpfe[s] Brüten' [brooding], and decides to honour her father 'durch die Tat' [[t]hrough deeds].

Before agreeing to succeed her father, Libussa makes it clear that she sees herself as a ruler within the terms of the social contract. At the end of Act I, Libussa explains the kind of relationship she wishes to have with her subjects. She tells the kneeling representatives to stand, which is clearly a rejection of their submission. She intends to move away from her father's method of government towards one in which she is not so much ruler as advisor:

> Es hielt euch fest des Vaters strenge Rechte
> Und beugt' euch in heilsam weises Joch.
> Ich bin ein Weib und, ob ich es vermöchte,
> So widert mir die starre Härte doch.
> Wollt ihr nun mein als einer Frau gedenken,
> Lenksam dem Zaum, so daß kein Stachel not,
> Will freudig ich die Ruhmesbahn euch lenken,
> Ein überhörtes wär' mein letzt' Gebot. (ll. 427–34)

[My father strictly ruled a land unstable;/ He made you subjects, but it was your gain./ I am a woman; even were I able/ To rule you harshly, that must cause me pain./ Be ever mindful 'tis a princess guideth;/ Obey the reins nor need the heavy hand,/ Then I will lead you on where fame abideth;/ One word ignored would be my last command. (p. 29)]

Domaslav happily accepts Libussa's offer, on his behalf and in the name of those he commands: 'Nimm unsern Schwur darauf und unsrer Untertanen' (l. 442) [This oath will we and all our subjects swear (p. 29)]. Libussa's reaction is to ban the word 'Untertan' (l. 443) [subject] and in doing so further develop her concept of ruling:

> In Zukunft herrscht nur Eines hier im Land:
> Das kindliche Vertraun. Und nennt ihrs Macht,
> Nennt ihr ein Opfer das sich selbst gebracht,
> Die Willkür, die sich allzu frei geschienen
> Und, eigner Herrschaft bang, beschloß zu dienen.
> Wollt ihr als Brüder leben, eines Sinns,
> So nennt mich eure Fürstin und ich bins;
> Doch sollt' ich Zwei'n ein zweifach Recht erdenken,
> Wollt' eher ich an euch euch selbst als Sklaven schenken.
> Seid ihrs zufrieden so? (ll. 444–53)

[Henceforth there's naught shall govern in our land/ But childlike trust. Not rule by force shall be./ Each freeman, seeming himself too free,/ Doubting his right to rule, shall make oblation/ Of privilege, and choose to serve the nation./ If you as brothers, of one mind, will live,/ I will accept the princely name you give./ But if a twofold law shall govern liege and lord,/ Then better you than I such justice should award./ Are you content with this? (p. 29)]

These two speeches are a more explicit indication of the influence of social contract theory than is offered in *Sappho*. As Robertson has already argued, Libussa determines to rule only with the approval of the Bohemian people: 'So nennt mich eure Fürstin und ich bins.'[114] Libussa sees her role as a guide and expects the people to live peacefully side by side. She does not want to use violence, so insists that the Bohemians must be 'lenksam dem Zaum', i.e. willing to accept her decisions. The second speech in particular makes clear that any power Libussa enjoys is only possible because it is willingly given to her by her subjects. The people choose Libussa — they are 'ein Opfer das sich selbst gebracht' — and they do so because they would not have been able to cope with absolute freedom. Libussa makes her reign contingent on her ability to rule fairly and promises to step down if she should fail to do so. At the end of the second speech Libussa asks if the people are satisfied, and all present reply in unison: 'Wir wollen!' (l. 453) [We are! (p. 30)]

As far as I am aware, only one critic, Ruth Florack, has recognized the influence of Rousseau's *Du contrat social* on *Libussa*, although Florack sees Primislaus as its voice in the drama. This approach ignores these speeches by Libussa, which evidence the influence of Rousseau, Locke and Hobbes, and which form the theoretical basis for her reign. It is perhaps this failure to grasp the influence of social contract in the foundation of Libussa's reign which leads Florack to criticize Libussa so harshly. Florack criticizes Libussa for propagating a class-based society, even though this is a solution which has the explicit approval of the populace.[115] Indeed, Rousseau supported aristocratic government in his work. Florack writes that Act II stresses 'die Demonstration der ums Schicksal eines jeden wissenden und besorgten Landesmutter' [the presentation of a mother of the nation who knows and is concerned about the fate of each individual], and that the people are not individualized with names but interchangeable figures who represent different aspects of communal life.[116] As to the first objection, Florack seems to be implying that this pastoral part of Libussa's role is a mere charade, which does not seem to be the case. This is confirmed by the fact that Libussa addresses at least two of her subjects directly and by name: she asks Brom how he is getting on with his wife and if they are reconciled with each other (ll. 616–17), and asks Risbak whether he has accepted his daughter's suitor (ll. 640–41).

Libussa's entrance in Act II is reminiscent of Sappho's arrival in Mytilene. Libussa uses a horticultural metaphor to explain her perception of her role:

> Was euch die Gärtnerin mit nächster Sorge,
> Verteilend hilfreich Naß und Wärm' und Schatten,
> Kann nützlich sein, das ist euch ja gewiß. (ll. 600–02)

[And as a gardener with his fostering care/ Distributes warmth and moisture, helpful shade,/ I shall, feel sure, be useful as I may. (p. 42)]

Libussa gives thanks for her people's respect and fondness. Sappho also thanks her subjects on her arrival in Mytilene, so perhaps it is a recognition of their mutually agreed reigns. Part of Libussa's role, as she sees it, involves ensuring that the work is not being forgotten. The discussion among her people indicates that there is a more communal approach to life and that wealth is shared rather than concentrated in the hands of the elite. So, for example, one of the returned workers tells an old man, 'Wir pflügten heut dein Feld' (l. 514) [We ploughed your field today. (p. 34)], and is thanked for his efforts. Another man, who protests his daughter's romantic relationship on the grounds that she is rich but her suitor 'hat kaum zu nagen' (l. 530) [lives in direst need (p. 37)], is rebuked by others and told to forget the old ways, for money is no longer the driving force of Bohemian society:

> Was kaufst du um dein Geld da wo nichts käuflich ist,
> Das Land ein breiter Tisch, an dem, wer hungert, ißt.
> Deshalb der Burschen Not, der Tochter dich erbarme,
> Er hat was ewig reich: ein Herz und rüst'ge Arme. (ll. 535–38)

> [When nothing is for sale, money is needed least./ The land is one broad board where all who hunger feast./ Take pity on the lad nor thwart your daughter's will./ His heart and powerful arms will bring them riches still. (p. 37)]

The scenes at the beginning of Act II, however, show that there is by no means universal delight at Libussa's innovations. An old man and a younger one discuss Libussa's reign, the elder fondly remembering Krokus who was a 'Held' [hero (p. 32)] and resepcted men's social position: '[Er] ließ den Mann am Herde nicht vertöffeln' (l. 485) [No man of us did e'er grow soft with leisure (p. 32)]. He clearly resents the 'unmasculine' emphasis of Libussa's reign which stresses peace and harmony rather than war. The younger man, however, praises Libussa and is thankful that peace has brought stability: 'der Löffel hat noch keinen Mund zerrissen/ [...]/ Ich lobe mir den Frieden.' (ll. 488, 492) [a spoon your mouth will never slit/ [...] Peace is the meat for me. (p. 33)]

In addition, over the whole of Libussa's reign hovers the spectre of state-imposed surveillance, which Neissl has already written about: 'Das Gesetz des kindlichen Vertrauens (V. 445) entpuppt sich als Grundlage für ein rigides Überwachungssystem, dessen Kontrolle die Aufgabe von Wlasta ist.'[117] [The law of naive trust turns out to be the basis for a rigid system of surveillance, the control of which is Wlasta's task.] Early in Act II, the stage directions give an idea of the threatening and pedantic nature of this surveillance: 'Ein Gewaffneter und Wlasta mit Brustharnisch und Helm an seiner Seite haben, wie beaufsichtigend, die Menge durchschritten' (p. 39) [A soldier, with Vlasta in a cuirass and helmet beside him, has entered and been walking through the crowd as if watching over them (p. 33)]. The armed man tells a group of people to keep their noise down, and later Wlasta makes sure that the workers leave punctually for their shift. The presence of Wlasta encourages the barkeeper to refuse alcohol to those who are already intoxicated because he fears trouble and remarks, 'Die Fürstin liebt das nicht' (l. 510) [The princess was ill pleased. (p. 34)]. Wlasta also questions those playing a board game. A player answers that no money is lost or won, and Wlasta replies, 'Ihr tut ganz recht, wollt ihr die Fürstin euch gewogen' (l. 521) [And rightly so, if you desire the princess' love. (p. 36)]. The presence of this surveillance team does not negate the values expounded by Libussa in Act I, for the people agreed to be led by her. However, the nature of her reign belies her self-proclaimed aversion to violence. While Wlasta is not violent, she is part of Libussa's coercive apparatus which represents a constant *threat* of violence. Hagl-Catling sees Wlasta as 'das nach außen projizierte Bild von Libussas Fähigkeit, auch hart zu sein' [the outward projection of Libussa's ability also to be tough].[118] Libussa's rule is different from her father's not because it is bereft of strict rules, but because those strict rules are dictated by Libussa with the consent of the people.

If the common people benefit from the equality ushered in by Libussa, the nobles are dissatisfied by their former serfs' gains. Lapak, observing the masses, remarks, 'Man ist recht glücklich hier' (l. 544) [Each one is happy now (p. 38)], and Domaslav replies, 'Und Jedermann ist satt' [And all have plenty, too (p. 38)]. Yet they are annoyed that the common people are no worse off than themselves, a situation which they feel undermines their standing. Although they praise Libussa — 'Ah, sie ist der Frauen Zierde!' (l. 549) [Ah, the crown of womankind. (p. 38)] — they do not approve of the new order. Lapak phrases his displeasure in terms of the new prominence of women: 'Die Weiber, dächt' ich, stellt sie allzuhoch.' (l. 560) [To set these maids so high is hardly wise. (p. 39)] Lapak and Domaslav hesitantly agree that Libussa, in her wisdom, knows what she is doing, but Biwoy gives voice to the fears we can reasonably assume they all share:

> Hör' ich die Klugen sprechen als im Fieber.
> Verkehrt ist all dies Wesen, eitler Tand,
> Und los aus seinen Fügen unser Land.
> Weiber führen Waffen und raten und richten,
> Der Bauer ein Herr, der Herr mit nichten. (ll. 570–74)

> [When wise folk talk with never rhyme nor reason./ This whole estate is wrong, vain, of no use./ Our country from its framework is torn loose./ Women carry weapons, advise and judge,/ New power for the peasant the noble debases. (p. 40)]

Biwoy calls Libussa's *Frauenherrschaft* a thing of fantasy, and fears for the country's safety should it come under attack. Although Lapak and Domaslav agree that Biwoy is exaggerating, they see a kernel of truth in his assessment, and Domaslav concludes: 'Daß ichs denn grad heraus nach meiner Einsicht deute,/ Dem Ganzen fehlt ein Mann, ein Mann an ihrer Seite.' (ll. 583–84) [I'll speak my mind and say what scarce can be denied:/The country needs a man, a good man at her side. (p. 41)]. Each suggests the others as possible candidates for Libussa's hand, but Biwoy is sceptical and asks: 'Doch frägt darnach das zarte Frauenbild?' (l. 590) [But does the tender maid ask for this? (p. 41)] Domaslav ignores his concern and says they should all present themselves as potential husbands and let Libussa choose one of them.

Libussa rejects the three noblemen because they fail to solve the riddle she sets them. At the same time, however, a man who was unsatisfied by Libussa's judgment in a boundary dispute, and who had already demanded the right to a male adjudicator, again raises his voice and demands a male ruler: 'Ich will mein Recht.

O wäre hier ein Mann,/ Der ernst entschiede wo es geht um Ernstes.' (ll. 958–59) [I want my rights! I would there were a man/ That he might gravely judge a grave affair. (p. 62)] Libussa agrees and says that a male ruler is necessary because she cannot be tough: 'Den Zügel führ' ich wohl mit weicher Hand,/ Doch hier bedarfs des Sporns, der scharfen Gerte.' (ll. 963–64) [I hold the reins, but with too light a hand,/ For here the spur, the stinging goad is needed. (p. 62)] Rather than the mild guidance offered by Libussa's metaphorical bridle, a man would lead with the whip. However, her decision to send for Primislaus is motivated not only by matters of state, but also by matters of the heart. Earlier in Act II, it becomes clear that Libussa's role, and her estrangement from her sisters, has caused her to feel a deep loneliness:

> Wer einsam wirkt spricht in ein leeres All,
> Was Antwort schien ist eigner Widerhall.
> Ha Wlasta komm! Ist irgend ein Geschäft,
> Ein Mühen, eine Sorge, eine Qual,
> Daß ich bevölkre meines Innern Wüste? (ll. 687–91)
>
> [At work alone, we speak but are not heard;/ What seemed an answer was our echoing word./ Ah, Vlasta, come. Is there no task to do/ Requiring labor, anxiousness, yes, pain,/ That I may people this vast void within me? (p. 46)]

Unlike Sappho, Libussa decides to raise Primislaus to a high position not only because of her private feelings; she does so for the good of the state, and with the explicit support of her subjects. However, because she acknowledges her loneliness and her admiration for Primislaus, it is obvious that her decision serves both political and private ends.

Although Libussa acquiesces in calls for a male leader, she clearly states her opposition to any change in the way the state is run. She accuses the people of being deaf to the reason she attempted to preach, and predicts that Primislaus will institute 'Recht, das Recht zugleich und Unrecht/ Und statt Vernunft gibt er euch ein Gesetz' (ll. 1000–01) [justice, just at once and unjust,/In place of reason he will give you law (p. 63)], and turn the state into a capitalist enterprise in which the individual is no longer valued: 'Bis ihr für euch nicht mehr, für Andre seid.' (l. 1003) [Till all you do for other men is done. (p. 63)] Libussa's words are bitter, and she warns the people that, once they have decided to elect Primislaus, there will be no return to the way things were, nor will there be recourse to her. In Act III, Libussa again shows how opposed she is to the idea of a husband. She voices her desire to return to her sisters, and declares it degrading that she should be forced to marry and spend her life among the common people. She believes that Primislaus should feel honoured because she remembered him kindly. So eager is Libussa to avoid marriage that she even suggests that Wlasta should marry and that Wlasta's children could rule. Nevertheless, Libussa shows herself willing to accept Primislaus as a husband, but rails against the people's demands for a male ruler:

> Ein Mann, ein Mann! Ich seh' es endlich kommen.
> Die Schwestern mein sie lesen in den Sternen,
> Und Wlasta führt die Waffen wie ein Krieger,

> Ich selber ordne schlichtend dieses Land;
> Doch sind wir Weiber nur, armsel'ge Weiber;
> Indes sie streiten, zanken, weinerhitzt,
> Das Wahre übersehn in hast'ger Torheit
> Und nur nach fernen Nebeln geizt ihr Blick,
> Sind aber Männer, Männer, Herrn des All! (ll. 1311–19)
>
> [A man, a man! How well I know what follows!/ My sisters, they read truth in Heaven's stars/ While Vlasta bears her weapons like a soldier/ And I give law and order to this land./ Yet we are only women, weak-souled women./ But though they fight and quarrel, hot with wine,/ Are blind to truth for folly and for haste,/ Their eyes fixed greedily on far illusions,/ They still are men, men, lords of all creation! (pp. 79–80)]

Libussa here again questions the patriarchal order, as she did at the beginning of Act II: 'Fühlt sich dein Knecht als Mensch dem Herren ähnlich,/ Warum soll sich dein Weib denn minder fühlen?' (ll. 629–30) [You feel your servant like you as a man;/Why should your wife not feel herself your equal? (p. 43)] This is a powerful statement of female self-determination, capability and independence which echoes Hero's words.

Primislaus's views on women show Libussa's concerns to be justified. He is a staunch representative of the patriarchal order and 'an unreconstructed male chauvinist' who makes no secret of his belief in male social dominance.[119] When Primislaus and Libussa meet for the first time, Libussa refuses to reveal her identity to him. As she leaves, he takes the ornament from her belt as he wants to know who she is. By doing so, he appropriates an important sign of Libussa's identity. Without it, she is rejected by her sisters and forced to accede to the throne. In his monologue at the beginning of Act III, Primislaus uses the analogy of an apiary to illustrate the degrading nature that female rule has on men. He rejects the idea of asking for Libussa's hand because receiving such an honour from a woman would damage his dignity and be contrary to natural male dominance: 'Denn es sei nicht der Mann des Weibes Mann,/ Das Weib des Mannes Weib, so stehts zu Recht.' (ll. 1028–29) [Let no man be the husband of his wife;/The woman be the man's wife, now and ever. (p. 66)] Primislaus sees male-female relationships exemplified in marriage, and female rule as an inversion of the natural order. It is for men to be dominant, to choose, and for women to accept their subordinate role. At the beginning of Act IV, he sees Wlasta examining weapons, and questions a woman's involvement in such matters. Wlasta challenges him to a duel, which he evades. He then approvingly remarks to Slawa, who rushes on stage saying 'O schützet mich!' (l. 1465) [Oh, lend me aid! (p. 87)]:

> Du bist das erste Weib
> An diesem Wunderort, das Schutz begehrt,
> Die andern sind vielmehr geneigt zu meistern. (ll. 1465–67)
>
> [No woman heretofore/ In all this wondrous place has asked protection,/ The others, rather, wish to play the master. (p. 87)]

In the final scene of Act IV, Libussa finally decides to accept Primislaus as her husband. The people, believing Primislaus to be in danger in Libussa's castle, demand his release. Primislaus shows himself to be a brave leader and wants to quell the uprising, and this proves to Libussa that he is the man who can help her rule. Primislaus challenges and ultimately destroys Libussa's society. In this respect, he plays a role similar to that of Phaon in *Sappho*. At the end of Act V, Libussa prophesies the demise of the society she has tried to establish. Libussa foresees that under Primislaus, the individual will cease to be of any importance, and will be subsumed in the mass of the state. Individuals will no longer be bound by the social contract, nor under the aegis of a solicitous ruler:

> Nicht Ganze mehr, nur Teile wollt ihr sein
> Von einem Ganzen, das sich nennt die Stadt,
> Der Staat, der jedes Einzelne in sich verschlingt,
> Statt Gut und Böse, Nutzen wägt und Vorteil
> Und euern Wert abschätzt nach seinem Preis. (ll. 2332–36)

> [No longer in yourselves complete, you would/ Be only parts of some large whole, the city,/ The state, which swallows up all single things,/ Not good and evil scans, but use and profit,/ And estimates your value at its price. (p. 124)]

Libussa paints a terrifying picture of life in this anonymous state, where the interpersonal relationships of the social contract no longer carry any weight, and even the gods coalesce into one impersonal deity. As personal relationships are devalued and feelings become mere words, words will spark wars and blood will be spilt. Rather than the communal approach which flourished under Libussa, self-interest will motivate the new society: 'Der eigne Nutzen wird dir zum Altar/ Und Eigenliebe deines Wesens Ausdruck.' (ll. 2373–74) [Your selfish purposes become your altar,/And self-love the expression of your soul. (p. 125)] Where once society had been harmonious, all human interaction will resemble war as the base elements of human nature dominate:

> Der Trug, die Hinterlist ersetzt das Schwert.
> Das Edle schwindet von der weiten Erde,
> Das Hohe sieht vom Niedern sich verdrängt.
> Und Freiheit wird sich nennen die Gemeinheit,
> Als Gleichheit brüsten sich der dunkle Neid. (ll. 2383–87)

> [Deceit and cunning will supplant the sword,/ Nobility will vanish from the earth,/ And high ideals be thrust aside by low./ Mean impudence will steal the name of freedom,/ Dark envy boast itself equality. (p. 125)]

Contrary to the expectations of Biwoy, Lapak and Domaslav, Primislaus's new order does not represent a return to the feudal hierarchy which they support. They had hoped that Libussa's marriage would return them to their positions of preeminence, but the changes they helped make possible actually facilitate a significant deterioration in their standing. Domaslav recognizes that the city, where the masses are concentrated, can only lead to a dilution of their power as society is depersonalized:

> Was ist auch diese schlauentworfne Stadt
> Als Schwächung unsers Ansehns, unsrer Macht?

> Wenn erst das Volk in großer Zahl vereint,
> Ist von uns jeder minder als er war,
> Der Mächt'ge kaum gewachsen so viel kleinen. (ll. 2289–93)
>
> [What means this city else, so slyly planned,/ Than weakening our influence and power?/ Let once the folk in numbers be united,/ Then each of us is less than heretofore,/ With all his might less strong that many weaklings. (p. 122)]

Primislaus's plans for Prague satisfy no one but himself. Crucially, they represent a drastic rejection of everything for which Libussa stands. The effort she needs to pronounce her prophecy drains what strength she has left, and at the end of the drama she collapses, despite the positive tone of her final monologue, in which she predicts a distant future which is the 'Zeit der Seher wieder und Begabten' (l. 2483) [days of prophets and of men of genius (p. 129)]. Libussa is taken off stage by her sisters, who to the very end are critical of her decision to engage with mankind. Kascha speaks the final lines of the drama, and blames the people's rejection of Libussa's society for her death. Specifically, it was their refusal to trust Libussa, to be 'lenksam dem Zaum', which necessitated her death. As Kascha says, 'Vertraun gehorcht, der Eigenwille denkt' (l. 2509) [Pure trust obeys, self-will seeks its own way (p. 130)]. Trust was the foundation of Libussa's rule, and when that principle was rejected, Libussa's sacrifice — that is, the renunciation of communion with her sisters — became meaningless and the continuation of her reign, impossible. Libussa's very being is defined by her relationships with mankind — 'Ich liebe [Menschen], und all mein Sein und Wesen/ Ist nur in ihrer Nähe was es ist' (ll. 2456) [I love them well, and all my self and being/Is only real when I am in their midst (p. 128)] — and so their rejection must destroy her.

Notes to Chapter 4

1. Grillparzer, 'Der Zauberwald. Eine komische Oper in 3 Aufzügen', in *HKA* II/iii, 87–91, p. 87.
2. Thomas Hobbes, *Leviathan*, ed. by J. C. A. Gaskin (Oxford: Oxford University Press, 2008), p. 89.
3. Ibid., p. 91.
4. Ibid., p. 114.
5. John Locke, *Two Treatises of Government*, ed. by Peter Laslett (Cambridge: Cambridge University Press, 1988), p. 74.
6. Ibid., p. 269.
7. Ibid., p. 283.
8. Ibid., p. 331.
9. Jean-Jacques Rousseau, 'The Social Contract', in *Discourse on Political Economy* and *The Social Contract*, trans. by Christopher Betts (Oxford: Oxford University Press, 1994), pp. 43–168 (p. 56).
10. Ibid., p. 103.
11. E.g. Marianne Burkhard, '"Die letzte Schuld des Lebens": Grillparzers "Sappho" als Tragödie der dichtenden Frau', *Monatshefte* 74 (1982), 122–38 (p. 125); Kokyo Morikawa, 'Grillparzers 'Sappho' — Entstehung und Erläuterung', *JdGG* 3. Folge 6 (1967), 101–19 (p. 108).
12. Alfred Freiherr von Berger, 'Das Szenische bei Grillparzer', *JdGG* 19 (1910), 29–38 (p. 33).
13. Griesmayer, *Das Bild des Partners in Grillparzers Dramen*, p. 263.
14. Grillparzer, 'Sappho', in *HKA* I/I, 263–373, ll. 1839–42.
15. Franz von Kleist, *Sappho. Ein dramatisches Gedicht* (Berlin: Vossische Buchhandlung, 1793), p. xi.

16. Ibid., p. xii.
17. Ibid., p. xvii.
18. Ibid., p. xviii.
19. Ibid., pp. xix–xxii.
20. Friedrich Wilhelm Gubitz, *Sappho. Monodrama* (Berlin: Maurersche Buchhandlung, 1816), p. 6.
21. Ibid., p. 8.
22. Friedrich Gottlieb Welcker, *Sappho, von einem herrschenden Vorurtheil befreyt* (Göttingen: Vandenhoek und Ruprecht, 1816), p. 6.
23. Joan DeJean, 'Sex and Philology: Sappho and the Rise of German Nationalism', in *Re-Reading Sappho. Reception and Transmission*, ed. by Ellen Greene (Berkeley, CA: University of California Press, 1996), pp. 122–45 (p. 127).
24. Ibid., p. 127–29.
25. Although I do not see a non-heterosexual theme in *Sappho*, Angela Steidele has argued that Sappho is attracted to Melitta. *'Als wenn du mein Geliebter wärest': Liebe und Begehren zwischen Frauen in der deutschsprachigen Literatur 1750–1850* (Stuttgart: Metzler, 2003), pp. 142–43.
26. Hägelin, *Denkschrift*, quoted in Glossy, 'Zur Geschichte der Wiener Theaterzensur', p. 317.
27. Welcker, *Sappho, von einem herrschenden Vorurtheil befreyt*, p. 8.
28. DeJean, 'Sex and Philology', p. 123.
29. Joan DeJean, *Fictions of Sappho, 1546–1937* (Chicago: The University of Chicago Press, 1989), p. 157.
30. Ibid., p. 158.
31. Ibid., p. 160.
32. DeJean, 'Sex and Philology', p. 123.
33. Joan DeJean, 'Portrait of the Artist as Sappho', in *Germaine de Staël. Crossing the Borders*, ed. by Madelyn Gutwirth, Avriel Goldberger and Karyna Szmurlo (New Brunswick, NJ: Rutgers University Press, 1991), pp. 122–37 (p. 125).
34. DeJean, *Fictions of Sappho*, p. 167.
35. Ibid., p. 160.
36. Ibid., p. 161.
37. Ibid., p. 176.
38. DeJean, 'Portrait of the Artist as Sappho', p. 124.
39. Ibid., p. 128.
40. Ibid., p. 136–37.
41. DeJean, *Fictions of Sappho*, p. 193.
42. Ibid., p. 194.
43. Ibid., p. 204.
44. Angelica Goodden, *Madame de Staël. Delphine and Corinne* (London: Grant and Cutler, 2000), p. 64.
45. Judith E. Martin, 'Nineteenth-Century German Literary Women's Reception of Madame de Staël', *Women in German Yearbook* 18 (2002), 133–57.
46. Ibid., p. 146.
47. Ibid., p. 151.
48. Josef Nadler, *Franz Grillparzer* (Vienna: Bergland, 1952), p. 142.
49. Marianne Burkhard, 'Love, Creativity and Female Role: Grillparzer's "Sappho" and Staël's "Corinne" Between Art and Cultural Norm', *Jahrbuch für Internationale Germanistik* 16 (1984), 128–46 (p. 130).
50. Littrow-Bischoff, *Aus dem persönlichen Verkehre*, p. 80.
51. Lori J. Marso, 'Defying Fraternity: Woman as Citizen in Germaine de Staël's *Corinne, or Italy*', *Women's Studies* 28 (1999), 645–74 (p. 656).
52. Burkhard, '"Die letzte Schuld des Lebens"', p. 125.
53. Politzer, *Das abgründige Biedermeier*, p. 88.
54. Steidele, p. 145.
55. Friedrich Schiller, 'Das Lied von der Glocke', in *Werke und Briefe*, 12 vols. ed. by Otto Dann et al. (Frankfurt a.M.: Deutscher Klassiker Verlag, 1992–2005), I (1992), pp. 56–68 (p. 59, ll. 106–07, 116–17).

56. Johann Wolfgang Goethe, 'Iphigenie auf Tauris', in *Sämtliche Werke, Briefe, Tagebücher und Gespräche*, 40 vols, ed. by Hendrik Birus et al. (Frankfurt a.M.: Deutscher Klassiker Verlag, 1986–2000), I/v (1988), pp. 553–619 (p. 556, ll. 24–26, 29).
57. Goodden, p. 65.
58. William C. Reeve, 'Orchestrated Death Scenes as a Means of Revenge: Schiller's *Maria Stuart* and Grillparzer's *Sappho*', *Seminar* 40 (2004), 122–34 (p. 130).
59. Gretchen Rous Besser has written that '[n]owhere in literature can we find anything like the triumphal procession celebrating female achievement that Staël offers in *Corinne*.' Besser is perhaps unaware of *Sappho*. It is possible that Sappho's triumphal entrance was inspired by Corinne's. Gretchen Rous Besser, *Germaine de Staël Revisited* (New York: Twayne, 1994), p. 85.
60. Yates, *A Critical Introduction*, p. 62.
61. Kerstin Aidenhoff et al., 'Vom Leid des Herrschers und vom Glück des Beherrschten: *Sappho*', in *Gerettete Ordnung: Grillparzers Dramen*, ed. by Bernhard Budde and Ulrich Schmidt (Frankfurt a.M.: Peter Lang, 1987), pp. 34–57 (p. 41).
62. Peter von Matt, *Der Grundriss von Grillparzers Bühnenkunst* (Zurich: Atlantis, 1965), p. 17.
63. Aidenhoff et al., 'Vom Leid des Herrschers und vom Glück des Beherrschten: *Sappho*', p. 35.
64. Caroline Anders, "... der Zündstoff liegt, der diese Mine donnernd sprengt gen Himmel." *Strategien der Ordnungsdestruktion in Franz Grillparzers dramatischem Werk* (Würzburg: Königshausen & Neumann, 2008), p. 49.
65. Janke, 'Gescheiterte Authentizität. Anmerkungen zu Grillparzers Frauenfiguren', p. 62.
66. Leitich, *Zwölfmal Liebe*, p. 65.
67. Werner M. Bauer, 'Kunst des Dramas. Drama der Kunst. Zu Grillparzers *Sappho*', *Études Germaniques* 47 (1992), 159–90 (pp. 182–83).
68. Ibid., p. 183.
69. Aidenhoff et al., 'Vom Leid des Herrschers und vom Glück des Beherrschten: *Sappho*', p. 41.
70. Locke, *Two Treatises of Government*, p. 398.
71. Ibid., p. 399.
72. Robert Pichl, 'Grillparzers dramaturgische Emanzipation von der Weimarer Klassik', *JdGG* 3. Folge 22 (2007–08), 51–62 (p. 55).
73. Bauer, 'Kunst des Dramas', p. 185.
74. Ibid., p. 186.
75. August Sauer, 'Über das Zauberische bei Grillparzer. (Drahomira, Medea, Libussa.) Vortrag, gehalten in der Grillparzer-Gesellschaft, am 17. Januar 1899', in *Gesammelte Reden und Aufsätze*, pp. 205–30 (p. 222).
76. Gisela Stein, *The Inspiration Motif in the Works of Franz Grillparzer. With Special Consideration of 'Libussa'* (The Hague: Martinus Nijhoff, 1955), p. 155.
77. Forster, 'Grillparzer', p. 44.
78. Ruth Florack, 'Nachruf auf die Landesmutter oder Vom unaufhaltsamen Aufstieg des Bürgerkönigs: *Libussa*', in *Gerettete Ordnung. Grillparzers Dramen*, ed. by Bernhard Budde and Ulrich Schmidt (Frankfurt a.M.: Peter Lang, 1987), pp. 238–54 (p. 238).
79. Ikuta, *Geschichte und Individuum in Grillparzers dramatischer Welt*, p. 167.
80. Ritchie Robertson, 'On the Threshold of Patriarchy: Brentano, Grillparzer, and the Bohemian Amazons', *German Life and Letters* 46 (1993), 203–19 (p. 218).
81. Forster, 'Grillparzer', p. 47.
82. Lorenz, 'Ambivalenz und Erkenntnis', pp. 52–53.
83. Ulrich Fülleborn, '"Der Gang der Zeit von Anfang". Frauenherrschaft als literarischer Mythos bei Kleist, Brentano und Grillparzer', *Kleist-Jahrbuch 1986*, ed. by Hans Joachim Kreutzer (Berlin: Erich Schmidt, 1986), pp. 63–80 (p. 68).
84. Yixu Lü, *Frauenherrschaft im Drama des frühen 19. Jahrhunderts* (Munich: iudicium, 1993), p. 104.
85. For more on Grillparzer and the Austrian Empire's national groups, see for example: Wilhelm Bücher, *Grillparzers Verhältnis zur Politik seiner Zeit. Ein Beitrag zur Würdigung seines Schaffens und seiner Persönlichkeit* (Marburg: N. G. Elwert'sche Verlagsbuchhandlung, 1913); Kostka, 'Grillparzer and the East'; Peter Kuranda, 'Grillparzer und die Politik des Vormärzes', *JdGG* 28 (1926), 1–21; Gerhart Reckzeh, *Grillparzer und die Slaven* (Weimar: Duncker, 1929).
86. Florack, 'Nachruf auf die Landesmutter', p. 238.

87. Emanuel Grigorovitza, *Libussa in der deutschen Litteratur* (Berlin: Duncker, 1901), p. 9.
88. Ibid., p. 10.
89. Udo Köster, 'Über das Verhältnis von Mythos und Geschichte am Beispiel der Bearbeitungen des Libussa-Stoffes bei Brentano, Ebert, Mundt und Grillparzer', in *Romantik. Mythos und Moderne*, ed. by Ulrich Wergin and Timo Ogrzal (Würzburg: Königshausen & Neumann, 2013), pp. 163–80 (p. 163).
90. Vaclav Hajek, *Böhmische Chronik*, trans. by Joannem Sandel (Leipzig: Fritschen, 1718), p. 17.
91. Ibid., p. 23.
92. Johann Karl August Musäus, 'Libussa', in *Volksmärchen der Deutschen* (Munich: Winkler, 1961), pp. 331–90 (p. 360).
93. Ibid., p. 365.
94. Ibid., p. 389.
95. Anonymous (Johann Friedrich Ernst Albrecht), *Die Töchter Kroks, Böheims Fürstinnen. Eine Geschichte des achten Jahrhunderts*, Erster Theil (Hamburg: Hoffmann, 1792), p. 158.
96. Ibid., p. 164.
97. Joseph Carl Bernard, *Libussa. Romantische Oper in drey Aufzügen* (Vienna: Wallishausser, 1823), p. 55.
98. Ibid., pp. 8–9.
99. Ibid., p. 50.
100. Grigorovitza, *Libussa in der deutschen Litteratur*, p. 10.
101. Clemens Brentano, *Die Gründung Prags. Ein historisch-romantisches Drama* (Pest: Hartleben, 1815), p. 140.
102. Karl Egon Ebert, *Wlasta. Böhmisch-nationales Heldengedicht in drei Büchern* (Prague: Calve, 1829), p. 15.
103. Köster, 'Über das Verhältnis von Mythos und Geschichte', p. 180.
104. Weiss, 'Opfer bei Grillparzer', p. 240.
105. Lü, *Frauenherrschaft*, p. 112.
106. Fülleborn, 'Der Gang der Zeit von Anfang', p. 70.
107. Dagmar C. G. Lorenz, 'Grillparzers *Libussa*: Eine Neubewertung', *JdGG* 3. Folge 14 (1980), 33–47 (p. 39).
108. Coenen, *Franz Grillparzer's Portraiture of Men*, p. 79.
109. Anna K. Kuhn, 'Myth, Matriarchy, *Männerphantasie*: Rereading Grillparzer's *Libussa*', in *Playing for Stakes: German-Language Drama in Social Context. Essays in Honor of Herbert Lederer* (Oxford: Berg, 1994), pp. 139–60 (p. 158).
110. Julia Neissl, 'Frauen, die das Geschick des Staates lenken. Geschlechterpositionen bei "Libussa" und "Penthesilea"', *JdGG* 3. Folge 20 (1997–2002), 240–77 (p. 263).
111. Grillparzer, 'Libussa', in *HKA* I/vi, 5–154, p. 12.
112. Fülleborn, 'Der Gang der Zeit von Anfang', p. 69.
113. Gmür, *Dramatische und theatralische Stilelemente in Grillparzers Dramen*, p. 15.
114. Robertson, 'Threshold of Patriarchy', p. 215.
115. Florack, 'Nachruf auf die Landesmutter', p. 240.
116. Ibid., pp. 244, 246.
117. Neissl, 'Frauen, die das Geschick des Staates lenken', p. 259.
118. Hagl-Catling, *Für eine Imagologie der Geschlechter*, p. 206.
119. Robertson, 'Threshold of Patriarchy', p. 216.

CHAPTER 5

Grillparzer and Kyriarchy

In previous sections, I demonstrate the breadth of Grillparzer's intellectual context, and the ways in which this plays out in his depictions of women in patriarchal societies. In *Sappho* and *Des Meeres und der Liebe Wellen*, we see that it is not just sex/gender, but also social class, which determines women's options in life. Sappho and Hero, for different reasons, are socially privileged, and this privilege elevates them above the realities of life encountered by Melitta and Janthe. In the chapters in this section, I will show that Grillparzer's portrayals of social disadvantage in *Das goldene Vließ* [*The Golden Fleece*] (1819) and *Die Jüdin von Toledo* [*The Jewess of Toledo*] (1855) are marked by a depiction of the numerous forces which converge to create patriarchal societies. The two dramas under consideration in this section incorporate ideas of 'otherness' into the discussion of intertwined social forces. Medea, a princess in her own right in Colchis, becomes the despised and disenfranchised outsider when dislocated in Corinth; Rahel, meanwhile, suffers because she is both a woman and Jewish.

The interpretations in this section have been influenced by the ideas of kyriarchy and intersectionality which have emerged from feminist theory in recent decades. Kyriarchy is a term coined by Elisabeth Schüssler Fiorenza, who states the purpose of her study *But she said: feminist practices of biblical interpretation* in the following terms:

> I seek to articulate a critical feminist interpretation on feminist political terms. Such an articulation requires a different understanding of patriarchy, one which does not limit it to the sex/gender system but conceptualizes it in terms of interlocking structures of domination [i.e. *kyriarchal*, elite male, relations of ruling (*Herr-schaft*)].[1]

Fiorenza's work is influenced by Third World and socialist-marxist feminists, who had previously argued for better understanding of complex systems of oppression. These feminists, writes Fiorenza, argued that women are oppressed by racism, classism and colonialism as well as sexism, and that women from racial minorities or less privileged classes were often more oppressed by elite white women than by men of their own class, race, religion etc. In Fiorenza's view, however, this 'adding on' approach is limited, for it

> ignores the fact that systems of oppression criss-cross and feed upon each other in women's lives. Such an "adding on" method conceptualizes the patriarchal

> oppression of women not as an interlocking, multiplicative, and overarching system, but as parallel oppressions that divide women against each other.[2]

Fiorenza seeks to reconceptualize patriarchy as a 'key heuristic category of feminist theology and biblical interpretation' so that it can 'make visible the complex interstructuring of the conflict-producing oppressions of different groups of women that are obscured by the ideology of patriarchy as binary sex-gender system'.[3] She coined the term kyriarchy to describe such a system in which power

> operates not only along the axis of gender but also along those of race, class, culture, and religion. These axes of power structure the more general system of domination in a matrix- (or better, patrix-) like fashion [...].[4]

Scholars working in intersectionality theory have common aims with Fiorenza. Intersectionality, a concept similar to kyriarchy, emerged from black feminist legal studies in the late 1980s, and 'in just two decades [...] has widely transformed notions of both theory and research [in women's and gender studies]'.[5] Intersectionality has also influenced research in history, sociology, literature, philosophy, anthropology, feminist studies, ethnic studies, queer studies, and legal studies.[6] Anna Carastathis argues that '[i]t has become commonplace within feminist theory to claim that women's lives are constructed by multiple, intersecting systems of oppression', and notes that intersectionality has extended beyond academic circles and influenced international human rights discourses.[7] Leslie McCall writes that intersectionality is perhaps 'the most important theoretical contribution that women's studies, in conjunction with related fields, has made so far'.[8] In 2008, Jennifer C. Nash referred to intersectionality as 'an institutionalized intellectual project' and 'the dominant tool for excavating the voices of the marginalized'.[9]

The metaphor of intersecting categories of discrimination was introduced by Kimberlé Williams Crenshaw, but the concept has a long history in black feminist thinking, and '[a]s early as the 19th century in the United States, Black feminists confronted the simultaneity of a "woman question" and a "race problem"'.[10] By the time Crenshaw introduced the term, the idea of intersecting axes of discrimination was already part of antiracist feminist discourse.

In her 1989 article, 'Demarginalizing the Intersection of Race and Sex: A Black Feminist Critique of Antidiscrimination Doctrine, Feminist Theory and Antiracist Politics', Crenshaw argued that black women were sometimes excluded from antiracist policy and feminist theory because these did not adequately comprehend the ways in which an individual could simultaneously suffer discrimination on the basis of both sex and race:

> Because the intersectional experience is greater than the sum of racism and sexism, any analysis that does not take intersectionality into account cannot sufficiently address the particular manner in which Black women are subordinated.[11]

Crenshaw claims that a lack of awareness of intersectionality has meant that courts as well as feminist and civil rights activists have failed to understand the unique situation in which black women find themselves. Crenshaw points out that feminist theory often evolves in a white racial context, which, though seldom acknowledged, limits the applicability of mainstream feminism for non-white women, whom it marginalizes:

> Not only are women of color in fact overlooked, but their exclusion is reinforced when white women speak for and as women. The authoritative universal voice — usually white male subjectivity masquerading as non-racial, non-gendered objectivity — is merely transferred to those who, but for gender, share many of the same cultural, economic and social characteristics. When feminist theory attempts to describe women's experiences [...] it often overlooks the role of race. Feminists thus ignore how their own race functions to mitigate some aspects of sexism and, moreover, how it often privileges them over and contributes to the domination of other women.[12]

Because feminist and antiracist discourses do not recognize the intersection of racism and sexism in real life, they cannot comprehend an individual whose lived experience is affected by identifying as both a woman and a person of colour, and so 'they relegate the identity of women of color to a location that resists telling'.[13]

That intersectionality is still a matter of debate in the twenty-first century is shown by the proceedings of a 2009 conference on the subject. Kathy Davis and Gail Lewis write that conference participants expressed 'repeated concern [...] about the need to move beyond metaphors that reproduce a framework of addition'.[14] This also shows that, despite making inroads in feminist thought, the concept of intersectionality is by no means universally accepted. Yvette Taylor confirms this, writing that the importance of intersectionality continues to be questioned, and that its 'buzzword status' could lead to further analysis of social inequalities being neglected.[15] Others note that intersectionality has been thoroughly critiqued within feminist studies, and is now even dismissed as outmoded.[16]

The suitability of *Die Jüdin von Toledo* and *Das goldene Vließ* for this type of analysis is apparent. In these dramas more than any other by Grillparzer, real or perceived differences become a central cause of conflict between characters. Although Grillparzer shows conflict between Germans and Hungarians in *Ein treuer Diener*, and between Germans and Bohemians in *Ottokar*, in neither of these dramas is one group's supposed superiority as keenly expressed, nor does it ignite conflict. Kunigunde's Hungarian background does not have an instrumental (negative) impact on her life at Ottokar's court, nor can it be argued that Erny's demise is necessitated by differences between German and Hungarian political factions. For Medea and Rahel, however, otherness exacerbates the difficulties they experience as female others in male-dominated societies. Most importantly, this otherness allows both women to become the victims of female aggression: Kreusa oppresses Medea, and Eleonore instigates Rahel's murder. While antagonism between male and female, and the subversion of the categories, is central to many of Grillparzer's dramas, particularly in the cases of Medea and Rahel we should heed Fiorenza's words and not allow this difference to obscure the

> complex interstructuring of patriarchal dominations inscribed *within* women and in the relationships of dominance and subordination *between* women, [and] the participation of white elite women and of Christian religion in patriarchal

oppression, insofar as both have served as the civilizing conduits of patriarchal knowledge, values, religion, and culture.[17]

'Sei eine Griechin du in Griechenland': Gender and Imperialism in *Das goldene Vließ*

Grillparzer's Medea trilogy most obviously suits a kyriarchy-influenced reading. Grillparzer's version of the myth, which presents not only Medea's life as a refugee with Jason in Corinth, but breaks with an established literary tradition to trace her story back to Colchis, her homeland, invites criticism of power structures predicated on supposed sex- and race-based superiority or inferiority. Indeed, this seems to have been his intention: Grillparzer, looking back to the composition of *Das goldene Vließ* in his *Selbstbiographie*, writes that he was primarily interested in 'der Charakter der Medea und die Art und Weise [...] wie sie zu der für eine neuere Anschauungsweise abscheulichen Katastrophe geführt wird' [the character of Medea and the way [...] in which she is led to the catastrophe which, from a modern point of view, appears abhorrent], and that this influenced his choice of a trilogy (*HKA* I/xvi, pp. 134–35). Christian Rogowski notes that the first two parts of the trilogy show the causes of Medea's later violent acts, and he argues that Grillparzer's decision to analyse 'ein weibliches, koloniales Subjekt' [a female colonial subject] from a psychological point of view indicates a 'kritische Perspektive auf sexistische und kolonialistische Zuschreibungen [...], welche Medea innerhalb einer männlich dominierten, aufgeklärten, westlichen Zivilisation als das fundamental "Andere" dämonisieren' [critical perspective on sexist and colonialist attributions [...] which demonize Medea as the fundamental "Other" within a male-dominated, enlightened, western civilization].[18] The conflict not just of male and female, but of Greek and Colchian, 'primitive' and 'advanced' societies, shows, to quote Fiorenza, the 'interlocking structures of domination' which dictate interpersonal relations in the drama. While the opening scenes of the trilogy seem to conform to a simple schema of male domination and female submission, this dichotomy is confused by the arrival of the Greeks, who would dominate because of perceived cultural superiority, not sex, and by Medea's life in Corinth, where she is marginalized not just by men because of her sex, but also by women because of her origins. My analysis of Grillparzer's attitude towards misogyny and imperialism has also been influenced by theories of stadial history which were popular in the Enlightenment era, and by Schiller's essay on universal history. Stadial history describes change in human societies as following a trajectory through successive stages — hunter-gatherer, pastoral, agricultural, commercial — each of which is defined by the means of subsistence on which the society was dependent. This theory is portrayed in the change in Medea's social standing between 'developing' Colchis and 'consumerist' Greece, as well as in the Greeks' imperialistic attitude towards Colchis and its inhabitants. Schiller's essay, *Was heißt und zu welchem Ende studiert man Universalgeschichte?* [*What Is, and to What End Do We Study, Universal History?*], describes the different levels of cultural, social and technological development among various groups of 'Wilden' [savages] that European travellers had come across. It was such comparisons of different societies which revealed the underlying laws and principles which affected history.[19]

Aietes' Colchis is not only a primitive, but also a patriarchal society. However, Medea and her women, at the beginning of *Der Gastfreund*, live in an Amazonian subculture insofar as they are an armed troop of women engaged in hunting and warfare — Dagmar Lorenz aptly terms it 'eine Art separatistischer Staat im Staat' [a type of separatist state within the state].[20] Hagl-Catling describes Medea as 'eine kühne, selbstbewußte und schöne Frau, für die Wollen und Handeln identisch sind und die die Liebesbindung an einen Mann als Schwäche verachtet' [a brave, self-confident and beautiful woman for whom desire and deed are identical and who despises romantic relationships with men as a weakness].[21] As we see from the opening lines of Gora's prayer, Medea and her women worship Darimba, a virgin female deity, as well as Peronto, who is the focus of the play's male protagonists. The opening scenes of *Der Gastfreund* show Medea hunting, while later she chastises a former companion for her romantic entanglement with a man.[22] Medea's possessiveness shows that she considers liaisons with men to be acts of treason against this female society in general, and, more specifically, against her. She views men with suspicion, an attitude which is also seen in her reaction to the Greeks' arrival: 'Und nahet ein Kühner, zahl' er's mit Blut!' (*DG*, l. 85.) [If anyone draws near, his blood shall pay. (p. 9)] The importance of female chastity in this society is also seen in the invocation to Darimba which hails the goddess as 'reine, magdliche' (*DG*, l. 9) [virtuous, virginal (p. 6)]. Medea shows the high regard in which she holds physical strength and other 'masculine' traits: 'Hinaus! hinaus!/ Und die am schnellsten rennt und die am leichtesten springt,/ Sei Königin des Tags' (*DG*, ll. 40–42) [Be off! Be off!/ And she who quickest runs, and she who farthest leaps,/ Be crowned our queen today (p. 7)], while she despises tameness: 'In deine Seele schäm' ich mich./ So feig, so zahm!' (*DG*, ll. 46–47) [I feel deep shame that should be yours./ So meek, so tame! (p. 7)]. Medea here berates a woman for traits which elsewhere in Grillparzer's dramas are used to chastise men.

Medea's society within a society immediately falls prey to the more powerful patriarchy governed by her father. Although Medea espouses ideals of individual freedom — 'Ei hört!/ Sie wollte nicht und tat's! Geh du sprichst Unsinn./ Wie konnt' es denn geschehen,/ Wenn du nicht wolltest.' (*DG*, ll. 63–66) [Oh hear!/ She would not, yet she did! — Why, that is nonsense./ How could that ever be,/ Did you not wish it? (p. 8)] — upon confrontation with her father he almost immediately imposes his will upon her. He uses a mixture of imperatives — 'Bleib jetzt!', 'Ich wills, du sollst!' (*DG*, l. 95) [Stay now!; You will do as I say! (p. 10)]; 'Bleib, sag ich, bleib!' (*DG*, l. 110) [Stay, I say stay! (p. 11)] — and blandishments — 'Du bist klug, du bist stark.' (*DG*, l. 112) [You are wise, you are strong. (p. 11)]; 'mein gutes Kind' (*DG*, l. 120) [my good, kind child (p. 11)]; 'mein gutes Mädchen' (*DG*, l. 131) [my good, kind daughter (p. 12)] — to persuade her to do his bidding. As Yixu Lü writes, *Der Gastfreund* charts Medea's change from 'die amazonenhafte, vermeintlich eine unbegrenzte Freiheit genießende Fürstin von Kolchis in die dem König recht mürrisch gehorchende Tochter des Aietes' [the Amazon-like princess of Colchis who supposedly enjoys boundless freedom to Aietes's daughter who obeys the king in a very surly manner].[23]

Medea eventually acquiesces in her father's requests, and it is as a result of the failure of Aietes' plan — the Colchian king denies Phryxus hospitality, seizing the fleece and murdering him — that, at the opening of *Die Argonauten*, Medea is again living in isolation, this time in a 'halbverfallener Turm' (p. 43) [a tower, partly in ruins (p. 5)]. This removal from the heart of Colchian society represents, more than anything, Medea's removal from the patriarchal society which subjugated her. Indeed, Medea eventually agrees to help her father again, but on condition that she be allowed to retreat forever into the solitude of the wilderness. Yet even in this physical isolation she is not safe from the machinations of her father who comes seeking her help against a new band of Greeks who have arrived. Absyrtus, her brother, and Aietes force Medea to descend from her tower, and Aietes scolds her for fleeing Colchis (*DA*, ll. 87–91). Aietes interprets Medea's retreat from society as an act of rebellion against his rule and against patriarchy. Medea has scorned the 'väterliche[s] Haus' [paternal house (p. 10)], which in nineteenth-century Austria was both refuge and prison for women, and for Aietes represents a civilizing force, in favour of the freedom of the wild. For the Greeks, Colchis is a barren wilderness, but for Aietes, Colchian settlements, which the Greeks consider primitive, provide the structures necessary for patriarchal rule and the submission of female wildness to male authority.

There exists a strong mutual enmity between the Greeks and the Colchians, in part a result of an antithesis as pronounced as that between their foremost female representatives, Kreusa and Medea. Grillparzer's notes on the trilogy in his *Selbstbiographie* show that he very deliberately exaggerated the 'barbarisch und romantisch' [barbaric and romantic] elements of Colchis in order to emphasize 'den Unterschied zwischen Kolchis und Griechenland [...], auf den alles ankam' [the difference between Colchis and Greece [...] on which everything depended].[24] Medea's unsocialized femininity is only one of the differences between these two cultures, which I shall further investigate in relation to the imperialistic theme in the trilogy.

In his 1993 study *Culture and Imperialism*, Edward Said writes that '[a]lmost all colonial schemes begin with an assumption of native backwardness and general inadequacy to be independent, "equal", and fit'.[25] Exactly this attitude towards Colchis and its inhabitants can be seen in Grillparzer's Greek characters. As will be shown, a similar attitude pervades in Greece with regard to women: Kreusa and Medea are expected to be subservient, submissive and decorative, as the assumption on the male side is that they are inferior. In *Der Gastfreund*, Phryxus' objectification of Medea is the first indication of the Greeks' *Weltanschauung* (*DG*, ll. 241, 244–48). Phryxus emphasizes the lightness of Medea's features ('der Wange Licht' [the radiance of these cheeks (p. 18)]), which is contrasted with the darkness of her hair. Rather than indicating a physical difference between Greek and Colchian, the text shows the physical similarities between the two peoples.

The events in the first part of the trilogy are set in motion by Aietes' overwhelming desire to possess the golden fleece. The arrival of Phryxus and his men in Colchis is significant for Aietes primarily because they come bearing '[r]eiche Beute' (*DG*, l. 100) [precious booty (p. 10)]. Aietes' reaction shows that the

Colchians are not merely the victims of Greek aggression, but equally scheming and eager to exploit. He abuses his role as host to the Greeks by murdering their leader and seizing the fleece. There are echoes of Schiller's inaugural lecture in this scene. The 'accuracy' of the words, '*Feind* heißt ihm [dem Wilden] alles was neu ist, und wehe dem Fremdling den das Ungewitter an seine Küste schleudert! [...] kein süßes Gastrecht [wird] ihn erfreuen' [everything new is the enemy, and woe to the stranger whom a storm has cast upon the coast [...] no sweet hospitality [will] comfort him],[26] can be seen in Aietes' cynical assessment of Phryxus' situation: 'Ich hab' ihm nicht Gastrecht geboten,/ Er nahm sich's, büß' er's der Tor!' (*DG*, ll. 384–85) [And never I offered him guest-rights;/ He took them; let the fool pay! (p. 24)] Medea's ominous prophecy at the end of the play — 'Sie kommen, sie nahen/ Sie umschlingen mich,/ Mich, dich, uns alle!/ Weh über dich!' (*DG*, ll. 515–18) [They come, they draw closer/ They lay hold on me,/ Me, you, us all!/ Woe upon you! (p. 32)] — is fulfilled by the Argonauts' arrival. Jason's declared aim is to regain the fleece. This desire is reflected in the language he uses towards Aietes in particular. Jason and his companions consistently refer to the Colchians as barbarians. Thus Jason's first words to Aietes — 'Hochmütiger Barbar, du wagst — ?' (*DA*, l. 808) [You, insolent barbarian, dare — ? (p. 47)] — are insulting, while his 'du wagst — ?' shows that, even in this foreign territory, he considers himself the lawgiver and Aietes, by virtue of his non-Hellenism, an insurgent subaltern.

In the same way that Kreusa is turned into a tool of patriarchal Greek oppression, so is Medea a tool in the Colchians' struggle against the foreigners. The conflict between natives and invaders comes to a head in *Die Argonauten* IV. Here, both Medea and the newly captured fleece become symbolic of the struggle between the two sides. Both are hotly contested objects, but Aietes' and Absyrtus' desire to possess the fleece, which leads them to renounce any patriarchal claims to Medea — 'Behalt sie, doch das Vließ gib mir heraus!' (*DA*, l. 1713) [You may keep her; but give the fleece to me! (p. 104)] — also leads to their deaths. Greek interference in Colchis, then, has led directly to the destruction of Medea's matriarchal subculture, as well to the capitulation of Colchian political power.

The fleece, which is the motif uniting the three parts of the trilogy, is important within the colonial framework of the trilogy as it represents the riches which stand to be gained from the exploitation of Colchis. The tripartite nature of Grillparzer's work, which has as its backdrop both Colchis and Greece, allows the playwright to position his depiction of colonization within the broader context of stadial history. Within this schema, it is possible to see the fleece as symbolic of 'wealth and world domination',[27] a luxury product procured from the underdeveloped (hunter-gatherer, pastoral) realms of Colchis for the highly-evolved consumer market in Corinth. In illustrating the development of social structures according to the world view of stadial historians, the influence of Schiller's historical thought might also be seen:

> Die Entdeckungen, welche unsre europäischen Seefahrer in fernen Meeren und auf entlegenen Küsten gemacht haben [...] zeigen uns Völkerschaften, die auf den mannichfaltigsten Stufen der Bildung um uns herum gelagert sind, wie

Kinder verschiednen Alters um einen Erwachsenen herum stehen [...]. Wie beschämend und traurig aber ist das Bild, das uns diese Völker von unserer Kindheit geben! und doch ist es nicht einmal die erste Stufe mehr, auf der wir sie erblicken.[28]

[The discoveries which our European mariners have made in distant oceans and on remote coastlines [...] show us tribes which surround us at the most diverse levels of culture, like children of different ages gathered around an adult [...]. But how shaming and sad is the picture these people give us of our childhood! And yet the level at which we see them is not even the first.]

The Greeks, as we have seen, clearly share Schiller's patronizing attitude towards other cultures.

Although her father and brother force her out of seclusion, it is Jason in *Die Argonauten* who most severely impinges on Medea's reclusive existence. Jason abuses Medea's love for him and enlists her treachery in his plans. She betrays her father and helps Jason capture the fleece. Their flight results in the death of both Aietes and Absyrtus and the removal of Medea from her native Colchis to Greece, where she suffers for her identity.

The themes of imperialism and misogyny most strongly coalesce in Jason and Medea's interaction, for their relationship strongly resembles that of a conqueror and the conquered. In *Die Argonauten* I, for example, Jason forces his way into Medea's tower 'mit bloßem Schwerte' (p. 63) [with sword unsheathed (p. 22)]. His naked blade is at once a sign of military power and a phallic metaphor of his power as a man over Medea. Indeed, his reaction on seeing Medea for the first time is to strike out with his sword, injuring her (p. 65). His language is imperious and derisive, making clear his contempt for Medea both as a Colchian and as a woman: '[v]erfluchte Zauberin' (*DA*, l. 421) [accursed sorceress (p. 24)]; 'Verruchte!' (*DA*, l. 425) [base creature (p. 24)]

Later, when he and Medea are alone again, he takes physical possession of her — 'Sie rasch anfassend und auf seinem Arm in die Höhe haltend' (p. 117) [seizes her quickly and lifts her high on his arm (p. 71)] — and refuses to release her until she complies with his wishes (*DA*, ll. 1160–62). Matthias Luserke-Jaqui writes that 'Jason gibt bereits hier die Sprach- und Handlungsmuster für Medea vor', and in doing so allows no 'Raum für den Aufbau oder gar die Präsentation einer eigenen weiblichen Identität oder menschlichen Individualität' [Here Jason is already specifying patterns of speech and behavior for Medea; room for the construction or even the presentation of her own female identity or human individuality].[29] Kreusa's socialization happened over the course of her upbringing, but here Jason attempts to expedite the process with force. In the same scene, he proceeds to treat her merely as his reflection and imposes on her feelings of love for himself (*DA*, ll. 1256–61). As Ingrid Spörk shows, Medea's silence in this scene provokes Jason to further assumptions about her, and this selective acknowledgment of her existence is part of the discourse of power in the scene. Based solely on his own perceptions, he places her in his own frame of reference.[30] This emotional assault is accompanied by repeated violent attacks against Medea's physical integrity. As in many of Grillparzer's plays, the stage directions are crucial to understanding the characters, and it is they that, in *Die Argonauten* III, show the true extent of Jason's aggressive mentality: 'Ihre Hand fassend und den Dolch entwindend' [takes her hand and wrests the dagger from it (p. 73)]; 'sie zurückhaltend' [holds her back (p. 73)]; 'Er faßt ihre Arme mit beiden Händen' [seizes her arm with both hands (p. 73)]; 'Er ringt mit der Widerstrebenden' (p. 119) [struggles with her as she offers resistance (p. 73)]; 'Er faßt ihre beiden Hände und wendet die sich Sträubende gegen sich' (p. 121) [takes both her hands and turns her toward him despite her resistance (p. 75)].

Jason's apparent love for Medea brings into sharp contrast the hypocrisy of his colonial attitude. For, while he claims to love her, he mercilessly abuses her love for him to ensure that he comes into possession of the fleece. The lure of the fleece is so strong that he ignores Medea's calls for him to stay, haughtily proclaiming, 'Nichts hält mich ab!' (*DA*, l. 1457) [Naught stops me now (p. 85)], until she eventually accedes to his will with the realization that he does not, in fact, love her: 'Die Liebkosung laß/ Ich habe sie erkannt!' (*DA*, 1466–67) [Now spare your caress;/ Its meaning I well know! (p. 86)]

Medea's cultural and geographical journey in *Das goldene Vließ* sees her transported from a quasi Amazonian society in Colchis to the severely restrictive confines of Greece, which Rogowski calls 'eine aufgeklärtere — aber nicht weniger grausame — patriarchale Welt' and 'unterdrückerisch[] patriarchal[]' [a more enlightened — but no less cruel — patriarchal world; oppressively patriarchal].[31] This transposition reflects the changes in women's place in society which took place in the late eighteenth and early nineteenth centuries. As Dagmar Lorenz writes, 'Grillparzer setzt einen historischen Prozess an, während dessen sich die Situation der Frau vis-à-vis den Männern progressiv verschlechtert' [Grillparzer begins a historical process during which the situation of women vis-à-vis men progressively worsens].[32] *Das goldene Vließ* therefore criticizes the disempowerment of women, and demonstrates the extent to which femininity, rather than being an innate quality, is the result of social constructs.[33] This aspect is particularly visible in the enlargement of Kreusa's role. In showing this, Grillparzer goes against the grain of contemporary theory which posited biological differences as necessarily determining the psychological characteristics of the sexes.

It is in the final part of the trilogy, *Medea*, that Grillparzer most harshly condemns repressive patriarchy. In *Die Argonauten*, Jason imposes his will on Medea. In taking her from her native Colchis to Greece, he forces her to comply with the demands that Greek society makes on women. Stadial history is portrayed in the change in Medea's social standing between Colchis and Greece. The initiatory hunt scene in *Der Gastfreund*, and the sociological information offered by the invocation to Darimba — 'Segne das Feld und den beutereichen Wald' (*DG*, l. 17) [Bless thou the fields and the booty-teeming wood (p. 6)] — indicate that Colchis is one of the less developed societies as defined by stadial history in general, and by Schiller in particular. Of particular interest for us is the surprise with which Schiller asserts, 'Hier war nicht einmal das so einfache Band der Ehe, dort noch keine Kenntniß des Eigenthums' (p. 364) [In some places, there was not even the simple bond of marriage, as yet no knowledge of property]. According to the precepts of both *Universalgeschichte* and stadial history, then, Greece is a more highly developed society than Colchis for it knows both marriage — of which there is no indication in Colchis — and, in its consumer culture, property. Schiller's assertion is also interesting because of its association of marriage with property. It seems, then, that it is the social development in Greece which means that Medea is considered to be (Jason's) property, whereas in Colchis she was, to an extent, independent. In any case, Medea's ability to hunt and fight elevates her above the merely decorative, as represented by Kreusa.

Gender conflict reaches its climax in *Medea*. The same is true of imperialism, and the closely related theme of cultural difference which also plays a role in the trilogy. Indeed, as Ortrud Gutjahr argues, the true power of the three parts as a cultural critique is only appreciable when they are seen as a single entity, for Grillparzer 'hat [...] die Liebestragödie zwischen Jason und Medea in eine Tragödie der Interkulturalität eingeschrieben' [has [...] written the tragedy of love between Jason and Medea into a tragedy of interculturality].[34] The opening stage directions of *Medea* I show that, since they fled from Colchis, Medea and Jason have been living in peripatetic alienation: they are residing in a tent '[v]or den Mauern von Korinth' (p. 168) [Before the walls of Corinth (p. 5)]. From the very beginning of the play they are outcasts in Corinth, dependent on the goodwill of Kreon. Medea's first act involves the burial of 'eine schwarze, seltsam mit Gold verzierte Kiste, in welche sie mancherlei Gerät [...] hineinlegt' (p. 168) [a black chest, strangely ornamented with gold, into which she lays various articles (p. 5)]. This is clearly an attempt at renouncing those elements of her Colchian identity which she fears will arouse Greek suspicion or hatred. She seems already to have internalized Jason's Hellenocentric attitude, for she too equates Greece with light, and her homeland with the darkness of ignorance:

> Zuerst den Schleier und den Stab der Göttin;
> Ich werd' euch nicht mehr brauchen, ruhet hier.
> Die Zeit der Nacht, der Zauber ist vorbei
> Und was geschieht, ob Schlimmes oder Gutes,
> Es muß geschehn am offnen Strahl des Lichts. (*M*, ll. 2–6)
>
> [Before all else the goddess' veil and staff;/ I shall not need you more; lie here at rest./ The dark of night, of conjury is past;/ And what will happen, whether good or evil,/ Must happen in the open light of day. (p. 5)]

Although Grillparzer makes it clear that, physically, there is little if any difference between Medea and the Greeks — after attacking Medea in *Die Argonauten*, Jason exclaims, 'Der *weiße* Arm, er blutet' (*DA*, l. 432. My emphasis) [I see your white arm bleeding (p. 25)] — Medea's 'otherness' nevertheless renders her an alarming figure for the Greeks. Medea's reputation has preceded her to Corinth, for Kreusa repeats gossip she has heard: 'Zuletzt verbanden sie als Gattin dir/ Ein gräßlich Weib, giftmischend, vatermörd'risch./ Wie hieß sie? — Ein Barbarenname war's —' (*M*, ll. 329–31) [And last they joined to you as wedded wife/ A monstrous, poison-mixing, father-slaying — / How was she called? — By some barbarian name — (p. 23)]. Aietes' malevolent prophecy in *Die Argonauten* III — 'Leb' im fremden Land, eine Fremde,/ Verspottet, verachtet, verhöhnt, verlacht' (*DA*, ll. 1370–71) [And in alien lands be an alien,/ Insulted, derided, scoffed at, despised (p. 81)] — has been fulfilled, for, as her nurse Gora reports, Greek society at large shies away from the sight of Medea: 'Ein Greuel ist die Kolcherin dem Volke' (*M*, l. 72) [No one but thinks the Colchian witch a monster (p. 9)].

Jason's reaction to his new surroundings allows his imperialistic hypocrisy and opportunism to come to the fore. While Medea was useful to him in Colchis, he feigned love for her, and even made her love him. Upon arrival in Corinth she is discarded. He is acutely aware of the effect Medea's presence has on the Corinthians, and, in a bitter tirade against both Medea and her barbaric people, warns her severely against the use of her magic:

> Man haßt das hier und ich — ich haß' es auch!
> In Kolchis sind wir nicht, in Griechenland,
> Nicht unter Ungeheuern, unter Menschen! (*M*, ll. 181–83)

[They hate that here and I — I hate it too!/ We are no more in Colchis but in Greece./ No more with monsters but with human kind! (p. 15)]

This is closely followed by his wholesale renunciation of Medea while in conversation with Kreon: 'nur mit Schaudern nenn' ich sie mein Weib.' (*M*, l. 475) [I must shudder when I call her wife. (p. 30)] This conversation in *Medea* I with Kreon reveals much about Jason's character. As well as his oblique but open admission that he used Medea, his denial of his involvement in Aietes' death with the words, 'Er fiel der Götter Hand' (*M*, l. 477) [The gods' hands smote him down (p. 31)], evidences the Greek rejection of cultural relativity so strongly expressed by Kreon: 'Nie recht ist Unrecht, Schlimmes nirgends gut.' (*M*, l. 458) [Wrong can never be right, bad nowhere good. (p. 30)] Jason expresses faith in the gods' approbation of his every action, which stands in stark contrast to Medea's reliance on self-approbation. Jason's use of Medea as a means rather than an end places both of them firmly within the imperialistic metaphor of the trilogy, Jason as conqueror and Medea as exploited native.

Medea's words to Kreusa in *Medea* II show just how big the difference between women's roles in Colchis and Greece is:

> Wie eine Magd will ich dir dienend folgen,
> Will weben an dem Webstuhl, früh zur Hand,
> Und alles Werk, das man bei uns verachtet,
> Den Sklaven überläßt und dem Gesind',
> Hier aber übt die Frau und Herrin selbst [...] (*M*, ll. 691–95)

[Will be a maid that follows you to serve,/ Before the loom will weave from early morn/ And all the tasks which we at home despise/ As fit for servants only and for slaves,/ But here all women practice, I will do (p. 40)]

In Greece, Medea's sphere of influence is strictly limited to the household, and the work she is expected to do appears menial. Despite these differences, Medea attempts to adapt to her new surroundings. While as a Colchian princess she was well versed in the art of war — 'Sieh, ich weiß, nicht den Pfeil nur vom Bogen,/ Schleuderst den Speer auch, die mächtige Lanze,/ Schwingest das Schwert in kräftiger Hand' (*DA*, ll. 981–83) [See, I know; not just arrows from bows,/ You hurl the spear too, the powerful lance./ You swing the sword with sinewy arm. (p. 60)] says Aietes to his daughter — in Greece she takes up the lyre, the symbol of Greek cultural achievement, as well as a decorative accomplishment expected of Greek women. The opening scene of *Medea* II sees Kreusa acting in what Konrad Kenkel has called her 'Vermittlerinrolle' [mediator role] between the spouses, which he argues is an innovation in Grillparzer's version of the myth.[35] She teaches Medea to play a song that Jason once sang. The two women have conflicting reactions to the song's lyrics, indicating the qualities that each society values in women. Medea thinks about the words and remarks ironically that Jason's prayers were answered. Kreusa's reaction to Medea's textual analysis reveals that independent thought is not encouraged among Greek women: 'Daran hatt' ich nun eben nie gedacht./ Ich sang's nur nach, wie ich's ihn singen hörte.' (*M*, ll. 613–14) [I never stopped to think of that before./ I only sang the songs which he had sung. (p. 37)] That mimetic existence is demanded of Greek women is also evident in Jason's attempts to elicit Medea's confession of love in *Die Argonauten* III: 'Sprich's aus Medea, sprich es aus: ich liebe!/ Fällt dir's so schwer ich will dich's lehren, Kind./ Sprich's nach: ich liebe dich!' (*DA*, ll. 1268–70) [Say it, Medea, say the words: I love!/ Is it so hard? Then I will teach you, child./ Repeat with me: I love you! (p. 75)]. It is this quality in Kreusa which contradicts Yvonne Parry's assertion that she 'is untouched by life and has not yet undergone a process of individuation'.[36] Precisely the opposite is true: she lacks individuation *because* she has been constructed to such an extent by the society of which she is part: she is 'eins mit den Herrschenden, mit dem herrschenden System' [one with the rulers, with the ruling system].[37]

Kreusa is held up by Greek society as the model of womanhood. Her behaviour establishes her as Medea's antithesis, for she is dedicated to the service of her male relatives, and by extension the patriarchy. Medea's description captures her inherent tenderness and purity which are valued by Greek society, and which the Colchian herself lacks (*M*, ll. 674–76). Medea emphasizes Kreusa's light complexion, while descriptions of Medea focus on the dark otherness of her appearance despite indications that she is also white. The dark-light dichotomy serves to accentuate the antithetical nature of the relationship between Medea and Kreusa, and by extrapolation of the relationship between Colchis and Greece. It is also interesting that Medea praises these qualities, especially in the light of her castigation of Peritta ('So feig, so zahm!'). Medea, perhaps, realizes just how out of place she is.

Medea's criticisms of Jason elicit from Kreusa an expression of shock, for she cannot comprehend that a wife might not wholeheartedly endorse her husband's every action: 'Ihr Götter! Spricht die Gattin so vom Gatten?' (*M*, l. 642) [Oh, gods! A wife reviles her husband thus? (p. 38)] Grillparzer seems to treat this unadulterated subservience sardonically, for he has Kreusa claim:

> [...] hätt' ich einen Gatten,
> So arg, so schlimm, als Deiner nimmer ist,
> Und Kinder, sein Geschenk und Ebenbild,
> Ich wollte sie lieben, töteten sie mich. (*M*, ll. 644–47)

[[...]if ever I should have a husband/ So base, so vile as yours could never be,/ And children too, his gifts, resembling him,/ I should still love them, if they struck me dead. (p. 38)]

Medea represents a threat to the Greek patriarchy, in which 'die Frau, wie Kreusa, bis zur Karikatur entstellt, domestiziert, zivilisiert und "weiblich" gemacht worden ist' [women, like Kreusa, have been distorted to caricatures, domesticated, civilized and made 'feminine'], because she diverges markedly from Greek expectations.[38] This is clearly a parody of the socialization of women in nineteenth-century Austria. In his negative portrayal of Kreusa, who is the epitome of this process of socialization in Kreon's Greece, Grillparzer distances himself not only from her, but also from the process as it was being carried out in contemporary Austria. Kreusa's supercilious treatment of Medea is amplified by her perfidy. She welcomes news of Jason's arrival with malicious gossip about Medea, and cries 'Entsetzen' (*M*, l. 332) [Oh, horror! (p. 24)] at the first sight of the Colchian. She immediately pities Medea and Jason's 'heimatlosen Waisen' (*M*, l. 345) [homeless waifs (p. 25)] and tells them 'ich will euch Mutter, Schwester sein!' (*M*, l. 349) [your mother, sister I shall be (p. 25)] Lorenz stresses the fact that Kreusa denies Medea any worth as a mother.[39] More crucially, Kreusa's use of the word 'Waisen' denies Medea worth as a *woman*, for within Greek society womanhood is strongly defined by motherhood. The children have rushed to her side, and when Medea calls them back, Kreusa, 'zu ihrem Vater emporblickend' (p. 190) [glances up at her father (p. 25)], asks 'Lass' ich sie hin?' (*M*, l. 354) [Shall I let them go?] With this attempted appropriation of Medea's children, Kreusa throws down the gauntlet, despite her later show of friendship. It is this betrayal by all members of Greek society — Jason and Kreon, who are openly hostile, but also two-faced Kreusa — which helps Grillparzer maintain sympathy with Medea despite her actions.

Kreusa's treatment of Medea is the best example in Grillparzer's dramas of kyriarchy. While Kreusa is disadvantaged within Corinthian society because of her sex, her status as a Greek allows her power over those who are not Greek, such as Medea. As Heike Bartel has previously argued, Kreusa 'appears mild and benevolent' but 'nevertheless perpetuates a male order that demands complete submission of the (female, ethnic, national) "Other"'.[40] Medea, therefore, is doubly oppressed, not just by men, but by women of the dominant national group. Fiorenza criticizes Western feminists who posit 'gender difference as the primary and originary difference' because this approach covers up the role which women from dominant groups play in the subjugation of female others. While sex does play a role in Medea's oppression, her cultural inferiority in the eyes of the Corinthians plays a key role for her in exile. Kreusa, as a Corinthian woman, is a conduit of Greek culture and values, and plays her part in the oppression of Medea when she mistreats the Colchian because of the latter's failure to adhere to Corinthian norms.

The children become the focal point of their parents' argument as Medea demands that they accompany her away from Greece, but Jason refuses, saying he plans to raise them '[h]ier in der Sitte Kreis' (*M*, l. 1583) [where Greek customs thrive (p. 81)]. Jason decides that one child will go with Medea while the other stays in Corinth, and he leaves the decision to the children. Kreusa brings the children, and emphasizes the strong bond she has developed with them (*M*, ll. 1622–25). Despite the sympathy that seemed to have developed between the two women, here it is clear that Kreusa cannot consider Medea a fit mother. Kreusa sees herself as emotional and caring where Medea is hard and savage, and for Kreusa the children's former life with Medea is an 'Unglück' [sad fate (p. 83)]. When Kreon tells Kreusa that one child will leave Corinth, she replies: 'Verlassen uns?' (*M*, l. 1627) [And leave us? (p. 83)] She stakes her claim to the children and their affections, again invalidating Medea as a mother.

Medea sees Kreusa as her enemy, and considers her children's loyalty to her to be treacherous:

> Was steht ihr dort
> Geschmiegt an meiner Feindin falsche Brust?
> O wüßtet ihr was sie mir angetan,
> Bewaffnen würdet ihr die kleinen Hände,
> Zu Krallen krümmen eure schwachen Finger,
> Den Leib zerfleischen, den ihr jetzt berührt.
> Verlockst du meine Kinder? Laß sie los! (*M*, ll. 1635–41)

[Why stand you there/ Heads nestled at the breast of my false foe?/ Oh, if you knew what she has done to me,/ You would take weapons in your little hands,/ To cruel claws would curve your feeble fingers,/ And rend in shreds the body you now touch./ Would you entice my children? Let them go! (p. 84)]

The children are scared of Medea and flee from her to Kreusa, despite their mother's attempts to lure them with blandishments. Medea blames Kreusa and is angry with the children, but Jason blames Medea, saying 'Dir selber dank' es, daß dein wildes Wesen/ Die Kleinen abgewandt, zur Milde hin.' (*M*, ll. 1699–1700) [You are yourself to blame if your harsh nature/ Inclined these little ones to gentle ways. (p. 86)] Kreon orders Kreusa to take the children inside, and the realization that she has been abandoned by her children increases Medea's desperation: 'Ich bin besiegt, vernichtet, zertreten' (*M*, l. 1710) [I am destroyed, defeated, downtrodden (p. 87)]. This turns Medea against Jason and Kreusa, and against her children. She does not want Jason to keep her sons, nor does she want them. In Act IV, partly because of Kreon's actions, opportunities for revenge present themselves. Kreon comes to speak to Medea, and finding her more reasonable than he expected, agrees to send the children to her one last time, and lets Medea send a gift to Kreusa. Alone with the children, Medea questions them and gets irrefutable proof that they fear her. This gives resolution to Medea's bloody plan — alluded to earlier by her reference to Althea '[d]ie den Sohn erschlug' (*M*, l. 1830) [Who slew her son? (p. 92)] — to kill the children. When the elder son wants to sleep, Medea's sinister response is 'Ihr werdet schlafen noch euch zu Genügen.' (*M*, l. 2055) [Not long and you will have your fill of sleep. (p. 104)] Gora hurries from the palace, which is in flames, and reports Kreusa's death. Aware that Kreon's guards are approaching, Medea hurries off stage to her children, leaving Gora to despair at the horror of Medea's revenge: 'Rache riet ich selbst; doch solche Rache!' (*M*, l. 2164) [Vengeance too I cried; but such a vengeance! (p. 108)] She is suddenly aware that the children are not present, and rushes after Medea. Gora returns to the stage, falls down and cries: 'Was hab' ich gesehn? — Entsetzen!' (*M*, l. 2168) [What have I seen? — Oh, horror! (p. 109)] Act IV closes with Medea's reappearance, dagger in hand.

Act V is full of recrimination. Kreon blames Gora for Kreusa's death, an act she accepts she unwillingly perpetrated. Gora, however, says that Kreusa got her comeuppance, and asks: 'Was griff sie nach des Unglücks letzter Habe?' (*M*, l. 2185) [Why did she seize misfortune's last possession? (p. 111)] Gora blames Jason, whom she calls 'heuchelnder Verräter' (*M*, l. 2242) [You hypocrite, you traitor! (p. 113)], and Kreon for their role in the children's murder:

> Habt ihr es nicht umstellt mit Jägernetzen
> Des schändlichen Verrats, das edle Wild,
> Bis ohne Ausweg, in Verzweiflungswut
> Es, überspringend euer Garn, die Krone,
> Des hohen Hauptes königlichen Schmuck
> Mißbraucht zum Werkzeug ungewohnten Mords.
> Ringt nur die Hände, ringt sie ob euch selbst! (*M*, ll. 2245–51)

[Did not you two pursue this noble quarry/ With nets of shameful treachery, stalking her/ Until without escape, in wild despair,/ She overleaped your snares and made the crown,/ The kingly ornament of royal brows,/ The awful tool of her unnatural crime./ Aye, wring your hands, but wring them for yourselves! (p. 113)]

Gora expresses verbally what the structure of the trilogy as a whole illustrates: the origin of Medea's act in her experiences and in her suffering at the hands of Jason, Kreon and Kreusa. Gora cannot sympathize with the Greeks; she feels that they have merely got what they deserve. For Gora, Medea's actions mean that she will no longer be an object of scorn for the Greeks: 'Ihr spottet nun nicht mehr der Kolcherin.' (*M*, l. 2257) [The Colchian woman you will mock no more. (p. 114)] In the end, Medea earned the notice and respect of Kreon and Jason not through assimilation and mimesis, but by channelling herself and those elements of her person which most horrified the Greeks. In Act IV, Medea lamented the loss of her identity, and the power inherited from her mother, which she had buried at the beginning of the drama out of love for Jason, and by which act she had become 'Den Feinden, statt ein Schrecken, ein Gespött!' (*M*, l. 1876) [to my foes/ No more a thing of terror but of scorn! (p. 94)] When Kreon demands the return of the fleece, Medea unearths the chest and is reunited with her Colchian paraphernalia. This reunion restores to Medea not just the instruments of Kreusa's demise, but her confidence in the otherness of her identity: 'Sei sicher, du erhältst, was dir gebührt,/ Medea bin ich wieder, Dank euch Götter!' (*M*, ll. 1952–53) [Be reassured, you will receive your due./ Once more I am Medea! Gods, be thanked! (p. 99)]

The return of Medea's identity also gives her the resolve to punish those who have persecuted her. Kreon's words give her the idea of sending Kreusa a gift, and Medea convinces Kreon to allow this despite the animosity between them (*M*, ll. 1960–63). Medea feigns acceptance of Kreusa's role as a replacement mother, but elsewhere makes clear that this is not the case. She worries that her sons will become slaves when she is no longer there, and that their step-siblings, the children of Jason and Kreusa, will '[h]öhnen sie, spotten ihrer/ Und ihrer Mutter,/ Der Wilden aus Kolchis.' (*M*, ll. 1790–92) [Mock them, cast insult on them/And on their mother,/ That savage of Colchis. (p. 91)] At the end of Act IV, Gora arrives with news of Kreusa's death, caused by the gifts which Medea sent, and Medea is jubilant:

> Bist du dahin, weiße Braut?
> Verlockst du mir noch meine Kinder?
> Lockst du sie? lockst du sie?
> Willst du sie haben auch dort?
> Nicht dir, den Göttern send' ich sie! (*M*, ll. 2155–59)

> [Your days are done, snow-white bride?/ And still would you entice my children?/ Charm them still? Charm them still?/ Would you have them even there?/ Not you, the gods shall have them now! (p. 108)]

The jealousy which motivates the murder of Kreusa and the children is obvious. Medea did not want Kreusa to raise her children, and resented the way in which the Greek had undermined her relationship with them. Murdering Kreusa is also the most effective way Medea has of punishing Kreon, and the king's reaction shows that Medea chooses the best form of revenge. His anger and sorrow are obvious in Act V, and, as a result of Kreusa's death, he turns on and banishes Jason, whom he blames for his daughter's death: 'Du hast die Tochter mir genommen!' (*M*, l. 2271) [You took my daughter from me! (p. 113)] Murdering Kreusa also creates symmetry, Medea taking Kreon's child as Kreusa took Medea's sons.

In *Das goldene Vließ*, Grillparzer presents a complex portrayal of the intersections between ethnicity and sex, and of the potential which perceived superiority has as a motivation for aggression, dehumanization and persecution. In Colchis, Medea's social status allows her certain freedoms, although her matriarchal subculture is ultimately subordinate to her father's society. The Greeks' arrival complicates the situation, and Medea finds herself disadvantaged both as a woman, and as a Colchian. In Greece, her standing is substantially worse, for the subordinate position she must accept as a woman is worsened by Greek fears of her otherness. In Colchis, Medea and her women were united by cultural practices and norms, but in Greece, she receives little support from Kreusa, who personifies the traits which Medea is supposed to display. Kreusa, due to her social standing as a Greek, is Medea's antagonist rather than her companion, and connives to deprive the foreigner of her children. The dynamics of Medea and Kreusa's relationship highlight the role which women play in supporting and enforcing the norms of patriarchal societies, even when these norms ultimately harm them too. In *Die Jüdin von Toledo*, Eleonore plays a similar role within Spanish society. In his trilogy, Grillparzer goes beyond the depiction of women's struggles in patriarchal societies, and shows that, in Fiorenza's words, 'systems of oppression criss-cross and feed upon each other in women's lives'.

'Vielmehr ich kann, beim Himmel, denn ich muß': Gender, Politics and Violence in *Die Jüdin von Toledo*

Criticism of Grillparzer's *Die Jüdin von Toledo* has largely sidelined the figure of Queen Eleonore. Perhaps because she is accorded so small a share of the action on stage, critics have failed to appreciate not only her importance for the drama, but also the subversive nature of her character in the context of the binary gender matrix which prevailed in the nineteenth century.[41] Almost without exception, scholars have focused their attention on the beguiling physicality of Rahel, on the relationship between her and Alfonso, and on the latter's subsequent failures, both political and personal. Eleonore, however, is clearly an exceptional female character, as displayed by her contribution to affairs of state in Act IV. A thorough investigation of Eleonore's actions will shed light upon Grillparzer's subversive portrayal of gender stereotypes, and upon the complex social structures which allow Rahel's murder to take place.

Grillparzer's drama shares with Shakespeare's *Macbeth* a murder as the central event. Grillparzer's thoughts on Shakespeare's drama are an important tool in analysing the subversive nature of Eleonore's involvement in the *Gräueltat* [atrocity] which is central to *Die Jüdin von Toledo*. In an 1817 assessment of the gender dynamics in the murder of King Duncan, Grillparzer writes:

> Einer der vortrefflichsten und, so viel ich weiß am wenigsten bemerkten Züge in Shakespeares Macbeth liegt in dem gerade umgekehrten Verhältniß des Antheils den Macbeth und seine Gattin am Entschluße zur That und dann an der That selbst nehmen. Shakespeare hat hier nicht bloß Macbeth und seine Gattin, er hat Mann und Weib überhaupt geschildert. In Lady Macbeths Seele ist im ersten Augenblicke der Entschluß reif. Sie ist das Weib, das nach Empfindungen, im guten und schlimmen, handelt. Macbeth sträubt sich lange gegen die Idee, [...] Lady Macbeth bestimmt ihn zur That. Aber jetzt da gehandelt werden soll, kehrt sich auf einmal das Verhältniß um. Macbeth schaudert aber handelt; Sein Weib, die Entmenschte, die Verlockerin, war vor ihm in Dunkans Zimmer, sie hatte die Dolche in der Hand, aber — had he not ressembled my father as he had slept, i had done't — (Nr. 218. *HKA* II/vii, pp. 99–100.)

> [One of the most excellent, and as far as I know least noticed, features in Shakespeare's *Macbeth* is the exactly reversed relationship of involvement which Macbeth and his wife have in the decision to act and then in the act itself. Here, Shakespeare has not merely depicted Macbeth and his wife, he has portrayed man and woman as such. At first the decision is fully developed in Lady Macbeth's soul. She is the woman who acts according to her emotions, in good and in bad. Macbeth resists the idea for a long time [...] Lady Macbeth prevails upon him to complete the deed. But now that it is time for action, the relationship is reversed. Macbeth shudders but acts. His wife, the inhuman, the temptress, was in Duncan's room before him, she had the daggers in her hand, but — had he not resembled my father as he slept, I had done't.]

For Grillparzer, the dichotomy of intent and action is a gendered dichotomy, which he sees enacted in Shakespeare's drama. While Lady Macbeth provides the impetus for the action, she is incapable of committing the deed. This inability, as presented by Shakespeare, results from her sex: intent can be, and in *Macbeth* is, connoted female as well as male, while action is connoted male. This extract is highly pertinent for my interpretation of *Die Jüdin von Toledo* because I investigate the gender dynamics which Grillparzer portrays, and which do not conform to the clear delineations which Grillparzer observes in *Macbeth*.

At first, Lady Macbeth's role is restricted to encouraging her husband to murder Duncan. She fears that his nature is too benevolent to be capable of murder, and determines to influence him in his task. Once she has been informed that Duncan will arrive that same evening, her perception of the role she has to play appears to change, and she lays claim to more active participation. In a second soliloquy directly before Macbeth's entrance, she pleads for the spirits' assistance in committing the deed she now sees as her own task, and not her husband's. She asks the spirits to 'unsex' her and endow her with 'direst cruelty'.[42] The notion that she will influence Macbeth's actions has disappeared, and she clearly sees herself as Duncan's murderer. This change of heart is confirmed by her words to Macbeth later in the scene: 'you shall put/ This night's great business into my dispatch' (I/v, ll. 66–67). What is more startling, and more relevant for a discussion of *Die Jüdin von Toledo*, is the gendered concept of action and cruelty which Lady Macbeth expounds. Womanhood is incompatible with so heinous a crime as murder, and the 'unsexing' entails the removal of her female physicality and feminine behaviour. It is only after the removal of feminine traits that she will be able to commit the murderous deed. Lady Macbeth, then, does more than just drive Macbeth to murder; she takes the role of murderer upon herself.

Lady Macbeth's concept of action as a male preserve is reinforced in I/vii, as she attempts to counter her husband's new qualms against their plan. She accuses him of cowardice, questioning his ambition when he shows himself unwilling to commit the murder. Macbeth responds with a defence of his own masculinity: 'I dare do all that may become a man;/ Who dares do more, is none.' (I/vii, ll. 46–47) This answer is unsatisfactory as far as his wife is concerned, and she retorts by questioning his masculinity. The analogy she uses in this scene — that of brutally murdering her child — displays the cruelty which she would gladly possess, but also the fact of her 'traditional' femininity: although she would kill her child if she had sworn to do so, her femininity and maternal instinct would make the deed as horrible to her as the thought of murdering Duncan is to Macbeth. Her passion and energy are relentless, and she unfolds the details of her plan: she will encourage Duncan's guards in their revelry, and bring them to a state of inebriation. Then, she says, 'What cannot *you and I* perform upon/ Th'unguarded Duncan?' (I/vii, ll. 70–71. My italics) At this point, right at the end of Act I, Lady Macbeth still sees the murder as an event in which she herself will be actively involved. Her role is not that of a mere 'Verlockerin', as Grillparzer calls her; rather, she intends to help effect Duncan's demise in an immediate, active capacity. It is partly this determination which leads to Macbeth's awed praise of his wife for defying the limits of her sex:

> Bring forth men-children only!
> For thy undaunted mettle should compose
> Nothing but males. (I/vii, ll. 73–75)

Despite her sex-defying determination, however, Lady Macbeth finds the execution of their plan beyond her capabilities. In II/ii, she has managed to bring Duncan's guards to a state of unconscious drunkenness, and boasts that '[t]hat which hath made them drunk hath made me bold' (II/ii, l. 1). Yet she is unable to commit the deed itself:

> I laid their daggers ready,
> [Macbeth] could not miss 'em. — Had [Duncan] not resembled
> My father as he slept, I had done't. (II/ii, ll. 11–13)

It is left to Macbeth to commit the murder, which he does. Grillparzer's analysis of the drama ends with the deed, and he neglects to address the effect which Macbeth's actions have on his state of mind. It is clear from the exchange between the protagonists in II/ii, directly after the deed has been done, that Macbeth has been psychologically disturbed. He ruminates on his actions, an activity which his wife knows is disadvantageous, and she warns him against such thoughts. Lady Macbeth may have been unable to commit the act, but in its wake it is she, and not Macbeth, who is in charge of herself and the situation. She directs the subsequent action, and indicates the faulty manner in which Macbeth committed the deed: clearly, Macbeth was not fully capable of the deed, as he has brought the guards' daggers, which incriminate him and his wife, from the scene of the crime. 'Why did you bring these daggers from the place?' (II/ii, l. 47), Lady Macbeth asks him, and then commands him to return them. Now it is Macbeth's turn to act in a sex-defying manner, another aspect of the drama that Grillparzer overlooks, claiming that he cannot return to Duncan's room and set eyes on the bloody scene. Lady Macbeth must take control, and in doing so scorns her husband. Macbeth's inability to act turns him into a child in her eyes, while her own 'undaunted mettle', within the gender matrix of Shakespeare's drama, is unexpected and unusual. When the murder has been discovered, Lady Macbeth appears on the scene and enquires as to the reason for the disturbance. For Macduff, news of the murder itself would be enough to kill a woman, and one can only infer from this that, for him, female participation in such a deed would be unthinkable:

> O gentle lady,
> 'Tis not for you to hear what I can speak:
> The repetition, in a woman's ear,
> Would murther as it fell. (II/iii, ll. 81–84)

In the light of Shakespeare's portrayal of his protagonists as individuals who subvert the behaviour and characteristics expected of their sex, Grillparzer's sketch of the drama seems superficial and overly simplified. The dichotomies of male and female, action and resolution, are not as clear-cut as Grillparzer would have them. And yet, for Grillparzer, Macbeth and his wife function not only as individuals, but as archetypes of their respective sexes, as 'Mann und Weib überhaupt'. What can Grillparzer's view of these dichotomies tell us about his attitude towards women? What is the significance of his own portrayal of Alfonso and Eleonore as gender-defying individuals in *Die Jüdin von Toledo* for his views on the differences between the sexes? And what can an examination of Eleonore, and in particular her complicity in Rahel's murder, reveal about Grillparzer's attitudes to female involvement in government and politics, as well as in society more generally?

The statements of various characters indicate that the Spain of the drama is defined by much the same gender stereotypes as those which prevailed in nineteenth-century Austria and to which Grillparzer alludes in his analysis of *Macbeth*. In Act I, Alfonso links bravery with masculinity and weakness with femininity:

> Im Grunde wunderlich,
> Ein feiger Mann er wird mit Recht verachtet
> Und dies Geschlecht ist stark erst wenn es schwach.[43]

[How strange in fact it is,/ A craven man quite justly is despised,/ While woman shows her strength by being weak. (p. 27)]

Women's weakness, then, is their strength insofar as it encourages the protection of brave men. In Act III, Alfonso acknowledges fear as 'Weiberrecht' [a woman's right (p. 51)], while simultaneously accusing Rahel of abusing her fear to gain his attention (l. 888). Garceran clearly values Doña Clara's reticence — 'Und meine Leidenschaft für Doña Clara?/ Die Schweigsamste von Allen die je schwiegen' (ll. 408–09) [my ardent love for Doña Clara — /Least prone to speak of all who never speak (p. 28)] — particularly when contrasted with the brash Rahel. Esther recounts the events directly preceding Rahel's death, and attributes her lack of consciousness to feminine cowardice — 'Das ist die rechte Feigheit, Weiberart.' (l. 1611) [That is true cowardice, a woman's way. (p. 84)] — even though it might have resulted from the physical impact of being thrown to the floor (ll. 1603–04). It is within this context that the characters and behaviour of Alfonso and Eleonore must be analysed.

As in other dramas by Grillparzer, the subversion of accepted gender roles is an important element in the action of *Die Jüdin von Toledo*. The presentation of Alfonso and Eleonore as opposing individuals is clear from the first act. Rahel enters, pursued by guards, and throws herself on the queen's mercy. Eleonore turns away from Rahel, who then appeals to Alfonso. After only a short verbal exchange, Alfonso is already under Rahel's spell. The queen, eager to remove herself from the presence of the Jewish family, asks the king if he will not go with her. His answer, 'Ihr seht, ich bin gefangen!' [You see that I am caught. (p. 23)] indicates not only that Rahel has rested her cheek on his leg, impeding movement, but also that he has been ensnared by her beauty. Eleonore leaves with the words, 'Seid Ihr gefangen, bin ich frei. Ich gehe.' (l. 334) [You may be caught, but I am free. I go. (p. 23)] It is his sensuality and the resultant subjugation of reason and duty to emotions and desire which lead to Alfonso's abandonment of his public role and the endangerment of the Spanish state. Alfonso's public and private failures do, however, create a space in which Eleonore can exercise more power, control and authority, and display her ability as a ruler. As Yates writes, it falls to Eleonore to maintain the rational order within the drama.⁴⁴ Despite the contemporary social context in which Grillparzer places the drama, and his expressed views regarding male action, his portrayal of Alfonso and Eleonore subverts gender-based expectations. Alfonso is invested with characteristics which were generally associated with women, such as irrationality and excessive sexuality, while Eleonore is a 'masculine' character insofar as she prioritizes rational behaviour, politics, and action. Indeed, in many ways Alfonso resembles Rahel, a character defined by her sensuality and impulsiveness.

The troubled gender matrix which Grillparzer portrays in Alfonso and Eleonore is not a simple reversal of contemporary gender binaries. Alfonso is not reduced to the role of a sensual man, ruled alone by his passions and devoid of learning or reason. Indeed, quite the opposite is true. Despite his own aversion to Jews, he has sufficient insight to realize that it is social prejudice and systemic discrimination which have forced the Jews to behave in the manner which the Spaniards find distasteful:

> Ich selber lieb' es nicht dies Volk, doch weiß ich,
> Was sie verunziert, es ist unser Werk;
> Wir lähmen sie und grollen, wenn sie hinken. (ll. 485–87)

[I love them not, these people, but I know/ That what disfigures them, we cause ourselves./ We lame them, then are angry if they limp. (p. 31)]

For Florian Krobb, this insight makes Alfonso a 'wohlwollend-absolutistischen Herrscher Josephinischer Prägung' [benevolent-absolute ruler in the Josephinian mould].⁴⁵ It is largely due to his upbringing that he allows himself to become involved in a sexual relationship with Rahel. Garceran laments the joyless youth of his king which he perceives as the cause of Alfonso's indiscretions:

> Oh, daß doch dieser König seine Jugend,
> Der Knabenjahre hast'gen Ungestüm
> In Spiel und Tand, wie mancher sonst, verlebt!
> [...]
> Selbst seine Ehe treibend als Geschäft,
> Kommt ihm zum erstenmal das Weib entgegen,
> Das Weib als solches, nichts als ihr Geschlecht
> Und rächt die Torheit an der Weisheit Zögling.
> (ll. 851–83, 857–60)

[Oh, why could not this king have spent his youth,/ The thoughtless turbulence of boyhood years,/ In play and trifling much as others do?/ [...] / his marriage even treated as a deal,/ He, for the first time, chances on a woman,/ A female being, nothing but her sex,/ Who venges folly on the child of wisdom. (p. 50)]

His difficult upbringing denied him the sexual experiences which otherwise would have been the right of a man of his standing. As Alfonso recounts, his first experience of woman was on his wedding day: 'Daß Weiber es auch gibt, erfuhr ich erst,/ Als man mein Weib mir in der Kirche traute' (ll. 182–83) [That women lived and breathed, I came to know/ In church the day I wedded her, my wife (p. 16)]. Eleonore, however, is not well matched for Alfonso, especially as he is sexually inexperienced. Eleonore is 'wirklich ohne Fehl' (l. 184) [a woman faultless (p. 16)], a description which alludes to her lack of sexual interest rather than a truly faultless character.

In Act II, Alfonso's infatuation leads him to damage the dignity of his office. He and Rahel are in the summerhouse when the queen and courtiers arrive. Alfonso hides in order, as he puts it, to spare the queen any pain and to preserve the dignity of the monarchy. Eleonore sees Rahel and realizes what is going on, for she thanks Garceran for doing his duty, even if that duty is unworthy of a knight. Alfonso realizes that he has acted in an undignified manner, and that his sense of shame results from his relationship with Rahel: 'Muß ich, noch gestern Vorbild aller Zucht,/ Mich heute scheun vor jedes Dieners Blicken?' (ll. 697–98) [Must I, decorum's model yesterday,/ Avoid today my servants' every glance? (p. 42)] Towards the end of the act, Alfonso is determined to go to Alarcos and join his troops in war, but Rahel's picture distracts him, and he recalls Retiro, the palace where his forefather and a Moorish mistress had amused themselves in seclusion. His intention to carry out his military duties is severely tested, and although he determines to imitate his ancestors 'in der Tapferkeit, dem Wert/ Und nicht in ihrer Schwäche niederm Sträucheln' (ll. 775–76) [in their bravery, their worth,/ Not in their weakness when they basely fall (p. 46)], Act III finds Alfonso and Rahel at the royal *Lustschloss*. Garceran arrives, and when Alfonso asks him how the army is faring, he replies reproachfully, 'Wie Ihr seit länger wißt./ Die Feinde rüsten sich.' (ll. 908–09) [As you long have known,/ The enemy prepares. (p. 52)] Still Alfonso will not leave Rahel, and he says that he will join his soldiers in a few days' time. Garceran tries to impress upon him the urgency of the situation, but Alfonso refuses to leave Retiro until Esther arrives with the news that Eleonore and Manrique have summoned the estates '[u]m zu beraten das gemeine Beste./ Als wäre herrenlos das Königreich/ Und Ihr gestorben, der Ihr Herr und König.' (ll. 1050–52) [to join in counsel for the common good/ As though the kingdom were without a head/ And you had died, who are its lord and king. (p. 58)] It is this direct threat to his authority which motivates Alfonso's action, and he leaves almost immediately despite Esther and Rahel's pleas that he stay. In doing so, however, Alfonso abandons the duty of care he owes his mistress, much as Bancbanus neglects to care properly for Erny. Alfonso recognizes Rahel's need for safety, and leaves her in the care of the castellan (ll. 1075–77). In Act II, Alfonso is aware that an affair with Rahel would compromise his authority: 'Was andern Laune ist beim Fürsten Schuld' [Caprice in others is in princes guilt (p. 43)] (l. 711). Here, at the end of Act III, however, he places part of the blame for his actions on Rahel. This is further proof of his inability to control himself and take full responsibility for his behaviour and its consequences.

Given Grillparzer's composition of Rahel as a care-free and sensual foil to Eleonore, it is easy enough to comprehend her attraction for Alfonso. Rahel represents 'die Erlösung aus kalter Pflicht, die Entdeckung der Vollnatur, der irrationalen Lieblichkeit und Seligkeit des Lebens' [relief from cold duty, discovery of the full nature, of the irrational sweetness and bliss of life].[46] Esther's words in Act II capture her personality: 'Es kam ihr ein, und also tat sie's eben' (l. 636) [She thought of it and did it, that is all. (p. 39)]. The first scene of the drama presents a capricious and confident woman who is well aware of her own sexual allure. Rahel is deaf to her father's warnings, and declares a desire to see the king, '[j]ung und schön' (l. 20) [young and fair (p. 10)], and court, 'und all ihr Wesen,/ All ihr Gold und ihr Geschmeide' (ll. 17–18) [and how they act,/ All their gold and precious jewels (p. 10)]. Her profligacy annoys Isaak, her father, who is characterized by a stereotypical obsession with money, and complains about her mother, his second wife, while Rahel sings, 'Bin ich nicht schön,/ Bin ich nicht reich?/ Und sie ärgern sich,/ Und mich kümmert's nicht. La la la la.' (ll. 41–44) [Am I not fair,/ Am I not rich?/ Though vexed they be,/ What's that to me? La-la, la-la. (p. 11)] Despite Eleonore's rejection of Rahel's pleas for protection, Alfonso entrusts the Jewish family to Garceran's care at the end of Act I. He is obviously taken with her beauty, and says to Garceran, 'Ich selbst hab' nie nach Weibern viel gesehn,/ Doch diese scheint mir schön.' (ll. 354–55) [I never looked on women much myself,/ But she seems fair to me. (p. 25)], but it is also her fear and emotionality which he finds alluring: 'Sie wankt noch immer. All ihr ganzes Wesen/ Ein Meer von Angst in stets erneuten Wellen.' (ll. 385–96) [She falters still. Her being, soul and body,/ A sea of fear with wave succeeding wave. (p. 27)]

Act II develops the traits which Alfonso finds attractive. Rahel's status as Eleonore's playful rival is highlighted when she dresses up as a queen. She takes a picture of the king and leaves her own portrait in its place: 'Das mag er ansehn, so wie seines ich/ Und mein gedenken, hätt' er mich vergessen.' (ll. 582–83) [So he can look at that as I at his/ And thus remember me if he forgot me. (p. 36)] She proceeds to mockingly imitate Eleonore, imagining the jealous queen's words to her husband:

> Die Jüdin, sie gefiel Euch, leugnet's nur!
> Und sie ist schön, bei meinem hohen Wort,
> Nur mit mir selber etwa zu vergleichen.
> [...]
> Ich, Eure Königin, nun duld es nicht,
> Denn eifersüchtig bin ich wie ein Wiesel. (ll. 598–602)

> [The Jewess pleased you, that you must admit!/ And she is fair upon my royal word,/ To be compared, I think, but with myself./ [...] But I will not allow it, I, your queen;/ For I am jealous, sharper than a weasel. (p. 37)]

Alfonso interrupts her jesting, startling her, and her fearful reaction endears her to him. Yet she also shows herself to be defiant and strong-willed, refusing to return Alfonso's picture, and risking his anger by playing at sorcery. This only serves to ignite Alfonso's passions, and he again comments on her beauty (l. 640). Eleonore and Manrique do not share Alfonso's enthusiasm, and when the queen encounters Rahel in Act II, she says disparagingly, 'Und hier die Jüdin.' (l. 661) [And here, the Jewess. (p. 40)] Manrique's assessment is damning, and he orders Rahel to remove her assumed outfit:

> Geschmückt, dem losgelaßnen Wahnsinn gleich,
> Mit all dem Flitterstatt des Puppenspiels.
> Leg ab die Krone, die dir nicht geziemt,
> Selbst nicht im Scherz; den Mantel von der Schulter! (ll. 662–65)

[Arrayed, like lunacy set loose and free,/ In all the tinseled state of puppet plays./ Take off the crown; which is not yours to wear,/ Not even as a jest; the mantle, too! (p. 40)]

In the end, however, Rahel's impetuous and irreverent behaviour ensnares Alfonso. He orders Rahel to return the picture, and Rahel feigns obedience, but resolves to have her way no matter what. She swaps her picture for Alfonso's before leaving. Rahel refuses to thank Alfonso, flirtatiously reserving her thanks for another time which, despite Alfonso's determination never to see her again, she is confident will arise. Only after they have left does Alfonso notice Rahel's trickery, and the renewed sight of her portrait forces him to abandon his plan of joining his troops, and at the end of Act II he follows Rahel rather than his duty.

Alfonso's resulting neglect of politics creates a situation in which Eleonore's decisiveness triumphs. Eleonore is able to thrive because she can subordinate desire to duty: 'Ich möchte, doch ich kann nicht./ Vielmehr ich kann, beim Himmel, denn ich muß.' (ll. 677–78) [I would, and yet I cannot;/ Rather, I can, by Heaven, for I must. (p. 41)] In the contrast between Alfonso's sensuousness and resultant negligence, and Eleonore's firm grip on matters of state, Grillparzer questions contemporary ideas regarding the nature of masculinity and femininity.

Previous scholarship has viewed Eleonore in one-dimensional, and almost entirely negative, terms. Roy Cowen, for example, writes that she is totally lacking in human understanding, and labels her 'selfrighteous, narrow-minded, intolerant and jealous'.[47] For Martha Helfer, Eleonore is a 'cold fish of a queen', jealous, and 'sexually unresponsive'.[48] Elie Lambert writes of 'die steife, streng tugendhafte Leonor' [the cold, strictly virtuous Leonor].[49] Dagmar Lorenz and Heinz Lippuner are slightly less critical of Eleonore, yet a negative image still emerges. Lorenz reduces Eleonore to the sum of her moral framework, portraying her as a 'Königin mit den höchsten Tugendidealen' [queen with the highest ideals of virtue],[50] while Lippuner presents Eleonore and her rival, Rahel, as representatives of boredom and amusement respectively.[51] For Alfonso, this boredom is certainly a result of Eleonore's robust morals. On closer inspection, however, Eleonore proves a much more interesting character if she is seen as a representative of the subversive gender constellations in the drama.

The gender dynamics in Grillparzer's drama mark Eleonore out as an unwomanly woman. Talking about Rahel, Garceran says: 'Das edle Weib ist halb ein Mann, ja ganz,/ Erst ihre Fehler machen sie zu Weibern.' (ll. 861–62) [Good women are in part, or wholly, men;/ It is their faults that turn them into women. (p. 50)] Combined with Alfonso's reproach of his spouse, whom, he says, he would love more, '[w]är' manchmal, statt des Lobs, auch etwas zu verzeihn' (l. 186) [were sometimes need, instead of praise, of pardon too (p. 16)], this statement serves to define the oppositional forces of Eleonore and Rahel in the drama. The concept of 'woman' as the sum of her faults, a concept which defines Rahel, calls to mind the Fall of Man, and particularly Eve's role as the temptress who caused man to sin. The parallels with the role of Rahel and her relationship with Alfonso in Grillparzer's drama are obvious.[52]

In the context of Rahel's sexuality, Eleonore acquires the role of sexual lawmaker. Her high moral standing and sexual frigidity have been noted already, and scholars have drawn attention to these facets of her personality. However, it is a mistake to underestimate Eleonore's importance for the gender dynamics of the drama and for Grillparzer's portrayal of misogynistic social conventions. In his portrayal of Eleonore, he illuminates the active role of women in the cultural, sexual and social subjugation of women. Eleonore is a more extreme example of the role played by Hero's mother in *Des Meeres und der Liebe Wellen* or Kreusa in *Medea*. She is, to use Fiorenza's terminology, a 'civilizing conduit[] of patriarchal knowledge, values, religion, and culture'.[53] Eleonore and her counterparts have internalized the oppressive message of patriarchal societies, and in turn oppress other women who do not conform, or do not wish to conform, to the standards of female existence and comportment enforced by androcentric social orders.

In Act I, Eleonore displays her power when she dismisses Doña Clara with a gesture, despite Alfonso's request that she stay. However, the extent of her political influence only becomes evident in the council scene in Act IV. The king's neglect of his state duties forces the councillors to meet in his absence in an attempt to find a resolution to the pressing political and military issues. The queen has been invited to the assembly in the king's stead to give the assembly a veneer of legitimacy (ll. 1148–54). Manrique, who chairs the meeting, explains the dangers of the situation: the Moors threaten Spain's safety, and it is the king's duty to raise an army and defend the land. Alfonso, however, is absent from court, '[v]erlockt von eines Weibes üpp'gem Sinn' (l. 1166) [lured by a woman's wantonness of heart (p. 64)]. It is clear to them what must be done: 'Da muß vor allem denn die Dirne fort.' (l. 1182) [But first the girl must go. (p. 65)], and permanently, to ensure the present and future security of the Spanish state. Several options are open to the council, including bribing Rahel or abducting her and taking her abroad. These options, however, are flawed, as Alfonso would be able to counter both. Manrique dares not voice the third possibility, particularly in the queen's presence as he believes women unequal even to a mere allusion to violence:

> Edle Frau, mit Gunst.
> Ihr seid zu mild für unser hart Geschäft
> [...]
> Zwar, wenn Ihr reden wollt, wohlan so sprecht.
> Welch Blumenschicksal, welche Schmeichelstrafe
> Glaubt Ihr dem Fehl der Buhlerin gemäß? (ll. 1189–90, 1196–98)

[Please, Your Majesty./ You are too gentle for our bitter task./ [...] Yet would you have your say, I beg you, speak./ What flowery fate, what flattering punishment/ Seems fitting for our monarch's paramour? (p. 65)]

Manrique assumes that Eleonore's verdict, because that of a woman, must be mild and forgiving, and the patronizing coinages 'Blumenschicksal' and 'Schmeichelstrafe' illustrate his own misogyny. Eleonore, however, defies his expectations of her as a woman, and, although quietly, she sentences Rahel to death, repeating 'Den Tod' (ll. 1199) [Death (p. 65)] twice. Manrique's concept of both men and women is challenged by Eleonore's firm resolution and capability for brutality:

> Ihr hört's, Ihr Herren.
> Das war der dritte Antrag, den ich früher,
> Obgleich ein Mann, nicht auszusprechen wagte. (ll. 1199–1201)

[You hear the words, my lords./ That was the third proposal which before,/ Although a man, I did not dare pronounce. (p. 65)]

Eleonore's words belie Roe's assertion that '[w]ith the backing of the Queen, the council of state decides to have Rahel killed'.[54] The queen is the catalyst for the murder and it is unclear what would happen without her resolve.

Eleonore justifies the necessity of Rahel's death with the latter's transgression against marriage and religion. Marriage, in Eleonore's understanding of the institution, is sanctioned by God and removes from sex the stain of sin, but Rahel threatens the royal family, 'und damit das christliche Familiensystem und die allgemeine Repression' [and with it the Christian family structure and the general repression].[55] Eleonore's manipulative use of language in this speech almost reaches demagoguery, and allows her to showcase her own skills as a politician. Although there is much historical precedent for male monarchs conducting extramarital affairs without endangering their legitimate heirs' rights of accession, and although the infidelity of Don Sancho, Alfonso's ancestor, is mentioned at the end of Act II, and has not prevented Alfonso from acceding, Eleonore argues successfully that Rahel's affair with Alfonso threatens to invalidate her own marriage with the king, making herself a sinner and their son a bastard. The affair, she argues, necessarily makes either herself or Rahel a sinner, thereby forcing the councillors to condemn Rahel.[56] Eleonore's language makes it difficult to support Thompson's claim that '[t]he state's representatives are depicted with sympathy' and that 'both Manrique and the queen argue reasonably and from a position of principle, seeking not bloody revenge, but justice'.[57] Eleonore again condemns Rahel to death, while adeptly maintaining the veneer of traditional femininity:

> Doch ist dies Weib der Schandfleck dieser Erde,
> So reinigt euren König und sein Land.
> Ich schäme mich, daß ich vor Männern spreche,
> Und was kaum schicklich auch, doch zwingt die Not. (ll. 1221–24)

[But if it be this woman taints our earth,/ Then cleanse your king of taint, his land of blight./ I am ashamed that men must hear me speak,/ And things scarce proper, too; but need compels. (p. 66)]

As Roe points out, Eleonore could have reasoned, as the nobles do, that Rahel endangered the security of Spain, and justified her death on these terms.[58] That her argument rests wholly on Rahel's infringement of sexual morality demonstrates both the importance of this morality as an inhibiting and proscriptive force on women's behaviour, and the extent to which Eleonore has internalized this morality. Eleonore condemns Rahel for offences against a code of behaviour which, given its patriarchal conception and configuration, has little, if anything, to offer either woman. In condemning Rahel for crimes against morality, Eleonore, whether she realizes or not, condones and utilizes the appendages of a system which also restricts her own actions and limits her possibilities.

In the final two lines of Eleonore's speech, Yates sees her admission, which is 'in keeping with the propriety basic in her character', that she finds it difficult to discuss private matters with the councillors.[59] Yet the king, in Act I, makes it clear that Eleonore shares in the business of state and takes part in council discussions; she is 'gewohnt an Rat und Krieg' (l. 229) [used to council and to war (p. 18)]. Although she may not be used to discussing her marriage with councillors, this is not where she sees the impropriety of their subject matter. Rather, Eleonore's self-representation as a conventional woman is necessitated by the death sentence she utters directly before, and which distances her from the councillors' perceptions of what is suitable for women. This avowal of feminine weakness serves to shroud her actions and pronouncements and prevent the censure of society. References to traditional femininity while performing actions which are distinctly unfeminine call to mind the techniques of female authors in the nineteenth century, who often published numerous literary works while simultaneously accentuating their own strict adherence to gender roles and even attacking other women writers.

Eleonore's speech is crucial for the nuanced portrayal of the subjugation of women, and, more generally, of the repression of sexual desire. Grillparzer represents marriage, and particularly marriages arranged for political or other reasons, rather than entered into by individuals who are capable of satisfying each other as lovers and companions, as a restrictive and oppressive social force. In touching on this matter, Grillparzer shows himself to be attuned to the concerns of some of the women in his circle. Caroline Pichler, for example, was a staunch opponent of marriages of convenience or of reason, and believed that only couples who loved and respected each other should be joined in matrimony. Pichler more than once writes of Maria Theresa's luck in being allowed to escape the political marriage that was the fate of most women of her rank and to choose 'den Gemahl [...], den schönen, liebenswürdigen [Franz Stephan]' [her husband [...] the handsome, kind [Franz Stephan]].[60] Grillparzer also shows that, much as women can become the representatives and enforcers of misogynistic social constructs, men can also be the victims of patriarchal structures which supposedly operate merely for the benefit of males. Garceran laments Alfonso's lost youth, a youth from which women and sex were exiled by the men who raised him. Although these men may have had good intentions, their actions, including the marriage arranged for Alfonso, are shown to have had overwhelmingly negative effects on the course of Alfonso's life.

Eleonore's condemnation of Rahel must also be seen in the context of the drama's antisemitic setting. Rahel, despite her personal wealth, is shown to belong to a marginalized social group. In Act I, Isaak warns Rahel against entering the garden because Jews are not permitted in the king's presence. Manrique repeats this interdiction when Rahel approaches Alfonso, although he ignores it. As Zdenko Škreb writes, 'Für den gesetzestreuen Juden ist vieles verboten, aber geradezu ein Reich des Verbotenen ist der Hof, und Herold und Vorkämpfer des Verbotenen ist die Königin' [For the law-abiding Jewish people much is forbidden, but the court is absolutely a realm of the forbidden, and the queen is herald and champion of the forbidden].[61] Eleonore's reaction to Rahel displays her own personal antipathy towards Jews, while Alfonso acknowledges widespread anti-Jewish discrimination. When Alfonso asks Garceran for advice about seduction, the latter indicates the social standing of Jews by admitting that soldiers often have liaisons with Moorish women, but that an affair with a Jew would be unthinkable: 'Auf Maurinnen sind Streiter wir der Grenze/ Zu Recht verwiesen, doch die Jüdin, Herr — ' (ll. 480–81) [As frontier fighters we have certain rights/ To Moorish women; but a Jewess, Sire — (p. 31)]. As a Jewish woman, Rahel is more suspect than the enemy besieging the kingdom. By portraying the antisemitic society in which both Eleonore and Rahel live, Grillparzer adds to his nuanced portrayal of gender relations. Anders has noted that Eleonore and Rahel are marginalized figures, the former because she is a woman, the latter because she is Jewish.[62] Eleonore's tirade against Rahel is successful partly because of the antisemitism of Spanish society, which means that Rahel is doubly disadvantaged: as a woman, and as a Jew. As Eda Sagarra notes, 'the mutilation of Rahel's body [has been seen] as paradigmatic of a society which marginalized and exercised violence on Jews and women.'[63] Eleonore, who is also subjected to social conceptions of femininity, asserts her dominance as a Christian and as a member of the ruling class over a woman who is less privileged. As Lippuner writes, 'Eleonore nimmt ihren angestammten Platz auf dem Thronsessel ein, sie spricht das Bluturteil — als wirkliche Herrscherin' [Eleonore takes her ancestral place on the throne, she delivers the bloody judgment — as the true ruler].[64]

Harshness is only one facet of Eleonore's character. Yates sees in Eleonore's pleas for mercy an emotional intensity which scholarship has generally denied her.[65] Her potential for genuine feeling is more apparent, however, in her conversation with Alfonso in Act IV. Although her cool reception of her husband offends him, her affection for him soon becomes apparent. She welcomes Alfonso's signs of repentance and hopes for a better future, giving him the sign of affection that she refused on his entrance. Once Alfonso has admitted his transgressions, Eleonore is quick to forgive him which Yates sees as proof that 'Eleonore's coldness *is* only apparent: it is at least in part a reserve which hides both determination and real feeling'.[66] Her role in the drama must be seen within the larger conflict between public and private. It is precisely this conflict which necessitates the opposing characteristics which Eleonore displays: harshness and brutality in her public role, and submission in her private role.

Eleonore's pleas of mercy for her rival help obfuscate the events which transpire between Acts IV and V. Most importantly, they shroud the identity of Rahel's executioner(s), as do the various statements in Act V. The final version of the drama therefore deviates from the certainty of Grillparzer's sources. In 1824, he noted that agency was clear in these: Rahel '[wurde] von den Großen des Reichs im Einverständniße mit der Königin ermordet' [[was] murdered by the grandees of the realm with the approval of the queen] (Nr. 1330. *HKA* II/viii, p. 139). This obfuscation, therefore, was Grillparzer's deliberate addition. He does not explain this decision, but it is possible that he wanted to create uncertainty regarding the identity of the murderer(s). Manrique's repudiation of Eleonore's guilt echoes Grillparzer's analysis of *Macbeth*. Eleonore wishes to make herself visible to Alfonso as the guiltiest of the plotters — 'Mich laßt voran, ich bin die Schuldigste.' (l. 1768) [Let me come first, I am the guiltiest. (p. 90)] — but Manrique stresses her innocence in deed, if not in intent:

> Nicht also, edle Frau! Ihr spracht das Wort,
> Doch als es kam zur Tat, habt Ihr gezittert,
> Euch widersetzt und Schonung anbefohlen [...] (ll. 1769–71)
>
> [Not so, Your Majesty! You spoke the word;/ But when we urged the deed, you showed your fear,/ Opposed us, pled for mercy (p. 90)]

This statement could be seen as confirming Helfer's conclusion that grandees, encouraged by Eleonore, kill Rahel.[67] Lorenz sees similar agency in the drama: Rahel is murdered by the 'empörten Hofschranzen unter der Leitung der Königin in einer pogromartigen Szene' [outraged sycophantic courtiers under the queen's leadership in a pogrom-like scene].[68] For Politzer, who likens Eleonore to Lady Macbeth, the queen's hesitation is not necessarily a sign of a change of heart.[69] If we take Manrique's statement at face value, Eleonore's role mirrors that of Lady Macbeth in Grillparzer's reading of *Macbeth*: she is the only courtier who can utter the death sentence, yet was too feminine to carry out the deed. And yet no one is ready to accept the principal blame in the affair. Manrique admits to a role in the events — 'Ich selber tat's. Zwar nicht mir meiner Hand,/ Allein mit Rat, mit furchtbar ernstem Mitleid. (ll. 1776–77) [I did the deed, not with my hand in truth,/ But yet with words, with dreadful stern compassion (p. 90)] — but not to the deed itself, and encourages Garceran 'zu vertreten/ Was du gehindert nicht, wenn nicht gefördert' (ll. 1779–80) [to answer [...]/ For not preventing what you did not further (p. 90)]. With both Garceran and Manrique acknowledging participation in Rahel's death but not execution of the deed, the perpetrator can only be Eleonore or one of the other grandees. Manrique clearly deems it necessary to protect Eleonore from Alfonso's wrath, which suggests that her hands may not be as clean as his earlier statement indicates (ll. 1773–75).

Grillparzer's decision to stage the murder between Act IV and Act V means that this argument must remain essentially speculative. This decision could have been motivated by a desire to avoid aggravating the censors, who may well have looked askance at the portrayal of a murderous queen. However, if we return to the council scene in which Eleonore sentences Rahel to death, we find an indication that the queen intended her involvement to go beyond the mere granting of approval. Asked by Manrique how Alfonso will bear the death of Rahel, Eleonore emphasizes the primacy of his duty as head of state, and foreshadows her own participation in Rahel's murder:

> Er wird wohl, weil er soll und darum muß.
> Auch bleibt ihm ja die Rache an den Mördern:
> Vor allem treff' er mich und diese Brust. (ll. 1226–28)
>
> [He will, because he should and therefore must./ He can also take revenge on the murderers:/ Above all, let him strike my breast.]

Eleonore, who after Rahel's death considers herself the guiltiest of the plotters, foresees in the council scene her own actions, and that she will be the murderer most deserving of Alfonso's revenge. The uncertain agency in Rahel's death is, in any case, a matter of secondary importance: Rahel's murder, if not committed by Eleonore, is nevertheless a symptom of her privilege and power. If Eleonore herself did not murder Rahel, then her violence merely reached its apogee in her speech in the council scene: her words were her weapon, but they were employed with skill and precision to engineer the desired result.

Given her support for the execution of Rahel and the extent to which her own interests, as well as those of the state, are served by this deed, it is not impossible that Eleonore herself carries out the death sentence which she demands in Act IV. Grillparzer colludes with his characters to conceal the ultimate agency in the drama. While Manrique and Garceran deny murdering Rahel, Eleonore, by her own admission, is the guiltiest of all. And, when we examine Manrique's version of events more carefully, he does not exculpate Eleonore, but indicates that she was aware of the magnitude and gruesomeness of the deed: she shuddered, resisted and begged for mercy on Rahel's behalf. These actions are not necessarily incompatible with murder: Macbeth experiences great unease before the murder of Duncan, and afterwards cannot bear to confront his actions: 'I am afraid to think what I have done;/ Look on't again I dare not.' (II/i, ll. 50–51) As Grillparzer writes, Macbeth 'schaudert aber handelt'. Could Eleonore have overcome her own misgivings in order to murder Rahel?

While it is interesting to investigate Eleonore's exact role in the murder of Rahel, *Die Jüdin von Toledo* offers a robust challenge to the gendered dichotomy of intent and action which Grillparzer sees portrayed in *Macbeth*, even if Eleonore is innocent. At the close of the drama, Alfonso departs for war, leaving his son as king and Eleonore as regent. Yet Eleonore's decisiveness and action, especially when contrasted with Alfonso's abandonment of matters of state, already marked her out as ruler of orphaned Spain. If she did not commit the murder herself, she can nevertheless consider herself the guiltiest of plotters, since she was the only member of the council meeting who was able to condemn Rahel to death. In a society where no one, not even the king, is capable of intent, let alone of action, Eleonore's strength of intent and purpose is connoted differently. In the absence of intent and action, intent is as good as action, and Eleonore's impassioned condemnation of Rahel and her exhortation of those around her to enforce her decision position her as the catalyst for Rahel's murder.

Die Jüdin von Toledo presents a world in which the links between masculinity and femininity, action and intent, are much more complex than the situation Grillparzer perceives in *Macbeth*. According to his notes on Shakespeare's play, there exists a simple dichotomy in which masculinity is paired with action, and femininity with intent. Like Lady Macbeth, Grillparzer writes, all women are incapable of action, although they may be capable of intent. Yet the action of *Die Jüdin von Toledo* does not corroborate this supposedly universal truth; nor does it present a simple reversal of the dichotomy. Alfonso is the beguiled king, unable to focus on affairs of state and unwilling to determine on any course of action. Eleonore is forced to make decisions in his stead, which she does with a strength foreign to Alfonso and the other men of state. The murder, between acts and off stage, conceals the identity of the agent, although Eleonore considers herself to be the guiltiest party. With Alfonso indecisive and prevaricating, Eleonore's fierce intent is enough to call into question both the conclusions Grillparzer draws from *Macbeth*, and the dominant cultural stereotypes which deemed women unworthy of public office. For Grillparzer, Lady Macbeth is 'das Weib, das nach Empfindungen, im guten und schlimmen, handelt'. While Eleonore's decision may be partially motivated by jealousy, there can be no doubt that, in the figure of Alfonso, whose sensuality renders him incapable of intent and action, Grillparzer has portrayed a character who deviates from the rationality and decisiveness expected of him.

Notes to Chapter 5

1. Elisabeth Schüssler Fiorenza, *But she said: feminist practices of biblical interpretation* (Boston: Beacon Press, 1992), pp. 7–8.
2. Ibid., p. 114.
3. Ibid., p. 115.
4. Ibid., p. 123.
5. Michelle Tracy Berger and Kathleen Guidroz, 'Introduction', in *The Intersectional Approach. Transforming the Academy through Race, Class, and Gender* (Chapel Hill, NC: The University of North Carolina Press, 2009), pp. 1–22 (p. 3).
6. Sumi Cho, Kimberlé Williams Crenshaw, and Leslie McCall, 'Toward a Field of Intersectionality Studies: Theory, Applications, and Praxis', *Signs* 38/4 (2013), 785–810 (p. 787).
7. Anna Carastathis, 'The Concept of Intersectionality in Feminist Theory', *Philosophy Compass* 9/5 (2014), 304–14 (p. 304).
8. Leslie McCall, 'The Complexity of Intersectionality', *Signs* 30/3 (2005), 1771–1800 (p. 1771).
9. Jennifer C. Nash, 'Re-thinking Intersectionality', *Feminist Review* 89 (2008), 1–15 (p. 13).
10. Carastathis, 'The Concept of Intersectionality in Feminist Theory', p. 305.
11. Kimberlé Crenshaw, 'Demarginalizing the Intersection of Race and Sex: A Black Feminist Critique of Antidiscrimination Doctrine, Feminist Theory and Antiracist Politics', *The University of Chicago Legal Forum* (1989), 139–67 (p. 140).
12. Ibid., p. 154.
13. Kimberlé Crenshaw, 'Mapping the Margins: Intersectionality, Identity Politics, and Violence Against Women of Color', *Stanford Law Review* 43/6 (1991), 1241–99 (p. 1242).
14. Kathy Davis and Gail Lewis, 'Celebrating Intersectionality? Debates on a Multi-faceted Concept in Gender Studies: Themes from a Conference', *European Journal of Women's Studies* 16/3 (August 2009), 203–10 (p. 205).
15. Yvette Taylor, 'Complexities and Complications: Intersections of Class and Sexuality', in *Theorizing Intersectionality and Sexuality*, ed. by Yvette Taylor et al. (Basingstoke: Palgrave Macmillan, 2011), pp. 37–55 (p. 37).
16. Yvette Taylor, Sally Hines and Mark Casey, 'Introduction', in *Theorizing Intersectionality and Sexuality*, pp. 1–12 (p. 3).
17. Fiorenza, *But she said: feminist practices of biblical interpretation*, p. 123.
18. Christian Rogowski, 'Erstickte Schreie. Geschlechtliche Differenz und koloniales Denken in Grillparzers Medea-Trilogie *Das goldene Vließ*', *JdGG* 3. Folge 21 (2003–06), 32–50 (p. 33).
19. Karen O'Brien, *Narratives of Enlightenment: Cosmopolitan History from Voltaire to Gibbon* (Cambridge: Cambridge University Press, 1997), p. 133.
20. Lorenz, *Dichter des sozialen Konflikts*, p. 69.
21. Hagl-Catling, *Für eine Imagologie der Geschlechter*, p. 177.

22. Grillparzer, 'Das goldene Vließ: Der Gastfreund. Die Argonauten. Medea', in *HKA* I/ii, 5–301. Quotations from 'Der Gastfreund' will be indicated with *DG*, from 'Die Argonauten' with *DA*, and from 'Medea' with *M* before line numbers. Here, *DG*, ll. 50–54.
23. Yixu Lü, *Medea unter den Deutschen. Wandlungen einer literarischen Figur* (Freiburg i. Br.: Rombach, 2009), p. 138.
24. Grillparzer, 'Selbstbiographie', in *HKA* I/xvi, p. 136.
25. Edward W. Said, *Culture and Imperialism* (London: Chatto and Windus, 1993), p. 96.
26. Friedrich Schiller, 'Was heißt und zu welchem Ende studiert man Universalgeschichte? Eine akademische Antrittsrede', in *Werke und Briefe*, VI (2000), pp. 411–31 (p. 418).
27. Francis Lamport, 'Three "Schopenhauerian" Trilogies: Grillparzer, Wagner, Hebbel', *Oxford German Studies* 39 (2010), 54–69 (p. 60).
28. Schiller, 'Universalgeschichte', pp. 416–17.
29. Matthias Luserke-Jaqui, *Medea. Studien zur Kulturgeschichte der Literatur* (Tübingen: Francke, 2002), p. 194.
30. Spörk, 'Gesten der Herrschaft — Zeichen der Macht', p. 218.
31. Rogowski, 'Erstickte Schreie', p. 46.
32. Lorenz, 'Frau und Weiblichkeit bei Grillparzer', p. 208.
33. Ibid.
34. Ortrud Gutjahr, 'Iphigenie — Penthesilea — Medea: Zur Klassizität weiblicher Mythen bei Goethe, Kleist und Grillparzer', in *Frauen: MitSprechen, MitSchreiben. Beiträge zur literatur- und sprachwissenschaftlichen Frauenforschung*, ed. by Marianne Henn and Britta Hufeisen (Stuttgart: Heinz, 1997), pp. 223–43 (p. 231).
35. Konrad Kenkel, *Medea-Dramen. Entmythisierung und Remythisierung. Euripides, Klinger, Grillparzer, Jahnn, Anouilh* (Bonn: Bouvier, 1979), p. 75.
36. Yvonne M. Parry, '*Das goldene Vließ*: The Tragedy of the Adventurer', in *Studies in Nineteenth Century Austrian Literature*, ed. by Brian O. Murdoch and Mark G. Ward (Glasgow: Scottish Papers in Germanic Studies, 1983), pp. 1–27 (p. 16).
37. Weiss, 'Opfer bei Grillparzer', p. 239.
38. Lorenz, 'Frau und Weiblichkeit bei Grillparzer', p. 208.
39. Ibid., p. 213.
40. Heike Bartel, 'Dressing the "Other", Dressing the "Self". Clothing in the Medea Dramas of Euripides and Franz Grillparzer', in *Unbinding Medea. Interdisciplinary Approaches to a Classical Myth from Antiquity to the 21st Century*, ed. by Heike Bartel and Anne Simon (London: Modern Humanities Research Association and Maney Publishing, 2010), pp. 161–75 (p. 169).
41. Prutti counts a mere 74 lines. Prutti, *Grillparzers Weltheater*, p. 350.
42. William Shakespeare, *Macbeth*, ed. by Kenneth Muir (London: Methuen, 1951), I/v, ll. 40–43, 47–48. Further quotations from this text will be indicated in parentheses in the body of the text.
43. Grillparzer, 'Die Jüdin von Toledo', in *HKA* I/vii, 5–105, ll. 388–90.
44. W. E. Yates, 'Grillparzer, *Die Jüdin von Toledo*', in *Landmarks in German Drama*, ed. by Peter Hutchinson (Oxford: Peter Lang, 2002), pp. 111–25 (p. 123).
45. Florian Krobb, '"Bleib zurück, geh nicht in' Garten!" Grillparzers *Jüdin von Toledo* als Traktat über die "Judenfrage"', in *Judenrollen. Darstellungsformen im europäischen Theater von der Restauration bis zur Zwischenkriegszeit*, ed. by Hans-Peter Bayerdörfer and Jens Malte Fischer (Tübingen: Niemeyer, 2008), pp. 125–42 (p. 137).
46. Johannes Volkelt, 'Die Psychologie der Liebe in Grillparzers Dramen', *JdGG* 19 (1910), 1–28 (p. 6).
47. Roy C. Cowen, 'The Tragedy of *Die Jüdin von Toledo*', *The German Quarterly* 37 (1964), 39–53 (pp. 40, 44).
48. Martha B. Helfer, 'Framing the Jew: Grillparzer's *Die Jüdin von Toledo*', *The German Quarterly* 75 (2002), 160–80 (pp. 164, 165, 168).
49. Elie Lambert, 'Eine Untersuchung der Quellen der "Jüdin von Toledo"', *JdGG* 19 (1910), 61–84 (p. 71).
50. Lorenz, *Dichter des sozialen Konflikts*, p. 103.

51. Heinz Lippuner, 'Grillparzers "Jüdin von Toledo". Untersuchung eines Paradigmas', *Orbis Litterarum* 27 (1972), 202–23 (p. 204).
52. Cf. Yates, 'Grillparzer, *Die Jüdin von Toledo*', p. 113.
53. Fiorenza, *But she said: feminist practices of biblical interpretation*, p. 123.
54. Roe, *An Introduction*, p. 252.
55. Lorenz, *Dichter des sozialen Konflikts*, p. 99.
56. Lorenz argues that the roles of Eleonore and Rahel are wholly compatible: 'Entscheidungen und Bewertungen werden gefordert, wo mit einem Sowohl-als-auch operiert werden könnte. Das Doktrinäre der westlichen Konventionen macht logisch Vereinbares unvereinbar. Ohne Doktrin könnten die Königin und Rahel koexistieren, denn ihre Interessen konfligieren kaum. Irrationale Faktoren — Konvention, Religion, Tradition und Sitte — stehen der rationalen Lösung entgegen.' This is probably true, but such a situation would degrade both women. Ibid., p. 104.
57. Thompson, *Franz Grillparzer*, p. 125.
58. Roe, *An Introduction*, p. 257.
59. Yates, 'Grillparzer, *Die Jüdin von Toledo*', p. 121.
60. Pichler, *Denkwürdigkeiten*, I, p. 12.
61. Zdenko Škreb, 'Rahel', in *Die andere Welt. Aspekte der österreichischen Literatur des 19. und 20. Jahrhunderts. Festschrift für Hellmuth Himmel zum 60. Geburtstag*, ed. by Kurt Bartsch et al. (Bern: Francke, 1977), pp. 97–105 (p. 100).
62. Anders, "... der Zündstoff liegt, der diese Mine donnernd sprengt gen Himmel.", p. 179.
63. Eda Sagarra, 'Grillparzer, the Catholics and the Jews: A Reading of *Die Jüdin von Toledo* (1851)', *Leo Baeck Institute Yearbook* 46 (2001), 67–80 (p. 78).
64. Lippuner, 'Grillparzers "Jüdin von Toledo"', p. 210.
65. Yates, 'Grillparzer, *Die Jüdin von Toledo*', p. 123.
66. Yates, *A Critical Introduction*, p. 188.
67. Helfer, 'Framing the Jew: Grillparzer's *Die Jüdin von Toledo*', p. 165.
68. Dagmar C. G. Lorenz, 'Die schöne Jüdin in Stifters *Abdias* und Grillparzers *Die Jüdin von Toledo*', *JdGG* 3. Folge 19 (1996), 125–39 (p. 128).
69. Politzer, *Das abgründige Biedermeier*, p. 346.

CONCLUSION

In the Introduction, I touched upon some of the contradictions and complexities regarding women which are present in Grillparzer's writing. This study has not reconciled these contradictory *Frauenbilder*, but that was not the aim. Indeed, given the length of Grillparzer's literary career, and the variety of genres in which these statements appear, these inconsistencies are perhaps inevitable and irreconcilable. What has been achieved, I hope, is a reimagining of the author which, while acknowledging his misogynistic statements, also takes into account the realities of his life and the positive female characters he created in his dramas.

Several important conclusions can be drawn from this study. First, by investigating the lives and writings of the women who were closest to Grillparzer during his lifetime, we can put paid to the idea that he was hostile to women who were active in the public sphere. Pichler, Weissenthurn, Paoli, Littrow-Bischoff, Ebner-Eschenbach, Schröder, Rettich and Wolter enjoyed Grillparzer's interest, respect and friendship. He encouraged their careers and welcomed their successes. Paoli and Littrow-Bischoff in particular argued for an improvement in women's social roles. While Grillparzer may not have made any direct statements regarding women's rights, the Frauen-Erwerb-Verein or other moves towards greater equality, the fact that he was friends with women who engaged with these issues indicates that he was not hostile to such ideas, and may have silently supported them.

Second, the writings of these authors on the *Frauenfrage* illustrate the aims and desires held by women of the age. Philosophical reflections on the relationship between the sexes are largely abandoned in favour of practical prescriptions for a changing society where women are increasingly left to fend for themselves. Pichler, Paoli, Littrow-Bischoff and other women whom Grillparzer knew advocated women's greater participation in the nation's economic life, as a way of providing for themselves and as a way of utilizing their skills and knowledge. They demanded improvements in women's education, and Littrow-Bischoff was instrumental in founding the Wiener Frauen-Erwerb-Verein, which realized some of the aims of the women's movement. By gaining a better understanding of the contemporary discourse, Grillparzer's dramas and their heroines can be put into a historical and social context. Grillparzer's dramas do not represent the kind of direct criticism of and challenge to specific contemporary issues facing women, as in Bauernfeld's *Bürgerlich und Romantisch*, or, indeed, Grillparzer's *Wer ist schuldig?*. Grillparzer, through his heroines, is nevertheless a harsh critic of prevailing social misogyny and restrictions placed on women, and a publicist for women's capabilities. The political and artistic talents, the devotion and steadfastness, the bravery, intelligence and determination of Hero, Kunigunde, Sappho, Libussa, and of the other figures who feature in this study, call into question contemporary assumptions and 'scientific facts' regarding women's capabilities. Grillparzer was therefore in tune with those women in nineteenth-century Austria who challenged the status quo and championed women's abilities.

As has been shown, Grillparzer's heroines should also be seen in the context of the author's wider intellectual context. I have argued for the influence of contemporary Austrian laws, European thinking on the social contract, Shakespeare, and the Enlightenment on the creation of these figures, and in doing so have shown the breadth of Grillparzer's intellectual interests. Where Grillparzer's dramas fit into existing literary traditions, he emphasizes the importance of female characters, demonstrating that they were of primary interest for him, and adds philosophical and political complexity as a framework for discussion of the *Frauenfrage*. Elaborating these various contexts, and the way Grillparzer manipulated existing traditions, demonstrates the emancipatory message of Grillparzer's dramas. I have also shown that Grillparzer's juvenilia, which address social issues more directly than his mature works, suggest that he censored these later works, and that they therefore might present only a weakened version of his opinions. It is possible that the portrayal of Kunigunde, the ambitious young woman whose aspirations are crushed by marriage, or of Berta, whose affections are the plaything of scheming male relatives, were criticisms of contemporary marriage. When he places Hero's desire for a life of self-determination in the context of Kant's philosophy, Grillparzer could be communicating a positive message regarding women's intellectual capabilities. When Grillparzer portrays the influence of social contract theory on Sappho's and Libussa's polities, he creates politically astute heroines who are victims of androcentric political coups rather than of their own physiology. Grillparzer's decision to create a backstory for the millennia-old Medea in which he sheds light on the misogynistic and xenophobic attitudes which drive her to extremes suggests an understanding of oppression. Arguing for *Die Jüdin von Toledo* to be seen in the context of Grillparzer's own pronouncements on *Macbeth*, particularly as regards the relationship between the sexes, means that Eleonore becomes a clever, if demagogic, politician capable of doing what is necessary when the men around her flounder, and that Grillparzer's misogynistic statements are contradicted by his own dramatic works. Taken together, Grillparzer's dramatic heroines represent a significant repudiation of Grillparzer's misogynistic statements, and of contemporary opinions regarding women's social role.

As stated in the Introduction, this is a study about Grillparzer's *ideas*. But what of his contemporary audiences and readers? Did they see his dramas as an intellectual response to the Austrian women's movement, or to discussions of the *Frauenfrage*? Although there was widespread discussion of women's emancipation and the *Frauenfrage*, including related developments abroad, in Austrian media during Grillparzer's life, his contemporaries do not seem to have linked his dramas to these discussions. In the Introduction, we saw that his heroines were praised, but primarily because contemporaries saw them as paragons of the female form, rather than as proponents of women's emancipation. Grillparzer's heroines attracted considerable critical attention, and contemporaries recognized the sympathy he showed for his female characters, but did not perceive this as social criticism or activism. One critic remarked that Grillparzer's Sappho was 'erhaben schön [...] gefühlvoll und wahr' [sublimely beautiful [...] sensitive and true], and his Medea was not 'die blutgetünchte Zauberin der Alten' [blood-covered sorceress of the ancients], but a 'tiefgekränkte Gattin und Mutter' [deeply aggrieved wife and mother],[1] while another noted the contrast Grillparzer created between Margarete's 'ideale[] Reinheit' and Kunigunde's 'moralische Blöße' [ideal purity; lack of morals].[2] After a performance of the first act of *Libussa* in 1840, the *Wiener Zeitschrift* wrote that the sisters 'scheinen mit jedem Worte über das gewöhnliche Maß der Frauengestalten hinauszuwachsen' [seem with each word to rise above the normal measure of female characters].[3]

This lack of contemporary critical recognition of the issues relating to women's emancipation which I see in these dramas is particularly surprising when we consider that at least some contemporaries noticed the 'Luft der wienerischen Verhältnisse' [air of Viennese conditions] in his dramas and argued that 'die Wahl der Stoffe oder die Formen, womit er seine Ideen umhüllt, verrathen uns, daß der Dichter in Wien lebt' [the choice of materials or the forms, in which he cloaks his ideas, betray to us that the poet lives in Vienna].[4] In the case of *Die Ahnfrau* criticism was concerned almost exclusively with the 'Schicksalsidee' [idea of fate], and with discussions regarding the drama's moral framework, which explains the lack of attention given to the female characters. But political issues were seen in other dramas. A critic in the *Neue Freie Presse* wrote that *Libussa* 'berührt in starkem Maße die Nationalitäten-Frage' [touches strongly on the question of nationality],[5] while *Die Neuzeit* saw *Die Jüdin von Toledo* as a drama about the place of Jews in society.[6] And references to the movement for women's emancipation were seen in works by other writers: a review of Roderich Benedix's *Doctor Wespe*, for example, stated that Elisabeth 'hat sich der modernen Frauenemancipation in die Arme geworfen' [has thrown herself into the arms of the modern movement for women's emancipation].[7] What can explain the lack of attention given to the emancipatory aspect of Grillparzer's dramas for which I argue here? It is possible that Grillparzer's historical and mythological settings, chosen to fool the censors, also fooled audiences. Although the Viennese flavour of Grillparzer's dramas was noted by some, others found his portrayals of foreign settings convincing and realistic: perhaps this prevented them from perceiving contemporary Austrian concerns in these dramas. Censorship, which affected Grillparzer's dramatic work, could also have played a role in critical reception: if the implications of Grillparzer's dramas were too controversial to be placed in a Viennese setting, perhaps their discussion was too sensitive for print. Another possibility is that contemporaries could not, or would not see Grillparzer's dramas, a source of national pride and often regarded as aspiring to the classicism of Goethe and Schiller, as ruminations on the *Frauenfrage* or women's emancipation, the latter in particular being treated with derision in much of the media coverage.

His contemporaries' lack of openness to the issues of women's social position which I see in these dramas cannot detract from the positive portrayal of Grillparzer's heroines. His sympathy with his heroines, women who defy the expectations their societies place on them, and the expectations Grillparzer's society placed on its female inhabitants, and the social criticism which he built into his dramas, however, suggest a much more generous attitude towards the *Frauenfrage* than do his diaries. In a letter to Caroline Pichler, Therese von Artner wrote: 'Allerdings hast du Recht, daß ich das schöne Bild, in dem mir Grillparzer früher erschien, nicht gern aufgebe, und völlig dagegen kämpfen möchte.' [You are certainly right that I do not wish to relinquish the beautiful image I had of Grillparzer in former times, and would like to struggle completely against it.][8] The present study represents a small contribution in the tradition of Artner and others who have defended the poet in the face of undue criticism or misunderstanding.

Notes to the Conclusion

1. 'Kritische Skizzen', in *Der Ungar*, 25.1.1842, 116-17 (p. 116).
2. 'Über Grillparzers Trauerspiel: "Ottokars Glück und Ende"', in *Abend-Zeitung*, 14.3.1825, 245-47 (p. 246).
3. 'K. K. Hoftheater nächst der Burg', in *Wiener Zeitschrift für Kunst, Literatur, Theater und Mode*, 5.12.1840, 1549-52 (p. 1551).
4. 'Dramatische Bücherschau für das Jahr 1839', in *Blätter für literarische Unterhaltung*, 28.7.1840, 845-47 (p. 845).
5. 'Feuilleton. Franz Grillparzer's sämmtliche Werke', in *Neue Freie Presse*, 21.6.1872, 1-4 (p. 2).
6. 'Die "Jüdin von Toledo"', in *Die Neuzeit*, 8.11.1872, 495-96 (p. 496).
7. 'K. K. Hoftheater nächst der Burg', in *Wiener Zeitschrift für Kunst, Literatur, Theater und Mode*, 16.2.1843, 261-63 (p. 261).
8. Therese von Artner to Caroline Pichler, 10.7.1828, Wienbibliothek im Rathaus, H.I.N. 362.

BIBLIOGRAPHY

Archival Sources, Wienbibliothek im Rathaus, Vienna

Nachlass Franz Grillparzer

H.I.N. 82372, [Verzeichnis der Kranzspenden zu Grillparzers Begräbnis], undated manuscript.

Nachlass Caroline Pichler/Fanny von Pelzeln

H.I.N. 362, Therese von Artner to Caroline Pichler, 10.7.1828.
H.I.N. 434, Caroline Pichler to Marie von Zay, 28.3.1821.
H.I.N. 589, Johanna Franul von Weissenthurn to Caroline Pichler, 21.4.1838.
H.I.N. 590, Johanna Franul von Weissenthurn to Caroline Pichler, 8.3.1843.

Sammlung Eufemia von Kudriaffsky

H.I.N. 39919, Eufemia von Kudriaffsky an Josephine von Knorr, 21.6.1861.

Other

H.I.N. 213829, Julie Rettich, 'Diktatschreiben an die Grüne Insel', no date.

Primary Sources

Grillparzer's Works (collected editions)

Sämmtliche Werke, ed. by Josef Weilen, 10 vols (Stuttgart: Cotta, 1872).
Sämtliche Werke, Historisch-kritische Ausgabe, 42 vols, ed. by August Sauer and Reinhold Backmann (Vienna: Gerlach & Wiedling, 1908–16; Vienna: Schroll, 1916–48).
Sämtliche Werke: Ausgewählte Briefe, Gespräche, Berichte, 4 vols, ed. by Peter Frank and Karl Pörnbacher (Munich: Hanser, 1960–65).

Grillparzer's Works (individual works)

'[Anfang einer Selbstbiographie]' (1835), in *HKA* I/xvi, pp. 17–20.
'[Anfänge einer Selbstbiographie]' (1822), in *HKA* I/xvi, pp. 11–15.
'Das goldene Vließ: Der Gastfreund. Die Argonauten. Medea', in *HKA* I/ii, pp. 5–301.
'Das Kloster bei Sendomir', in *HKA* I/xiii, pp. 5–33.
'Der Zauberwald. Eine komische Oper in 3 Aufzügen', in *HKA* II/iii, pp. 87–91.
'Des Meeres und der Liebe Wellen', in *HKA* I/iv, pp. 81–211.
'Die Ahnfrau', Trauerspiel in fünf Aufzügen (erste Auflage: Wien 1817; sechste Auflage: Wien 1844), in *HKA* I/i, pp. 9–148.
'Die Ahnfrau', Trauerspiel in vier Aufzügen (erste Fassung), in *HKA* I/i, pp. 153–256.

'Die Jüdin von Toledo', in *HKA* I/vii, pp. 5–105.
'Drahomira. III', in *HKA* II/iv, pp. 361–72.
'Ein treuer Diener seines Herrn', in *HKA* I/iii, pp. 183–314.
'König Ottokars Glück und Ende', in *HKA*, I/iii, pp. 5–177.
'Libussa', in *HKA* I/vi, pp. 5–154.
'Sappho', in *HKA* I/I, pp. 263–373.
'Selbstbiographie', in *HKA* I/xvi, pp. 63–231.
'Wer ist schuldig?', in *HKA* II/iv, pp. 93–136.

Translations of Grillparzer's Works

A Faithful Servant of his Master, trans. by Arthur Burkhard (Yarmouth Port, MA: The Register Press, 1941).
The Golden Fleece, trans. by Arthur Burkhard (Yarmouth Port, MA: The Register Press, 1942).
Hero and Leander, trans. by Arthur Burkhard (Yarmouth Port, MA: The Register Press, 1962).
Libussa, trans. by Henry H. Stevens (Yarmouth Port, MA: The Register Press, 1941).
The Jewess of Toledo. Esther, trans. by Arthur Burkhard (Yarmouth Port, MA: The Register Press, 1953).
King Ottocar, His Rise and Fall, trans. by Arthur Burkhard (Yarmouth Port, MA: The Register Press, 1962).
Sappho, trans. by Arthur Burkhard (Yarmouth Port, MA: The Register Press, 1953).

Other Primary Sources

Allgemeines bürgerliches Gesetzbuch für die gesammten deutschen Erbländer der Oesterreichischen Monarchie (Vienna: k.k. Hof- und Staats-Druckerey, 1811).
ANONYMOUS (Johann Friedrich Ernst Albrecht), *Die Töchter Kroks, Böheims Fürstinnen. Eine Geschichte des achten Jahrhunderts*, Erster Theil (Hamburg: Hoffmann, 1792).
AUGUST, OTTO (Auguste Littrow-Bischoff), *Die sociale Bewegung auf dem Gebiete der Frauen* (Hamburg: Hoffmann und Campe, 1868).
BAUERNFELD, EDUARD VON, *Bauernfelds ausgewählte Werke in vier Bänden*, 4 vols, ed. by Emil Horner (Leipzig: Hesse, no date).
——*Eduard von Bauernfelds Gesammelte Aufsätze*, ed. by Stefan Hock, Schriften des Literarischen Vereins in Wien IV (Vienna: Verlag des Literarischen Vereins in Wien, 1905).
——'Die schöne Literatur in Österreich', in *Eduard von Bauernfelds Gesammelte Aufsätze*, pp. 137–75.
BERNARD, JOSEPH CARL, *Libussa. Romantische Oper in drey Aufzügen* (Vienna: Wallishausser, 1823).
BRENTANO, CLEMENS, *Die Gründung Prags. Ein historisch-romantisches Drama* (Pest: Hartleben, 1815).
EBERT, KARL EGON, *Wlasta. Böhmisch-nationales Heldengedicht in drei Büchern* (Prague: Calve, 1829).
EBNER-ESCHENBACH, MARIE VON, *Meine Erinnerungen an Grillparzer. Aus einem zeitlosen Tagebuch* (Berlin: Gebrüder Paetel, 1916).
——*Kritische Texte und Deutungen*, ed. by Karl Konrad Polheim, Carsten Kretschmann and Jens Stüben, 8 vols (Tübingen: Niemeyer, 1999–2012).
GOETHE, JOHANN WOLFGANG, *Sämtliche Werke, Briefe, Tagebücher und Gespräche*, 40 vols, ed. by Hendrik Birus et al. (Frankfurt a.M.: Deutscher Klassiker Verlag, 1986–2000).

———*Iphigenia in Tauris*, trans. by Roy Pascal, ed. by Martin Swales (London: Angel Books, 2014).
GUBITZ, FRIEDRICH WILHELM, *Sappho. Monodrama* (Berlin: Maurersche Buchhandlung, 1816).
HOBBES, THOMAS, *Leviathan*, ed. by J. C. A. Gaskin (Oxford: Oxford University Press, 2008).
KANT, IMMANUEL, *Werke in sechs Bänden*, ed. by Wilhelm Weischedel (Frankfurt a.M.: Insel, 1956–64).
——— 'An Answer to the Question: "What is Enlightenment?"' in *Political Writings*, ed. by Hans Reiss, trans. by H. B. Nisbet (Cambridge: Cambridge UP, 1991), pp. 54–60.
KLEIST, FRANZ VON, *Sappho. Ein dramatisches Gedicht* (Berlin: Vossische Buchhandlung, 1793).
LOCKE, JOHN, *Two Treatises of Government*, ed. by Peter Laslett (Cambridge: Cambridge University Press, 1988).
MARLOWE, CHRISTOPHER, and GEORGE CHAPMAN, *Hero and Leander* (Chiswick: C. Whittingham, 1821).
MCDONALD, LYNN (ed.), *Florence Nightingale on Society and Politics, Philosophy, Science, Education and Literature*, Collected Works of Florence Nightingale, vol. 5 (Waterloo, Ontario: Wilfred Laurier University Press, 2003).
MERBACH, PAUL ALFRED, 'Zwei Aufsätze von Johanna Franul v. Weissenthurn. Aus der Handschrift mitgeteilt', *JdGG* 24 (1913), 211–24.
MILL, JOHN STUART, *Additional Letters of John Stuart Mill*, ed. by Marion Filipiuk, Michael Laine, John M. Robson (Toronto: University of Toronto Press; London: Routledge, 1991).
MUSÄUS, JOHANN KARL AUGUST, *Volksmärchen der Deutschen* [1782–86] (Munich: Winkler, 1961).
OVID, *The Heroïdes or Epistles of the Heroines, The Amours, Art of Love, Remedy of Love, and Minor Works*, trans. by Henry T. Riley (London: Bohn, 1852).
Betty Paolis Gesammelte Aufsätze, ed. by Helene Bettelheim-Gabillon, Schriften des Literarischen Vereins in Wien IX (Vienna: Verlag des Literarischen Vereins in Wien, 1908).
PAOLI, BETTY, *Was hat der Geist denn wohl gemein mit dem Geschlecht?*, ed. by Eva Geber (Vienna: Mandelbaum, 2001).
PICHLER, CAROLINE, *Sämmtliche Werke*, 60 vols (Vienna: Anton Pichler, 1828–45).
——— *Denkwürdigkeiten aus meinem Leben*, 2 vols, ed. by Karl Blümml (Munich: Georg Müller, 1914).
ROUSSEAU, JEAN-JACQUES, *Discourse on Political Economy* and *The Social Contract*, trans. by Christopher Betts (Oxford: Oxford University Press, 1994).
SCHILLER, FRIEDRICH, *Werke und Briefe*, 12 vols, ed. by Otto Dann et al. (Frankfurt a.M.: Deutscher Klassiker Verlag, 1992–2005).
——— *Song of the Bell*, trans. by W.H. Furness (Philadelphia, PA: C. Sherman, Printer, 1849).
——— *Poet of Freedom*, 4 vols, II (Washington, D.C.: Schiller Institute, 1988).
SCHREYVOGEL, JOSEPH, *Joseph Schreyvogels Tagebücher 1810–1823*, ed. by Karl Glossy, II. Schriften der Gesellschaft für Theatergeschichte III (Berlin: Verlag der Gesellschaft für Theatergeschichte, 1903).
Briefe von Sophie Schröder (1813–1868), ed. by Heinrich Stümcke (Berlin: Selbstverlag der Gesellschaft für Theatergeschichte, 1910).
SHAKESPEARE, WILLIAM, *Macbeth*, ed. by Kenneth Muir (London: Methuen, 1951).
Statuten des Wiener Frauen-Erwerbs-Vereines (Vienna: Verlag des Wiener Frauen-Erwerbs-Vereines, 1866).

WEISSENTHURN, JOHANNA FRANUL VON, *Schauspiele von Johanna Franul v. Weissenthurn, gebornen Grünberg, kaiserl. königl. Hofschauspielerinn*, 15 vols (Vienna: Degen, 1809–48).

Periodicals

'Die "Jüdin von Toledo"', in *Die Neuzeit*, 8.11.1872, 495–96.
'Dramatische Bücherschau für das Jahr 1839', in *Blätter für literarische Unterhaltung*, 28.7.1840, 845–47.
'Feuilleton. Franz Grillparzer's sämmtliche Werke', in *Neue Freie Presse*, 21.6.1872, 1–4.
"Gelegenheitsworte für unsere Zeit. Die schöne Wienerin", in *Der Österreichische Zuschauer. Zeitschrift für Kunst, Wissenschaft und geistiges Leben*, 11.5.1842, 549–51.
'Grillparzers männliche und weibliche Charaktere', in *Wienerbote. Beilage zu den Sonntagsblättern*, 9.1.1848, p. 10.
'Johann, Herzog von Finnland', in *Wiener Zeitschrift für Kunst, Literatur, Theater und Mode*, 31, 12.3.1818, 251–52.
'K. K. Hoftheater nächst der Burg', in *Wiener Zeitschrift für Kunst, Literatur, Theater und Mode*, 5.12.1840, 1549–52.
'K. K. Hoftheater nächst der Burg', in *Wiener Zeitschrift für Kunst, Literatur, Theater und Mode*, 16.2.1843, 261–63.
'Kritische Skizzen', in *Der Ungar*, 25.1.1842, 116–17.
LAUBE, HEINRICH, 'Dramaturgische Briefe über das Burgtheater', in *Blätter für Theater, Musik und Kunst*, 8.9.1865, 285–86.
—— 'Franz Grillparzer', in *Neue Freie Presse*, 28.1.1872, pp. 1–3.
'Literarische Nachrichten', Review of Carl Ebner's *Versuch zur Vertheidigung der angeborenen Rechte des Frauengeschlechtes*, in *Wiener Zeitung*, 27.6.1845, 1371–72.
MEISSNER-DIEMER, FANNY, 'Auguste Littrow-Bischoff. (Erinnerungsblatt einer Freundin)', in *Neue Freie Presse* Nr. 9279, 24.6.1890, Abendblatt, 2.
NORBERT, E., 'Weissenthurn', in *Die Gegenwart. Politisch-literarisches Tagblatt*, 22.5.1847, 545–46.
'Öffentliches Leben in Wien', in *Der Österreichische Zuschauer. Zeitschrift für Kunst, Wissenschaft und geistiges Leben*, 31.5.1839, 666–67.
Review of *Frauen-Emancipation* by Wilhelm Marchland, in *Wiener Zeitschrift für Kunst, Literatur, Theater und Mode*, 28.5.1839, 511–12.
'Ruprecht Graf zu Horneck', in *Wiener Zeitschrift für Kunst, Literatur, Theater und Mode*, 20, 15.2.1820, 158–60.
'Schauspiel. Die Ahnfrau', in *Wiener-Moden-Zeitung und Zeitschrift für Kunst, schöne Literatur und Theater*, 5.2.1817, 87–88.
THALER, KARL VON, 'Frauenarbeit. ("Das Recht der Frauen auf Erwerb." Blicke auf das Frauenleben der Gegenwart von Louise Otto)', in *Bücher-Zeitung. Neue Freie Presse*, 23.11.1866, no pagination.
'Theatersalon. Theater in der Josephstadt', in *Der Humorist*, 3.9.1840, 711–12.
'Über Grillparzer's Trauerspiel: "Ottokar's Glück und Ende"', in *Abend-Zeitung*, 14.3.1825, 245–47.
'Wien', in *Wiener Zeitung*, 8.9.1848, 606 (page number incorrectly printed as 595).

Secondary Sources

ADEL, KURT, 'Grillparzers Hero-Drama (und Kleists "Penthesilea")', *JdGG* 3. Folge 7 (1969), 143–201.
AIDENHOFF, KERSTIN, MATTHIAS BRAUCKMANN and ANDREA EVERWIEN, 'Vom Leid des Herrschers und vom Glück des Beherrschten: *Sappho*', in *Gerettete Ordnung: Grillparzers*

Dramen, ed. by Bernhard Budde and Ulrich Schmidt (Frankfurt a.M.: Peter Lang, 1987), pp. 34–57.

ANDERS, CAROLINE, *"... der Zündstoff liegt, der diese Mine donnernd sprengt gen Himmel." Strategien der Ordnungsdestruktion in Franz Grillparzers dramatischem Werk* (Würzburg: Königshausen & Neumann, 2008).

ANGRESS, R. K., 'Das Gespenst in Grillparzers *Ahnfrau*', *The German Quarterly* 45 (1972), 606–19.

ARONS, WENDY, *Performance and Femininity in Eighteenth-Century German Women's Writing. The Impossible Act* (New York: Palgrave Macmillan, 2006).

BACHLEITNER, NORBERT, 'The Habsburg Monarchy', in *The Frightful Stage. Political Censorship of the Theater in Nineteenth-Century Europe*, ed. by Robert Justin Goldstein (New York: Berghahn, 2009), pp. 228–64.

BACKMANN, REINHOLD, 'Entwicklungsgeschichtliches zu Grillparzers "Ahnfrau"', *JdGG* 28 (1926), 22–42.

BARTEL, HEIKE, 'Dressing the "Other", Dressing the "Self". Clothing in the Medea Dramas of Euripides and Franz Grillparzer', in *Unbinding Medea. Interdisciplinary Approaches to a Classical Myth from Antiquity to the 21st Century*, ed. by Heike Bartel and Anne Simon (London: Legenda, 2010), pp. 161–75.

BAUER, MAGDALENA, 'Therese von Artner und Marianne Neumann von Meißenthal. Zwei Repräsentantinnen der ersten Generation schreibender Frauen im österreichischen Raum. (Studien zu einer Doppelbiographie.)', 2 vols (unpublished dissertation, University of Vienna, 1992).

BAUER, ROGER, 'Grillparzers Aufklärung', in *Zwischen Weimar und Wien. Grillparzer — Ein Innsbrucker Symposion*, ed. by Sieglinde Klettenhammer (Innsbruck: Institut für Germanistik, 1992), pp. 13–30.

BAUER, WERNER M., 'Kunst des Dramas. Drama der Kunst. Zu Grillparzers *Sappho*', *Études Germaniques* 47 (1992), 159–90.

BAUM, WILHELM, 'Einleitung', in *Weimar — Jena — Klagenfurt. Der Herbert-Kreis und das Geistesleben Kärntens im Zeitalter der Französischen Revolution*, ed. by Wilhelm Baum (Klagenfurt: Kärntner Druck- und Verlagsgesellschaft, 1989), pp. 6–21.

BECK, FRIEDRICH, 'Betty Paoli', *Österreichischer Rundschau* 9 (1906), 260–72.

BECKER-CANTARINO, BARBARA, 'Caroline Pichler und die "Frauendichtung"', *Modern Austrian Literature* 12 (1979), 1–23.

—— *Der lange Weg zur Mündigkeit. Frau und Literatur (1500–1800)* (Stuttgart: Metzler, 1987).

BÉRENGER, JEAN, *Die Geschichte des Habsburgerreiches 1273 bis 1918*, trans. by Marie Therese Pitner (Vienna: Böhlau, 1995).

BERGER, ALFRED FREIHERR VON, 'Das Szenische bei Grillparzer', *JdGG* 19 (1910), 29–38.

BERGER, MICHELLE TRACY, and KATHLEEN GUIDROZ, 'Introduction', in *The Intersectional Approach. Transforming the Academy through Race, Class, and Gender* (Chapel Hill, NC: The University of North Carolina Press, 2009), pp. 1–22.

BERGHAUS, GÜNTER, 'Rebellion, Reservation, Resignation: Nestroy und die Wiener Gesellschaft 1830–1860', in *Viennese Popular Theatre: A Symposium*, ed. by W. E. Yates and John R. P. McKenzie (Exeter: University of Exeter, 1985), pp. 109–22.

BESSER, GRETCHEN ROUS, *Germaine de Staël Revisited* (New York: Twayne, 1994).

BETTELHEIM-GABILLON, HELENE, 'Zur Charakteristik Betty Paolis. Nach alten und neuen Quellen', *JdGG* 10 (1900), 191–250.

BOUSSKA, VLADIMIRA, 'Der Salon der Johanna Bischoff von Altenstern und ihrer Tochter Auguste von Littrow-Bischoff', *Meidling, Blätter des Bezirksmuseums* 42 (1996), 30–37.

BOVENSCHEN, SILVIA, *Die imaginierte Weiblichkeit. Exemplarische Untersuchungen zu kulturgeschichtlichen und literarischen Präsentationsformen des Weiblichen* (Frankfurt a.M.: Suhrkamp, 1979).

BRAMKAMP, AGATHA C., *Marie von Ebner-Eschenbach. The Author, Her Time and Her Critics* (Bonn: Bouvier, 1990).
BÜCHER, WILHELM, *Grillparzers Verhältnis zur Politik seiner Zeit. Ein Beitrag zur Würdigung seines Schaffens und seiner Persönlichkeit* (Marburg: N. G. Elwert'sche Verlagsbuchhandlung, 1913).
BURKHARD, MARIANNE, '"Die letzte Schuld des Lebens": Grillparzers "Sappho" als Tragödie der dichtenden Frau', *Monatshefte* 74 (1982), 122–38.
—— 'Love, Creativity and Female Role: Grillparzer's "Sappho" and Staël's "Corinne" Between Art and Cultural Norm', *Jahrbuch für Internationale Germanistik* 16 (1984), 128–46.
CARASTATHIS, ANNA, 'The Concept of Intersectionality in Feminist Theory', *Philosophy Compass* 9/5 (2014), 304–14.
CHO, SUMI, KIMBERLÉ WILLIAMS CRENSHAW, and LESLIE MCCALL, 'Toward a Field of Intersectionality Studies: Theory, Applications, and Praxis', *Signs* 38/4 (Summer 2013), 785–810.
CLARK, LINDA L., *Women and Achievement in Nineteenth-Century Europe* (Cambridge: Cambridge University Press, 2008).
COENEN, FREDERIC E., *Franz Grillparzer's Portraiture of Men* (Chapel Hill, NC: University of North Carolina Press, 1951).
COENEN, FREDERIC E., 'Review of *The Inspiration Motive in the Works of Franz Grillparzer. With Special Consideration of "Libussa"*', *Monatshefte* 49/3 (1957), 131–32.
COWEN, ROY C., 'The Tragedy of *Die Jüdin von Toledo*', *The German Quarterly* 37 (1964), 39–53.
—— 'Franz Grillparzer', in *Major Figures of Nineteenth-Century Austrian Literature*, ed. by Donald G. Daviau (Riverside, CA: Ariadne, 1998), pp. 252–77.
CRENSHAW, KIMBERLÉ, 'Demarginalizing the Intersection of Race and Sex: A Black Feminist Critique of Antidiscrimination Doctrine, Feminist Theory and Antiracist Politics', *The University of Chicago Legal Forum* (1989), 139–67.
—— 'Mapping the Margins: Intersectionality, Identity Politics, and Violence Against Women of Color', *Stanford Law Review* 43/6 (1991), 1241–99.
DAVIS, KATHY, and GAIL LEWIS, 'Celebrating Intersectionality? Debates on a Multi-faceted Concept in Gender Studies: Themes from a Conference', *European Journal of Women's Studies* 16/3 (2009), 203–10.
DEJEAN, JOAN, *Fictions of Sappho, 1546–1937* (Chicago: The University of Chicago Press, 1989).
—— 'Portrait of the Artist as Sappho', in *Germaine de Staël. Crossing the Borders*, ed. by Madelyn Gutwirth, Avriel Goldberger and Karyna Szmurlo (New Brunswick, NJ: Rutgers University Press, 1991), pp. 122–37.
—— 'Sex and Philology: Sappho and the Rise of German Nationalism', in *Re-Reading Sappho. Reception and Transmission*, ed. by Ellen Greene (Berkeley, CA: University of California Press, 1996), pp. 122–45.
DILCHER, GERHARD, 'Die Ordnung der Ungleichheit. Haus, Stand und "Geschlecht"', in *Frauen in der Geschichte des Rechts. Von der Frühen Neuzeit bis zur Gegenwart*, ed. by Ute Gerhard (Munich: Beck, 1997), pp. 55–72.
DOPPLER, ALFRED, '*König Ottokars Glück und Ende*. Das Verhältnis von dargestellter Zeit, Zeit der Darstellung und gegenwärtiger Rezeption', in *Grillparzer und die Europäische Tradition. Londoner Symposium 1986*, ed. by Robert Pichl, Alexander Stillmark, Fred Wagner, and W. E. Yates (Vienna: Hora, 1987), pp. 21–29.
DUSINI, ARNO, *Die Ordnung des Lebens. Zu Franz Grillparzers "Selbstbiographie"* (Tübingen: Niemeyer, 1991).
—— '"...wenn nicht vernichtet, so doch verkümmert...". Zur Struktur der Grillparzerschen Selbstbiographie', in *Autobiographien in der österreichischen Literatur. Von Franz Grillparzer bis Thomas Bernhard*, ed. by Klaus Amann and Karl Wagner (Innsbruck: Studien Verlag, 1998), pp. 27–43.

EISENBERG, LUDWIG, *Großes Biographisches Lexikon der Deutschen Bühne im XIX. Jahrhundert* (Leipzig: List, 1903).
ESSLER, HILDEGARD, 'Die Frau Grillparzers' (unpublished dissertation, University of Vienna, 1945).
EVANS, RICHARD J., *The Feminist Movement in Germany 1894–1933* (London: Sage, 1976).
—— *The Feminists. Women's Emancipation Movements in Europe, America and Australasia 1840–1920* (London: Croom Helm, 1977).
FIORENZA, ELISABETH SCHÜSSLER, *But she said: feminist practices of biblical interpretation* (Boston: Beacon Press, 1992).
FISCHER, ERNST, 'Franz Grillparzer', in *Von Grillparzer zu Kafka. Sechs Essays* (Vienna: Globus, 1962), pp. 9–56.
FLORACK, RUTH, 'Nachruf auf die Landesmutter oder Vom unaufhaltsamen Aufstieg des Bürgerkönigs: *Libussa*', in *Gerettete Ordnung. Grillparzers Dramen*, ed. by Bernhard Budde and Ulrich Schmidt (Frankfurt a.M.: Peter Lang, 1987), pp. 238–54.
FLOSSMANN, URSULA, 'Die beschränkte Grundrechtssubjektivität der Frau. Ein Beitrag zum österreichischen Gleichheitsdiskurs', in *Frauen in der Geschichte des Rechts. Von der Frühen Neuzeit bis zur Gegenwart*, ed. by Ute Gerhard (Munich: Beck, 1997), pp. 293–324.
FORSTER, ELLINOR, 'Handlungsspielräume von Frauen und Männern im österreichischen Eherecht. Geschlechterverhältnisse im 19. Jahrhundert zwischen Rechtsnorm und Rechtspraxis' (unpublished dissertation, University of Innsbruck, 2008).
FORSTER, FRANZ, 'Grillparzer — ein Dichter des Alternativen, mit besonderer Berücksichtigung des Dramas "Libussa"', in *Franz Grillparzer 1791–1991. Vorträge anläßlich einer Grillparzer-Gedenkfeier an der Universität Oslo 25.–26. September 1991*, ed. by Kurt Erich Schöndorf and Elsbeth Wessel (Oslo: Germanistisches Institut der Universität Oslo, 1993), pp. 37–66.
FRIEBERGER, KURT, 'Bancbanus und Franz Deák', *JdGG* 3. Folge 3 (1960), 94–105.
FRIEDRICH, MARGRET, 'Versorgungsfall Frau? Der Wiener Frauen-Erwerb-Verein — Gründungszeit und erste Jahre des Aufbaus', *Studien zur Wiener Geschichte. Jahrbuch des Vereins für Geschichte der Stadt Wien* 47/48 (1991/92), 263–308.
FRIMMEL, JOHANNES, *Literarisches Leben in Melk. Ein Kloster im 18. Jahrhundert im kulturellen Umbruch* (Vienna: Böhlau, 2005).
FRONIUS, HELEN, *Women and Literature in the Goethe Era 1770–1820. Determined Dilettantes* (Oxford: Oxford University Press, 2007).
FÜLLEBORN, ULRICH, '"Der Gang der Zeit von Anfang". Frauenherrschaft als literarischer Mythos bei Kleist, Brentano und Grillparzer', in *Kleist-Jahrbuch 1986*, ed. by Hans Joachim Kreutzer (Berlin: Erich Schmidt, 1986), pp. 63–80.
GEBER, EVA, 'Mir aber ward solch sanfte Milde von der Natur nicht eingeflößt', in Betty Paoli, *Was hat der Geist denn wohl gemein mit dem Geschlecht?*, ed. by Eva Geber (Vienna: Mandelbaum, 2001), pp. 7–65.
GESTRICH, ANDREAS, *Geschichte der Familie im 19. und 20. Jahrhundert*, Enzyklopädie deutscher Geschichte Band 50 (Munich: Oldenbourg, 2010).
GLOSSY, KARL, 'Aus Bauernfelds Tagebüchern', *JdGG* 5 (1895), ix–xviii, 1–217.
—— 'Zur Geschichte der Wiener Theaterzensur', *JdGG* 7 (1897), 238–340.
GMÜR, HANS, *Dramatische und theatralische Stilelemente in Grillparzers Dramen* (Winterthur: Keller, 1956).
GOODDEN, ANGELICA, *Madame de Staël. Delphine and Corinne* (London: Grant and Cutler, 2000).
GOKHALE, VIBHA BAKSHI, 'Geschlechtscharaktere', in *The Feminist Encyclopedia of German Literature*, ed. by Friederike Eigler and Susanne Kord (Westport, CT: Greenwood, 1997), pp. 211–12.

GRIESMAYER, NORBERT, *Das Bild des Partners in Grillparzers Dramen. Studien zum Verständnis ihrer sprachkünstlerischen Gestaltung* (Vienna: Braumüller, 1972).

GRIGOROVITZA, EMANUEL, *Libussa in der deutschen Litteratur* (Berlin: Duncker, 1901).

GUTJAHR, ORTRUD, 'Iphigenie — Penthesilea — Medea: Zur Klassizität weiblicher Mythen bei Goethe, Kleist und Grillparzer', in *Frauen: MitSprechen, MitSchreiben. Beiträge zur literatur- und sprachwissenschaftlichen Frauenforschung*, ed. by Marianne Henn and Britta Hufeisen (Stuttgart: Heinz, 1997), pp. 223–43.

HÄGELIN, FRANZ KARL, *Denkschrift*, quoted in Glossy, 'Zur Geschichte der Wiener Theaterzensur', *JdGG* 7 (1897), 238–340.

HAGL-CATLING, KARIN, *Für eine Imagologie der Geschlechter. Franz Grillparzers Frauenbild im Widerspruch* (Frankfurt a.M.: Peter Lang, 1997).

HAJEK, VACLAV, *Böhmische Chronik*, trans. by Joannem Sandel (Leipzig: Fritschen, 1718).

HAUCH, GABRIELLA, *Frau Biedermeier auf den Barrikaden. Frauenleben in der Wiener Revolution 1848* (Vienna: Verlag für Gesellschaftskritik, 1990).

HEADY, KATY, *Literature and Censorship in Restoration Germany. Repression and Rhetoric* (Rochester, NY: Camden House, 2009).

HELFER, MARTHA B., 'Framing the Jew: Grillparzer's *Die Jüdin von Toledo*', *The German Quarterly* 75 (2002), 160–80.

HOCK, STEFAN, 'Briefe Betty Paolis an Leopold Kompert', *JdGG* 18 (1908), 177–209.

HOLTHÖFER, ERNST, 'Die Geschlechtsvormundschaft. Ein Überblick von der Antike bis ins 19. Jahrhundert', in *Frauen in der Geschichte des Rechts. Von der Frühen Neuzeit bis zur Gegenwart*, ed. by Ute Gerhard (Munich: Beck, 1997), pp. 390–451.

HORMAYR, JOSEPH, *Oesterreichischer Plutarch, oder Leben und Bildnisse aller Regenten und der berühmtesten Feldherren, Staatsmänner, Gelehrten und Künstler des österreichischen Kaiserstaates*, 20 vols (Vienna: Doll, 1807–14).

IKUTA, MASATO, *Geschichte und Individuum in Grillparzers dramatischer Welt. Zur Entwicklung der Grillparzerschen Geschichtsdramatik* (Frankfurt a.M.: Peter Lang, 1990).

JANKE, PIA, 'Gescheiterte Authentizität. Anmerkungen zu Grillparzers Frauenfiguren', *Lenau-Jahrbuch* 26 (2000), 57–72.

KENKEL, KONRAD, *Medea-Dramen. Entmythisierung und Remythisierung. Euripides, Klinger, Grillparzer, Jahnn, Anouilh* (Bonn: Bouvier, 1979).

KOMMERELL, MAX, 'Grillparzer. Ein Dichter der Treue' [1936], in *Franz Grillparzer*, ed. by Helmut Bachmaier (Frankfurt a.M.: Suhrkamp, 1991), pp. 88–98.

KORD, SUSANNE, *Ein Blick hinter die Kulissen. Deutschsprachige Dramatikerinnen im 18. und 19. Jahrhundert* (Stuttgart: Metzler, 1992).

—— 'Eternal Love or Sentimental Discourse? Gender Dissonance and Women's Passionate "Friendships"', in *Outing Goethe and His Age*, ed. by Alice A. Kuzniar (Stanford, CA: Stanford University Press, 1996), pp. 228–49.

—— 'Erudite Woman/Gelehrte', in *The Feminist Encyclopedia of German Literature*, ed. by Friederike Eigler and Susanne Kord (Westport, CT: Greenwood, 1997), pp. 124–26.

KOSTKA, EDMUND, 'Grillparzer and the East', *Monatshefte* 47 (1955), 273–84.

KÖSTER, UDO, 'Über das Verhältnis von Mythos und Geschichte am Beispiel der Bearbeitungen des Libussa-Stoffes bei Brentano, Ebert, Mundt und Grillparzer', in *Romantik. Mythos und Moderne*, ed. by Ulrich Wergin and Timo Ogrzal (Würzburg: Königshausen & Neumann, 2013), pp. 163–80.

KRIPPENDORFF, EKKEHART, 'Grillparzer, der Fortschrittliche', in *Politics in Literature. Studies on a Germanic Preoccupation from Kleist to Améry*, ed. by Rüdiger Görner (Munich: iudicium, 2004), pp. 83–98.

KROBB, FLORIAN, '"Bleib zurück, geh nicht in' Garten!" Grillparzers *Jüdin von Toledo* als Traktat über die "Judenfrage"', in *Judenrollen. Darstellungsformen im europäischen Theater von der Restauration bis zur Zwischenkriegszeit*, ed. by Hans-Peter Bayerdörfer and Jens Malte Fischer (Tübingen: Niemeyer, 2008), pp. 125–42.

KRUG, MICHAELA, *Auf der Suche nach dem eigenen Raum. Topographien des Weiblichen im Roman von Autorinnen um 1800* (Würzburg: Königshausen & Neumann, 2004).

KUHN, ANNA K, 'Myth, Matriarchy, *Männerphantasie*: Rereading Grillparzer's *Libussa*', in *Playing for Stakes: German-Language Drama in Social Context. Essays in Honor of Herbert Lederer* (Oxford: Berg, 1994), pp. 139–60.

KURANDA, PETER, 'Grillparzer und die Politik des Vormärzes', *JdGG* 28 (1926), 1–21.

LAMBERT, ELIE, 'Eine Untersuchung der Quellen der "Jüdin von Toledo"', *JdGG* 19 (1910), 61–84.

LAMPORT, FRANCIS, 'Three "Schopenhauerian" Trilogies: Grillparzer, Wagner, Hebbel', *Oxford German Studies* 39 (2010), 54–69.

LAQUEUR, THOMAS, *Making Sex: Body and Gender from the Greeks to Freud* (Cambridge, MA: Harvard University Press, 1990).

LASHER-SCHLITT, DOROTHY, 'Grillparzers "Hero und Leander". Eine psychologische Untersuchung', *JdGG* 3. Folge 3 (1960), 106–14.

LATTMANN, PETER, *Franz Grillparzer. Untersuchungen zu seinem Drama* Ein treuer Diener seines Herrn (Zurich: Juris Druck+Verlag, 1971).

LAUBE, HEINRICH, *Franz Grillparzers Lebensgeschichte* (Stuttgart: Cotta, 1884).

LEITICH, ANNA TIZIA, *Zwölfmal Liebe. Frauen um Grillparzer* (Vienna: Georg Fromme & Co., 1948).

—— *Genie und Leidenschaft. Die Frauen um Grillparzer* (Vienna: Speidel, 1965).

LEWINSKY, JOSEF, *Gedenkrede auf Betty Paoli* (Vienna: Verlag des Vereins der Schriftstellerinnen und Künstlerinnen in Wien, 1895).

LIPPUNER, HEINZ, 'Grillparzers "Jüdin von Toledo". Untersuchung eines Paradigmas', *Orbis Litterarum* 27 (1972), 202–23.

LITTLE, WILLIAM A., 'Grillparzer's Excursions into Autobiography', *Kentucky Foreign Language Quarterly* 11 (1964), 142–51.

LITTROW-BISCHOFF, AUGUSTE VON, *Aus dem persönlichen Verkehre mit Franz Grillparzer* (Vienna: Rosner, 1873).

LOHBERGER, HANS, 'Anton Prokesch über "Caroline Pichler und ihr Kreis"', *Blätter für Heimatkunde* 46 (1972), 80–83.

LORENZ, DAGMAR C. G., 'Grillparzers *Libussa*: Eine Neubewertung', *JdGG* 3. Folge 14 (1980), 33–47.

—— *Grillparzer. Dichter des sozialen Konflikts* (Vienna: Böhlau, 1986).

—— 'Frau und Weiblichkeit bei Grillparzer', in *Der Widerspenstigen Zähmung. Studien zur bezwungenen Weiblichkeit in der Literatur vom Mittelalter bis zur Gegenwart*, ed. by Sylvia Wallinger and Monika Jonas (Innsbruck: Institut für Germanistik, Universität Innsbruck, 1986), pp. 201–16.

—— 'Grillparzer, Dichter des sozialen Konflikts', in *Grillparzer oder Die Wirklichkeit der Wirklichkeit*, ed. by Bernhard Denscher and Walter Obermaier (Vienna: Historisches Museum der Stadt Wien, 1991), pp. 31–38.

—— 'Ambivalenz und Erkenntnis in Franz Grillparzers Werk', in *Grillparzer heute — wiederentdeckt oder vergessen?* (Vienna: Picus, 1993), pp. 51–66.

—— 'Die schöne Jüdin in Stifters *Abdias* und Grillparzers *Die Jüdin von Toledo*', *JdGG* 3. Folge 19 (1996), 125–39.

LUSERKE-JAQUI, MATTHIAS, *Medea. Studien zur Kulturgeschichte der Literatur* (Tübingen: Francke, 2002).

LÜ, YIXU, *Frauenherrschaft im Drama des frühen 19. Jahrhunderts* (Munich: iudicium, 1993).

—— *Medea unter den Deutschen. Wandlungen einer literarischen Figur* (Freiburg i. Br.: Rombach, 2009).

MARSO, LORI J., 'Defying Fraternity: Woman as Citizen in Germaine de Staël's *Corinne, or Italy*', *Women's Studies* 28 (1999), 645–74.
MARTIN, JUDITH E., 'Nineteenth-Century German Literary Women's Reception of Madame de Staël', *Women in German Yearbook* 18 (2002), 133–57.
MARX, JULIUS, *Die österreichische Zensur im Vormärz* (Vienna: Verlag für Geschichte und Politik, 1959).
MATT, PETER VON, *Der Grundriss von Grillparzers Bühnenkunst* (Zurich: Atlantis, 1965).
MCCALL, LESLIE, 'The Complexity of Intersectionality', *Signs* 30/3 (Spring 2005), 1771–1800.
MEYER, MARSHA, 'The Depictions of Women in Gutzkow's *Wally, die Zweiflerin* and Mundt's *Madonna*', in *Beyond the Eternal Feminine. Critical Essays on Women and German Literature*, ed. by Susan L. Cocalis and Kay Goodman (Stuttgart: Heinz, 1982), pp. 135–58.
MIKOLETZKY, HANNS LEO, *Österreich. Das große 18. Jahrhundert. Von Leopold I. bis Leopold II.* (Vienna: Austria-Edition, 1967).
MORIKAWA, KOKYO, 'Grillparzers 'Sappho' — Entstehung und Erläuterung', *JdGG* 3. Folge 6 (1967), 101–19.
MORRIEN, RITA, *Sinn und Sinnlichkeit. Der weibliche Körper in der deutschen Literatur der Bürgerzeit* (Cologne: Böhlau, 2001).
MORRIS, I. V., 'The "Ahnfrau" Controversy', *The Modern Language Review* 62 (1967), 284–91.
NADLER, JOSEF, *Franz Grillparzer* (Vienna: Bergland, 1952).
NAGL, J. W., JAKOB ZEIDLER and EDUARD CASTLE, *Deutsch-Österreichische Literaturgeschichte*, 4 vols (Vienna: Fromme, 1914–37).
NASH, JENNIFER C., 'Re-thinking Intersectionality', *Feminist Review* 89 (2008), 1–15.
NEISSL, JULIA, 'Frauen, die das Geschick des Staates lenken. Geschlechterpositionen bei "Libussa" und "Penthesilea"', *JdGG* 3. Folge 20 (1997–2002), 240–77.
O'BRIEN, KAREN, *Narratives of Enlightenment: Cosmopolitan History from Voltaire to Gibbon* (Cambridge: Cambridge University Press, 1997).
OLENHUSEN, IRMTRAUD GÖTZ VON, 'Das Ende männlicher Zeugungsmythen im Zeitalter der Aufklärung: Zur Wissenschafts- und Geschlechtergeschichte des 17. und 18. Jahrhunderts', in *Ordnung, Politik und Geselligkeit der Geschlechter im 18. Jahrhundert*, ed. by Ulrike Weckel et al. (Göttingen: Wallstein, 1998), pp. 259–83.
PAOLI, BETTY, *Julie Rettich. Ein Lebens- und Charakterbild* (Vienna: Sommer, 1866).
—— 'Studie über Grillparzer' (1872), *Grillparzers Gespräche und die Charakteristiken seiner Persönlichkeit durch die Zeitgenossen*, ed. by August Sauer (Schriften des Literarischen Vereins in Wien I. Vienna: Verlag des Literarischen Vereins in Wien, 1904), pp. 243–71.
—— *Grillparzer und seine Werke* (Stuttgart: Cotta, 1875).
PARRY, YVONNE M., '*Das goldene Vließ*: The Tragedy of the Adventurer', in *Studies in Nineteenth Century Austrian Literature*, ed. by Brian O. Murdoch and Mark G. Ward (Glasgow: Scottish Papers in Germanic Studies, 1983), pp. 1–27.
PETER, BIRGIT, 'NS-ideologische Metamorphosen am Beispiel von Heinz Kindermann: Ferdinand Raimund und Franz Grillparzer als deutsche Volksdramatiker', in *Der Dichter und sein Germanist. Symposium in Memoriam Wendelin Schmidt-Dengler*, ed. by Stephan Kurz, Michael Rohrwasser and Daniela Strigl (Vienna: New Academic Press, 2012), pp. 81–95.
PICHL, ROBERT, 'Grillparzers dramaturgische Emanzipation von der Weimarer Klassik', *JdGG* 3. Folge 22 (2007–08), 51–62.
POLAK, GABRIELA, 'Das Familienrechtsmodell des ABGB (1811) in Konfrontation mit den Modernisierungstendenzen bürgerlich-fortschrittlicher Frauenvereine bis zur 1. Teilnovelle im Jahre 1914' (unpublished dissertation, University of Vienna, 1991).

POLITZER, HEINZ, 'Der Schein von Heros Lampe', *Modern Language Notes* 72 (1957), 432–37.
—— *Franz Grillparzer oder das abgründige Biedermeier* (Vienna: Molden, 1972).
PROHASKA, GERTRUDE, *Der literarische Salon der Karoline Pichler* (unpublished dissertation, University of Vienna, 1946).
PRUTTI, BRIGITTE, *Grillparzers Welttheater: Modernität und Tradition* (Bielefeld: Aisthesis, 2013).
RECKZEH, GERHART, *Grillparzer und die Slaven* (Weimar: Duncker, 1929).
REEVE, WILLIAM C., 'Orchestrated Death Scenes as a Means of Revenge: Schiller's *Maria Stuart* and Grillparzer's *Sappho*', *Seminar* 40 (2004), 122–34.
REINHARDT, GEORGE W., 'Female Self-Determination in the Early Dramas of Franul von Weissenthurn', in *Austria in the Age of the French Revolution 1789–1815*, ed. by Kinley Brauer and William E. Wright (Minneapolis, MN: Centre for Austrian Studies, University of Minnesota, 1990), pp. 151–62.
ROBERT, ANDRÉ, *L'idée nationale autrichienne et les guerres de Napoléon. L'apostolat du Baron de Hormayr et le salon de Caroline Pichler* (Paris: Alcan, 1933).
ROBERTSON, RITCHIE, 'On the Threshold of Patriarchy: Brentano, Grillparzer, and the Bohemian Amazons', *German Life and Letters* 46 (1993), 203–19.
—— 'Der patriotische Minister in Grillparzers *Ein treuer Diener seines Herrn* und Hebbels *Agnes Bernauer*', *Hebbel-Jahrbuch* 2010, 95–119.
ROE, IAN F., *An Introduction to the Major Works of Franz Grillparzer, 1791–1872, German Dramatist and Poet* (Lewiston, NY: The Edwin Mellen Press, 1991).
—— *Franz Grillparzer: A Century of Criticism* (Columbia, SC: Camden House, 1995).
—— 'The Comedies of Johanna von Weissenthurn', in *The Austrian Comic Tradition. Studies in Honour of W. E. Yates*, ed. by John R. P. McKenzie and Lesley Sharpe (Austrian Studies IX. Edinburgh: Edinburgh University Press, 1998), pp. 41–57.
ROGOWSKI, CHRISTIAN, 'Erstickte Schreie. Geschlechtliche Differenz und koloniales Denken in Grillparzers Medea-Trilogie *Das goldene Vließ*', *JdGG* 3. Folge 21 (2003–06), 32–50.
ROIDER, KARL A., 'The Pragmatic Sanction', *Austrian History Yearbook* 8 (1972), 153–58.
ROSE, FERREL, 'Betty Paoli', in *Major Figures of Nineteenth-Century Austrian Literature*, ed. by Donald G. Daviau (Riverside, CA: Ariadne, 1998), pp. 387–416.
ROSSBACHER, KARLHEINZ, *Literatur und Bürgertum. Fünf Wiener jüdische Familien von der liberalen Ära zum Fin de Siècle* (Vienna: Böhlau, 2003).
SAGARRA, EDA, 'Grillparzer, the Catholics and the Jews: A Reading of *Die Jüdin von Toledo* (1851)', *Leo Baeck Institute Yearbook* 46 (2001), 67–80.
SAID, EDWARD W., *Culture and Imperialism* (London: Chatto and Windus, 1993).
SAUER, AUGUST, '"Ein treuer Diener seines Herrn"', *JdGG* 3 (1893), 3–40.
—— *Gesammelte Reden und Aufsätze zur Geschichte der Literatur in Österreich und Deutschland* (Vienna: Fromme, 1903).
SAUER, WERNER, *Österreichische Philosophie zwischen Aufklärung und Restauration. Beiträge zur Geschichte des Frühkantianismus in der Donaumonarchie* (Amsterdam: Rodopi, 1982).
SCHAUM, KONRAD, 'Grillparzers "Des Meeres und der Liebe Wellen": Seelendrama und Kulturkritik', *JdGG* 3. Folge 11 (1974), 95–114.
—— 'Grillparzers "König Ottokars Glück und Ende" — historische Tragödie und Zeitkritik', *JdGG* 3. Folge 15 (1983), 51–63.
SCHEIDER, ANGELA, 'Auguste und Carl von Littrow. Detailstudie einer bürgerlichen Familie des 19. Jahrhunderts' (unpublished dissertation, University of Vienna, 1999).
SCHEIT, GERHARD, 'Grillparzer und die deutschen Männer', in *Stichwort Grillparzer*, ed. by Hilde Haider-Pregler and Evelyn Deutsch-Schreiner (Vienna: Böhlau, 1994), pp. 51–58.

SCHNITZLER, GÜNTER, 'Grillparzer und die Spätaufklärung', in *Franz Grillparzer. Historie und Gegenwärtigkeit* (Freiburg i. Breisgau: Rombach, 1994), pp. 179–201.

SCHÖFFMANN, BARBARA, 'Immanuel Kant und die Aufklärung in Kärnten', in *Weimar — Jena — Klagenfurt. Der Herbert-Kreis und das Geistesleben Kärntens im Zeitatler der Französischen Revolution*, ed. by Wilhelm Baum (Klagenfurt: Kärntner Druck- und Verlagsgesellschaft, 1989), pp. 90–100.

SCHOLZ, HANNELORE, *Widersprüche im bürgerlichen Frauenbild. Zur ästhetischen Reflexion und poetischen Praxis bei Lessing, Friedrich Schlegel und Schiller* (Weinheim: Deutscher Studien Verlag, 1992).

SEIBERT, PETER, *Der literarische Salon. Literatur und Geselligkeit zwischen Aufklärung und Vormärz* (Stuttgart: Metzler, 1993).

SEITTER, WALTER, *Unzeitgemäße Aufklärung. Franz Grillparzers Philosophie* (Vienna: Kant, 1991).

SONNLEITNER, JOHANN, '"Krasse Sinnlichkeit und frömmelnde Tendenzen". Wiener Salonszenen und Ansichten der Romantik', in *Paradoxien der Romantik. Gesellschaft, Kultur und Wissenschaft in Wien im frühen 19. Jahrhundert*, ed. by Christian Aspalter, Wolfgang Müller-Funk, Edith Saurer, Wendelin Schmidt-Dengler, Anton Tantner (Vienna: Facultas, 2006), pp. 256–72.

SPÖRK, INGRID, 'Gesten der Herrschaft — Zeichen der Macht. Zur Annektierung des Anderen bei Grillparzer', *Études Germaniques* 47 (1992), 215–34.

STAIGER, EMIL, 'Grillparzer. König Ottokars Glück und Ende' [1943], in *Franz Grillparzer*, ed. by Helmut Bachmaier (Frankfurt a.M.: Suhrkamp, 1991), pp. 69–87.

STEIDELE, ANGELA, *'Als wenn du mein Geliebter wärest': Liebe und Begehren zwischen Frauen in der deutschsprachigen Literatur 1750–1850* (Stuttgart: Metzler, 2003).

STEIN, GISELA, *The Inspiration Motif in the Works of Franz Grillparzer. With Special Consideration of 'Libussa'* (The Hague: Martinus Nijhoff, 1955).

STEINER, CARL, 'Franz Grillparzer and Marie von Ebner-Eschenbach: A Father-Daughter Relationship', in *Für all, was Menschen je erfahren, ein Bild, ein Wort und auch das Ziel. Beiträge zu Grillparzers Werk*, ed. by Joseph P. Strelka (Bern: Peter Lang, 1995), pp. 211–29.

STEINHAGEN, HARALD, 'Grillparzers *König Ottokar*. Drama, Geschichte und Zeitgeschichte', *Jahrbuch der Deutschen Schiller-Gesellschaft* 14 (1970), 456–87.

STIRNWEIS, CARMEN, 'Verborgene Schuld in Franz Grillparzers *Die Ahnfrau*. Ein Beitrag zur Relativierung der angeblichen Schicksalstragödie', *JdGG* 3. Folge 22 (2007–08), 80–108.

STEYSKAL, LUDMILLA ANTONIA, 'Johanna Franul von Weissenthurn als Schauspielerin am Burgtheater' (unpublished dissertation, University of Vienna, 1963).

STÖRI, FRITZ, *Grillparzer und Kant* (Frauenfeld: Huber, 1935).

STRICH, FRITZ, *Franz Grillparzers Ästhetik* (Berlin: Duncker, 1905).

SURYNT, IZABELA, *Erzählte Weiblichkeit bei Marie von Ebner-Eschenbach* (Opole: Wydawnictwo Uniwersytetu Opolskiego, 1998).

ŠKREB, ZDENKO, *Grillparzer. Eine Einführung in das dramatische Werk* (Kronberg: Scriptor, 1976).

—— 'Rahel', in *Die andere Welt. Aspekte der österreichischen Literatur des 19. und 20. Jahrhunderts. Festschrift für Hellmuth Himmel zum 60. Geburtstag*, ed. by Kurt Bartsch, Dietmar Goltschnigg, Gerhard Melzer, Wolfgang Heinz Schober (Bern: Francke, 1977), pp. 97–105.

TANZER, ULRIKE, 'Grenzgänge in Franz Grillparzers Trauerspiel "Des Meeres und der Liebe Wellen"', in *Grenzgänge und Grenzgänger in der österreichischen Literatur. Beiträge des 15. Österreichisch-Polnischen Germanistentreffens Kraków 2002*, ed. by Maria Kłańska, Krzysztof Lipiński, Katarzyna Jaśtal, Agnieszka Palej (Kraków: Wydawnictwo Uniwersytetu Jagiellońskiego, 2004), pp. 77–86.

——'Konzeptionen des Glücks im Werk Marie von Ebner-Eschenbachs', *Seminar* 47 (2011), 254–67.
TAYLOR, YVETTE, 'Complexities and Complications: Intersections of Class and Sexuality', in *Theorizing Intersectionality and Sexuality*, ed. by Yvette Taylor, Sally Hines and Mark Casey (Basingstoke: Palgrave Macmillan, 2011), pp. 37–55.
——, SALLY HINES and MARK CASEY, 'Introduction', in *Theorizing Intersectionality and Sexuality*, ed. by Yvette Taylor, Sally Hines and Mark Casey (Basingstoke: Palgrave Macmillan, 2011), pp. 1–12.
THOMPSON, BRUCE, *Franz Grillparzer* (Boston: Twayne, 1981).
VOGEL, URSULA, 'Gleichheit und Herrschaft in der ehelichen Vertragsgesellschaft — Widersprüche der Aufklärung', in *Frauen in der Geschichte des Rechts. Von der Frühen Neuzeit bis zur Gegenwart*, ed. by Ute Gerhard (Munich: Beck, 1997), pp. 265–92.
VOLKELT, JOHANNES, 'Die Psychologie der Liebe in Grillparzers Dramen', *JdGG* 19 (1910), 1–28.
WAGNER, MEIKE, *Theater und Öffentlichkeit im Vormärz. Berlin, München und Wien als Schauplätze bürgerlicher Medienpraxis* (Berlin: Akademie Verlag, 2013).
WARD, MARK G., 'Some Notes on Grillparzer's *König Ottokar* and the "entfernte Ähnlichkeit"', *German Life and Letters* 34 (1981), 214–22.
WEISS, WALTER, 'Opfer bei Grillparzer', *Études Germaniques* 47 (1992), 235–43.
WEISSENSTEINER, FRIEDRICH, 'Karoline Pichler', in *Zwischen Idylle und Revolution. Ungewöhnliche Biedermeierporträts* (Vienna: Ueberreuter, 1995), pp. 257–66.
WELCKER, FRIEDRICH GOTTLIEB, *Sappho, von einem herrschenden Vorurtheil befreyt* (Göttingen: Vandenhoek und Ruprecht, 1816).
WOLF-CIRIAN, FRANCIS, *Grillparzers Frauengestalten* (Stuttgart: Cotta, 1908).
WOZONIG, KARIN S., *Die Literatin Betty Paoli. Weibliche Mobilität im 19. Jahrhundert* (Vienna: Löcker, 1999).
——'Betty Paoli, Journalistin', in Betty Paoli, *Was hat der Geist denn wohl gemein mit dem Geschlecht?*, pp. 66–77.
——'Betty Paoli, die Lyrikerin als Journalistin', *The German Quarterly* 76 (2003), 56–67.
——'Betty Paoli und die schönen Frauen', *Nestroyana. Blätter der Internationalen Nestroy-Gesellschaft* 29 (2009), 72–81.
WURM, ERNST, 'Grillparzers erste Medea — Sophie Schröder', *JdGG* 3/6 (1967), 121–37.
WURZBACH, CONSTANT VON, *Biographisches Lexikon des Kaiserthums Oesterreich*, 58. Theil (Vienna: Hof- und Staatsdruckerei, 1889).
YATES, DOUGLAS, *Grillparzer. A Critical Biography* (Oxford: Blackwell, 1946).
YATES, W. E., *Grillparzer. A Critical Introduction* (Cambridge: Cambridge University Press, 1972).
——*Humanity in Weimar and Vienna: The Continuity of an Ideal. An Inaugural Lecture delivered in the University of Exeter on 30 April, 1973* (Exeter: University of Exeter, 1973).
——'Nestroy, Grillparzer, and the Feminist Cause', in *Viennese Popular Theatre: A Symposium/ Das Wiener Volkstheater. Ein Symposion*, ed. by W. E. Yates and John R. P. McKenzie (Exeter: University of Exeter, 1985), pp. 93–107.
——'Grillparzer and the Fair Sex', in *Grillparzer und die Europäische Tradition. Londoner Symposium 1986*, ed. by Robert Pichl, Alexander Stillmark, Fred Wagner, W. E. Yates (Vienna: Hora, 1987), pp. 71–83.
——'*König Ottokars Glück und Ende* und *Der Traum ein Leben*: Realitätsbezug und Rezeptionsproblematik', *Études Germaniques* 47 (1992), 201–14.
——*Theatre in Vienna. A Critical History, 1776–1995* (Cambridge: Cambridge University Press, 1996).
——'Grillparzer, *Die Jüdin von Toledo*', in *Landmarks in German Drama*, ed. by Peter Hutchinson (Oxford: Peter Lang, 2002), pp. 111–25.
——and ULRIKE TANZER, 'Theater und Gesellschaft im Wien des 19. Jahrhunderts. Zur

Einführung', in *Theater und Gesellschaft im Wien des 19. Jahrhunderts. Ausgewählte Aufsätze. Zum 25-jährigen Bestehen der Zeitschrift* Nestroyana, ed. by W. E. Yates and Ulrike Tanzer (Vienna: Lehner, 2006), pp. 7–18.

ZEILLER, FRANZ VON, *Abhandlung über die Principien des allgemeinen bürgerlichen Gesetzbuches für die gesammten deutschen Erbländer der österreichischen Monarchie* [1816–20], ed. by Wilhelm Brauneder (Vienna: Manz, 1986).

ZSIGMOND, ANIKÓ, *Marie von Ebner-Eschenbach. Das Frauenbewußtsein einer österreichischen Aristokratin* (Szombathely: Maedinfo, 2001).

INDEX

1848 Revolution 12, 42

actresses 17, 31, 44, 50
    Grillparzer's attitude to 45
    social status of 44
Adel, Kurt 101, 111
Albrecht, Johann Friedrich Ernst:
    Die Töchter Kroks, Böheims Fürstinnen 137–38
Allgemeines bürgerliches Gesetzbuch (ABGB) 43, 56–58, 62, 69, 72, 75, 90, 91
    guardianship 58, 90, 91
Allgemeines Landrecht für die Preußischen Staaten 57
Anders, Caroline 129, 181
Angress, R. K. 59
Arons, Wendy 27
Artner, Therese von 32, 33, 50, 115, 190
    Rogneda und Wladimir 115
August, Otto, *see* Auguste Littrow-Bischoff

Backmann, Reinhold 38, 59
Bartel, Heike 166
Barthélemy, Jean-Jacques:
    Voyage du jeune Anacharsis en Grèce 124
Bauer, Roger 81
Bauer, Werner M. 130–31, 132, 133
Bauernfeld, Eduard von 9, 42
    Bürgerlich und Romantisch 10, 187
    opinion of Johanna Franul von Weissenthurn 35
    Xenien 9
Becker-Cantarino, Barbara 26
Berger, Alfred von 121
Berghaus, Günter 12
Bernard, Joseph Carl 136
    Libussa 138
Besser, Gretchen Rous 152 n. 59
Bettelheim-Gabillon, Helene 39
Brentano, Clemens 136
    Die Gründung Prags 138
Burgtheater 4, 6, 11, 35, 36, 38, 46, 47, 48, 49, 86
Burkhard, Marianne 125–26

Carastathis, Anna 155
censorship 4, 5, 9, 10, 11, 12, 13, 14, 28, 62, 123, 135, 189
    in Austria 11–12
    of books 11
    of theatre 11–12

Charles VI, Holy Roman Emperor 63, 64
Chaussard, Pierre-Jean-Baptiste:
    Fêtes et courtisanes de la Grèce 124
Chézy, Wilhelmine von 9, 48, 49
Clark, Linda L. 28
Code civil 57
Coenen, Frederic E. 23 n. 56, 89, 93, 101, 140
Cowen, Roy C. 11, 20, 177
Crenshaw, Kimberlé Williams 155–56

D'Auvigny, Jean Du Castre:
    L'Histoire et les amours de Sapho de Mytilène 124
Davis, Kathy 156
DeJean, Joan 123, 124, 125
Dilcher, Gerhard 26
Doppler, Alfred 71
Douville, Jean-Baptiste:
    Voyage au Congo 8, 115
Dusini, Arno 2, 3

Ebert, Karl Egon 136
    Wlasta. Böhmisch-nationales Heldengedicht 139
Ebner, Karl:
    Versuch zur Vertheidigung der angebornen Rechte des Frauengeschlechtes 30
Ebner-Eschenbach, Marie von 1, 31, 32, 42, 43, 44, 50, 187
    Grillparzer on her early poetry 43–44
    Maria Stuart in Schottland 115
    Marie Roland 8
    Meine Erinnerungen an Grillparzer 5–6
Elizabeth I 115, 116
Enlightenment 16, 27, 57, 85, 86, 87, 88, 89, 102, 105, 109, 110, 157, 188
Essler, Hildegard 21
Evans, Richard J. 28, 43, 57

Fichte, Johann Gottlieb von:
    Grundriß des Familienrechts 25
Fiorenza, Elisabeth Schüssler 154–55, 156–57, 166, 169, 178
Fischer, Ernst 21, 101
Florack, Ruth 134, 144
Forster, Ellinor 58
Forster, Franz 18, 134
Forster, Georg 32
Frank, Peter 48, 102, 122, 136

Frauenbild 25–28
Frauenfrage 10, 11, 14, 15, 17, 19, 25, 28–31, 33, 39, 41, 43, 44, 59, 70, 187, 188, 189, 190
French Revolution 15, 56, 123, 140
Frieberger, Kurt 94, 95,
Friedrich, Margret 43
Fröhlich, Katharina 2, 4, 6, 15, 19, 45
Fronius, Helen 27, 28
Fülleborn, Ulrich 134, 140, 142

Geber, Eva 39
gelehrte Frau 27, 37, 40
Gerold, Rosa von 1
Geschlechtscharaktere 25–27, 35, 44, 51 n. 11, 103,
Glossy, Karl 9
Gmür, Hans 74, 142
Goethe, Johann Wolfgang 86, 189
  Iphigenie auf Tauris 127
Gouges, Olympe de:
  Déclaration des droits de la femme et de la citoyenne 25, 26
Greiner, Charlotte (mother of Caroline Pichler) 26, 32, 33
Griesmayer, Norbert 59, 121
Grillparzer, Franz:
  antisemitism 1, 20
  as Austrian national author 20–21
  and Caroline Pichler 33
  censorship 4, 5, 10, 11, 55 n. 138, 189
  father 7, 19
  and the *Frauenfrage* 59, 70, 188, 190
  and German nationalism 20–21
  and Johann Franul von Weissenthurn 35
  mother 19
  in Nazi Germany 20
  portrayal of women 17–21, 188–89
  reception 17–21, 188–89
  Reichsrat 5
  romantic relationships with women 1–2
  self-censorship 14, 135
  and Sophie Schröder 46–47, 55 n. 138
  support for women writers 43–44, 48–49
  works:
    Das goldene Vließ 16, 66, 77, 154, 156, 157–69
    Das Kloster bei Sendomir 14–15
    Der Zauberwald 16, 117–18
    Des Meeres und der Liebe Wellen 16, 48, 85, 88, 92, 100–12, 154, 178
    Die Ahnfrau 11, 12, 16, 46, 57, 59–70, 74, 189
    Die Jüdin von Toledo 11, 16, 20, 38, 69, 78, 92, 96–100, 154, 156, 169, 170–84, 188, 189
    'Drahomira' 116
    'Drahomira III' 116–17
    Ein treuer Diener seines Herrn 16, 85, 88–100, 156
    König Ottokars Glück und Ende 16, 17, 55 n. 138, 56, 70–82, 94, 121, 156

    Libussa 11, 16, 112, 115, 118, 120, 132, 133, 134–50, 188, 189
    'Rudolf und Ottokar' 74
    Sappho 11, 16, 17, 45, 46, 49, 60, 77, 78, 79, 92, 101, 115, 117, 121–33, 144, 147, 149, 154
    Selbstbiographie 2–4, 7, 11, 46, 60–61, 121, 157
    Wer ist schuldig? 13–14, 16, 117, 187
Gubitz, Friedrich Wilhelm:
  Sappho. Monodrama 122–23
Gurney, Archer 17
Gutjahr, Ortrud 163

Hägelin, Franz Karl:
  Denkschrift 11, 62
Hagl-Catling, Karin 9, 14, 19–20, 28, 146, 158
Hahn-Hahn, Ida Gräfin von 9
  Gräfin Faustine 125
Hajek, Vaclav:
  Böhmische Chronik 71–72, 136–37, 138, 139
Hauch, Gabriella 57
Helfer, Martha 177, 182
Herder, Johann Gottfried 136
Hippel, Theodor Gottlieb von:
  Ueber die bürgerliche Verbesserung der Weiber 25
Hobbes, Thomas 115, 120, 144
  De cive 118
  Leviathan 118–19, 129–30
Holthöfer, Ernst 57
Hormayr, Joseph 33
  Österreichischer Plutarch 71–72
Humboldt, Wilhelm von 28, 34
Hume, David:
  History of England 115

Ikuta, Masato 20, 134
intersectionality 16, 154–57
  see also kyriarchy

Janke, Pia 6, 21, 129
Joseph I, Holy Roman Emperor 63
Joséphine, Empress of the French 71

Kant, Immanuel 16, 26, 85–88, 89, 99, 100, 105, 107, 110, 112, 134, 188
  Beantwortung der Frage: Was ist Aufklärung? 87–88
  Kritik der reinen Vernunft 85–86
  Kritik der Urteilskraft 86
Kenkel, Konrad 165
Kleist, Franz von:
  Sappho. Ein dramatisches Gedicht 122
Kleist, Heinrich von 19
  Penthesilea 115
Kommerell, Max 92
Kord, Susanne 27
Kostka, Edmund 76
Krippendorff, Ekkehart 20

Krobb, Florian 174
Krug, Michaela 26
Kudriaffsky, Eufemia von 1, 32, 38
Kuhn, Anna 140
kyriarchy 16, 154–57, 166
   see also intersectionality

Lambert, Elie 177
Lantier, Etienne:
   Voyages d'Anténor 124
Laqueur, Thomas 15
Lattmann, Peter 92, 94
Laube, Heinrich 3, 4, 6, 19, 20, 38, 48, 135–36
Laube, Iduna 1, 32
Leitich, Anna Tizia 6, 18, 129
Leopold I, Holy Roman Emperor 63
Lewis, Gail 156
Lippuner, Heinz 177, 181
Little, William A. 3–4,
Littrow-Bischoff, Auguste von 1, 6, 32, 38, 41, 48, 50, 187
   Aus dem persönlichen Verkehre mit Franz Grillparzer 4–5, 41–42
   Die sociale Bewegung auf dem Gebiete der Frauen 42
   and Florence Nightingale 42
   and John Stuart Mill 42
   and the Wiener Frauen-Erwerb-Verein 43
Locke, John 115, 118, 144
   Two Treatises of Government 119–20, 131
Lorenz, Dagmar C. G. 14, 18–19, 20, 68, 90, 93, 94, 101–02, 103, 104, 111, 134, 140, 158, 162, 166, 177, 182
Lü, Yixu 158
Luserke-Jacqui, Matthias 161

Marchland, Wilhelm:
   Frauen-Emancipation 28–29
   Gefährliches Mittel 29
Maria Theresa 39, 63, 73, 180
   Grillparzer's opinion on 115
Marie Antoinette 8, 115
Marlowe, Christopher:
   Hero and Leander 102
Marso, Lori 126
Martin, Judith 125
Martini, Karl Anton von 56
Mary Stuart 115–16
Matt, Peter von 129
McCall, Leslie 155
Metternich, Klemens von 12, 33
Mill, John Stuart 9, 42
Morrien, Rita 26
Mühlbach, Luise:
   Der Zögling der Natur 125
Musäus, Johann Karl August 136
   Volksmärchen der Deutschen 137

Nadler, Josef 20, 125,
Napoleon 33, 71, 124, 134
Nash, Jennifer C. 155
Neissl, Julia 140, 145
Nestroy, Johann 12
   Der Kobold 12
   Freiheit in Krähwinkel 12
Neumann von Meißenthal, Marianne 32, 50, 73
Nightingale, Florence 42

Olenhusen, Irmgard Götz von 27
Otto, Luise:
   Das Recht der Frauen auf Erwerb 30
Ovid:
   Heroides 102

Pactum mutuae successionis 63
Paoli, Betty (Barbara Elisabeth Glück) 1, 32, 38, 41, 42, 47, 50, 187
   'Die Wandlungen der Frauenfrage' 40
   'Ein Wort Pombals' 39–40
   'Eine Zeitfrage' 39
   Grillparzer und seine Werke 5, 6
   on women's education 39
   on women's employment 39–40
Parry, Yvonne 165
Peter, Birgit 21
Pichl, Robert 131
Pichler, Caroline 17, 26, 31, 37, 38, 39, 42, 49, 50, 180, 187, 190
   and Austrian national literature 32–33
   education 33
   on Germaine de Staël 35, 126
   reading Wollstonecraft and de Gouges 26, 32
   salon 32–33
   on the role of women 34–35
   on women's education 34–35
   works:
      Gleichnisse 32
      'In Erinnerung an einige merkwürdige Frauen' 73
      'Kindererziehung' 34
      'Über die Bildung des weiblichen Geschlechtes' 34
      'Über Mißheirathen' 73
Polak, Gabriela 57
Politzer, Heinz 6, 91, 94, 101, 103, 104, 126, 182
Pörnbacher, Karl 48, 102, 122, 136
Pragmatic Sanction 63
Prohaska, Gertrude 32
Prutti, Brigitte 18, 76, 79

Reeve, William C. 127
Reinhardt, George 35, 36
Rettich, Julie (née Gley) 17, 31, 44, 47, 48, 187
   Betty Paoli on 47

Grillparzer's esteem for 48
and the Wiener Frauen-Erwerb-Verein 47
Robertson, Ritchie 89, 93, 134, 144
Roe, Ian 2, 36, 71, 89, 179
Rogowski, Christian 157, 162
Rose, Ferrell 41
Rousseau, Jean-Jacques 26, 28, 115, 118, 130
   Du contrat social 118, 120, 144
   Émile 26

Saar, Ferdinand von 32, 42
Sagarra, Eda 181
Said, Edward 159
salons 17, 32, 33
   and politics 33
Sauer, August 3, 60, 87, 95, 134
Sauer, Werner 85
Schaum, Konrad 71, 103, 104
Scheit, Gerhard 104
Schiller, Friedrich 86, 189
   'Hero und Leander' 102
   'Lied von der Glocke' 127
   Maria Stuart 11, 115
   'Was heißt und zu welchem Ende studiert man Universalgeschichte?' 157, 160, 161, 162–63
Schlegel, Dorothea von 34
Schnitzler, Günter 87,
Schopenhauer, Johanna:
   Gabriele 125
Schreyvogel, Joseph 11, 60, 85, 86
   and *Die Ahnfrau* 60–61, 62
Schröder, Sophie 17, 31, 44, 45, 187
   Grillparzer's esteem for 45–46
   playing Grillparzer's heroines 45, 46, 126
   support for Grillparzer 45, 46, 47
Shakespeare, William 188
   A Midsummer Night's Dream 117
   King Lear 11
   Macbeth 170–72, 183
Škreb, Zdenko 180
social contract theory 16, 118–20, 122, 125, 129, 130, 131, 132, 133, 136, 138, 140, 144, 188
Spörk, Ingrid 26, 161
Staël, Germaine de 8–9, 20, 32, 35, 123–24, 125, 133
   Corinne, ou l'Italie 35, 127
      influence on Grillparzer's *Sappho* 125–26
   Delphine 35, 124
   Dix années d'exil 9
   Sapho 124
Staiger, Emil 76, 78
Stein, Gisela 134
Steinhagen, Harald 71
Stifter, Adalbert 38
Stirnweis, Carmen 66, 68, 70
Störi, Fritz 86–87

Strich, Franz 86
Surynt, Izabela 44

Tanzer, Ulrike 44, 103, 111
Taylor, Yvette 156
Thaler, Karl von 30–31
Thompson, Bruce 20, 71, 89, 94, 95, 179
Todesco, Sophie von 32

Varnhagen, Rahel von 8, 45
Verri, Alessandro:
   Le Avventure di Saffo 124
Vogel, Ursula 57, 58
Vormärz 12, 28, 125, 126

Wagner, Meike 12
Weissensteiner, Friedrich 34
Weissenthurn, Johann Franul von 17, 32, 35–38, 49, 187
   and Caroline Pichler 37–38
   Johann, Herzog von Finnland 36
   reception of 36
   and the role of women 37
   Ruprecht Graf zu Horneck 36
Welcker, Friedrich Gottlieb:
   Sappho, von einem herrschenden Vorurtheil befreyt 123
Werner, Zacharias:
   Wanda, Königin der Sarmaten 115
Wertheimstein, Josefine von 1, 32, 33
Wieland, Christoph Martin 86
Wolf-Cirian, Francis 18, 94
Wollstonecraft, Mary:
   A Vindication of the Rights of Woman 25, 40
   in Europe 26, 33
   German translation of 26
Wolter, Charlotte 17, 31–32, 44, 48, 187
   playing Grillparzer's heroines 48
women:
   education 26, 28, 31, 34, 39, 40, 42, 47, 50, 187
   employment 28, 30–31, 39, 40, 43, 50
   legal position 28, 43, 56–59
   social roles 28, 34, 47
women's emancipation 12, 32, 42, 50, 187, 188–89
   aims of contemporary women's movement 30, 40
   debates about:
      in Austria 28–31
      in the press 28–31, 39
Wiener Frauen-Erwerb-Verein 1, 28, 32, 39, 47, 187
Wozonig, Karin 38, 39, 41, 44, 47

Yates, Douglas 6
Yates, W. E. 1, 12, 76, 89, 94, 128, 173, 180, 181

Zay, Marie von 32, 50, 73
Zeiller, Franz von 58